PORT CHALMERS - the pen-ultimate vessel built for the fleet and looking the worse for wear following a period of lay-up. (World Ship Society Photograph Library)

PORT LINE

Incorporating

James P. Corry & Company
Thomas B. Royden & Company
Wm. Milburn & Company
G. D. Tyser & Company
The Commonwealth & Dominion Line Ltd.

By

H. C. Spong

In association with
J. Dobson

http://www.worldshipsociety.org

CONTENTS

ACKNOWLEDGEMENTS 3
INTRODUCTION 4
NOTES ON THE SHIP HISTORIES 4
PART No. 1 5
  The Ancestoral Companies. 5
  JAMES P. CORRY 5
  THOMAS ROYDEN 18
    Inver Steamships Ltd 33
    Royden Chartered Ship 34
    Santa Clara Steamship Company 34
    Managed for the Admiralty. 35
  WILLIAM MILBURN 36
    William Milburn 46
    Wm. & T. L. Milburn 47
    Edmund Hannay Watts 47
    Watts, Milburn & Company. 48
    Managed Vessels 63
    Wm. Milburn & Company. 63
    Anglo-Australasian Steam Navigation Company Ltd 82
    Milburn Line Ltd 83
    Milburn Family - as Mortgage Lenders 83
    Ashington Coal Company Ltd. 84
    Milburn And Hawthorn, Leslie 84
  TYSER LINE 87
PART No. 2 98
  Post Amalgamation. 98
    1. The Commonwealth & Dominion Line Ltd. 98
    2. Post-War Reconstruction. 103
    3. Port Line Ltd. 107
    4. Another War. 120
    5. New For Old. 133
    6. Port Line Railway Locomotive. 136
    7. Rationalisation And Co-operation. 139
    8. Under Pressure. 147
  The Commonwealth & Dominion Line Ltd. / Port Line Ltd., Fleet 152
    The Commonwealth & Dominion Line - Managed Vessels. 196
    Port Line - Managed Vessels. 196
    Port Line - Chartered vessels. 201
APPENDIX No. 1 - Ships Machinery 205
APPENDIX No. 2 - M.A.N.Z. Line 208
APPENDIX No. 3 - Port Line Masters in September 1939 214
APPENDIX No. 4 - HMS PORT NAPIER 215
APPENDIX No. 5 - PORT MACQUARIE 225
APPENDIX No. 6 - M.I.L.A.G. 227
APPENDIX No. 7 - Refrigeration 229
APPENDIX No. 8 - PORT VICTOR Correspondence 232
APPENDIX No. 9 - Port Line At War 235
APPENDIX No. 10 - Conversions For War 239
What's In A Name ? 246
BIBLIOGRAPHY 251
INDEX 252

Front cover shows **PORT AUCKLAND** undergoing sea-trials. (Turner Photography / Company Archives)

ACKNOWLEDGEMENTS

During the course of my many years of research into the "Port Line" numerous people have been of value to my research efforts. To them I offer my sincere thanks :-

The Central Record Team of the World Ship Society - namely Martin Benn, Bernard Lawley, Harold Appleyard, John Bartlett, and Kevin O' Donoghue.

Individuals:-

Geoff Amos, Lee Andrews, J. Ashburner, Andrew Bell, Bob Balmer, Vic Baxter, Ken Bottoms, T. Britt, Dr. Ian Buxton, Joe Clarke, M. Condie, Ann Cowne, Richard Cornish, Dave Crolley, Cathy Donoghue N.M.M., Mrs S. Duggan, Peter Eyres, Ian Farquhar, Roy Fenton, J. Fisher, Warwick Foote, Ron French, Peter Gosson, The late Rowan Hackman, T. A. Harman, P. C. Hogben, The late John Hole, Paul Hood, Dave Hunt, D. H. Johnzon, Barbara Jones, Michael Jones, Dick Keys, William Ferguson Knight, Bernard Lawley, John Maber, Dr. R. H. Osborne, Joachim Pein, Ian Rae, George Ransome, Peter Rattue, Captain J. Robson, Bill Schell, Robert Shopland, Andrew Smith, Dave Sowden, Christine Sutton, Emma Taaffe, E. N. Taylor, Dave Vincent. Michael Vincent, Vic Young, Ian Wells, E.D.Walter

My special thanks go firstly to my wife Carole for the endless task of typing and retyping numerous drafts as the work progressed and for the constructive comments throughout, and for putting up with the periods of absence during the research and formulation period, and secondly to Bill Harvey without whose guidance and hours of effort, this work would not have been produced to final state as smoothly as it has within the timescale set.

The research work for this book started back in 1988 at the behest of Michael Crowdy. It proved however to be a daunting task, and in response to my advertised quest for information I was contacted by my associate author John Dobson, who in turn proved to be a mine of information on the Milburn business empire and their part in the formation of Port Line. For that free-flowing passage of information I am eternally grateful and it has been a pleasure to work with him over the years. Thanks also to his wife Jennifer for putting up with my constant questions dragging John away for hours on end to supply the answers.

Having thanked all the aforementioned, I also pass on the same gratitude to anyone that may have been overlooked.

Illustrations:
These have been provided as captioned, and I thank the relevant people, including Tony Smith - custodian of the World Ship Society Photograph Library, for trawling their archives to provide a varied selection of views.

~ 0 ~

Published in the United Kingdom by The World Ship Society Ltd., Mayes House, Vansittart Estate, Arthur Road, Windsor SL4 1SE.

© 2004   H. C. Spong, J. Dobson & The World Ship Society Ltd.

Edited and Produced by W. J. Harvey and H. C. Spong.

All rights reserved. No part of this work may be reproduced, stored in a retrieval system or transmitted in any form or by means, electronic, mechanical, photocopying, recording or otherwise, without the written permission of the publisher.

The right of H. C. Spong & J. Dobson to be identified as the authors of this work has been asserted by them in accordance with the Copyright, Design and Patent Act 1998.

ISBN 0 - 9543310 - 2 - 8

Typeset by The Highlight Type Bureau Ltd., 2, Clifton Villas, Bradford, BD8 7BY.
Printed by The Amadeus Press, Ezra House, West 26 Business Park, Cleckheaton, BD19 4TQ.

INTRODUCTION

In 1914, four companies engaged in the trade to New Zealand and Australia amalgamated to form the Commonwealth & Dominion Line, just prior to the outbreak of World War One, and the vagaries that that imposed on shipping.

Within two years, the fledgling Commonwealth & Dominion Line was acquired by the Cunard Steamship Company, anxious to expand their business into the Antipodean market.

This book tells the individual stories of the four companies before the amalgamation and the creation of this new enterprise, together with the subsequent story of the Commonwealth & Dominion Line that was transformed into Port Line during the 1930's.

This is a story of a company that became renowned for building some of the finest designs of cargo liners to serve one of the best-maintained fleets in the British Merchant Navy, through both peace and war.

Port Line sadly fell victim to the container age, coupled with long-haul air travel, two factors that quickly overshadowed their long distinguished career, wherein, the company was served loyally by their staff. This sadly is something not often seen in modern businesses. Port Line throughout its career was an efficient transporter of people and cargo, and due to that efficiency, ran like a well-oiled machine, giving job satisfaction to all those who were employed.

To all those "Port Liners" either in retirement enjoying their memories, or still sailing the seven seas, I offer you this work as a record of a once greatly respected company.

H. C. Spong
29th February 2004.

NOTES ON THE SHIP HISTORIES

The first line contains the combined fleet chronology number, ship name, the number of vessels that have carried the name in the fleet, the period in the fleet and type of vessel (wood, iron or steel).

The second line contains the **O. N.** = Official Number, (where known) **g.** = gross and **n.** = net tonnages, followed by the dimensions between perpendiculars for earlier vessels given in feet and tenths of feet. From 1956 overall dimensions were given in feet and inches. Lloyds Register changed to metric dimensions in 1975. These latter dimensions are identified by oa at the end of the line.

(*) N.B. Occasionally vessels are lengthened, re-measured or rebuilt resulting in new figures being quoted. In these instances they are added in new lines commencing with the effective year. They also have an effect on which line commences the machinery details.

(*) The third line normally contains the number of engines (if more than one). This is followed either by **C.**= compound; **T.**= Triple expansion, followed by the number of cylinders, for steam reciprocating machinery, or for motor machinery, the number of cylinders is followed by **S. C**= stroke cycle and **S. A.**= single acting. Both types are succeeded by then by machinery type, (where known) and the manufacturer thereof, followed by the figure and whichever of the following denominators that is applicable:- **HP** = horse power, **IHP** = indicated horse power, **RHP** = registered horse power, **NHP** = nominal horse power, **SHP**= shaft horse power, **BHP** = brake horse power. (e.g. 2,500 ihp). That is then followed by the vessel speed and any supplementary technical information. If a vessel has new machinery fitted then that is detailed immediately below the original machinery details, commencing with the relevant date.

The final section contains the ship history commencing with keel laying, launch or completion dates (whichever are known), the shipbuilder, (Yard No.) etc., followed by the vessel's career.

PART No. 1

The Ancestoral Companies.

JAMES P. CORRY

Belfast

The shipowning activities of the Corry family began in the middle of the nineteenth century following the establishment in, 1814, of a timber business in Belfast. Initially a partnership between John Corry and William Montegomery, the business became known as James P. Corry & Son from 1851 and by this time they were well established as building contractors. As the firm expanded, Robert Corry, a son of the founder, decided to charter ships to import timber from Canada. They eventually moved into shipownership in January 1849, with the purchase of the UNITED KINGDOM, built in Quebec in 1840 for Duncan Gibb of Liverpool. Later in March of the same year, the Canadian built NELSON VILLAGE and CHIEFTAIN (1) were purchased. Further secondhand acquisitions followed until, in June 1852, the SAINT HELENA, a new building, was delivered. Surprisingly, the SUMMERHILL a fourteen-year old wooden barque of only 198 tons, built in Norway in 1840, was added to the fleet two years later. Further secondhand vessels of wooden construction were added to the growing fleet until, in 1860, the JANE PORTER the first iron-built ship was delivered. Named after the wife of William Corry, she was a ship of 953 tons and had the distinction of being the first sailing ship completed by Harland & Wolff. She was destined to serve in the Corry fleet for 29 years.

The association with Harland & Wolff continued with the construction of a further eleven ships all named "STAR OF ....". Most of the company's sailing ships were running from London to Calcutta with coal and returning home with jute, and it was only occasionally that a Corry vessel ventured into the Australian trade.

Shortly after the start of the American Civil War in April 1861, Corry purchased the CRESCENT, built at Thomaston, Maine in 1840. She was a ship of 1,334 tons and was probably a bargain, as during that period many of the Northern shipowners were desperate to rid themselves of their ships. Harland & Wolff completed four ships for Corry during the period of this war (1861-1865). Each ship was approximately 1,000 tons, and they were named STAR OF ERIN, STAR OF DENMARK, STAR OF SCOTIA and the STAR OF ALBION.

The first vessel for which costs survive is Harland & Wolff, Yard No. 24, STAR OF SCOTIA, completed for J. P. Corry in 1864. This sailing ship was priced at £14,498 and earned the firm £350 in profit, a return of less than 2%. Unlike most of the early contracts, this was paid for by means of bills of exchange 'drawn on' Harland & Wolff and accepted by J. P. Corry, which in effect gave J. P. Corry credit for a fixed period of time at a specified rate of interest. Ten years later, when the STAR OF BENGAL was delivered, the builders sustained a loss of £2,000 because of a sharp rise in material costs.

Corry's last sailing ship, the STAR OF AUSTRIA, a steel ship of 1,781 tons, was launched in February 1886 by Workman, Clark & Company, by which time members of the Corry family had married into the Workman family. Due to this family connection, all subsequent steamers built for the "Star Line" between 1887 and 1914 were delivered from the yard of Workman, Clark & Company, Belfast.

Completed in 1887, the Golden Jubilee year of Queen Victoria, Corry's first steamer the STAR OF VICTORIA (1), was joined two years later by the STAR OF ENGLAND (1). Initially chartered out for voyages to India, they were taken in 1889 by Tyser & Company for a number of voyages to New Zealand. Both ships were equipped with refrigerating machinery at the expense of Tysers, but after 6 voyages that equipment was purchased by Corry and the ships continued to load on the Tyser berth on a commission basis.

Over the next few years a valuable association developed between the Tyser Line and the Star Line and the latter company built several new ships specifically for the frozen meat trade.

By comparison with the Tyser Line, James P. Corry's Star Line had a comparatively easy entry into the New Zealand trade. Tyser had all the drive and business initiative whereas Corry had the capital and made sure their ships on the Tyser berth had the best refrigeration equipment. Furthermore, the first Chief Engineer of Corry's, Alexander McDonald, was an expert in refrigeration methods and directed the installation and maintenance of the equipment in both Tyser and Corry ships over a number of years before becoming the first Superintendent Engineer for the Commonwealth & Dominion Line.

In 1898 the last four sailing ships in the fleet, the STAR OF BENGAL, STAR OF ITALY, STAR OF RUSSIA and the STAR OF FRANCE, were all sold, being destined eventually to hoist the flag of the

Alaska Packers Association. One of the quartet, the STAR OF BENGAL was wrecked in May 1908 with very heavy loss of life.

STAR OF AUSTRALIA (Ambrose Greenway collection)

An interesting description of one of the early refrigerated Corry steamers appeared in a local Australian newspaper during late 1899:

> "14.12.1899: STAR OF AUSTRALIA: Captain John Simpson, arrived Melbourne 22.11.1899
>
> She is the fifth from Workman, Clark and is commanded by the Commodore. She has 5 cargo holds, rigged as a brigantine. *(she was actually the fourth steamer built for Corry, H.C.S).*
>
> She has 3 insulated holds capable of containing 2,400 tons of meat and for refrigerated purposes dependence is placed on one of Benjamin Goodfellows duplex-tandem cold air machines which is capable of dealing with 240,000 cu ft of air per hour. Fitted with 10 large winches, 10 extra strong derricks and one portable derrick capable of lifting 30 tons. Fitted with electric light. She is a 12 knot ship with a 3 cyl-triple expansion engine, steam being supplied by four double ended boilers, the furnaces being assisted in their work by Howdens system of forced draught.
>
> The engines and refrigeration are in the charge of Alex MacDonald and Mr Coombes."

On a smaller scale the Corry Line also participated in the carriage of frozen meat from South America with the STAR OF IRELAND and an earlier steamer, the STAR OF NEW ZEALAND being used, but for the most part their activities were centered on the New Zealand trade.

After the completion of their first steamer the fleet expanded steadily, with a new ship being completed approximately every four years. The STAR OF JAPAN, launched by Miss Corry in August 1906, had the misfortune, in April 1908, whilst on her fourth voyage to the Antipodes, to run aground on a reef on the West coast of Africa. She proved impossible to salvage and after £60,000 worth of cargo was removed during July 1908, she was abandoned. Shortly afterwards the shipping press reported that her replacement had been ordered and was to be named STAR OF CHINA. In fact, she was launched as the STAR OF CANADA in August 1909 and was no more fortunate than her predecessor. Whilst laying off Gisborne, New Zealand, in June 1912, during the worst storm experienced for many years, she dragged her anchors and was driven quickly ashore on Kaiti Beach. Within two weeks her back was broken and she was abandoned to the underwriters. However, various fittings were salvaged and her bridge was used as part of a house in Childers Road, Gisborne for many years before being presented to Gisborne Museum. Thirty-seven years later the PORT BOWEN was to suffer a similar fate at Wanganui. All in all, 1912 was not the happiest of years for the Star Line. In August of that year the STAR OF NEW ZEALAND collided with the SLIEVE BLOOM off Holyhead and was so badly damaged that she was run ashore and beached. Furthermore, during October 1912, the STAR OF AUSTRALIA had the bad luck to suffer a broken tailshaft and had to be towed over 600 miles to Aden for repair.

STAR OF CANADA 26th June 1912 (Richard Cornish collection)

Corry also joined Tysers, Roydens and Milburns in the provision of specialist migrant carriers (under contract to the State Government of Victoria), for the carriage of emigrants from the United Kingdom to Melbourne. An order was placed in 1913 for the construction of two 9,000 ton gross twin-screw steamers with Workman, Clark, Belfast for delivery in early 1914. Fine looking ships, they had promenade decks which extended for half the length of the ship and tween decks which could be converted to passenger accommodation in a matter of weeks. There was a shortage of riveters at the time due to naval demands and the experiment was tried of using hydraulic and pneumatic riveting for the whole of the ships' bottom. Both were delivered within three months of one another, the first, the STAR OF VICTORIA (2) being completed in January 1914 and delivered to the Star Line whilst her sister, the STAR OF ENGLAND, was delivered on 8th April 1914, to the newly formed Commonwealth & Dominion Line. The latter vessel after calling at Barry for bunkers enroute from Belfast to London, sailed on her first voyage from the latter port on 14th May 1914. However, the two largest steamers never really saw the service for which they were intended, as the Great War intervened later in 1914. The STAR OF ENGLAND was requisitioned by the Australian Government as troopship A 15 whilst the STAR OF VICTORIA, became troopship A 16.

The company contributed five large modern ships to the formation of the Commonwealth & Dominion Line in 1914. As well as the two newest and largest, the STAR OF ENGLAND and STAR OF VICTORIA, which each gave thirty-four years of sterling service both in peacetime and through two world wars, whilst three others, the STAR OF INDIA, STAR OF AUSTRALIA and the STAR OF SCOTLAND, were also transferred.

Despite the change of ownership, the Corry family retained a prominent involvement with Cunard and the Commonwealth & Dominion Line. Sir William Corry and Robert Corry were the original Corry directors on the board of the new company, while Herbert W. Corry was Resident Director in Sydney from 1915. He joined the main board in 1923 and was Chairman, subsequently, of both the Port Line Ltd. and T. & J. Brocklebank Ltd.. The family line continued into subsequent generations, as Sir James P. I. M. Corry succeeded to the baronetcy on the death of Sir William in 1926 and became Secretary of the Port Line for thirty-one years as well as serving on the Board for fourteen years. An obituary in the 'Shipbuilding and Shipping Record' of the 17th June 1926 stated:

> "Death of Sir William Corry, Bart, aged 68, was the second baronet. He was educated at Eton and Trinity College, Cambridge. His father, Sir James P. Corry, in association with his grandfather Mr Robert Corry and his uncles John and Robert founded the

Belfast shipping line Corry & Company in 1859, a company which was celebrated for its fast sailing ships, which as time wore on, became associated with Australian and New Zealand trades".

John Corry, the eldest son of Herbert, served as a Director of Port Line from 1957 to 1967. Although he represented the last Corry link with Port Line, other members of the family still manage the family timber and construction business, trading as James P. Corry & Company Ltd, Belfast. In more recent years the yards have been subjected to repeated vandalism and terrorist attacks associated with the religious and political struggles in Northern Ireland. Despite these troubles, the company still remains one of the leading construction concerns in Belfast.

The Star Line ships had black hulls and white upperworks with the same buff funnel with black top as the Tyser Line. The house flag was a red heart on a white background with two red stripes top and bottom. Although no longer flying at sea, it still flies on the company headquarters in Belfast.

The Corry Fleet

C 1. UNITED KINGDOM (1849 - 1858) Wooden Ship
O.N. 33046. 1,257 tons. 199.3 x 31.9 x 21.9 feet.
5.5.1840: Launched by J. Munn, Quebec, for Duncan Gibb, Liverpool. 29.1.1849: Purchased by R. Corry, Belfast. 1858: Whilst on a voyage from Quebec to Belfast, was abandoned. 15.11.1858: Crew picked up by the American vessel DANIEL WEBSTER. 26.11.1858: Wreck was sighted by CAROLINE in position 48 N., 30 W, waterlogged.

C 2. NELSON VILLAGE (1849 - 1852) Wooden Barque
384 tons. 106.1 x 29.4 x 20.2 feet.
1826: Launched at Miramichi, New Brunswick, for Wilson & Company, Belfast. 1833: Sold to Casement, Belfast. 9.1847: Sold to H. Bowden, Belfast. 22.3.1849: Sold to R. Corry, Belfast. 19.10.1852: Parted anchors and was driven ashore at Bathurst Bay, Chaleur, Gulf of St. Lawrence, Canada. 11.1852: Condemned and sold with cargo.

C 3. CHIEFTAIN (1) (1849 - 1852) Wooden Barque
325 tons. 104.10 x 26.7 x 18.0 feet.
1826: Launched at Montreal, for Parlane & Company, Liverpool. 4.1838: Sold to A & J. Smyth, Belfast. 1846: Sold to Herdman, Belfast. 21.2.1849: Sold to William Wilson, Belfast. 22.3.1849: Sold to R. Corry, Belfast. 26.11.1852: Whilst on a voyage from Belfast to Savannah, seriously damaged when she ran ashore in Dundrum Bay, Ireland and was declared a total loss. Crew saved.

C 4. HERCULES (1851 - 1853) Wooden Barque
551 tons. 129.3 x 26.9 x 18.0 feet.
1849: Launched at Hampton, New Brunswick. 9.12.1850: Sold to R. Corry, Belfast. 29.11.1852: With damage to her bulwarks and stanchions, departed from Belfast bound for repairs at Liverpool. 28.12.1852: Anchored off Walney, Barrow in Furness, after losing her fore and main masts. She was subsequently taken in tow by a steamer and brought into Fleetwood. 19.2.1853: After repair, departed from Fleetwood bound for New Orleans. 7.3.1853: Foundered in 39N., 73W. Crew saved.

C 5. ALABAMA (1852 - 1869) Wooden Barque
O.N. 4590. 519 tons. 129.0 x 26.0 x 18.2 feet.
6.1852: Launched at St. Martins, New Brunswick, for R. Corry, Belfast. 18.5.1869: Arrived at Miramichi, New Brunswick from Belfast. 6.1869: Lost in St. Georges Bay, Newfoundland.

C 6. SAINT HELENA (1852 - 1862) Wooden Ship
O.N. 26469. 811 tons. 147.0 x 29.0 x 21.0 feet.
18.6.1852: Launched at St. Andrews, New Brunswick, for R. Corry, Belfast. 1876: Sold to Paul Rodgers, Carrickfergus. 6.5.1881: Abandoned at sea in position 36N., 46.39W.

C 7. SUMMER HILL (1854 - 1860) Wooden Barque
O.N. 14325. 198 tons. 89.0 x 21.0 x 15.0 feet.
1840: Built at Bergen, Norway. 1854: Sold to R. Corry, Belfast. 7.10.1860: Whilst on a voyage in ballast, from Belfast to Bathurst, New Brunswick, was abandoned in position 50N., 43W., after springing a leak. Her crew were rescued by the HELMUTH & MARIA, and landed at Greenock.

C 8. JAMES CARSON (1855 - 1859) Wooden Ship
O.N. 8153. 1,189 tons. 169.0 x 32.0 x 22.0 feet.
Post 1856 1,080 tons.
30.7.1851: Launched by Thomas. H. Oliver, Quebec. 4.11.1851: Sold to Edward Oliver, Liverpool. 27.11.1851: Sold to Dunn & Son, Belfast. 18.1.1855: Sold to R. Corry, Belfast. 27.9.1856: Tonnage amended. 6.7.1859: Whilst on a voyage from the Clyde to Bombay, was abandoned in position 28 S., 26 W., in a sinking condition. Her master and crew were put on board the ship MELBOURNE and returned to Liverpool.

C 9. PERSIAN (1855 - 1863) Wooden Ship
O.N. 23347. 1,132 tons. 171.3 x 34.0 x 22.8 feet.
1851: Launched by James Nevins, St. John, New Brunswick (Yard No. 3), for Carter & Company, London. 1855: Sold to R. Corry, Belfast. 25.1.1863: Whilst on a voyage from Manila to Liverpool, was abandoned in position 34N., 31W.

C 10. CHARGER (1857-1876) Wooden Ship
O.N. 35098. 1,060 tons. 174.5 x 37.7 x 22.6 feet.
8.1856: Launched by James. T. Smith at St. John, New Brunswick (Yard No. 30). 9.1857: Sold to R. Corry, Belfast. 1876: Sold to T. Dixon, Belfast. 1882: Owners restyled as T. Dixon & Sons. 15.11.1890: Whilst on a voyage from Dalhousie to Belfast with a cargo of deals, was abandoned and drove ashore on the coast of Kerry, South West Ireland,

C 11. CHIEFTAIN (2) (1859 - 1863) Wooden Ship
O.N. 22770. 795 tons. 137.2 x 29.2 x 22.0 feet.
9.1841: Launched by James Briggs, St. John, New Brunswick. 6.11.1843: Sold to Davies & Company, Beaumaris. Reduced to a barque. 12.5.1849: Sold to David Scott & Company, Leith. 1857: Sold to J. Jamieson, Glasgow. 1859: Sold to R. Corry, Belfast. 1.4.1863: Whilst on a voyage in ballast, from Belfast to Bathurst, New Brunswick, sprang a leak and run aground at Bolsa, Isle of Islay. Became a total loss

C 12. ALBERTA (1860 - 1861) Wooden Barque
O.N. 12989. 628 tons. 129.1 x 27.9 x 20.3 feet.
7.1849: Launched at St. John, New Brunswick. 25.1.1850: Sold to James Campbell Buchanan, Greenock. 1860: Sold to R. Corry, Belfast. 20.5.1861: Whilst on a voyage from Liverpool to Quebec foundered near St. Pauls. Crew saved.

C 13. GREENOCK (1859-1863) Wooden Ship
O.N. 25920. 1,285 tons. 199.6 x 34.8 x 23.4 feet.
29.7.1840: Launched at Buctouche, New Brunswick, for Duncan Gibb, Liverpool. 14.3.1859: Sold to R. Corry, Belfast. 26.11.1863: Lost.

C 14. QUEEN OF THE WEST (1859 - 1875) Wooden Ship
O.N. 18301. 1,433 tons. 181.7 x 38.0 x 21.7 feet.
1843: Launched by Brown & Bell, New York. 25.1.1855: Sold by public auction at Llanelly, South Wales, to J. & R. Jones, Public Works Contractors. 1.1856: Sold to J. & J. Johnson, Liverpool. 1859:

Stranded near Carrickfergus, purchased by R. Corry, Belfast, and refloated. 1875: Sold to W. M. Corner, London. 1878: Dismantled.

C 15. JANE PORTER (1860 - 1889) Iron Ship
O.N. 28835. 953g. 200.5 x 32.0 x 21.5 feet.
1.9.1860: Launched by Harland & Wolff, Belfast (Yard No. 5), for J. P. Corry & Company, Belfast. 15.9.1860: Completed as the first iron ship owned by Corry. 1889 Sold to W. Ross, Liverpool. 1896: Sold to H. Burmeister & Company, Hamburg, and renamed NANNY. 1902: Sold to J. E. Olsen, Gothenburg, and renamed TRICHERA. 2.6.1905: Whilst on a voyage from Bunbury to East London with a cargo of Jarrah sleepers, wrecked 1 mile from Aliwal Shoal

C 16. CRESCENT (1861 - 1868) Wooden Ship
O.N. 28837. 1,334 tons. 189.1 x 37.7 x 24.8 feet.
28.11.1856: Launched as MARQUETTE by Cushing & Watts, Thomaston, Maine. U. S. A., for Creighton, Robinson & Watts, a partnership, Thomaston, Maine. 4.7.1861: Sold to R. Corry, Belfast, and renamed CRESCENT. 4.5.1868: Whilst on a voyage from Liverpool to the United States, was abandoned in a sinking condition.

C 17. STAR OF ERIN (1862 - 1889) Iron Ship
O.N. 45122. 949g. 200.0 x 32.0 x 21.9 feet.
9.10.1862: Launched by Harland & Wolff, Belfast (Yard No. 16), for J. P. Corry & Company, Belfast. 31.10.1862: Completed. 8.1863: Whilst on a voyage from Calcutta to London, she was stopped by the Confederate States Ship ALABAMA, in a position 325 miles N.W. by W., from the Cape of Good Hope, in order that three captured United States citizens could be put aboard. 17.1.1888: Reduced to a barque. 11.1889: Sold to Park Bros, London. 6.2.1892: Whilst on a voyage from Bluff Harbour to London with a cargo of wool, grain and tallow, wrecked at Waipapa, New Zealand,

C 18. STAR OF DENMARK (1863 - 1889) Iron Ship
O.N. 47182. 998g. 208.7 x 32.0 x 21.9 feet.
19.6.1863: Launched by Harland & Wolff, Belfast (Yard No. 20), for J. P. Corry & Company, Belfast. 15.7.1863: Completed. 30.4.1877: Reduced to a barque. 1889: Sold to F. M. Tucker, London. 1889: Sold to Hine Bros, Belfast, and renamed DENTON HOLME. 10.5.1890: Registry transferred to Maryport. 25.9.1890: Whilst on a voyage from Glasgow to Fremantle with a cargo of iron pipes and general, stranded at Rottnest Island near Fremantle.

C 19. STAR OF SCOTIA (1864 - 1887) Iron Ship
O.N. 47190. 999g. 212.0 x 32.1 x 21.8 feet.
1.1864: Launched by Harland & Wolff, Belfast (Yard No. 24), for J. P. Corry & Company, Belfast. 15.7.1879: Reduced to a barque. 27.6.1887: Whilst on a voyage from San Francisco to Queenstown (for orders), wrecked at Bull Point, East Falkland. The Chief Officer and 7 of her crew were drowned.

C 20. STAR OF ALBION (1864 - 1886) Iron Ship
O.N. 49713. 999g. 214.0 x 32.1 x 21.5 feet.
20.7.1864: Launched by Harland & Wolff, Belfast (Yard No. 29), for J. P. Corry & Company, Belfast. 1.2.1879: Reduced to a barque. 25.9.1886: Whilst on a voyage from Cardiff to Calcutta, stranded on Long Sand, Hooghly River, Calcutta.

C 21. STAR OF PERSIA (1868 - 1893) Iron Ship
O.N. 60312. 1,289g. 227.0 x 35.0 x 22.2 feet.
23.6.1868: Launched by Harland & Wolff, Belfast (Yard No. 55), for J. P. Corry & Company, Belfast. 14.6.1893: Sold to C. M. Matzen, Hamburg, and renamed EDITH. 19.3.1903: Whilst on a voyage from Port Ludlow, Puget Sound to Port Pirie with a cargo of lumber, wrecked on Nereus Shoal, New Caledonia.

C 22. STAR OF GREECE (1868 - 1888) Iron Ship
O.N. 60313. 1,289g. 227.0 x 35.0 x 22.2 feet.
19.9.1868: Launched by Harland & Wolff, Belfast (Yard No. 57), for J. P. Corry & Company, Belfast.
13.7.1888: Whilst on a voyage from Adelaide to London, wrecked on the Willunga Reef, South Australia.

STAR OF GERMANY

(World Ship Society Photograph Library)

C 23. STAR OF GERMANY (1872 - 1897) Iron Ship
O.N. 63949. 1,337g. 232.0 x 35.0 x 22.0 feet.
11.3.1872: Launched by Harland & Wolff, Belfast (Yard No. 82), for J. P. Corry & Company, Belfast.
20.5.1872: Completed. 1897: Sold to W. K. Parrett, Belfast. 1897: Sold to Foley & Company, London. 1900: Sold to Star of Germany Ship Company Ltd., (W. A. Rainford & Company, managers), Belfast. 1906: Sold to Acties Grid (A. Bech, Tvedestrud), Norway, and renamed GRID. 8.9.1906: Arrived at Barbados dismasted. 1907: Sold and hulked at Trinidad.

STAR OF BENGAL (World Ship Society Photograph Library)

C 24. STAR OF BENGAL (1874 - 1898) Iron Ship
O.N. 63957. 1,877g. 262.8 x 40.2 x 23.5 feet.
3.1.1874: Launched by Harland & Wolff, Belfast (Yard No. 86), for J. P. Corry & Company, Belfast. 7.3.1874: Completed. 24.6.1898: Sold to J. J. Smith, San Francisco. 1906: Sold to Alaska Packers Association, San Francisco. 20.5.1908: Whilst on a voyage from Wrangell to San Francisco, wrecked on Coronation Island, Alaska. There were only 27 survivors from a total complement of 137.

STAR OF RUSSIA (World Ship Society Photograph Library)

C 25. STAR OF RUSSIA (1874 - 1898) Iron Ship
O.N. 63958 1,981g 275.5 x 40.6 x 24.2 feet.
12.12.1874: Launched by Harland & Wolff, Belfast (Yard No. 88), for J. P. Corry & Company, Belfast. 1898: Sold to Shaw, Savill & Company, London. 1898: Sold to J. J. Moore & Company, Honolulu.

1901: Sold to Pacific Colonial Shipping (J. J. Moore & Company Ltd.). 1906: Sold to Alaska Packers Association, San Francisco. 1926: Sold to Burns, Philip & Company, San Francisco, (Burns, Philip & Company, Sydney, managers), renamed LA PEROUSE, under French flag, and reduced to hulk at Apia, Samoa.

STAR OF ITALY (World Ship Society Photograph Library)

C 26. STAR OF ITALY (1877 - 1898) Iron Ship
O.N. 78103. 1,644g. 257.1 x 38.0 x 22.8 feet.
7.1877: Launched by Harland & Wolff, Belfast (Yard No. 113), for J. P. Corry & Company, Belfast. 17.3.1898: Sold to J. J. Moore, Honolulu. 1898: Sold to Pacific Colonial Shipping Company (J. J. Moore, managers), San Francisco. 1905: Sold to Alaska Packers Association, San Francisco. 1927: Sold to Darling-Singer, San Francisco. 1934: Sold to Cia Colombia Maritima, Colombia. 1936: Sold to Alberto Quijano, Colombia, and reduced to a hulk at Buenaventura, Colombia.

C 27. STAR OF FRANCE (1877-1898) Iron Ship
O.N. 78105. 1,644g. 258.0 x 38.0 x 22.8 feet.
21.11.1877: Launched by Harland & Wolff, Ltd., Belfast (Yard No. 114), for J. P. Corry & Company, Belfast. 1898: Sold to J. J. Moore, Honolulu. 1898: Sold to Alaska Packers Association, San Francisco. By 1928: was being used as a Sea Scouts Training Ship at San Francisco. 1932: Sold to L. Rothenberg, San Francisco. 1933: Sold to Capt J. M. Anderson, for use as a fish barge. By 1937: Was owned by Hermosa Amusement Corporation, Hermosa, California, as a fish barge named OLYMPIC 11. 4.9.1940: Run down by SAKITO MARU off San Pedro, California and sunk.

C 28. STAR OF AUSTRIA (1886 - 1895) Steel Ship
O.N. 93152. 1,781g. 264.7 x 38.7 x 23.1 feet.
8.2.1886: Launched by Workman, Clark & Company, Belfast (Yard No. 37), for J. P. Corry & Company, Belfast. 25.3.1895: Departed from Santa Rosalia, Mexico bound for Swansea with a cargo of copper and copper ore. 1.4.1895: Last sighted in the Gulf of California.

C 29. STAR OF VICTORIA (1) (1887 - 1911)
O.N. 93164. 3,451g. 2,230n. 361.7 x 42.7 x 26.4 feet.
T.3-cyl. steam engine manufactured by J. & J. Thomson & Company, Glasgow. 361nhp. 12.1903: New donkey boiler fitted. 10kts.

24.1.1887: Launched by Workman, Clark & Company, Belfast (Yard No. 39), for the Star of Victoria Steamship Company Ltd. (J. P. Corry & Company, managers), Belfast. 1903: Sold to the Star Line Ltd. (same managers), Belfast. 1911: Sold to Fratelli Cosulich, Trieste (Austro-Hungarian Flag), and renamed FRIGIDA. 1915: Sold to Soc. Anon di Nav. Sud Atlantica, Argentine, and renamed MOINHO FLUMINENSE. 1916: Sold to Soc Nationale d'Affretements, France, and renamed MARSEILLE. 20.3.1917: Lost in a collision off Ile d'Yeu.

C 30. STAR OF ENGLAND (1) (1889 - 1913)
O.N. 93180. 3,696g. 2,424n. 371.8 x 44.2 x 27.2 feet.
T.3-cyl. steam engine manufactured by J and J. Thomson & Company, Glasgow. 400 nhp. 10kts.
2.2.1889: Launched by Workman, Clark & Company Ltd., Belfast (Yard No. 58), for the Star of England Steamship Company Ltd. (J. P. Corry & Company, managers), Belfast. 3.1889: Completed. 11.11.1903: Sold to the Star Line Ltd. (same managers), Belfast. 23.5.1913: Sold to T. Gazzolo fu A., Italy, and renamed PURIFICAZIONE. 1915: Sold to Soc. Anon. Ilva, Italy. 8.9.1915: Whilst on a voyage from Genoa to Norfolk, Virginia, in ballast, was abandoned in the North Atlantic.

STAR OF NEW ZEALAND (Ambrose Greenway collection)

C 31. STAR OF NEW ZEALAND (1895 - 1915)
O.N. 104459. 4,417g. 2,833n. 393.5 x 46.8 x 28.0 feet.
T.3-cyl. steam engine manufactured by the shipbuilder. 457 nhp. 11kts.
24.1.1895: Launched by Workman, Clark & Company Ltd., Belfast (Yard No. 94), for the Star of New Zealand Steamship Company Ltd. (J. P. Corry & Company, managers), Belfast. 20.3.1895: Completed. 11.11.1903: Sold to the Star Line Ltd. (same managers), Belfast. 21.9.1912: Collided with SLIEVE BLOOM near Holyhead, beached and later refloated. 13.5.1914: Collided with the pilot cutter W. W. JONES off Cardiff. 5 of the pilots on board the cutter were drowned. 28.11.1915: Whilst on a voyage from Montevideo to Le Havre with a cargo of meat and maize, ran aground on Ile de Molene, France. 4.12.1915: Abandoned as a total wreck.

C 32. STAR OF AUSTRALIA (1899 - 1914)
O.N. 110507. 6,179g. 3,985n. 440.0 x 55.1 x 29.7 feet.
T.3-cyl. steam engine manufactured by the shipbuilder. 579 nhp. Refrigerated capacity 217,442 cu.ft. 12kts.
24.6.1899: Launched by Workman, Clark & Company Ltd., Belfast (Yard No. 157), for the Star of Australia Steamship Company Ltd. (J. P. Corry & Company, managers), Belfast. 7.9.1899: Completed. 11.1903: Sold to the Star Line Ltd. (same managers). 2.7.1904: Rescued the crew of Canadian Barque SWANSEA, abandoned in the North Atlantic. 28.10.1912: Whilst on a voyage from Sydney to Dunkirk,

her tailshaft snapped. 4.11.1912: Taken in tow by the British vessel GLENLOCHY (4,654g./1896), and towed over 600 miles to Aden. 10.11.1912: Arrived at Aden. 14.2.1914: Transferred to The Commonwealth & Dominion Ltd., London. 12.10.1916: Renamed PORT STEPHENS. 1.8.1918: In collision with NORTH CAMBRIA, approximately 70-80 miles west of Ushant, as a result of the collision the NORTH CAMBRIA sank. 1924: Refrigerated and insulated machinery removed at Hull. 14.3.1924: Sold to G. E. Amedeo Lombardo for demolition then resold to L. E. Coati & Figli and demolished in Italy.

C 33. STAR OF IRELAND (1903 - 1916)
O.N. 116006. 4,331g. 2,743n. 380.0 x 48.7 x 28.3 feet.
T.3-cyl. steam engine manufactured by the shipbuilder. 452 nhp. 12kts.
29.6.1903: Launched by Workman, Clark & Company Ltd., Belfast (Yard No. 200), for the Star Line Ltd. (J. P. Corry & Company, managers), Belfast. 18.8.1903: Completed. 1916: Sold to Nelson Steam Navigation Company Ltd. (H. & W. Nelson Ltd., managers), and renamed HIGHLAND STAR. 1927: Laid up at Dunston on Tyne. 4.1930: Sold to Thos. W. Ward Ltd., Sheffield, for demolition at their Inverkeithing facility.

STAR OF SCOTLAND (World Ship Society Photograph Library)

C 34. STAR OF SCOTLAND (1904 - 1914)
O.N. 120702. 6,230g. 4,001n. 440.3 x 55.3 x 30.3 feet.
T.3-cyl. steam engine manufactured by the shipbuilder. 579 nhp. 12kts.
15.9.1904: Launched by Workman, Clark & Company Ltd., Belfast (Yard No. 212), for the Star Line Ltd. (J. P. Corry & Company, managers), Belfast. 29.10.1904: Completed. 23.3.1914: Transferred to The Commonwealth & Dominion Line Ltd., London. 13.9.1916: Renamed PORT CAMPBELL. 7.4.1918: Whilst on a voyage from London to New York, was damaged with a torpedo by the German submarine U 53, 115 miles W.S.W. from Bishop Rock. 9.4.1918: Sank.

C 35. STAR OF JAPAN (1906 - 1908)
O.N. 120717. 6,236g. 4,000n. 440.3 x 55.3 x 30.3 feet.
T.3-cyl. steam engine manufactured by the shipbuilder. 601nhp. 12kts
23.8.1906: Launched by Workman, Clark & Company Ltd., Belfast (Yard No. 235), for the Star Line Ltd., (J. P. Corry & Company, managers), Belfast. 2.10.1906: Completed. 2.4.1908: Whilst on a voyage

from London to Hawkes Bay, New Zealand with general cargo, stranded on a reef at St. Cyprians Bay, Pedro de Galha, West Africa. 8.7.1908: £60,000 worth of cargo was transhipped to other vessels, and the wreck declared as a constructive total loss.

STAR OF CANADA (Ambrose Greenway collection)

C 36. STAR OF CANADA (1909 - 1912)
O.N. 129627. 7,280g. 4,623n.   470.3 x 58.4 x 31.6 feet.
Two T.3-cyl. steam engines manufactured by the shipbuilder. Twin screw. 749 nhp. 13kts.
17.8.1909: Launched by Workman, Clark & Company Ltd., Belfast (Yard No. 283), for the Star Line Ltd. (J. P. Corry & Company, managers), Belfast. 5.10.1909: Completed. 22.6.1912: Whilst at Gisborne, New Zealand, loading for the United Kingdom, dragged her anchors during a storm and wrecked at Kaiti Beach. 3.7.1912: Broke her back in the vacinity of her foremast and was abandoned to the underwriters.

STAR OF INDIA operated as HMNZT No. 8 during WW1 (Ambrose Greenway collection)

C 37. STAR OF INDIA (1910 - 1914)
O.N. 129635. 7,316g. 4,602n. 470.1 x 58.4 x 31.6 feet.
Two T.3-cyl. steam engines manufactured by the shipbuilder. Twin screw. 756nhp. 12kts. Refrigerated capacity 299,727 cu.ft.
22.9.1910: Launched by Workman, Clark & Company Ltd., Belfast (Yard No. 297), for the Star Line Ltd. (J. P. Corry & Company, managers), Belfast. 29.10.1910: Completed. 14.2.1914: Transferred to The Commonwealth & Dominion Line Ltd., London. 28.9.1916: Renamed PORT PIRIE. 10.1935: Sold to T.

W. Ward Ltd., Sheffield, for demolition at their Briton Ferry facility. 8.11.1935: Handed over. 13.11.1935: Arrived at Briton Ferry.

C 38. STAR OF VICTORIA (2) (1914)

O.N. 132046. 9,152g. 5,852n. 501.3 x 63.3 x 33.6 feet.
Two T.3-cyl. steam engines manufactured by the shipbuilder. Twin screw. 979nhp. 13kts. Refrigerated capacity 387,000 cu.ft.
7.1929: Additionally fitted with two low-pressure turbines, reduction geared with hydraulic couplings. Now 1,181 nhp.
13.11.1913: Launched by Workman, Clark & Company Ltd., Belfast (Yard No. 328), for the Star Line Ltd. (J. P. Corry & Company, managers), Belfast. 13.1.1914: Completed. 14.2.1914: Transferred to The Commonwealth & Dominion Line Ltd., London. 20.6.1916: Renamed PORT MELBOURNE. 1931: Whilst laid up in the River Blackwater suffered fire damage, and was later repaired and laid up on the Tyne. 12.1947: Whilst on a voyage from Montreal to Liverpool with a cargo of dairy produce, suffered a serious fire in her bunkers. The food cargo that included 13,535,640 eggs was saved but there was damage to a consignment of timber. 13.5.1948: Arrived at Blyth for demolition by Hughes, Bolckow Ltd.

C 39. STAR OF ENGLAND (2) (1914)

O.N. 136660. 9136g. 5835n. 501.3 x 63.3 x 33.6 feet.
Two T.3-cyl. steam engine manufactured by the shipbuilder. Twin screw. 979nhp. 13kts. 5,000 ihp. Refrigerated capacity 387,100 cu.ft.
5.1929: Additionally fitted with two low-pressure turbines, reduction geared with hydraulic couplings. Now 1,181 nhp.
16.2.1914: Launched by Workman, Clark & Company Ltd., Belfast (Yard No. 329), for The Commonwealth & Dominion Line Ltd., London. 8.4.1914: Completed. 27.4.1916: Renamed PORT SYDNEY. 26.10.1948: Arrived Liverpool. 30.11.1948: Sold via the British Iron & Steel Corporation, to T. W. Ward Ltd., Sheffield, for demolition at their Preston facility. 17.12.1948: Arrived in tow at Preston from Liverpool. 1.1949: Demolition commenced.

THOMAS ROYDEN

Liverpool

The founder of the company, Thomas Royden, was born at Frankby, Cheshire in 1792 and, because of family connections, had strong links with the shipbuilding industry in Liverpool. In 1808, at the age of sixteen, he was apprenticed to Charles Grayson whose family had been connected with Liverpool shipbuilding for over half a century. Subsequently Royden (in partnership with James Ward) commenced a shipyard in 1818 at Baffin Street, on the west side of Queens Dock, the firm being known as Royden and Ward. This arrangement was dissolved in 1824 when Ward retired due to ill health.

In April 1825 Thomas Royden married Anne Dean in Liverpool. Later that year a devastating fire destroyed some of the shipyard and two of the vessels on the stocks. In 1828 the business became Thomas Royden & Company with the admission of John Watson as a partner. This ceased seven years later and the company name was changed to Thomas Royden.

Thomas Royden had three sons, one died in infancy, but the other two, Thomas Bland born in 1831 and Joseph, born in 1833, both served their apprenticeship with the firm and duly became partners. Royden built his first vessel, THE DUKE completed in 1843, specifically for himself and other investors although there is some unconfirmed evidence that he was involved in shipowning before this, with an interest in a ship named KINGSTON (built in 1794).

In 1850 the yard was moved from Baffin Street at the south end of Liverpool to the Queen's Dock, where it remained until its closure in 1893. The barquentine ISMYR (1) was completed for Royden's own account in 1850 and she was followed at regular intervals by a succession of wooden vessels starting with the barque CHILENA completed in 1853 followed by the ship ANNE ROYDEN named after his wife and completed in 1856. Subsequently the LA ZINGARA, a barque of only 287 tons, was delivered during 1860, while the SPRINGWOOD, the final wooden vessel built by the yard, was completed in 1862 also for Royden's own account. In the early years Royden's ships were, perhaps, better known in the Calcutta and River Plate trades.

The Company's shipowning was still something of a sideline, but when the yard was slack its workmen were kept busy with ships which ran under the family flag, at least until a purchaser could be found. During 1859, with the admission of the eldest son into partnership, the firm became Thomas Royden & Son. It was not until 1862 that the yard started iron shipbuilding, with the SILVIA, completed in 1863, being the first. Most of the steamers that the yard built were of quite modest size but some of the sailing ships completed were big for those days. They included several noteworthy vessels, among them the HADDON HALL (1146 tons), which distinguished herself by her speed on Alexander's Hall Line service. The decision to build in iron was not without its problems. For example, when Thomas Royden heard that his son Thomas. B. Royden was considering accepting an order to build two iron ships, he threatened to leave the yard. The order was accepted and Thomas Royden left the yard never to return. During 1866 the firm changed its name to Thomas Royden & Sons when Joseph, the youngest son, was made a partner.

The sailing vessels of the Royden fleet were now engaged in a variety of trades: Liverpool to India via the Cape; to South America and also to Australia. The first important steamer Roydens built was FRANCE, (3572 tons gross) completed in 1867 for the National Line, however her launch was marred by the collapse of the staging, although casualties were limited to two people with serious injuries.

In September 1868 Thomas Royden died and was succeeded by his sons, Thomas Bland and Joseph, who carried on the dual business of shipbuilders and shipowners. An unusual event during this year was the re-purchase of the SIR JOHN LAWRENCE, built in 1859 for Farnworth and Jardine of Liverpool. She was probably taken in part exchange for four other vessels that the firm had recently completed for this local shipowner. This was not the first time that Roydens had re-purchased a ship of their own manufacture, as the brig BARKHILL of 175 tons had been similarly re-acquired in 1857.

The yard had some remarkably faithful clients. For example, Hall Line's HADDON HALL was succeeded by LOCKSLEY HALL and others, whilst Singlehurst & Company, who were later amalgamated with the Booth Line, went to them for their first four steamers between 1869 and 1871. Roydens had the distinction of building the only two ships which the White Star Line ever ordered from any yard other than Harland & Wolff, the ASIATIC and TROPIC, (approximately 2,000 tons gross), which were purchased on the stocks. Other orders came from the Allan Line and from the Leyland Company in its early days.

In 1877 Royden's own fleet consisted of nine sailing ships, three of them wooden, which had been built in their own yard. Orders for steamers from other firms were increasing.

The Company suffered their first maritime loss in 1871 when the CLIFFORD, an iron ship of 915 tons built in 1864, was abandoned off Cape Horn, fortunately without loss of life. Further losses occurred when ISMYR (2) was wrecked in 1879 and the BEATRICE was posted missing in 1883. In both cases there were no survivors. The final sailing ship loss was sustained in January 1884 when the LATHOM (1) stranded in the Thames Estuary inward bound from Calcutta.

Their first steel hull was the ARISTIDES of 1881 built for Layborn, Legge & Company, Liverpool, and, unluckily, lost within a few months. Most of the Company's subsequent ships were of steel construction.

In 1888, having run down their fleet of sailing ships for some time, Royden's built the first steamer for their own fleet. This ship was the INDRA of 3,583 tons gross, and registered under the ownership of the Indra Steamship Company with T. Royden as managers. The management was afterwards transferred to Macvicar, Marshall & Company, for whom they had built several ships. The pioneer steamer was soon followed by the INDRANI and INDRAPURA. Subsequently many of their steamers were employed in a service between New York and the Far East operating under the name of the United States-China-Japan Line.

The final sailing vessel laid down for Roydens' own account was the LATHOM (2) completed in 1891 and sold on completion to a single ship company managed by Macvicar, Marshall & Company who been associated with Roydens for a number of years.

In the early 1890's the long-standing difference of opinion between the Mersey Docks & Harbour Board and the surviving Liverpool shipyards came to a head. The once thriving shipbuilding centre had suffered badly because the Board considered that this activity was of only secondary importance compared with that of ensuring the efficient passage of cargo through the port. After moving the yards further out from site to site as the docks expanded, the Board refused to allow builders to take out long leases when existing ones expired. A limit of six months at a time was imposed and, not unnaturally, builders felt that they were not justified in laying down expensive plant on such an uncertain tenure.

Thomas. B. Royden (who was created a Baronet in 1905 and died, at the age of 86, in 1917) together with Joseph (who died in 1919) retired from the firm in 1893, to be succeeded by the junior partners, the cousins Thomas and Joseph. B. Royden. A new ship repair company was formed, and went on to finish the last ship to be laid down under the old regime number 260 on the original building list; this was the four masted barque PRINCE ROBERT (2,846 tons gross) which later became the ROBERT DOLLAR. The plans to concentrate on repair work were not proceeded with and before the end of the year the shipyard was given up. The site vacated by the shipyard was later used for dock extensions and warehouses whilst the firm concentrated on running the ships of the Indra Line, which later contributed to the Commonwealth & Dominion amalgamation. Prior to this, in 1879, a serious fire had destroyed all the company's files and when the yard was finally closed all subsequent records were not preserved, thus making the writing of a company history extremely difficult.

Roydens' connection with Australasia started when the INDRA was chartered by Tyser & Company to carry wool from Australia and New Zealand. The second steamer to run for Tysers was the INDRAMAYO, built in 1889, and she was fitted out for the carriage of frozen meat three years later. Later ships of the Indra Line operating to Australasia were also insulated.

The INDRAPURA, launched in January 1890 for Macvicar, Marshall & Company, was completed in March of that year for Indrapura S. S. Company Ltd, and managed by T. B. Royden. Subsequent ships completed in the period up to 1901 were also registered under single ship companies, with Roydens acting as managers. After that, new buildings were completed for the Indra Line Ltd, a company formed to run services between New York and the Far East with T. B. Royden as managers.

In common with William Milburn, the Roydens were not averse to selling vessels nearing completion to other owners if the opportunity arose. The INDRADEVI was sold off in 1898 to Houlder, Middleton of London and in 1905 the INDRABARAH was disposed of to the Admiralty after a tempting offer was received.

After the closure of their own shipyard in 1893 (which had completed three steamers for the company) the Roydens went to a variety of shipbuilders for their new buildings, before finally settling on Charles Connell & Company as their favoured supplier. Between 1896 and 1913 Connells completed a total of twelve steamers for the Royden group.

Close connections were established with both the Tyser and Corry companies which led to some of Roydens fleet running in conjunction with the vessels of the other companies. This resulted in probably the only Royden ship specifically laid down for the Australia/New Zealand trade being built. She was the INDRAPURA of 1911 and was completed by Swan, Hunter Wigham & Richardson to take advantage of a contract awarded to Tyser & Company by the Victorian State Government for the carriage of migrants. At over 8,000 tons she was the largest ship ever owned by Roydens and had accommodation for approximately 1,000 steerage passengers in her upper tween decks.

In addition to human passengers the Royden steamers would often carry zoological specimens from the Far East for New York's Zoo. On one such voyage, the cargo broke adrift in a gale and many of the animals, including a Bengal tiger and a large python, got loose and began roaming the deck; all the crew took fright and locked themselves in their cabins. Eventually the tiger and python battled together on the deck, and when the fight was over the crew emerged to discover, the python as victor engaged in eating the tiger.

Casualties amongst those early steamers were few, the most notable being the stranding of the INDRABARAH near Wanganui in 1913. Ashore for over two months, she was eventually refloated and repaired at Port Chalmers.

When the Commonwealth & Dominion Line was formed in 1914, it was first reported in the shipping press that the complete fleet of the Indra Line of T. B. Royden & Sons, Liverpool, was to be taken over as part of that company's contribution to the new concern. However, only three ships were transferred to the new company, with INDRALEMA, (built 1901), INDRABARAH (built 1910) and INDRAPURA (built 1911) being renamed PORT ALMA, PORT ELLIOT and PORT ADELAIDE respectively.

Of the four concerns merged in 1914, the contribution of the Indra Line was the smallest, but the Royden family connection with the group was significant and may well have been a factor in the purchase of the Commonwealth & Dominion Line by Cunard Steamship Company in 1916. Thomas Royden joined the Commonwealth & Dominion Board in 1914 but he was already a director of Cunard, as well as other shipping companies. Subsequently he served on the Commonwealth & Dominion and Port Line boards from 1914 until his death in 1950. Furthermore he was Chairman of Cunard from 1922 to 1930 and remained on the board as a director for a further twenty years.

An early casualty during World War One was the two-year-old steamer INDRANI, which was captured by the German cruiser KARLSRUHE in September 1914, and later sunk by her after use as a collier.

In August 1915 the Indra Line with its seven steamers totalling 38,072 tons was sold to Alfred Holt & Company, a purchase that enabled Holts to obtain a place on the New York - China conference. The purchase was arranged by Sir Thomas Royden, who met Richard Holt at the Admiralty in London and negotiated a sale price of £750,000, a sum recorded as prodigious by Richard Holt. Holt's shareholders were not told the full terms of the deal, only that the purchase price was reasonable. Following the purchase all seven ships were renamed with Homeric names commencing with "Eury" and one of them, the EURYADES built in 1913 as INDRA (3) remained in Blue Funnel service until 1948. For a time the American trades were, indeed, very successful, but with the return of peace, constant conference problems, low freight rates, and the impact of the great slump on America after 1929 all combined to make the American venture far less profitable than Richard Holt had hoped.

Although Roydens transferred three ships to the Commonwealth & Dominion Line in 1914 and sold seven ships to Alfred Holt & Company in 1915, they still retained a shipping interest through the Santa Clara Steamship Company Ltd., which was registered in Liverpool on 30th March 1911, operating a total of five vessels between 1911 and 1933. The first two vessels owned by this company were purchased from Scrutton, Sons & Company and were registered, at first with Inver Steamships Ltd before being transferred to the Santa Clara concern. The Santa Clara S.S Company Ltd, was set up to run a feeder service from the West Indies to New York and within three years its first two secondhand ships had been replaced by two new buildings from the yard of Dunlop, Bremner, of Port Glasgow. Unfortunately, the SANTA ISABEL (completed in 1914) was sunk off the Cape Verde Islands in April 1918 by gunfire from U 153. Her replacement, a "C" type standard cargo ship was delivered in March 1920 and on her sale in 1933 to the Bristol City Line of Steamers, the company was wound up.

Inver Steamships was a subsidiary company set up by Roydens in 1906. They took over their first steamer, the INVERCLYDE in 1906, followed by the INVERESK in 1907. The latter was wrecked at Juan de Nova in 1911 and the company was wound up on the sale of the INVERCLYDE to Alfred Holt in 1915.

During World War One, the SANTA MARGHERITA, an experimental diesel, engined tanker was managed on behalf of the Admiralty, as was an ex - German vessel the PROVIDENTIA which was renamed PROVIDENCE.

The livery of Indra Line was a red funnel with black top and a black hull with green boot topping, whilst upperworks and masts were white and derricks were painted light brown. The house flag was swallow tailed with a pattern of two equal horizontal halves of blue and red with a white diamond in the centre. Royden's house flag (with the addition of a maple leaf on the white diamond) was used between 1936 and 1971 as the emblem of the Montreal, Australia and New Zealand Line (MANZ Line), Port Line having a one third interest in this company.

On 28th April 1955 the Shipbuilding and Shipping Record reported that a new company to be known as Thomas Royden & Sons Ltd. had been formed. It was a Private company with a capital of £250, and its objectives were to carry on the business of shipowners and brokers, shipping and travel agents. The directors were Sir Ernest B. Royden, Bt., John L Royden. Thomas Hind, James M. Harrison and Raymond B Jones. The registered office was located at the Cunard Building Liverpool 2.

The Royden Fleet

R 1. THE DUKE (1843 - 1854) Wooden Ship
O.N. 15028. 765 tons. 128.5 x 28.5 x 21.7 feet.
1843: Launched by Thomas Royden, Liverpool (Yard No. 38), for T. Royden & others, Liverpool. 1854: Sold to George Kendall, Liverpool. 1.1867: Whilst on a voyage from Cardiff to Kingston, Jamaica with a cargo of coal she struck the North Reef, Barbuda and became a total wreck. Crew saved.

R 2. ISMYR (1) (1850 - 1866) Wooden Barqantine
O.N. 27052. 245 tons. 98.8 x 20.7 x 15.0 feet.
10.6.1850: Launched by Thomas Royden, Liverpool (Yard No. 52), for T. Royden & John Sanders, Liverpool. 1866: Sold to Evans & Company, Bideford. 1876: Sold to J. M. Cock, Liverpool. 1882: Sold to J. Evans, Liverpool. 1883: Sold to J. Knott, North Shields. 1888: Sold to W. Milburn, North Shields. 1.12.1893: Whilst on a voyage from Burry Port to Woolwich with a cargo of coal, wrecked on Rat Island, Lundy Island.

R 3. CHILENA (1853 - 1872) Wooden Barque
O.N. 14784. 408 tons. 121.0 x 21.0 x 18.4 feet.
30.12.1853: Launched by Thomas Royden, Liverpool (Yard No. 59), for T. Royden, Liverpool. 1872: Sold to R. McMorland, Greenock. 1884: Sold to T. Rhys, Greenock. 1886: Sold to West of Scotland Shipping Company, Greenock. 1887: Sold to W. Polkinghorne, Greenock. 1888: Sold for demolition.

R 4. ANNE ROYDEN (1856 - 1883) Wooden Ship.
O.N. 13581. 1,175 tons. 174.5 x 35.5 x 22.5 feet.
11.1.1856: Launched by Thomas Royden, Liverpool (Yard No. 61), for T. Royden, Liverpool. 1883: Sold to P. Landberg, Zoon & B. C de Jong, Batavia, and renamed CORNELIA ELIZABETH. 1886: Reduced to a barque. 1892: Sold to Giesberger & Company, Batavia. 14.4.1892: Lost by fire in Batavia Roads.

R 5. BARKHILL (1857 - 1863) Wooden Brig
O.N. 25787. 175 tons. 83.7 x 19.2 x 13.6 feet.
1845: Launched by Thomas Royden, Liverpool (Yard No. 41), for S. & J. Job, Liverpool. 1.1857: Sold to Thomas Royden. 1863: Sold to J. Thompson, Liverpool. 13.7.1869: Sold to Foreign Owners.

R 6. FRANKBY (1857 - 1874) Wooden Barque
O.N. 20457. 437 tons. 131.6 x 26.7 x 18.0 feet.
11.1857: Launched by Thomas Royden, Liverpool (Yard No. 62), for T. Royden, Liverpool. 1874: Sold to J. B. Walmsley & Company, Liverpool. 1875: Sold to R. D. Hearn, Liverpool. 10.1877: Sold to Lucas Bros & Company, Bristol. 1889: Hulked, but later restored to service. 1895: Wrecked in the Cameroons River, West Africa.

R 7. LA ZINGARA (1860 - 1867) Wooden Barque
O.N. 29144. 287 tons. 125.6 x 23.5 x 14.1 feet.
15.9.1860: Launched by Thomas Royden, Liverpool (Yard No. 67), for T. Royden, Liverpool. 27.3.1867: Sold to R. Brown, Liverpool. 4.1870: Sold to R. & W. Poole King, Bristol. 1888: Whilst on a voyage from the west coast of Africa to the Azores, disappeared.

R 8. SPRINGWOOD (1862 - 1884) Wooden Ship
O.N. 45437. 990 tons. 180.7 x 34.2 x 22.5 feet.

22.11.1862: Launched by T. Royden & Son, Liverpool (Yard No. 71), for T. Royden & Son, Liverpool. 1884: Sold to Irwell Shipping Company Ltd., Liverpool. 20.7.1887: Whilst anchored at Redonda Island, West Indies, having loaded a full cargo of erude phosphate, for Booth Bay, Maine, parted her anchor-chains during a severe S.S.E., gale and was driven aground. 28.9.1887: Broke up during a heavy swell.

R 9. CLIFFORD (1864 - 1871) Iron Ship
O.N. 51011. 915 tons. 198.1 x 32.0 x 20.4 feet.
20.9.1864: Launched by T. Royden & Son, Liverpool (Yard No. 76), for T. Royden & Son, Liverpool. 7.4.1871: Whilst on a voyage from Calcutta to Dundee, was in collision with BRITISH LION, 20 miles W.S.W of Beachy Head. 22.4.1871: Having undergone temporary repairs, arrived at Dundee in tow. 30.9.1871: Whilst on a voyage from Shields to San Francisco, was totally dismasted and abandoned in about 58S., 65W., south of Cape Horn The crew were taken off by the S. CURLING and landed at Callao.

R 10. BEATRICE (1864 - 1883) Iron Barque
O.N. 50471. 610 tons. 172.2 x 27.8 x 17.7 feet.
20.7.1864: Launched by T. Royden & Son, Liverpool (Yard No. 79), for T. Royden & Son, Liverpool. 7.2.1883: Departed from Llico, Chile bound for Falmouth with a cargo of wheat and disappeared.

R 11. ISMYR (2) (1868 - 1879) Iron Barque
O.N. 60049. 610 tons. 171.8 x 27.9 x 17.5 feet.
1.1868: Launched by T. Royden & Sons, Liverpool (Yard No. 100), for T. Royden & Sons, Liverpool. 9.3.1868: Registered. 2.1879: Whilst on a voyage from Port Pirie to the United Kingdom with a cargo of wheat, disappeared and believed wrecked on Reef Head near Althorpe Island, Spencer Gulf.

R 12. L'ALLEGRO (1868 - 1885) Iron Barque
O.N. 60077. 612 tons. 172.0 x 28.6 x 17.5 feet.
5.1868: Launched by T. Royden & Sons, Liverpool (Yard No. 105), for T. Royden & Sons, Liverpool. 3.7.1868: Registered. 15.1.1885: Sold to M. Burmeister, Hamburg, and renamed NANNY. 13.5.1890: Stranded Santos Bar, Brazil.

R 13. SIR JOHN LAWRENCE (1868 - 1882) Wooden Ship
O.N. 27139. 1,090 net. 188.5 x 36.0 x 22.9 feet.
1859: Launched by T. Royden, Liverpool (Yard No. 64), for Farnworth & Jardine, Liverpool. 1868: Sold to T. Royden & Sons, Liverpool. 24.5.1882: Sold to Ole Larsen, Tonsberg, Norway. 1885: Sold to O. L. Roed, Tonsberg, Norway. 1896: Sold to Hjalmar Roed, Norway. 1.10.1904: Whilst on voyage in ballast, from London to Fredrikstad, wrecked in Kristiania Fjord, Fredrikstad.

R 14. SABRINA (1874 - 1884) Iron Barque
O.N. 70863. 792 tons. 187.2 x 31.7 x 19.9 feet.
7.1874: Launched by T. Royden & Sons, Liverpool (Yard No. 161), for T. Royden & Sons, Liverpool. 26.8.1974: Registered. 1884: Sold to J. Newton & Company, Liverpool. 1906: Sold to E. & J. Chiappe, Callao, Peru. 1908: Sold to Fratelli Chiappe. 7.10.1910: Wrecked at Chinchas whilst loading Guano.

R 15. LURLEI (1875 - 1884) Iron Barque
O.N. 74468. 835 tons. 185.0 x 31.7 x 19.8 feet.
8.1875: Launched by T. Royden & Sons, Liverpool (Yard No. 170), for T. Royden & Sons, Liverpool. 1884: Sold to J. B. Walmsley, Liverpool. 1906: Sold to Oelckers Hermanos, Valparaiso, Chile. 1913: Sold to Carlos Oelckers. 1918: Sold to Irala y Ugalde, Bilbao, and renamed ALBERTO. 1923: Reduced to hulk, owners now Cia. de Remolcador Ibaizabal. (Sota Aznar, managers).

R 16. LUCILE (1877 - 1881) Iron Ship
O.N. 76498. 1491 tons. 232.0 x 37.9 x 22.8 feet.
3.1877: Launched by T. Royden & Sons, Liverpool (Yard No. 177), for T. Royden & Sons, Liverpool. 1881: Sold to Thompson, Anderson & Company, Liverpool. 1882: Renamed SIERRA CORDOVA. 1888: Owners now Sierra Shipping Company (Thompson, Anderson & Company, managers). 1902: Sold to L. Gundersen, Porsgrund, Norway, and renamed HEIMDAL. 1903: Sold to Acties Heimdal (Leif Gundersen). 25.1.1913: Damaged by collision and abandoned 7 miles west of the Sandettie Lightship. Subsequently towed into Dunkirk derelict, and later taken to Boulogne and demolished.

R 17. LARNACA (1878 - 1881) Iron Ship
O.N. 78816. 1,497 tons. 234.5 x 38.0 x 23.0 feet.
9.1878: Launched by T. Royden & Sons, Liverpool (Yard No. 193), for T. Royden & Sons, Liverpool. 1881: Sold to Johnston Sproule & Company, Liverpool. 10.1894: Sold to the Liver Shipping Company, (Johnston & Sproule, managers), Liverpool. 11.10.1898: Sold to G. Maresca fu G, Castellamare di Stabia, Italy, and renamed ELISA. 10.1911: Demolished at Genoa.

R 18. LATHOM (1) (1883 - 1884) Iron Ship
O.N. 86286. 2,048 tons. 269.0 x 41.6 x 24.3 feet.
1883: Launched by T. Royden & Sons, Liverpool (Yard No. 217), for T. Royden & Sons, Liverpool. 6.3.1883: Registered. 1.1884: Whilst on a voyage from Calcutta to London with general cargo, stranded on Kentish Knock, Thames Estuary, and became a total wreck.

R 19. LATHOM (2) (1891) Steel Barque
O.N. 99304. 3082 tons. 324.0 x 46.0 x 25.2 feet.
1891: Launched by T. Royden & Sons, Liverpool (Yard No. 259), for T. B. Royden, Liverpool, and sold on completion to the Steel Sailing Ship "Lathom" Company Ltd., (Macvicar, Marshall & Company, managers), Liverpool. 1896: Sold to D. H. Watjen & Company, Bremen, and renamed BERTHA. 10.1900: Lost West Coast South America.

R 20. INDRA (1) (1888 - 1896)
O.N. 93769. 3,582g. 2,337n. 361.8 x 44.3 x 27.1 feet.
T.3-cyl. steam engine (3791) manufactured by Fawcett, Preston & Company, Liverpool. 348 nhp.
3.1888: Completed by T. Royden & Sons, Liverpool (Yard No. 230), for the Indra Steamship Company Ltd. (T. B. Royden) (Macvicar, Marshall & Company, managers), Liverpool. 10.3.1888: Trials. 26.11.1896: Sold to William Thompson, Dundee. 13.1.1897: Sold to Steamship Kildona Company Ltd. (W. Thomson & Sons, managers), Dundee, and renamed KILDONA. 14.12.1907: Whilst on a voyage from the River Tyne to Portland, Maine with general cargo, wrecked on Brazil Rocks near Cape Sable, Nova Scotia.

R 21. INDRANI (1) (1888 - 1892)
O.N. 93798. 3,584g. 2,337n. 361.8 x 44.3 x 27.0 feet.
T.3-cyl. steam engine (3792) manufactured by Fawcett, Preston & Company, Liverpool. 348 nhp. 1909: New donkey boiler fitted.
5.1888: Launched by T. Royden & Sons, Liverpool (Yard No. 248), for the Indrani Steamship Company Ltd. (T. B. Royden) (Macvicar, Marshall & Company, managers), Liverpool. 8.1888: Completed. 21.4.1892: Sold to Donaldson Bros, Glasgow. 11.1913: Sold to Donaldson Line Ltd. 27.6.1915: Whilst on a voyage from the Clyde to Montreal with general cargo, was captured by and then torpedoed by the German submarine U 24 off the Tusker Light, Southern Ireland.

INDRANI - seen in Donaldson Line funnel colours. (R. M. Parsons)

INDRAMAYO (Tom Rayner)

R 22. INDRAMAYO (1) (1889 - 1901)
O.N. 96302. 4,110g. 2,662n.   400.2 x 45.1 x 20.2 feet.
T.3-cyl. steam engine manufactured by the shipbuilder. 421nhp. 11kts. 1921: New donkey boiler fitted.
3.4.1889: Launched by London & Glasgow Engineering & Iron Shipbuilding Company Ltd., Govan, Glasgow (Yard No. 259), for the Indramayo Steamship Company Ltd. (T. B. Royden) (Macvicar, Marshall & Company, managers), Liverpool. 5.1889: Completed. 1901: Sold to Houlder Line Ltd. (Houlder Bros & Company Ltd., managers), Liverpool, and renamed THORPE GRANGE. 1930: Sold to J. J. King & Company, for demolition at Garston.

R 23. INDRAPURA (1) (1890 - 1897)
O.N. 97761. 3,859g. 2,510n.   369.8 x 44.0 x 27.7 feet.
T.3-cyl. steam engine manufactured by Fawcett, Preston & Company Ltd., Liverpool. 372nhp. 10kts. 1907: New Donkey Boiler fitted.
21.1.1890: Launched by T. Royden & Sons, Liverpool (Yard No. 253), for Macvicar, Marshall & Company, Liverpool. 3.1890: Completed for the Indrapura Steamship Company Ltd. (T. B. Royden, managers), Liverpool. 1897: Sold to Raeburn & Verel, Glasgow, and renamed WESTMINSTER. 1901: Transferred to the Steamship Westminster Company Ltd. (Raeburn & Verel, managers), Glasgow. 1904:

Sold to Ukon Gonzayemon, Osaka, Japan, and renamed FUKUI MARU. 1918: Sold to Uchida Kisen Kabushiki Kaisha, Amagasaki. 27.10.1921: Whilst on a voyage from Seattle and Tacoma to Yokohama and Kobe with lumber, was abandoned at sea 375 miles from Cape Flattery.

R 24. INDRALEMA (1) (1894 - 1900)

O.N. 102133. 3,150g. 2,020n. 330.0 x 41.5 x 25.1 feet.
T.3-cyl. steam engine manufactured by the Central Marine Engineering Works, West Hartlepool. 264 nhp. 10kts.
1.8.1893: Keel laid by C. S. Swan & Hunter, Newcastle (Yard No. 187), for the Indralema Steamship Company Ltd. (T. B. Royden, managers), Liverpool. 23.12.1893: Launched. 22.2.1894: Completed. 30.4.1900: Sold to the Ulster Steamship Company Ltd., (G. Heyn & Sons, managers), Belfast, and renamed BRAY HEAD. 14.3.1917: Whilst on a voyage from St. Johns, New Brunswick to Belfast, with general cargo, she was attacked with gunfire by the German submarine U 44, of the 3rd U-boat Flotilla operating from Emden and commanded by Kapitan Leutnant Paul Wagenfuhr, and sunk in position 52.04N., 18.50W., approximately 375 miles N.W. by W., from the Fastnet. 21 lives including the captain were lost.

R 25. INDRANI (2) (1894 - 1911)

O.N. 102152. 4,994g. 3,226n. 400.0 x 48.2 x 29.3 feet.
T.3-cyl. steam engine manufactured by the shipbuilder. 532 nhp. 11kts.
29.4.1894: Launched by The Naval Construction & Armaments Company Ltd., Barrow (Yard No. 225), for the Indrani Steamship Company Ltd. (T. B. Royden, managers), Liverpool. 5.1894: Completed. 21.2.1902: Transferred to the Indra Line Ltd. (same managers), Liverpool. 5.1911: Sold to Kishimoto Kisen Kabushiki Kaisha, Japan, and renamed SHINBU MARU. 1922: Sold to Taiyo Kaiun Kabushiki Kaisha, Japan. 1930: Sold to Yagi Honten K.K., Japan, and renamed JINBU MARU. 1932: Sold to Yagi Gyogyo K.K. 1932: Sold to Taihei Gyogyo K.K., Hakodate. 1938: Owners restyled Taiheiyo Gyogyo K.K., and renamed ZINBU MARU. 11.6.1943: Torpedoed and sunk by United States submarine S 28 in position 50.23N., 155.36E.

INDRAGHIRI (Ambrose Greenway collection)

R 26. INDRAGHIRI (1) (1896 - 1910)

O.N. 105384. 4,927g. 3,181n. 400.4 x 48.2 x 29.0 feet.
T.3-cyl. steam engine manufactured by D. Rowan & Son, Glasgow. 485 nhp. 11kts.
5.3.1896: Launched by Charles Connell & Company, Glasgow (Yard No. 225), for the Indraghiri Steamship Company Ltd. (T. B. Royden, managers). 27.4.1896: Completed. 18.7.1900: Badly damaged by fire while loading at Woolwich. The cargo included explosives. 1901: Transferred to the Indra Line Ltd., (same managers), Liverpool. 17.4.1907: Grounded in the Suez Canal near Ismailia. 11.1910: Purchased by the Brodstone Steamship Company Ltd. (William Raphael Outram, manager), Liverpool, and renamed BRODSTONE. 1912: Management transferred to The Blue Star Line Ltd. 15.8.1917: Whilst on a voyage from Cardiff to Zarate, Argentine Republic, was torpedoed and sunk by the German submarine UB 40, 95 miles W. ¼ S., from Ushant, France. 5 members of her crew were lost.

R 27. INDRA (2) (1897 - 1913)
O.N. 106839. 6,057g. 3,923n.   430.0 x 51.3 x 30.8 feet.
T.3-cyl. steam engine manufactured by D. Rowan & Son, Glasgow. 476 nhp. 11kts.
30.12.1896: Launched by Charles Connell & Company, Glasgow (Yard No. 235), for the Indra Steamship Company Ltd. (T. B. Royden, managers), Liverpool. 16.2.1897: Completed. 8.1900: Stranded. 3.12.1901: Transferred to the Indra Line Ltd., (same managers), Liverpool. 29.11.1912: Registry closed upon sale to unspecified Japanese owners but was later reposessed upon collapse of the sale. 27.3.1913: Sold to Samuel Samuel, London, and renamed INDRO. 11.1913: Sold to Goshi Kaisha Kishimoto Shokai, Japan, and renamed BANKOKU MARU. 1919: Owners Taisho Kisen K.K., (Taiyo Kaiun K.K., managers). 6.3.1929: Whilst on a voyage from Sydney to Keelung, with a cargo of wheat, wrecked on Kama Island, West Caroline Islands. 1933: Salvaged and demolished in Japan.

R 28. INDRAPURA (2) (1897 - 1911)
O.N. 106872. 4,899g. 3,152n.   400.0 x 49.2 x 28.3 feet.
T.3-cyl. steam engine manufactured by D. Rowan & Company, Glasgow. 476 nhp. 11kts.
21.6.1897: Launched by Charles Connell & Company, Glasgow (Yard No. 238), for the Indrapura Steamship Company Ltd. (T. B. Royden, managers), Liverpool. 8.1897: Completed. 30.5.1911: Sold to Osaka Shosen Kabushiki Kaisha, Japan, and renamed INDO MARU. 1925: Owners restyled as Utsubo Shosen K.K., Osaka. 1931: Sold for demolition in Japan.

R 29. INDRAVELLI (1897 - 1912)
O.N. 106891. 4,899g. 3,152n. 400.0 x 49.2 x 28.3 feet.
T.3-cyl. steam engine manufactured by D. Rowan & Company, Glasgow. 476 nhp. 11kts.
31.8.1897: Launched by Charles Connell & Company, Glasgow (Yard No. 239), for the Indravelli Steamship Company Ltd. (T. B. Royden, managers), Liverpool. 12.1897: Completed. 1.2.1902: Transferred to the Indra Line Ltd., (same managers), Liverpool. 25.7.1912: Sold to Meiji Kaiun Kabushiki Kaisha, Japan, and renamed NANKAI MARU. 1926: Sold to Mikami K.K., Japan. 1932: Sold to Fuji Tachiji Fuchumura. 1932: Sold to Toyo Kyoyeisha K.K. 1933: Sold for demolition in Japan.

R 30. INDRADEVI (1) (1898 - 1898)
O.N. 109997. 2,993g. 1,917n. 328.0 x 47.7 x 21.1 feet.
T.3-cyl. steam engine manufactured by J. Dickinson & Son, Sunderland. 300 nhp. 10kts.
1.10.1898: Launched by J. Blumer & Company, Sunderland (Yard No. 145), for the Indradevi Steamship Company Ltd. (T. B. Royden, managers), Liverpool. Sold before completion to Houlder, Middleton & Company, London, and renamed WHITGIFT. 27.10.1898: Completed. 13.11.1899: Sold to the Buenos Ayres Great Southern Railway Company (A. Holland, manager), London, and renamed ALFALFA. 27.4.1917: Sunk by the German submarine UB 32, 30 miles south west of the Isles of Scilly. Her crew of 30 were lost.

R 31. INDRADEVI (2) (1900 - 1911)
O.N. 110639. 5,683g. 3,702n. 420.6 x 53.2 x 29.4 feet.
T.3-cyl. steam engine manufactured by J. Dickinson & Sons Ltd., Sunderland. 615 nhp. 10kts.
14.12.1899: Launched by Sir J. Laing & Sons Ltd., Sunderland (Yard No. 573), for the Indradevi Steamship Company Ltd. (T. B. Royden, managers), Liverpool. 3.1900: Completed. 1911: Sold to Furness Withy & Company Ltd., and renamed CHASE SIDE. 1912: Sold to the British & Argentine Steam Navigation Company Ltd. (Furness, Withy & Company Ltd., managers), and renamed EL CORDOBES. 2.8.1917: Chased by a submarine in the Atlantic but escaped. 10.1926: Sold to M. Querci & O. Rosini, Genoa, and renamed PRATOMAGNO. 1931: Sold for demolition in Italy.

INDRADEVI (Tom Rayner)

R 32. INDRALEMA (2) (1901 - 1914)
O.N. 113469. 6,669g. 4,344n. 450.6 x 55.0 x 30.8 feet.
T.3-cyl. steam engine manufactured by D. Rowan & Company, Glasgow. 615 nhp. 12kts. Refrigerated capacity 238,549 cu.ft.
3.1901: Launched by Charles Connell & Company, Glasgow (Yard No. 259), for the Indralema Steamship Company Ltd. (T. B. Royden, managers), Liverpool. 6.1901: Completed for the Indra Line Ltd. (same manager). 31.12.1904: Damaged in collision with the British vessel MANCHESTER CORPORATION (5,467g./1899), outside Eastham Lock entrance. INDRALEMA was beached having suffered extensive damage to her starboard bow plating. Subsequently repaired, and returned to service. 25.4.1911: Collided with and sank TROOPER (958g./1902), owned by Fisher, Renwick & Company, off Dungeness. 1914: Transferred to The Commonwealth & Dominion Line Ltd., London. 12.10.1916: Renamed PORT ALMA. 1923: Reported as being sold for demolition but later in the year was sold for £15,000, to Vianda Steamship Company Ltd. (Wm. H. Muller & Company (London) Ltd., managers), London, and renamed VIANDA. 1927: Sold for £14, 000, to Soc. Anon.Di Nav. "Unione" (Pietro Ravano fu Marco, managers), Genoa, and renamed FIDELITAS. 1927: Refrigeration machinery removed. 10.1927: Ran ashore off the coast of Virginia U.S.A. Subsequently refloated after 1,600 tons of her cargo of coal had been jettisoned. 2.1932: Class Withdrawn. 5.1932: Sold for demolition in Italy.

R 33. INDRASAMHA (1901 - 1915)
O.N. 115214. 5,197g. 3,367n. 410.1 x 49.3 x 29.6 feet.
T.3-cyl. steam engine manufactured by D. Rowan & Company, Glasgow. 500 nhp. 11kts.
2.9.1901: Launched by Charles Connell & Company, Glasgow (Yard No. 262), for the Indra Line Ltd. (T. B. Royden, managers), Liverpool. 8.10.1901: Completed. 8.1915: Sold to the China Mutual Steam Navigation Company Ltd. (A. Holt & Company, managers), Liverpool, and renamed EURYDAMAS. 6.6.1924: Sold to Jugoslovensko Amerikanska Plovidba, Jugoslavia, and renamed JUGOSLAVIJA. 1928: Owners restyled as Jugoslavenski Lloyd A.D. 4.1934: Sold for £6,500, to Ruigi Balbi, Genoa for demolition.

INDRASAMHA (Ambrose Greenway collection)

R 34. INDRAMAYO (2) (1902 - 1914)
O.N. 115264. 5,200g. 3,370n.   410.4 x 49.3 x 29.5 feet.
T.3-cyl. steam engine manufactured by D. Rowan & Company, Glasgow. 500 nhp.   11kts.
20.2.1902: Launched by Charles Connell & Company, Glasgow (Yard No. 266), for the Indra Line Ltd. (T. B. Royden, managers), Liverpool. 22.3.1902: Completed. 4.3.1914: Sold to Ryoto Kisen Kabushiki Kaisha (Mitsui Bussan Kaisha Ltd., managers), Japan, and renamed KONGOSAN MARU. 1.3.1928: Whilst on a voyage from Dairen to Miike, with general cargo, wrecked on the Japanese Coast near Osezaki Lighthouse, Goto Island.

INDRAWADI (Ambrose Greenway collection)

R 35. INDRAWADI (1902 - 1915)
O.N. 115294. 5,194g. 3,369n.   410.3 x 49.3 x 29.5 feet.
T.3-cyl. steam engine manufactured by D. Rowan & Company, Glasgow. 500 nhp.   11kts.
20.5.1902: Launched by Charles Connell & Company, Glasgow (Yard No. 268), for Indra Line Ltd. (T. B. Royden, managers), Liverpool. 6.1902: Completed. 8.1915: Sold to the Ocean Steamship Company Ltd. (A. Holt & Company, managers), Liverpool, and renamed EURYMEDON. 1922: Sold to Southern Whaling & Sealing Company Ltd. (N. C. Watt, manager), London. Later in 1922: Sold to Skibs A/S

Southern Queen (T. Thorssen, managers). Norway, and renamed SOUTHERN QUEEN. Converted for carrying whale oil in bulk. 24.2.1928: Whilst working in the whale fishing grounds, was lost in the ice, east of the South Orkney Islands, She was carrying a large cargo of whale oil at the time of her loss.

R 36. INDRABARAH (1) (1905)

Admiralty dimensions:- 6,900g. 11,300disp. 470.0 x 55.00 x 41.0 feet
Two, T.3-cyl. steam engines manufactured by Richardsons, Westgarth. Twin screw. 3,500ihp. 11^1/$_2$kts.
2.11.1905: Launched by Sir James Laing & Sons Ltd., Sunderland (Yard No. 609), for T. B. Royden, Liverpool. 1.12.1905: Purchased for £90.000, before completion, by the Admiralty, for use as a depot ship. 1906: Completed as HMS CYCLOPS, a fleet repair ship. The shipbuilders lost £100,000 on this conversion and as a result, found themselves in financial difficulties. 1922: Converted into a submarine depot ship, and stationed in Mediterranean. 1937: Stationed near Oran during Spanish civil war to support two squadrons of RAF flying boats that were patrolling the Mediterranean. 10.1939: Attached to the Home fleet with the 3rd Submarine Flotilla (nine S class boats) stationed at Rothesay on the Clyde. 29.6.1947: Arrived at Newport for demolition by John Cashmore Ltd.

INDRADEO (A. Duncan)

R 37. INDRADEO (2) (1910 - 1915)

O.N. 128023. 5,559g. 3,507n. 430.2 x 50.2 x 30.7 feet.
T.3-cyl. steam engine manufactured by D. Rowan & Company, Glasgow. 517 nhp. 12kts.
12.1.1910: Launched by Charles Connell & Company Ltd., Glasgow (Yard No. 331), for the Indra Line Ltd. (T. B. Royden, managers), Liverpool. 3.1910: Completed. 8.1915: Sold to the Ocean Steamship Company Ltd. (A. Holt & Company, managers), Liverpool, and renamed EURYBATES. 12.1926: Sold to R. & J. Thomas & Company Ltd., Holyhead, and renamed CAMBRIAN PEERESS. 1928: Transferred to William Thomas Shipping Company Ltd. (R. & J. Thomas & Company Ltd., managers), Liverpool. 6.1931: Sold to Petrograd Steamers Ltd., (Wm. Thompson & Company, managers), Leith, and renamed BENDORAN. 1941: Sold to Ben Line Steamers Ltd., (same managers), Leith. 28.3.1944: Sold to The Ministry of War Transport, London. 9.6.1944: Sunk as a block-ship to form part of Mulberry Harbour (Gooseberry No. 4) at Arromanches, Normandy. 8.1946: Refloated. 19.5.1947: Arrived in tow at Blyth for demolition by Hughes Bolckow Shipbreaking Company Ltd.

R 38. INDRABARAH (2) (1910 - 1914)

O.N. 131279. 7,395g. 4,664n. 471.0 x 58.4 x 31.6 feet.
Two T.3-cyl. steam engines manufactured by Richardsons, Westgarth & Company Ltd., Hartlepool. Twin screw. 755 nhp. 12kts. Refrigerated capacity 289,337 cu.ft.
8.6.1910: Launched by Swan, Hunter & Wigham Richardson Ltd., Wallsend on Tyne (Yard No. 855), for the Indra Line Ltd. (T. B. Royden, managers), Liverpool. 8.1910: Completed. 2.5.1913: Whilst on a voyage from Gisborne to Wanganui, to load meat for London, ran aground 7 miles north of Wanganui. 7.1913: Refloated. 29.7.1913 until 10.9.1913: Docked at Port Chalmers for repair. 6.3.1914:

Transferred to The Commonwealth & Dominion Line Ltd., London. 30.3.1916: Renamed PORT ELLIOT. 12.1.1924: Whilst on a voyage from New York to Auckland and Wellington, with a cargo of motor vehicles, oils and general cargo, wrecked on Horeora Point, 80 miles north of Gisborne, New Zealand.

INDRABARAH ashore 10th May 1913. (World Ship Society Photograph Library)

INDRAPURA (Ambrose Greenway collection)

R 39. INDRAPURA (3) (1911 - 1914)
O.N. 131403. 8,144g. 5,147n. 490.6 x 61.3 x 32.4 feet.
Two T.3-cyl. steam engines manufactured by the Wallsend Slipway Company Ltd., Newcastle. Twin screw. 931 nhp. 13kts. Unspecified refrigerated capacity.
10.10.1911: Launched by Swan, Hunter & Wigham Richardson Ltd., Newcastle (Yard No. 887), for the Indra Line Ltd. (T. B. Royden, managers), Liverpool. 30.11.1911: Completed. 24.3.1914: Transferred to The Commonwealth & Dominion Line Ltd., London. 3.5.1916: Renamed PORT ADELAIDE. 3.2.1917: Whilst on a voyage from London to Sydney, N.S.W., was sunk by the German submarine U 81 in the North Atlantic in position 48.49N., 11.40W., 180 miles west south west of Fastnet. Her master was taken prisoner.

INDRAGHIRI as **EURYLOCHUS** (Tom Rayner)

R 40. INDRAGHIRI (2) (1912 - 1915)

O.N. 131424. 5,723g. 3,600n.   430.5 x 53.9 x 30.3 feet.
T.3-cyl. steam engine manufactured by the shipbuilder. 672 nhp. 12kts.
20.12.1911: Launched by the London & Glasgow Engineering & Iron Shipbuilding Company Ltd., Glasgow (Yard No. 361), for the Indra Line Ltd. (T. B. Royden, managers), Liverpool. 3.1912: Completed. 8.1915: Sold to the China Mutual Steam Navigation Company Ltd. (A. Holt & Company, managers), Liverpool, and renamed EURYLOCHUS. 22.7.1918: Chased by surfaced submarine when off Madeira and escaped. 29.1.1941: Whilst on a voyage from Liverpool to Takoradi with a cargo of aeroplanes, was captured and sunk by the German raider KORMORAN west of Freetown in position 08.15N., 25.04W. 15 of her crew of 82 were killed in the attack, 38 were taken prisoner, the remainder were picked by the Spanish ship MONTE TEIDE.

R 41. INDRANI (3) (1912 - 1914)

O.N. 131440. 5,706g. 3,615n.   430.1 x 54.0 x 30.4 feet.
T.3-cyl. steam engine manufactured by Dunsmuir & Jackson Ltd., Glasgow. 687 nhp. 12kts.
22.4.1912: Launched by Charles Connell & Company Ltd., Glasgow (Yard No. 345), for the Indra Line Ltd. (T. B. Royden, managers), Liverpool. 5.1912: Completed. 17.9.1914: Whilst on a voyage from Norfolk, Virginia to Rio de Janeiro with a cargo of coal, was captured by the German cruiser KARLSRUHE, 145 miles N. W. of Cape St Rogue. Used as a collier by the Germans, and renamed HOFFNUNG. 9.11.1914: Scuttled in position 11.27N., 63.10W.

INDRAKUALA as **EURYPYLUS** (World Ship Society Photograph Library)

R 42. INDRAKUALA (1912 - 1915)
O.N. 131445. 5,691g. 3,607n.   430.0 x 54.0 x 30.5 feet.
T.3-cyl. steam engine manufactured by Dunsmuir & Jackson Ltd., Glasgow. 687 nhp. 12kts.
15.6.1912: Launched by Charles Connell & Company Ltd., Glasgow (Yard No. 346), for the Indra Line Ltd. (T. B. Royden, managers), Liverpool. 7.1912: Completed. 8.1915: Sold to China Mutual Steam Navigation Company Ltd. (A. Holt & Company Ltd., managers), Liverpool, and renamed EURYPYLUS. 1938: Sold for £17,500 to Continental Transit Company Ltd., London, and renamed TRADE. 1939: Sold for £20,000, to The Board of Trade (later Ministry of Shipping and later Ministry of War Transport (Sir William Reardon Smith & Sons Ltd., managers), London, and renamed BOTAVON as part of the part of the Merchant Shipping Reserve.   2.5.1942: Whilst on a voyage from Middlesbrough to Murmansk with Government stores, was damaged by enemy aircraft torpedo, North West of North Cape in position 73.02.N., 19.46.E.   3.5.1942: Sunk by escort destroyer HMS BADSWORTH. At the time of her sinking she was the commodore ship of convoy PQ.15. 21 of her crew of 78 were lost.

INDRA as **EURYADES** (World Ship Society Photograph Library)

R 43. INDRA (3) (1913 - 1915)
O.N. 135488. 5,713g. 3,620n.   430.0 x 54.0 x 30.4 feet.
T.3-cyl. steam engine manufactured by Dunsmuir & Jackson Ltd., Glasgow. 592 nhp. 12kts.
23.6.1913:Launched by Charles Connell & Company Ltd., Glasgow (Yard No. 353), for the Indra Line Ltd., (T. B. Royden, managers), Liverpool. 8.1913: Completed. 8.1915: Sold to the Ocean Steamship Company Ltd. (A. Holt & Company, managers), Liverpool, and renamed EURYADES. 2.2.1918: Missed by torpedo in the Irish Channel. 1948: Sold via the British Iron & Steel Corporation to T. W. Ward Ltd., Sheffield, for demolition at their Briton Ferry facility. 15.10.1948: Left Glasgow for delivery voyage to shipbreakers. 19.10.1948: Arrived at Briton Ferry. 3.12.1948: Demolition commenced.

SANTA MARGHERITA as **TRIGONIA** (Authors collection)

R 44. SANTA MARGHERITA (1916 - 1920) Motor Tanker
O.N. 137509. 7,499g. 4,364n. 440.0 x 54.3 x 36.4 feet.
Two 8-cyl. 4 S. C. S. A., oil engines manufactured by the shipbuilder geared to twin screw shafts. 1921: New Donkey Boiler fitted.
Post 1928: 12-cyl. 4 S. C. S. A, oil engine manufactured by N. V. Werkspoor, Amsterdam.
1913: Laid down as OLYMPIA by Vickers Ltd., Barrow (Yard No. 445), for the Admiralty, London. 23.10.1915: Launched as SANTA MARGHERITA for Thomas Royden, Liverpool. 26.5.1916: Completed. 22.3.1920: Sold to the Anglo-Saxon Petroleum Company Ltd., London. 19.4.1920: Renamed MARINULA. 15.11.1927: Renamed TRIGONIA. 5.1928: Re-engined. 1939-1945: Employed as an oil storage hulk at Sierra Leone. 7.1945: Transferred as an oil storage hulk to Durban. 20.6.1946: Transferred to the Shell Company of Gibraltar Ltd., London, and became an oil storage hulk at Gibraltar. 2.1947: Class Withdrawn at Owners Request. 1951: Sold to John Cashmore Ltd., for demolition at Newport, Mon. 5.4.1951: Arrived at Newport, Mon.

Inver Steamships Ltd

IS 1. INVERCLYDE (1906 - 1915)
O.N. 124001. 4,995g. 3,214n. 400.6 x 52.3 x 29.3 feet.
T.3-cyl. steam engine manufactured by Dunsmuir & Jackson Ltd., Glasgow. 495 nhp. 11kts.
10.7.1906: Launched by Charles Connell & Company, Glasgow (Yard No. 306), for Inver Steamships Ltd. (T. B. Royden, managers), Liverpool. 10.1906: Completed. 8.1915: Sold to the Ocean Steamship Company Ltd. (A. Holt & Company, managers), Liverpool, and renamed EURYMACHUS. 11.6.1917: Chased by a U-boat in the Atlantic. 12.2.1926: Sold to Jugoslovensko Amerikanska Plovidba, Jugoslavia, and renamed NIKOLA MIHANOVIC. 1928: Owners restyled as Jugoslavensk: Lloyd A.D. 15.4.1929: Badly damaged by fire at Rotterdam. 16.4.1929: Fire extinguished. 1929: Sold to shipbreakers T. W. Ward Ltd., Sheffield, for demolition at their Inverkeithing facility.

IS 2. INVERESK (1907 - 1911)
O.N. 124042. 4,986g. 3,206n. 400.0 x 52.3 x 29.3 feet.
T.3-cyl. steam engine manufactured by Dunsmuir & Jackson Ltd., Glasgow. 495 nhp. 11kts.
29.1.1907: Launched by Charles Connell & Company Ltd., Glasgow (Yard No. 307), for Inver Steamships Ltd. (T. B. Royden, managers), Liverpool. 3.1907: Completed. 22.3.1911: Whilst on a voyage from New York to Yokkaichi, Japan, with a cargo of steel rails and bridge girders, wrecked at Juan de Nova, Mozambique Channel.

SAVAN at Bristol (World Ship Society Photograph Library)

IS 3. SAVAN / SANTA CLARA (1910 - 1911)
O.N. 105889.   2,585g. 1,668n.   312.6 x 41.2 x 14.9 feet.
T.3-cyl. steam engine manufactured by the shipbuilder. 260 nhp.
5.9.1896: Launched as SAVAN by John Readhead & Sons, South Shields (Yard No. 318), for Scrutton, Sons & Company. 19.10.1896: Completed. 10.11.1910: Sold to Inver Steamships Ltd. (T. B. Royden, managers). 14.11.1910: Renamed SANTA CLARA. 12.4.1911: Sold to Santa Clara Steamship Company Ltd. (T. B. Royden, managers), Liverpool. 9.10.1914: Sold to American & Cuban Steamship Line Inc. New York. 1923: Demolished by Boston Iron & Metal Company, Boston. U.S.A.

IS 4. SABA / PINAR DEL RIO (1) (1911 - 1911)
O.N. 105713. 2,504g. 1,608n.   306.2 x 41.1 x 14.9 feet.
T.3-cyl. steam engine manufactured by the shipbuilder. 262 nhp.
8.6.1895: Launched as SABA by John Readhead & Sons, South Shields (Yard No. 307), for Scrutton, Sons & Company. 24.7.1895: Completed. 18.1.1911: Sold to Inver Steamships Ltd. (T. B. Royden, managers). 23.1.1911: Renamed PINAR DEL RIO. 12.4.1911: Sold to Santa Clara Steamship Company Ltd. (T. B. Royden, managers), Liverpool. 16.9.1914: Sold to American & Cuban Steamship Line. Inc. New York. 8.6.1918: Captured and sunk by gunfire by the German submarine U 151, in a position 36.16N., 73.55W.

Royden Chartered Ship

RC 1. INDRADEO (1) (1902 - 1907)
O.N. 115315. 5,315g. 3,457n.   410.2 x 50.2 x 29.2 feet.
T.3-cyl. steam engine manufactured by J. Dickinson & Sons Ltd., Sunderland. 493 nhp.
8.7.1902: Launched by Sir James Laing & Sons Ltd., Sunderland (Yard No. 592), for Wright, Graham & Company, Liverpool. 8.1902: Completed for Falls Line Steamship Company Ltd. (T. B. Royden, chartering-managers), Liverpool. 1907: Returned to the Falls Line Steamship Company Ltd. (Wright, Graham & Company, managers), Liverpool, and renamed FALLS OF MONESS. 1913: Sold to the Teakwood Steamship Company Ltd. (J. I. Jacobs & Company, managers), London, and renamed TEAKWOOD. 28.4.1917: Whilst on a voyage from Port Arthur to Port Said, was sunk by submarine torpedo 26 miles S.W. by W., from Sapienza Island. All her crew were saved.

Santa Clara Steamship Company
Founded 1911
U.S. And West Indies service.

SC 1. SANTA CLARA   (1911 - 1914) see ship No. IS 3. above.

SC 2. PINAR DEL RIO (1) (1911 - 1914) see ship No. IS 4. above.

SC 3. SANTA THERESA   (1914 - 1924)
O.N. 135578. 2,016g. 1,208n.   290.7 x 42.2 x 19.4 feet.
T. 3 cyl. steam engine manufactured by the shipbuilder. 236 nhp.
9.4.1914: Launched by Dunlop, Bremner & Company Ltd., Port Glasgow (Yard No. 280), for the Santa Clara Steamship Company Ltd. (T. B. Royden, managers), Liverpool. 5.1914: Completed. 28.9.1924: Whilst on a voyage from Cardanas, Cuba to New York with a cargo of sugar, foundered 100 miles off Savannah.

SC 4. SANTA ISABEL (1914 - 1918)
O.N. 135587. 2,023g. 1,211n.   290.7 x 42.2 x 19.4 feet.
T.3-cyl. steam engine manufactured by the shipbuilder. 236 nhp.
21.5.1914: Launched by Dunlop, Bremner & Company Ltd., Port Glasgow (Yard No. 281), for the Santa Clara Steamship Company Ltd. (T. Royden & Sons, managers), Liverpool. 15.6.1914: Completed. 14.4.1918: Whilst on a voyage from Cardiff to Sierra Leone, with a cargo of coal, was captured and sunk with gunfire by the German submarine U 153, 15 miles west of Cape Verde Islands, in a position 14.40N., 17.54W.,   1 member of her crew was lost.

PINAR DEL RIO (2) as **MONTREAL CITY** at Bristol. (World Ship Society Photograph Library)

SC 5. PINAR DEL RIO (2) (1920 - 1933)
O.N. 143621. 3,069g. 1,830n. 331.1 x 46.7 x 23.2 feet.
T.3-cyl. steam engine manufactured by Buckley & Taylor Ltd, Oldham. 378 nhp.
23.12.1919: Launched by North of Ireland Shipbuilding Company Ltd., Londonderry (Yard No. 90), for the Santa Clara Steamship Company Ltd. (T. Royden & Sons, managers), Liverpool. 18.3.1920: Completed. 26.4.1933: Sold to the Bristol City Line of Steamers Ltd (Charles Hill & Sons, managers), Bristol. 29.4.1933: Renamed MONTREAL CITY. 21.12.1942: Whilst on a voyage from Bristol to New York with a cargo of 1,800 tons of china clay and general cargo, and a straggler from convoy O.N. S.152, was sunk by the German submarine U 591, (K/L H. Zetzche) in position 50.23N., 38.00W. Her crew of 33 and 7 gunners were lost.

Managed for the Admiralty.

SCM 1. PROVIDENCE (1915 - 1917)
O.N. 135361. 2,970g. 1,904n. 301.4 x 43.2 x 18.9 feet.
T.3-cyl. steam engine manufactured by the shipbuilder.
1903: Completed as PROVIDENTIA by A. G. 'Neptun', Rostock, for Dampfschiffe Reederi 'Hom' A. G., Lubeck. 13.1.1915: Requisitioned by the Admiralty, renamed PROVIDENCE, and registered at Manchester, (Santa Clara Steamship Company Ltd. (T. Royden & Sons, managers), Liverpool, appointed as managers). 22.3.1917: Whilst on a voyage from Cork to France with a cargo of hay, she struck a mine laid by the German submarine UC 48, in the St Georges Channel 1¼ miles S. by W. ½ W., from the Barrels light vessel and sank.

WILLIAM MILBURN

The North East element of the Port Line story was founded at Blyth in Northumberland in 1851 by William Milburn (1826-1903), when he formed a partnership with Edmund H. Watts (1830-1902), and from 1857 until 1879 when the partnership was dissolved the company traded as Watts, Milburn & Company. In the mid-nineteenth century Blyth was a small port exporting coal, but it was overshadowed by the more important commercial centre of Newcastle upon Tyne which dominated the trade in the area. However, Blyth's position should not be underestimated as, for example, it exported 172,946 tons of coal in 1,067 vessels (trading both coastwise and foreign) in 1856. The shipping community of which Milburn was about to become a member must have debated the early use of steam power at great length. Steam had been introduced on the new railways opened from 1840 onwards in the Blyth area, and between 1842 and 1846 the twin-screw steamship BEDLINGTON, traded between Blyth and the Tyne. These new developments in the use of steam for transport purposes created a lasting impression on Milburn and would have contributed to his decision to move into steamships in the mid 1860s.

William Milburn the eldest of nine children was born in 1826 on a farm called Sparrow House near Bothal, Northumberland. His father, George, had several occupations as the family grew up, starting as a farm labourer and becoming a butcher in about 1838. This occupation was followed by William who had his own butcher's shop in the busy port of Blyth from about 1852. William Milburn, (the founder of the company) was a typical example of a Victorian entrepreneur, he started his working life as a butcher in the small town of Blyth, Northumberland, and when he died on 12th November 1903, his estate was valued at almost £248,000, which included several large houses and estates, as well as a major shareholding in a large Northumberland coal mining company, the Ashington Coal Company Ltd.

During that time he built up one of the largest and most successful shipping concerns on the North East coast, his shipping company eventually merging with three others in 1914 to become the Commonwealth & Dominion Line Ltd, which subsequently became part of the Cunard Steamship Company Ltd. When in 1879 he bought Rosedale Abbey and its estates in North Yorkshire he became Lord of the Manor. An obituary in the Newcastle Chronicle, described him as a well-known Newcastle shipowner, Chairman of Ashington Coal Company Ltd, Director of York City and County Banking Company Ltd and several steamship insurance associations. However, in his Will he modestly referred to himself as "a merchant".

William Milburn's entry into shipowning followed conventional lines for the period. Having established himself as a butcher, he made an investment in two collier brigs.

In 1849, when he was 22 years old William Milburn, the butcher, joined the ranks of Blyth collier brig owners when he acquired a quarter share (16/64) of the JOHN TWIZELL (owned by the Blyth pilot John Twizell) and, a year later, he purchased a shareholding (8/64) in another brig, the VOLANT. On the 23rd October 1850 William Milburn, the founder of the Company, married Mary Davison (1830-1909), the daughter of John and Catherine Davison, a local mill and shipowning family. The newly married couple set up house in Bridge Street, Blyth, later moving to Sussex Street to live over the butcher's shop.

The appeal of being involved in shipping (apart from supplying victuals), together with the profits from his initial venture into shipowning, led Milburn in May 1851 to purchase the one-year old 212-ton brig PERO built at Sunderland. When Milburn acquired the PERO he contained the risk and profit between himself and the vessel's master by reverting to the tradition of dividing a vessel into thirds (Milburn 43/64 and the master, John Cole, 21/64). Making the master a shareholder in his vessel was a shrewd move, because it gave the master the additional incentive to look after his own property! It was not uncommon for the master to agree to take a share in his command; indeed it was the practice of some owners to make this part of the master's wages. No doubt at the beginning of his shipping career William Milburn would have welcomed an experienced master to help to handle the ship's business, whilst he gained practical knowledge in shipowning at Blyth.

Several facets combined to make it a favourable time for a young man to enter the shipping business. The Navigation Acts were repealed in 1850 encouraging free trade, whilst trading vessels built on the Wear were available at a reasonable price and there was a steady demand for coal, thereby ensuring a flourishing trade for both the coastal and export vessels.

The Navigation Acts had been designed to ensure that most of the imports and exports for Britain and her Empire were carried in British owned and British built-vessels manned by British seamen, as well as to provide a Naval Reserve of trained seamen for possible use by the Royal Navy in time of war. This effectively removed a monopoly situation and therefore encouraged free trade.

Another advantage of joining the ranks of the shipowners at this time was the availability of reasonably priced vessels built on the Wear, where shipbuilding practices at the time were unique and where wooden shipbuilding continued long after shipyards on other rivers had changed over to iron. Wear shipbuilders often consisted of small groups of shipwrights, in all probability financed by a local timber merchant, who built ships "on spec" before looking for a buyer. The shipwrights' real skills lay in the way they extracted the most from the timbers with which they worked. Complementing this was the low-cost land bordering the river where timber could be spread out to be worked in the most economical manner. The more fortunate shipbuilders would be in a position to build a top-class vessel, whilst at the same time being able to construct a smaller craft using the surplus materials from the former.

William Milburn's second vessel, the brig, HALICORE (1) represented the beginning of a life- long parochial influence in shipping matters. The HALICORE (1) was built at Blyth for Milburn by Margaret Jane Stoveld, widow of the shipbuilder whose house was in the same street as Milburn's butchers shop. Once again the Master, J. Turnbull, was made part owner with 16/64th shares to Milburn's 48/64th. During 1855 Milburn continued to add to his shipping interests with the brig WHALTON, in which he acquired a quarter share and became the managing owner. In October the new barque EQUINOX was delivered from Sunderland and Milburn must have been feeling very confident because this time he held all the shares (64/64th). Two years later these four vessels were to be his contribution to a new partnership that he formed in 1857 with another young man from Blyth, Edmund Hanney Watts. Watts had a rope and sail-making business in the town and had started shipowning in 1853 with the brig CARRON, and by the following year, he owned a half share in the snow ARETHUSA plus a third share in the snow BRILLIANT. This was soon to be followed by investment in several other vessels.

The story of Watts' entry into shipowning was similar to that of Milburn's, in that they were both involved in servicing ships and had risen from being small businessmen to becoming shipowners. The difference between them was that Watts' father had had a share (8/64th) in the brig VIBILIA for about 22 years from 1834, whereas William Milburn was the first member of his family to enter shipping in any form. Watts invested in several vessels and his contribution to the new partnership consisted of five vessels - the brigs BRILLIANT, CACTUS and SULTAN with the barques ST. CLAIR and GUARDIANA. This new enterprise took the title Watts, Milburn & Company and at about this time Milburn sold his investment shareholding in the JOHN TWIZELL and the VOLANT to other parties.

Milburn and Watts entered shipowning in a gradual way, at first buying 64th shares in collier brigs managed by others as an investment, whilst carrying on their own businesses (butcher and sailmaker respectively), and then becoming part-time shipowners, managing their own vessels Eventually they became full-time shipowners and, as well as managing their own ships, they acted as agents in the ports of Blyth and Newcastle.

Shipowning in those days had several facets and, apart from owning vessels, some shipping companies acted as managers for a fee or commission (with the advent of steamers this sometimes materialised in the form of one ship companies). During their early days Milburn and Watts operated some of the sailing vessels they owned in this way, as in several of them, only one of the partners had a shareholding. For example, the GUADIANA was Watts' controlled (24/64th) but the only survivor of her loss reported to Milburn first when he got back to the North East from Yarmouth.

Walter Runciman in his book "Collier Brigs and their Sailors" describes a facet of the life that the young Milburn was about to enter:-

> "The people who owned them (collier brigs) were all of the small shopkeeping and tradesman class, who, by frugal habits and the help of other industrious, saving people, were enabled to buy cheap, worn out coffins that made large profits at that period, which enabled them to purchase ship after ship, some new, others second-hand, of larger tonnage and sounder condition." Also in the same book is a description of " Stout Old Dinsdale" a shipmaster in the Milburn fleet.

When Milburn and Watts were owners of sailing vessels the accepted shareholding was often a third (21/64th) or greater (up to 64/64th) but a change came when they moved into iron steamships, which called for much greater investment. The pattern with the steamers was for one of the partners (usually W. Milburn or E. H. Watts but sometimes another shareholder such as J. D. Milburn, H. Philipson, C. Mitchell or W. Milburn the younger) to register the vessel as the holder of all the 64 shares. However most were subsequently sold to people who would like to make an investment and would buy perhaps one or two shares. The other partner (Watts or Milburn) would buy approximately 5/64th shares but this varied. The vessel would be entered in Lloyds Register under the name of the registered owner - W. Milburn or E. H. Watts etc. and not as Watts, Milburn & Company. This led to circumstances where several vessels were recorded in Lloyds Register under W. Milburn of Newcastle as an individual not a company.

As shipowners, Milburn and Watts were not pioneers in new developments but they kept near the edge of current technology, a tradition which was continued when Commonwealth & Dominion Line ordered motor ships in the 1920s. In 1859, with the initial expansion of the business, an office was opened at 21, Broad Chare, Newcastle and in 1864 the Milburn family moved from Blyth to reside in Eldon Street, Newcastle, but the company still maintained an office in Blyth.

The Milburns were level-headed businessmen, who took a parochial stance when ordering new ships and machinery which they always purchased from local firms thereby providing the local community with work. From 1853 to 1914 over 120 new vessels were delivered to the company who, during this period, recognised the future of steam and the importance of the Suez Canal. As well as running their own shipping business Milburns were instrumental in the founding of two important companies, the Hamburg South America Line and the Federal Steam Navigation Company. The partnership of Milburn and Watts steadily built up a fleet from nine sailing vessels in 1857 to a peak of 39 steamers and sailing vessels. When Milburn and Watts started out in shipowning the shipping world was dominated by coal. The wooden hulled sailing vessels they owned and managed were taking coal from the Northumberland and Durham coalfield to London and the near Continental ports. Some cargoes were sent to the Baltic in both steam and sailing vessels that would often return to London or Leith with a cargo of grain. The bigger sailing vessels that were designed and named (HINDOOSTAN and EASTERN QUEEN), for trading to India and China including the ports in between. Rangoon for example was often where a cargo of rice was loaded. Coal was a regular outward cargo, it was carried to bunkering stations and on occasion for use on the emerging railways in that part of the world. When Watts, Milburn took delivery of steamships particularly post 1870, coal was often the main cargo carried, but with the steamships it was not just north east coal, ships which had discharged in the Thames or Mersey would often make their way to one of the South Wales ports to load coal for Mediterranean destinations such as Gibraltar, Malta and Alexandria. This was followed by a passage to the Black Sea to load grain for the United Kingdom or Continent. When the Milburns became major shareholders in the Ashington Coal Company, they returned to their roots by delivering coals from Northumberland to London and across the North Sea mainly to Hamburg. They were prompted to acquire three second-hand colliers, renaming one of them ASHINGTON and this was followed in 1892 with a new ASHINGTON. Although coal was an important cargo it was not the only commodity to be exported by Great Britain, the ships that traded out to the east in particular carried general cargo. They also had frequent sailing's from the Mediterranean to the United States. The voyage would start with coal from the United Kingdom to a Mediterranean coaling station. After discharge, the vessel would then sail in ballast to load for North America and after discharge there, would then load for either Liverpool or London.

The company developed an eastern trade pattern, which found employment for some ships in the Japanese coal trade and in conjunction with Siessmen & Company of Hamburg and Hong Kong, they also operated on the China coast. The loss of the CHU KIANG on the morning of 6th February 1872 illustrates some aspects of the operation on the China coast. CHU KIANG left Shanghai on 4th February with a cargo of rice and sundries, a crew of 40, which included seven European officers, and 17 passengers. The ship was proceeding at full speed in fog when breakers were seen ahead, the helm was put hard over but the wheel rope broke and she struck Reef Island and was wrecked. Another incident took place in 1886 when the PLAINMELLER was engaged in the Japanese coal trade. She left Otaree (Island of Yesso), Japan on the 9th November with a coal cargo for Yokohama and was not heard of again. The Milburns slowly withdrew from these various trading patterns and concentrated on Australia, which they first became involved in when Anderson, Anderson & Company, chartered the ST. OSYTH in 1874. This was closely followed by Flint chartering WHAMPOA for his Colonial Line service. As the Milburn business gained strength financially the shareholding was retained by the family and after the partnership was dissolved in 1879 with Watts continuing in business as Watts, Ward & Company, and subsequently becoming the well known Watts, Watts & Company, only members of the Milburn family held shares in the new steamers. Some of the latter were registered as wholly owned by the Anglo-Australasian Steam Navigation Company, of which the Milburn family were the principal shareholders, having formed this Company in 1883 and they were instrumental in the foundation of the Federal Steam Navigation Company in 1895.

Before a truly economical marine steam engine in the form of the two cylinder compound had been developed, Milburn and his shareholders had invested in iron steamships with simple expansion engines. The partners' first iron steamship, the SHEARWATER, built at North Shields in 1864 by T. & W. Smith. She was not a lucky ship, being abandoned on the 1st November 1865 in the Atlantic whilst on passage to Alexandria with a cargo of coal. This disaster must have been instrumental in the selling off of their next steamship, the three-month old LEVANT, six weeks later on the 16th December 1865. However, a further eight simple expansion steamships were built, but, unfortunately four of these were also lost, their average service life being four years. The remaining four were sold to continue a useful life with other owners. Moving from sail into steam-propelled ships was a very important landmark in the careers of William Milburn and his partner E. H. Watts Jr.

It is very difficult for us at the beginning of the 21st Century to be able to empathise with shipowners of the mid-nineteenth century and to appreciate the predicament in which some shipowners found themselves with the advent of steam. Most of them had built up successful fleets of sailing vessels and were naturally reluctant to change from something they knew well into something which was unknown and unproven. They faced quite a dilemma. On the one hand they wanted to be involved in this new idea, which, if successful, would increase trade and profits by ensuring a regular service, independent of the wind. On the other hand many of them were reluctant to take the chance until steam had been proven.

At the British Association meeting held in Newcastle during September 1863, Charles M. Palmer (1822-1907) discussed the progress of iron shipbuilding and also promoted the steam collier as opposed to the sailing brig. Palmer stated:

> "The JAMES DIXON made fifty-seven voyages to London in one year, and in that year delivered 62,842 tons of coals, and this with a crew of only twenty-one persons. To accomplish this work on the old system with sailing colliers would have required sixteen ships and 144 hands to man them".

Less than two months later, on the evening of the 7th November 1863, the steam collier JAMES DIXON was departing the Tyne loaded with coal when she collided with the brig ELI entering the Tyne under tow and became a wreck on the foundations of the South Pier, which was under construction at that time. Some of her cargo was recovered, before she was salvaged and towed to Newcastle to be rebuilt at St. Peters. Completed in 1865 and renamed ARCHIMEDES, she was virtually a new ship and was purchased as such by Watts, Milburn. During 1867-1868 she was chartered to lay a cable from Newbiggin just north of Blyth to Denmark for the Great Northern Telegraph Company. Unfortunately she was wrecked on the 3rd September 1869 on Gotland in the Baltic during bad weather when returning from Cronstadt to London with a cargo of wheat and oats. The news of her loss would have been telegraphed along the cable she had laid the year before.

The Hartlepool shipbuilder John Punshon Denton (1800-1871) bought the barque ZETUS probably in part exchange for the composite ship TAUNTON that had just been launched. The TAUNTON may have been an experimental vessel as she was the only composite craft built by Denton, Gray & Company and the only one of this type owned by Watts, Milburn & Company. The TAUNTON and an iron hulled sistership, the LUTTERWORTH, were both full-rigged ships and were built in 1868 at Hartlepool, becoming the last sailing vessels built for the company.

In 1869 E. H. Watts moved from Blyth to open an office in London, a decision influenced by the opening of the Suez Canal in November. During that year Elders' patent on the compounding of the steam engine expired and gave an impetus to the building of iron screw steamships and the practical development of the compound steam engine. The former was already a priority with the company and with the co-operation of Charles Mitchell (1820-1895) the Tyneside shipbuilder, this new technology was soon installed in the next generation of ships. Thus, in 1869, Watts, Milburn took delivery of their first compound engines that were supplied by three different manufacturers and duly installed them in the SURBITON, CHU KIANG and the OTTERBURN.

When the Suez Canal opened in 1869 it became the steamship route to India and China helping to provide prompt delivery of the new season's tea to the London markets as well as enhancing key colonial links. The appropriately named CHU KIANG, was the first company vessel to use the canal and arrived at Hong Kong from London in 66 days on 29th March 1870, she then proceeded to Shanghai arriving on the 7th April. The opening of the Suez Canal in 1869 initially caused a lapse in the improvement to services. Because the Canal project was essentially a French idea, the British deliberately denigrated its importance and, as a consequence, were unprepared for the opportunities that it afforded. Watts, Milburn along with Alfred Holt may have been the exceptions.

Shipowning on the scale practised by Watts, Milburn & Company involved much shipbuilding and a relationship must have developed with iron shipbuilders such as Charles Mitchell and Andrew Leslie (1818-1894). There was regular construction for the company by C. Mitchell & Company until 1879; which was followed by a similar pattern of building across the Tyne at Hebburn by A. Leslie & Company, which lasted until Milburn ceased shipowning. In 1886 A. Leslie & Company, was restyled R. & W. Hawthorn, Leslie & Company

The iron shipbuilder Charles Mitchell at Low Walker became both a regular builder of Watts, Milburn ships (although some may have been built on 'spec' and bought completed) and a shareholder in Watts, Milburn vessels. This involvement of shipbuilder and shipowner was taken a step further when both Milburn and Mitchell became partners with a Hamburg shipping agent thus forming the Hamburg Brazilian S.S. Company. This company started operations in 1869 using Mitchell, built`and Watts, Milburn owned vessels. At first chartering the CRITERION and the BRAZILIAN which proved successful they purchased the appropriately named SANTOS, BRAZILIAN and RIO. It soon developed into the famous German shipping company the Hamburg South America Line and is still in existence today, under the umbrella of Columbus Ship Management of Hamburg.

In November 1871 two Tyneside shipowning companies, Watts, Milburn & Company, and Nelson, Donkin & Company, combined with C. Mitchell & Company to form the Wallsend Slipway Company, thereby providing much needed iron steamship repairing facilities on the Tyne. During 1875 Wallsend Slipway Company commenced manufacturing boilers and marine engines but, surprisingly, this facility was not often used by Watts, Milburn. The first engine bought from them by the company was installed in the SURBITON (2) which was built in 1877 by C. Mitchell, and the next engine and boilers were built in 1883 for the PORT PHILLIP (1), which was constructed by A. Leslie, but, in the intervening period, Milburns had used other local firms to supply them with a total of 22 engines.

Watts and Milburn, in addition to developing business links with two local shipbuilders, also supported other undertakings. These included the Willington Quay yard of Cole Brothers, which lasted only from 1871 until 1876, and subsequently reopened as the Tyne Iron Shipbuilding Company. (1876-1928), in addition to W. Dobson at Low Walker (1883-1928) and the Scotswood shipbuilders Campbell, Mackintosh and Bowstead.

William Milburn - Senior (1826 - 1903)
(J. Dobson collection)

With the increase in the number of steamships owned on Tyneside, the owners of these vessels arranged a meeting that was held in the Mayor's Chambers at the Guildhall, Newcastle on Friday 24th March 1871. William Milburn suggested that the 22 owners present should form themselves into a Steamship Owners Association. This Association, known as the North of England Steamship Owners Association, was to be an alliance of shipowners who shared experiences, and it was also a pressure group to promote mutual interests. At the next meeting on 3rd April William Milburn was elected onto the committee.

In 1873 Watts, Milburn proposed the concept of a six-ship passenger service from London to Melbourne with backing which had Australian and New Zealand support. The company entered into a consortium with other interests, forming the Anglo-Australian Steam Navigation Company that was floated with a capital of £1,250,000. The backing for this project, which, had been promised from both Australia and New Zealand failed to materialize, and the scheme collapsed. Of the original six ships planned only three were built and their potential was soon recognised by other shipowners who soon placed them on the trade they were designed for.

The ST OSYTH, one of the trio, left London on 31st October 1874 for Melbourne via the Cape under charter to Anderson, Anderson & Company, who were the forerunners of the Orient Steam Navigation Company. This ship was the first full-powered steamship to run between London and Australia via the Cape and, by completing the passage in 42 days, she beat the regular P & O service via Suez. Subsequently the other two sister ships, WHAMPOA and HANKOW, took up regular running to Melbourne and Sydney via the Cape operating under John H. Flint's Colonial Line of Australian Packets which was founded in 1873.

At that time, because Australia only imported goods and emigrants, there was very little prospect of a return cargo, and consequently Watts, Milburn vessels obtained an outward charter to Melbourne before proceeding north to China in ballast to load tea for the homeward passage to London by way of the Suez Canal.

An advert extolling the virtues of one of the Watts, Milburn ships appeared in the press on Wednesday, 9th February 1876:

> *"Colonial Line of Packets. Their celebrated steamship WHAMPOA 5,000 tons burthen, 300 h.p. effective. W. J. Hynes Commander. South West India Dock, embarking passengers at Gravesend on 13th March and calling at Plymouth. Unrivalled accommodation for all classes of passengers. Last passage to Melbourne 45 days including all stoppages. Passage money from 15 to 70 guineas".*

After completion of the Swing Bridge at Newcastle in 1876 two shipyards were opened above the bridges. The well known one at Elswick, for Sir W. G. Armstrong, was part of the reason for the building of an opening bridge. The other at Scotswood is probably less well known; it lasted only from 1881 until 1885, operating under the grand title of Campbell, Mackintosh & Bowstead. One of the partners of this shipyard was John McLeod Campbell (1841-1903) who had been working as shipyard manager at Wigham Richardson & Company from 1877 until he started the shipbuilding business in 1881 at Scotswood. Unfortunately, the business did not succeed and in 1885 the partnership was dissolved with Campbell becoming the manager of Robert Stephenson's yard at Hebburn. However, in that short period three iron screw steamships were built for the Millburn's and another yard was started up a little later by William Dobson (1832-1907) who had been manager for Charles Mitchell until he set up business next door to his former employer as W. Dobson & Company. This yard lasted until 1928 but only built ships for Milburn in the early years.

In July 1879 the partnership between E. H. Watts and William Milburn came to an end. The formal announcement of the dissolution was reported in the BLYTH WEEKLY NEWS of the 22nd September 1877:-

> *"The LONDON GAZETTE of Friday night last, states that the partnership existing between the following has been dissolved: Edmund Hannay Watts, William Milburn, and Edward Stout, ship and insurance brokers and general commission agents, at Newcastle and Blyth, under the firm of Watts, Milburn, & Company This was a repeat of an item which appeared in the Newcastle Journal of Saturday 15th September 1877".*

Sold on for further service	**Watts, Ward**	**William Milburn & Company**
BUSTON VALE	ACTON	AMOY
EASTERN QUEEN	BLYTHWOODE	CHIN KIANG
HARE BELL	CHISWICK	CONSETT
HINDOOSTAN	COLOMBO	GILSLAND
LORD COLLINGWOOD	GOSFORTH	HANKOW
ST OSYTH	NANKIN	MAHARAJAH
WHAMPOA	RICHMOND	MARCIA
	SULTAN	NINGPO
		TAUNTON
		WEST STANLEY
		YANGTZE

In the 21 months following the announcement all the loose ends were tied up including the Milburn half of the partnership relocating to a new address in London. During this period several new steamships joined the fleet and were managed by Watts, Milburn, although owned by either Milburn or Watts. The Watts ships were the SINGAPORE, KENSINGTON, CAMDEN, JESMOND and the SURBITON. The Milburn ships were the FERNWOOD, PLAINMELLER, COMPTON, and the CLANDON. In July 1879 Watts, Milburn & Company, became Watts, Ward & Company and W. Milburn &

Company, respectively and the fleet operated by the former company was divided into three; part was sold off, and the remainder was transferred to either Watts or Milburn. Watts kept the brig SULTAN as her master was an old family friend.

The termination of the partnership with Watts in July 1879, created opportunities for the sons to join their fathers in the business.

John Davison Milburn
(J. Dobson collection)

William Milburn - junior.
(J. Dobson collection)

In the case of the Milburns the eldest son John Davison was put in charge of the Newcastle office, William and Charles opened the new London office and subsequently Fred the youngest son ran the Cardiff office for many years. The Milburns also expanded their empire by diversifying into coal and land by acquiring a substantial share in the Ashington Coal Company and also purchasing the manor of Rosedale, North Yorkshire. They did not, however, neglect the shipping side of their business and continued to expand their fleet of steamships. To complement the operation of the deep sea fleet they had built, two twin-screw shallow draught coasters, which were specifically designed to carry 500 tons of grain across the Sea of Azoff. This enabled ships that had loaded at Taganrog to be topped up once they were over the Kertch bar and into the deeper water of the Black Sea. These vessels were built in 1880 by C. Mitchell & Company for W. Milburn & Company on behalf of Berthold, Smith & Company of Taranrog, their operators, and named the OMSK and TOMSK. They were the first vessels to be constructed of steel for W. Milburn & Company.

Coal mining at 'Ashington' began in about 1846 when the first shaft was sunk at a pit called Fell-Em-Doon, being referred to as Ashington Colliery in the first edition of the Ordnance Survey. At the time William Milburn was living only about a mile away to the south, at Sparrow House, and he would no doubt have been aware of this important event but it is very doubtful whether he would have thought, that one day he would be chairman of Ashington Coal Company, the subsequent owner of Fell-Em-Doon. At what is described as the regular meeting of the partners of Ashington Coal Company on 10th August 1869 it was decided that additional capital was required to finance the sinking of a new shaft. Consequently it was proposed to create eight additional shares in the colliery and agreed that the constitution should be amended from 32 to 40 parts or shares. The eight shares, valued at £1,500 per share, were offered to Watts, Milburn & Company but, at the following meeting of the Ashington Coal Company, on 7th September 1869, it was reported that the offer had been declined, unfortunately with no reason being given. Watts, Milburn did however become coal owners in 1873 when they acquired three coalmines in South Wales in partnership with Charles Mitchell. In 1879, William Milburn accepted the offer of the late Mr Carl Lange's interest in the Ashington Coal Company, thereby starting the Milburn family's long involvement in the Ashington Coal Company, which lasted until nationalisation in 1947. In 1893, when the company was reconstructed, William Milburn became the first Chairman, a post he held until his death in 1903, when his eldest son John Davison Milburn took over until his own death four years later.

One of the unfortunate aspects of shipowning is the loss of a vessel, its cargo and often the crew. This was a particularly frequent occurrence during the nineteenth century and of the 140 or so vessels owned by the Milburns from 1851 until the merger of the company in 1914, one - third were either wrecked or disappeared without trace, being referred to officially as "and has not since been heard of". In 1884 several prominent North East shipowners were trying to reduce the cost of insurance. A self-insurance scheme proposed by W. Milburn & Company to their shareholders was favourably received. One feature of the scheme was a bonus payment to the vessels master who had completed 12 consecutive months without an incident. In 1887 during an interview John D. Milburn said "a few years ago we commenced a self-insurance scheme and although the risks taken were heavy, total losses actually increased". As in the period 1884 to 1887 ten vessels were wrecked or missing. J. D. Milburn continues "Being determined to succeed in this matter a rule has been laid down that every captain shall underwrite the vessel under his control to the extent of £200, receiving the same premium as would be payable at Lloyds. In addition to this premium every captain receives an extra premium, provided he has navigated his vessel safely during the year". Whether the Milburns thought this scheme was a success is difficult to assess without documentation. However, the facts are that the fleet in total of ships was decreasing and from 1887 to 1895 three ships were lost and three ships sold on to others following either collision or stranding. Holts of Liverpool also operated a similar system of insurance.

There are many examples of good relationships between shipowners and shipbuilders. Milburns was with the Hebburn shipyard of Hawthorn, Leslie and the following incidents illustrate how the relationship usually favoured the shipowner. In 1888, the PORT CAROLINE (1) when almost completed was sold to the Russian Volunteer Fleet and renamed KOSTROMA. The February board meeting of R. & W. Hawthorn, Leslie & Company Ltd was informed that the price realised (£50,700) was to be divided between the company (builder of the ship), Wigham Richardson (builder of the machinery) and W. Milburn & Company. The directors of Hawthorn, Leslie however were not best pleased with the profit Milburns were making on the deal. In the early 1890s another interesting transaction was struck between Hawthorn, Leslie and the Milburns; when two vessels about ten years old were taken in part exchange for two new vessels to be built (a common practice at the time). However, at the Hawthorn, Leslie monthly board meeting of June 1892 it was resolved that no part exchange deals could be entered into by any director, either for the old ships or in respect of shares in new vessels. The meeting was also appraised of the situation with regard to the PORT JACKSON (1), which was the first "PORT" ship, having been built at Hebburn nine years previously and was taken by the company as part payment for the new building PORT MELBOURNE (1). Two directors, Arthur Coote and J. H. Ridley, were registered as joint owners and in effect the shipbuilder became a reluctant shipowner until the PORT JACKSON (1) was sold to an Italian owner in 1895. A. Coote, who was Andrew Leslie's partner until the latter retired, had negotiated the merger with R. & W. Hawthorn. Interestingly in 1919, a further example of the good relationship which existed between shipowner and shipbuilder occurred when the twin-screw geared turbine passenger and cargo vessel PORT NICHOLSON (2) was delivered by R. & W. Hawthorn, Leslie & Company to the Commonwealth & Dominion Line Ltd she was described by the technical journal 'The Shipbuilder' as: *"the thirty-eighth vessel"* to be constructed for W. Milburn & Company: who were the pioneers of the "steamer" trade to Australia. They were the first company to bring Tasmanian apples to England and introduced insulation for the carriage of frozen meat to this country'. To consider the new Commonwealth & Dominion Line Ltd to be W. Milburn & Company in 1919 shows a misplaced loyalty by the "The Shipbuilder", which was a local publication.

Milburns decision to concentrate on the Australasian trade was because of the improvement in return cargoes that consisted of mainly wool and the difficulties they encountered in obtaining return cargoes in the China trade. The following extract taken from David Macgregor's book 'The China Bird' explains.

> *"In 1884, the steamer PORT PHILLIP tried to load at Hankow in May but she could only obtain limited amounts to enable her to load slowly at £1-10-0 to £2-0-0 while the Conference steamers such as the GLENOGLE and GLENELG were getting £5 and £3 respectively. But it was noted that the outsider would inevitably enforce lower rates all round. Later it was reported that the PORT PHILLIP had been so overlooked that she could not even obtain one ton of cargo at the low rate of £1-10-0 a ton. She was owned by the Anglo-Australasian Steam Navigation Company Ltd and was 2671 tons gross".*

> *"Holt ships were getting £2-7-6d. The following year another outsider, s.s. ASCALON, was more successful. First she loaded part of her cargo at Hankow at £2-0-0 while the Glens and Holts got £2-17-6 and the Shires and Bens £2-15-0, and was fixed to complete her cargo with 500 tons of tea at Foochow at £2-0-0. In consequence the Conference ships reduced their rates, Holt ships offering £1-12-6 and mail ships £1-15-0 instead of £3-0-0".*

In 1883 the Milburns made an unusual decision with their commitment to Australia by founding the subsidiary, Anglo-Australasian Stean Navigation Company (members of the Milburn family being the only directors). The object was to trade between London to Adelaide, Melbourne and Sydney via the Cape. This new company ran in conjunction with the parent company (W Milburn & Company) to trade to Australia on a monthly service with both cargo and passengers. A monthly service was advertised which expanded in 1890 to fortnightly. The new company maintained the parent company's livery and naming system, the only difference was the house flag which was a double pennant; the upper one red with WM & Co in white letters and the lower one, white with A-ASNCo in red letters. The inaugural sailing by the CHOLLERTON from London to Adelaide, Melbourne and Sydney, via Cape Town, took place on 30th April 1883. New ships were ordered, all bearing a name with the prefix "Port", and the first of the new tonnage, PORT JACKSON (1), sailed from London on 10th November 1883 for Adelaide, via Plymouth, followed by PORT PHILLIP (1) on the 15th December. In addition to cargo, migrants were carried in temporary accommodation in the 'tween decks. Some of the ships called at Antwerp when outward bound, and Hobart was added on occasions to the list of Australian ports of call. Within two years the first triple-expansion engined ship to join the fleet, the PORT VICTOR (1), was delivered.

All the new "Port" ships were named after Australian harbours, and, even in those early days the name "Port Line" was often used. The long name, Anglo-Australasian Steam Navigation Company when used in advertisements was, from 1890, thereafter supplemented with Milburn Line.

In 1892 it was decided to stop passenger carrying on a large scale and during the next few years the passenger ships were disposed of including, the PORT ALBERT (1) and the PORT HUNTER (1) which were sold to Japan in 1894 for use as troopships for the war against China.

It was not until 1912, two years before the merger with the other companies, that the company again carried passengers, but this time it was for the emigrant trade promoted by the Government of Victoria. Two new vessels, the PORT MACQUARIE (1) and the PORT LINCOLN (1), each providing 600 steerage berths, were built for the service.

The strategy of chartering ships and building ships for a new company employed by W. Milburn senior when he was involved with the foundation of what ultimately became the Hamburg South America Line was repeated by his son William with his involvement with the Federal Steam Navigation Company the name had just been adopted in May 1895, exactly a year later C. Wigham authorised the company to use his late firm's flag and they made a payment of 20 guineas to Lloyds Patriotic Fund.

The Milburns made an important contribution to the newly named company firstly by arranging suitable tonnage for charter. This included the SEVERUS completed in December 1894 which was specially fitted for the frozen meat trade, and made her maiden voyage for the Federal Steam Navigation Company. They also arranged the purchase of their PORT CHALMERS (1) to help out until the new ships were delivered. William Milburn was also made a director of the Federal Steam Navigation Company with the unusual provision that his brother Charles would deputise for him when he was not available. The new ships were in two lots all built by Milburns old friends Hawthorn, Leslie. The first order was for two ships which became the CORNWALL and DEVON. Milburn received almost 2% brokerage fee for handling these two ships on behalf of the Federal Steam Navigation Company and the shipbuilder made just over 5% profit building them. The second order was for three ships with an option for the fourth, they were duplicates of the CORNWALL but with four masts. The arrangements for payment and delivery of these ships was also put in the hands of W. Milburn & Company. It was the intention of the Federal Steam Navigation Company board not to take delivery of the fourth ship but to sell her on. As it turned out Shaw, Savill and Albion bought the third of the series and named her KARAMEA, obtaining a delivery to suit their requirements. In 1903 Milburns as individuals held $12^1/2$% of the total shareholding in the Federal Steam Navigation Company. In 1904 Hawthorn, Leslie were completing two ships for W. Milburn & Company and before completion Milburns sold them both, the second one PORT PHILLIP (3) was sold to the Federal Steam Navigation Company and renamed DURHAM. New Zealand Shipping Company purchased all the shares of the Federal Steam Navigation Company on 29th April 1912.

William Milburn died in 1903 at the age of 77 and his sons carried on the business; the eldest, John Davison Milburn, was created a baronet two years before he died in 1907. His eldest son, Charles Stamp Milburn, who, with his uncles, ran the business, succeeded him. Later his son, Charles T. Milburn, took over control and became a Director of the Commonwealth & Dominion Line from 1914 to 1922. He was also a Director of the Cunard Line from 1916 until his death in 1922 and members of the Milburn family were shareholders in Cunard for many years thereafter.

William Milburn & Company and Tyser & Company were both largely responsible for the decision to merge the four separate interests that subsequently became the Commonwealth & Dominion Line. The two companies had worked closely together for some years, with Milburns having the larger involvement with Australia and Tysers being stronger in the New Zealand trade. The Star Line vessels, owned by James P. Corry, were linked to Tysers in the frozen meat trade from New Zealand, while

Royden steamers operated predominantly in the southbound Tyser service from New York to Australia and New Zealand. Both Corry and Roydens were also involved in the transport of migrants under a contract awarded by the State Government of Victoria.

Towards the end of 1913 the amalgamation of all four interests was agreed, becoming effective the following year. The last ship ordered by Milburns, the PORT ALBANY (1), was launched on 12th February 1914 by Mrs Boulton, sister of Sir Charles Milburn. This was the 36th vessel ordered by Milburn from Hawthorn, Leslie and she was delivered three months later to the newly formed Commonwealth & Dominion Line Ltd.

In 1919 another company, William Milburn & Company Ltd. was incorporated. This was a private concern with a capital of £200,000, although only 70,500 shares were paid up and this firm returned to shipowning in 1927 with two tramp steamers. One was sold to Italians before the outbreak of war in 1939 and the other was sunk during hostilities. In January 1952, the registration of a new company named William Milburn & Company Ltd. to take over the existing business of a firm of the same name was reported. This was expected to mean the reappearance in the shipping world of a flag of the highest repute on the North East Coast. The directors of the new firm were the same as of the old - Sir Leonard J. Milburn Bt., and Mr Archibald W. Milburn - the capital was to be £250,000 and the object was to act as shipowners, managers, brokers, etc., but it was not to be.

The lasting legacy of one of Tyneside's great shipping companies is the Edwardian office block, Milburn House, Newcastle, built in 1905 under the supervision of John D Milburn. Situated very close to the old commercial centre and the Quayside, part of this building became Milburns offices until 1964. A subsidiary company The Milburn Estates Ltd maintained an office there until 1997. Another reminder is the Milburn Arms Hotel situated in the village of Rosedale, North Yorkshire.

The Milburn Fleets

William Milburn
Blyth
(Butcher)
As a minority shareholder

A 1. JOHN TWIZELL (1849 - 1854) Brig
O.N. 2440. 195 tons. 80.5 x 22.0 x 13.8 feet.
2.1849: Launched at Sunderland by Hodgson & Garner for John Twizell & Company, Blyth. William Milburn, butcher of Blyth had 16/64th shares. 27.2.1854: W. Milburn sold his 16 shares to J. Twizell. 27.10.1880: Whilst on a voyage in ballast, from Caen to Llanelly lost masts off St. Govan's Head, Pembrokeshire and was later condemned at Milford.

A 2. VOLANT (1850 - 1856) Snow
O.N. 2441. 166 tons. 70.0 x 20.2 x 12.6 feet.
1833: Launched by John Mowbray Gales, Hylton, County Durham, for his own account. 1836: Registry transferred to Newcastle. 14.2.1850: Sold to Richard Lough, Blyth, and registry transferred to Shields. William Milburn had 8/64th shares. 1856: Sold to Ebenezer Nicholas, Rochester, Kent. 18.1.1861: Sold to Felix Allen, Sunderland. 3.11.1861: Whilst on a voyage from Sunderland to London, sprang a leak and foundered off the Galloper (in the Thames Estuary). The crew were saved and landed at Deal.

William Milburn,
Blyth
(1851 - 1857)
(1857 - 79 See under Watts, Milburn & Company)

M 1. PERO (1851 - 1864) Snow
O.N. 12901. 212 tons. 88.6 x 22.2 x 14.5 feet.
6.1850: Launched by T. Lightfoot, Sunderland, for T. Pearce and W. Thackrey, Timber Merchants, Sunderland. 3.5.1851: Sold to W. Milburn, Blyth. 1857: Watts, Milburn & Company, appointed as managers. 18.1.1864: Sold to J. Bedlington, Whitby. 12.2.1866: Whilst on a voyage in ballast, from London to West Hartlepool, was driven ashore on the North beach, Yarmouth. Her crew were saved. 4.3.1866: Wreck sold by auction.

M 2. HALICORE (1) (1853 - 1864) Snow
O.N. 16147. 259 tons. 97.0 x 23.2 x 15.4 feet.
10.1853: Launched by Margaret Jane Stoveld, Blyth, for W. Milburn. Blyth. 1857: Watts, Milburn & Company, appointed as managers. 6.12.1864: Whilst on a voyage from the Tyne to Copenhagen, struck a rock near New Hellesund, Norway and was abandoned in the North Sea.

M 3. WHALTON (1855 - 1859) Snow
O.N. 18422. 226 tons. 88.6 x 22.2 x 14.8 feet.
8.1854: Launched by Jopling & Willoughby, Sunderland for Headley & Company, Blyth. 7.2.1855: Sold to W. Milburn. 1857: Watts, Milburn & Company, appointed as managers. 15.1.1859: Whilst in ballast and at anchor off Beyrout, driven ashore along with four other vessels. Her crew were saved. 2.1859: Condemned.

M 4. EQUINOX (1855 - 1869) Barque
O.N. 4974. 406 tons. 124.85 x 27.3 x 17.55 feet.
10.1855: Launched at Sunderland for W. Milburn. 1857: Watts, Milburn & Company, appointed as managers. 23.3.1869: Sold to J. P. Denton and W. Gray. Shipbuilders, West Hartlepool. (Taken in part

exchange for LUTTERWORTH see ship No. WMi30). 8.1879: Offered for sale by auction at Hartlepool but withdrawn as the reserve price of £350 was not achieved. 1880: Sold to an unspecified Swedish owner and registered at Bergqvara. 29.3.1880: Left Hartlepool for Malmo with a cargo of coal and subsequently disappeared.

M.5. HALICORE (2) (1865 - 1868) Brig
O.N. 51381. 256 tons. 104.6 x 25.75 x 15.7 feet.
18.11.1865: Launched by D. A. Douglass, Southwick, Sunderland, for W. Milburn (Watts, Milburn & Company, managers), Newcastle. 5.3.1868: Whilst on a voyage from Blyth to Sagua la Grande, Cuba with a cargo of coal, lost at Morant Bay, Jamaica. Crew saved.

Wm. & T. L. Milburn
Blyth

W&TLM 1. CALLIOPE (1866 - 1871) Brig
O.N. 20261. 213g. 96.9 x 24.9 x 14.7 feet.
1858: Built by unspecified shipbuilders, at Bill Quay on Tyne for J. Carr, Newcastle. 1866: Sold to Thomas Lawson Milburn, and William Milburn, (32/64th shares each), (Thomas L. Milburn, manager), Blyth. 8.2.1871: whilst on a voyage from Faro, Portugal to Newcastle with a cargo of locust beans, wrecked at Seaford.

NB. This vessel was managed by William Milburns younger brother, and in his Will, T. L. Milburn stated "I desire to express my gratitude to my brother William for his kindness in the assistance rendered to me on commencing business".

Edmund Hannay Watts
Blyth
(1853 - 1857)
(1857 - 79 See under Watts, Milburn & Company)

W 1. CARRON (1) (1853) Snow
O.N. 3584. 238 tons. 90.3 x 25.3 x 17.3 feet.
1801: Launched at Alloa for Carron & Company. 1814: Sold to S Watson, Newcastle. 3.1851: Owned by A. Strong, North Shields. 16.1.1852: Sold to J. Morrison, Newcastle.1.3.1853: Sold to E. H. Watts, Blyth. 28.11.1853: Sold to E. F. Newton, Blyth. 31.5.1865: Lost in the Kattegat.

W 2. ARETHUSA (1854-1855) Snow
O.N. 24906. 199 tons. 84.0 x 21.4 x 14.5 feet.
1842: Launched at Montrose for Milne & Company, Arbroath. 28.1.1854: Sold to E. H. Watts, Blyth. Registry transferred from Arbroath to Shields. 1.1.1855: Sold to Soulsby, Blyth. 6.1.1861: Whilst on a voyage from Shields to Dieppe with a cargo of coal, lost on Cross Sand, near Yarmouth during a snow storm. Her crew was saved by the Caister lifeboat.

W 3. BRILLIANT (1854-1863) Snow
O.N. 23426. 204 tons. 81.3 x 20.9 x 14.9 feet.
1839: Launched at Montrose for Sherret & Company, Montrose.1844: Sold to Walker & Company, Montrose. 28.1.1854: Sold to E. H. Watts, Blyth. 1857: Watts, Milburn & Company, appointed as managers. 19.2.1863: Sold to Bedlington & Taylor, Sunderland. 1881: Sold to G. Hardy, West Hartlepool. 1886: Sold to W. J. Hardy, West Hartlepool. 1889: Sold for demolition.

W 4. ST. CLAIR (1855-1867) Barque
O.N. 23849. 268 tons. 119.6 x 22.3 x 14.9 feet.
1855: Launched by John Watt, Dysart, Fife, for E. H. Watts, Blyth. 1857: Watts, Milburn & Company, appointed as managers. 6.4.1867: Sold to Marshall Twedell, Sunderland. 2.5.1867: Sold to William Hill, Whitby. 22.3.1881: Whilst on a voyage from Newcastle to Middleburg, Holland with a cargo of coal, was driven ashore at Zoutelande and lost. The crew were saved.

W 5. GUADIANA (1855-1866) Barque
O.N. 4993. 258 tons. 102.9 x 25.2 x 15.0 feet.
10.1855: Launched at Sunderland for E. H. Watts, Blyth. 1857: Watts, Milburn & Company, appointed as managers. 1862: Re-rigged as a brig. 30.11.1866: Whilst on a voyage from St. Petersburg to London with a cargo of grain, was lost on the Winterton Ridge, near Yarmouth. One crew member saved.

W 6. CACTUS (1856-1867) Snow
O.N. 22587. 203 tons. 87.9 x 25.4 x 14.5 feet.
1846: Launched by J. T. Alcock, Sunderland, for his own account. 19.3.1851: Sold to William Tose, South Shields. 27.2.1856: Sold to E. H. Watts, Blyth. 1857: Watts, Milburn & Company, appointed as managers. 21.2.1867: Sold to John Manners, Blyth. 7.2.1883: Whilst a voyage from Blyth to Gravesend with a cargo of coal, was wrecked on the Black Middens at the mouth of the River Tyne. Crew saved.

W 7. SULTAN (1856-1879) Snow
O.N. 11573. 223 tons. 97 x 24.7 x 14.3 feet.
1850: Launched at Sunderland by Sykes & Company, for W. Burdis, Sunderland. 27.12.1856: Sold to E. H. Watts, Blyth. 1857: Watts, Milburn & Company, appointed as managers. 10.1876: Registry transferred to London. 7.1879: Transferred to Watts, Ward & Company. 25.11.1880: Whilst on a voyage from Lisbon to Vlaaridingen, Holland, with a cargo of salt, was lost near Brouwershaven, Holland. All the crew were saved.

Watts, Milburn & Company.
Blyth, Newcastle And London
(1857 - 1879)

WMi 1. VIBILIA (1859) Brig
O.N. 11583. 327 tons. 93.0 x 26.3 x 19.1 feet.
12.1818: Launched at South Blyth by Patrick Holland & Company for their own account. 1.1819: Sold to E. H. Watts & Others, Blyth. 11.4.1825: Hodgson & Company, London. 19.2.1856: Sold to J. Hodgson, Blyth. 23.8.1858: Sold to William Robson Crawford, Blyth. 2.7.1859: Sold to Watts, Milburn & Company. 29.12.1859: Whilst on a voyage from Newcastle to Corunna, was lost off St. Gildas, Bay of Biscay, France. Crew saved.

WMi 2. LOTHIAN (1860 - 1872) Snow
O.N. 28578. 235 tons. 97.9 x 26.2 x 15.0 feet.
8.1860: Launched by Bowman, Blyth for Watts, Milburn & Company. Cost: Hull, Masts and Rigging £1,960 Total Cost ready for sea £2,960-0-6d. 13.1.1872: Whilst on a voyage from Boulogne in ballast, ran aground off Blyth. 9.3.1872: Whilst on a voyage from Blyth to Malmo, with a cargo of coal, stranded in dense fog and abandoned off Vedero Island, Sweden. 10.3.1872: Pulled off by a steam tug and taken to Elsinore. 25.3.1872: Declared beyond economical repair.

WMi 3. ZETUS (1860-1868) Barque
O.N. 28587. 300 tons. 110.1 x 26.15 x 16.5 feet.
8.1860: Launched by Pace & Blumer, Sunderland (Yard No. 4), for Watts, Milburn & Company.

11.5.1868: Sold to J. P. Denton, Shipbuilder, Hartlepool, who took her in part exchange for TAUNTON. (see ship No. Wmi 27).   4.6.1868: Sold to J. Turnbull, Amble.   11.11.1868: Whilst on a voyage from Sulina, Romania to Malta she was wrecked on the Monchair Reef, Malta. Crew saved.

WMi 4. CARRON (2) (1861 - 1867) Snow
O.N. 29714. 242 tons. 100.5 x 25.9 x 15.4 feet.
8.1861: Launched by the Floating Dock Company, Blyth for Watts, Milburn & Company. Cost: Hull, Masts and Rigging £2,100-0-0. Total cost ready for sea £3,179-9-10d.   21.3.1867: Whilst on a voyage from Troon to Cuba with a cargo of coal she was wrecked near Campbeltown off Patterson's Rock. Crew saved.

WMi 5. ALN (1862 - 1867) Barque
O.N. 2029. 335 tons. 108.3 x 26.0 x 16.4 feet.
4.1855: Launched by G. Bowman & T. Drummond, Blyth for their own account. 22.7.1861: Mortgage for £600.0.0 between G. Bowman owner of 16 shares and E. H. Watts jnr, R. & W. Milburn. 29.3.1862: Mortgage discharged and vessel bought by Watts, Milburn & Company.   1864: Re-rigged as a brig. Tonnage reduced to 269 tons. 6.11.1867: Whilst on a voyage from St. Petersburg to Dundee, wrecked near Onstmahorn, Holland.

WMi 6. ULRICA (1862 - 1874) Snow
O.N. 8586. 291 tons. 100.6 x 26.5 x 16.8 feet.
3.1851: Built by Austin & Mills, Sunderland for their own account. 1859: Sold to H. Stone, Poole. 5.1862: Sold to Watts, Milburn & Company. 18.2.1874: Sold to J. Manners, Blyth.   1886: Sold to G. Marshall, North Shields.   25.11.1891: Sold to J. Watson, Newcastle.   1906: Sold to K. McKenzie, Newcastle. 9.7.1912: Destroyed by fire in Stornaway harbour.

WMi 7. HINDOOSTAN (1863 - 1879) Barque
O.N. 45169. 479tons.   138.9 x 29.4 x 18.0 feet.
19.6.1863: Launched by J. Gill, Sunderland (Yard No. 476), for Watts, Milburn & Company, Newcastle. 6.1863: Completed.   1864: Chartered by the Black Ball Line, Liverpool for their London to Australia service.   9.1871: Registry transferred to London. 16.12.1879: Sold to J. Gibson, Blyth. 25.12.1881: When entering into the Tyne from Hamburg, in collision with s.s. CRAMLINGTON.   5.1887: Sold by public auction at Rouen, France, to J. Horney (Master and Owner) Blyth.   5.1892: Sold to John and Jonathan Holt of Liverpool.   8.1892: Sold to Claud Maxwell MacDonald Mayor, H.B.M., Commissioner and Consul General Oil River Protectorate. Dismasted and used as a house for Government officials on the Benni River, Algio Coast Protectorate.   23.12.1898: Registry closed.

WMi 8. SAVANNAH LA MAR (1863 - 1869) Brig
O.N. 20129. 242 tons. 107.85 x 23.4 x 14.95 feet.
1857: Launched at Alloa for A. King, Glasgow.   1861: Sold to Friend & Company, Liverpool. 7.1863: Sold to Watts, Milburn & Company. 19.9.1869: Whilst on a voyage from Cronstadt to London with a cargo of wheat, stranded on the Skaw Reef at the entrance to the Kattegat, and became a total loss. Crew saved.

WMi 9. BUSTON VALE (1863 - 1879) Barque
O.N. 47765. 421 tons. 133.3 x 28.0 x 17.6 feet.
11.9.1863: Launched by Hutchinson, Newcastle for Watts, Milburn & Company, Newcastle. 19.4.1864: Ran aground near Karachi, but refloated. 12.11.1879: Sold to G. Paterson and T. J. Webster, Liverpool. 1880: Sold to F. G. Fry & Company, London. 1.8.1884: Sold to the Government of India. 1894: Hulked.

WMi 10. MAITLAND (1863 - 1867) Brig
O.N. 23354. 301 tons. 105.2 x 26.4 x 17.0 feet.
9.1851: Launched as a barque by W. Pile, Sunderland for J. R. Kelso, North Shields. 2.10.1851: Completed. 9.6.1863: Sold to J. Hodgson, Blyth. 7.11.1863: Sold to Watts, Milburn & Company and re-rigged as a brig. 11.1864: Damaged by ice near Cronstadt. Wintered in Russia. 14.3.1867: Abandoned about 180 miles south-west of Cape Clear. Crew saved.

WMi 11. HARTLEPOOL (1864 - 1868) Snow
O.N. 16287. 208 tons. 95.1 x 24.8 x 14.5 feet.
17.7.1856: Launched by James Hardie, Sunderland for A. Scotson & G. Porteus, Sunderland. 1861: Sold to Henry Longstaff, Sunderland. 11.3.1864: Sold to Watts, Milburn & Company. 1.2.1868: Sold to Wm. Pickersgill, shipbuilder. Sunderland, in part exchange for the barque FLODDEN. (see No. WMi 25). 5.2.1868: Sold to G. Stokeld, Seaham, and registered at Sunderland. 4.3.1873: Sold to T. Storm, Robin Hoods Bay. 11.1880: Whilst on a voyage in ballast, from London to Shields, and in a gale, stranded two miles north of Kettleness, near Staithes, and became a total loss.

WMi 12. EASTERN QUEEN (1864 - 1879) Barque
O.N. 49620. 481 tons. 140.2 x 29.2 x 18.2 feet.
8.6.1864: Launched by R. Thompson jnr, Southwick (Yard No. 22), for Watts, Milburn & Company, Newcastle. 6.1864: Completed. 24.12.1879: Sold to R. Thomas, Criccieth. 6.3.1888: Whilst on a voyage from Hull to Natal with a cargo of coal, foundered in the North Atlantic in a position 46.10N., 11.40W. Her crew were picked up by the LOUIS M. LAMB and transferred to the Wales-bound, Italian barque SIMPATIA. 10.3.1888: Landed at Cardiff.

WMi 13. SHEARWATER (1864 - 1865) Iron Ssteamship
O.N. 49623. 682g.   198.1 x 28.0 x 16.45 feet.
Simple 2-cyl. steam engine manufactured by R. & W. Hawthorn, Newcastle. 90 nhp.
5.7.1864: Launched by T. & W. Smith, North Shields (Yard No. 23), for Watts, Milburn & Company. 1.11.1865: Whilst on a voyage from Cardiff to Alexandria with a cargo of coal and railway materials, was abandoned in position 48.41N., 7.28W., with 8ft. of water in the engine-room. Crew saved by the Dutch barque, ZEENYMPH that later transferred them to CERES that in turn landed them at Falmouth.

WMi 14. CHIPCHASE (1865 - 1871) Barque
O.N. 49649. 369 tons. 120.2 x 27.65 x 16.8 feet.
1.1865: Launched by Tully, Sunderland, for Watts, Milburn & Company.
16.11.1871: Whilst on a voyage from Liverpool to Bahia with a cargo of coal, sank off Liverpool about 2 miles W.N.W., of the North West Lightship after colliding with and sinking the barque MARY BAKER of Bermuda. The complete crew of 15 from the CHIPCHASE were lost.

WMi 15. HANNAH PARK (1865) Snow
O.N. 7395. 259 tons. 98.1 x 25.3 x 16.1 feet.
3.7.1856: Launched by W. Crown, Sunderland for Duncan McBrayne Park. 10.3.1865: Sold to Watts, Milburn & Company. 14.9.1865: Whilst on a voyage from Cronstadt to London with a cargo of wheat, was sunk in the Gulf of Finland, in a collision with the LENA of London. Crew saved.

WMi 16. LUCERNE (1865 - 1867) Brig
O.N. 40784. 280 tons. 105.6 x 26.3 x 16.3 feet.
9.1865: Launched by Floating Dock Company, Blyth for Watts, Milburn & Company. Cost: Hull, masts and rigging £2,175-0-0. Total cost ready for sea £2,996-14-1d. 6.1.1867: Whilst on a voyage from London to Blyth, in ballast, wrecked at the South Pier, mouth of the River Tyne,

WMi 17. LEVANT (1865) Iron Screw Steamer
O.N. 51378. 723g. 209.0 x 28.7 x 16.3 feet.
Simple 2-cyl. steam engine manufactured by Fossick, Blair & Company, Stockton. 90 nhp.
1873: New C. 2-cyl. steam engine and boiler manufactured by Ouseburn Engine Works, Newcastle. 90 nhp.
7.10.1865: Launched by Denton, Gray, Hartlepool (Yard No. 61), for Watts, Milburn & Company. 11.1865: Completed. 16.12.1865: Sold to J. P. Denton & W. Gray, Hartlepool. 3.1870: Sold to H. Taylor, Liverpool. 1873: Sold to Taylor, Cameron & Company, Liverpool. 12.1887: Sold to W. Runciman, South Shields. 24.3.1888: Sailed from Cardiff bound to Oporto with a cargo of coal and believed to have foundered.

WMi 18. ARCHIMEDES (1866 - 1869) Iron Screw Steamer
As built   O.N. 27912. 1,053g. 235.8 x 32.7 x 17.2 feet.
Post 1865   O.N. 51369. 1,086g. 239.9 x 32.8 x 17.3 feet.
Simple 2-cyl. steam engine (E1064) manufactured by R. & W. Hawthorn, Newcastle. 120 nhp.
20.8.1859: Launched as JAMES DIXON by Palmers Shipbuilding & Iron Company Ltd., Jarrow on Tyne (Yard No. 88), for W. Cory jnr., London. 7.11.1863: Collided with the Austrian brig ELI on the Tyne Bar and then ran onto the foundations of the South Pier becoming a total wreck. Wreck subsequently salvaged and rebuilt by the Tyne Iron Shipbuilding Company, Ltd., Newcastle. 10.1865: Mistakenly re-registered for Crawshay, Scott & Jameson, Newcastle, having been renamed ARCHIMEDES. 20.1.1866: Sold to Watts, Milburn & Company. 1867: Chartered to lay cable from Newbiggin, Northumberland to Denmark. 1.9.1869: Whilst on a voyage from Cronstadt to London with a cargo of hemp, wheat and oats, wrecked on the coast of Gotland. Crew saved. Masters certificate suspended for 9 months.

WMi 19. ST. BEDE (1866 - 1870) Iron Screw Steamer
O.N. 51385. 748g.   201.4 x 28.1 x 17.43 feet.
Simple 2-cyl. steam engine manufactured by the shipbuilder. 90 nhp.
11.12.1865: Launched by Palmers Shipbuilding & Iron Company Ltd., Jarrow on Tyne (Yard No. 193), for Watts, Milburn & Company, Newcastle. 2.1866: Completed. 7.1.1870: Whilst on a voyage from Newcastle to Huelva with a cargo of pig iron, coal and coke, foundered after collision with BLACK SWAN off Flamborough Head. 18 of her crew of 19 were lost.

WMi 20. GOSFORTH (1866 - 1879) Iron Screw Steamer
O.N. 51395. 833g. 214.5 x 29.2 x 17.55 feet.
Post 1873: 1,064g. 244.5 x 29.2 x 17.4 feet.
Simple 2-cyl. steam engine (E1362) manufactured by R. & W. Hawthorn, Newcastle. 100 nhp.
1873: New C. 2-cyl. steam engine (E1581) fitted by R. & W. Hawthorn, Newcastle. 110 nhp.
4.1866: Launched by T. & W. Smith, North Shields (Yard No. 31), for Watts, Milburn & Company, Newcastle. 1872: Registry transferred to London. 1873: Lengthened and machinery compounded. 7.1879: Transferred to Watts, Ward & Company. 4.4.1881: Whilst on a voyage from Newport to Savona with a cargo of coal, wrecked in approximate position 45N., 10W.

WMi 21. JOHN MIDDLETON (1) (1866 - 1870) Iron Screw Steamer
O.N. 56042. 772g. 212.0 x 28.15 x 17.4 feet.
Simple 2-cyl. steam engine manufactured by the shipbuilder. 90 nhp.
15.8.1866: Launched by Palmers Shipbuilding & Iron Company Ltd., Howdon (Yard No. 209), for Watts, Milburn & Company. 20.12.1867: In collision with the EQUITA. 21.4.1868: Ran aground in the River Danube. 21.8.1868: Ran aground in the Dardanelles. 1.9.1870: Foundered whilst on a voyage from Cronstadt to Leith. Crew saved and landed at Christiansand.

WMi 22. CARRON (3) (1867 - 1879) Barque
O.N. 56495. 344 tons. 120.1 x 27.2 x 17.0 feet.
16.4.1867: Launched by J. Crown, Southwick, Sunderland, for Watts, Milburn & Company. 3.3.1879:

Whilst on a voyage from New Orleans to Leith with a cargo of oil cake, sank after a collision with the Spanish BILBOA about 12 miles E.N.E., of the North Sand Light. Crew saved.

WMi 23. MARION (1867 - 1870) Barque
O.N. 45156. 460 tons. 131.55 x 29.45 x 17.95 feet.
1.1863: Launched by Davison & Stokoe, Sunderland, for Collingwood Tully, Newcastle. 24.10.1867: Sold by Mortgagee in Possession, to Watts, Milburn & Company, together with LORD COLLINGWOOD (see No.WMi 24). 25.9.1870: Whilst on a voyage from Colombo to Calcutta with a cargo of about 100 tons of coconut oil, struck a rock when entering the harbour at Galle, S.W. Ceylon, to load more cargo, and was beached but soon became a total wreck. Her hull and fittings were sold for £315.

WMi 24. LORD COLLINGWOOD (1867 - 1879) Barque
O.N. 43596. 407 tons. 123.0 x 28.8 x 17.8 feet.
8.7.1861: Launched by Davison & Stokoe, Sunderland for Collingwood Tully, Newcastle. 25.10.1867: Sold by Mortgagee in Possession, to Watts, Milburn & Company, together with MARION (ship WMi 23). 27.8.1879: Sold to John Robertson and J. J. Marks, Liverpool.1885: Sold to R. Barazarte, Valparaiso, Chile, and renamed JUAN JOSE LATORRE. 1896: Sold to D. Z. de Barazarte. 1904: Sold to A. Ibarra, Ancud, Chile. 1909: Deleted from Lloyds Register.

WMi 25. FLODDEN (1867 - 1875) Barque
O.N. 56520. 343 tons. 120.0 x 27.2 x 16.9 feet.
10.12.1867: Launched by Wm. Pickersgill, Sunderland for Watts, Milburn & Company. HARTLEPOOL (ship WMi 11) was taken in part exchange for her. 1875: Sold to Robert Rae, Melbourne, Victoria. Australia. 27.8.1883: Whilst on a voyage from Albany, Western Australia to Shanghai with a cargo of sandalwood, wrecked on the South bank of the River Yangtse.

WMi 26. CLAREMONT (1868 - 1873) Iron Screw Steamer
O.N. 56098. 799g. 533n. 214.6 x 29.2 x 17.6 feet.
Simple 2-cyl. steam engine manufactured by Thompson, Boyd & Company, Newcastle. 100 nhp.
1900: New C. 2-cyl. Steam engine fitted by H. Brandenburg, Hamburg.
9.5.1868: Launched by C. Mitchell & Company, Newcastle (Yard No. 164), for Watts, Milburn & Company, Newcastle. 24.10.1869: Whilst on voyage from the Tyne to the Baltic was in collision with and sank the steamship OSSIAN, that was on a voyage from Copenhagen to the Tyne, with the loss of six passengers and five crew. 21.6.1871: Judgment given against the CLAREMONT concerning the collision with the OSSIAN. 2.1872: Registry transferred to London. 6.1873: Sold to F. G. Schmidt, Hamburg, and renamed GAMMA. 14.12.1881: Collided with and sank the steamer METROPOLITAN in the Thames off Woolwich. 1884: Sold to A. Kirston, Hamburg. 1900: Re-engined. 1914: Sold to Sardegna Trasporti Marrittimi (S. Rocca Anci, managers), Cagliori, Italy and renamed SARDEGNA. 1917: Sold to F. Lagorio fu g., Italy. 1918: Sold to Ravano & Corrado, Italy, and renamed SANTI AGOSTINO. 1924: Sold to Unione Linea Gran Cabotaggio Soc.Anon di Nav., Italy. 1925: Sold to P. Consigliere, Italy. 1926: Sold for demolition.

WMi 27. TAUNTON (1868 - 1879) Composite Ship
O.N. 60830. 705g. 688n. 181.5 x 32.0 x 17.7 feet.
19.6.1868: Launched by Denton, Gray & Company, West Hartlepool (Yard No. 73), for Watts, Milburn & Company. ZETUS (ship WMi 3) was taken in part exchange. 7.1879: Transferred to W. Milburn & Company, Newcastle. 2.10.1880: Whilst on a voyage from Tyne to Le Havre, ran down and sank the schooner CURLEW. Five of the schooner's crew were drowned. 30.12.1881: Sold to G. B. Meager, Swansea, and re-rigged as a barque. 1892: Sold to J. A. Ferreira & Company, Lisbon, and renamed EMILIA. 17.7.1898: Whilst on a voyage, in ballast, from Lourenco Marques to New Orleans, struck Thunderbolt Rock, and was later towed to Port Elizabeth where she sank.

WMi 28. FENHAM (1868 - 1875) Iron Screw Steamer
O.N. 56099. 880g.   224.5 x 29.2 x 17.6 feet.
Simple 2-cyl. steam engine (E1433) manufactured by R. & W. Hawthorn, Newcastle. 100 nhp.
1875: C. 2-cyl. steam engine manufactured by T. Richardson & Son, Hartlepool. 99 nhp.
20.6.1868: Launched by C. Mitchell & Company, Newcastle (Yard No. 166), for Watts, Milburn & Company.   17.7.1869: Whilst on a voyage Ibralia to Antwerp, put into Plymouth with machinery damage.   13.11.1869: Whilst on a voyage from Antwerp to the Tyne, collided with the brig SEA VENTURE off Whitby. 2.1872: Registry transferred to London. 1875: Sold to J. Fawcett & Greenwell, Newcastle, and re-engined. 29.12.1882: Whilst on a voyage from Dede Agatch, Turkey to Schiedam with a cargo of rye, wrecked, at the entrance to the New Cut, Rotterdam Her crew were saved. 30.12.1882: Wreck sold for 110 florins, 304 tons of cargo saved.

WMi 29. CRITERION (1868 - 1877) Iron Screw Steamer
O.N. 56100. 965g. 647n.   224.5 x 29.3 x 17.5 feet.
Post 1873: 1,109g 834n.   248.8 x 29.3 x 17.4 feet.
Simple 2-cyl. steam engine manufactured by Thompson Boyd & Company, Newcastle. 100 nhp.
1873: C. 2-cyl. steam engine re-manufactured by Thompson Boyd & Company, Newcastle. 99 nhp.
29.1.1868: Keel laid by C. Mitchell, Newcastle (Yard No. 169), for Watts, Milburn & Company, Newcastle. 24.7.1868: Launched. 27.8.1868: Completed. 1872: Registry transferred to London. 1873: Lengthened and machinery compounded. 21.7.1877: whilst on a voyage from Cronstadt to London with a cargo of wheat and oats, foundered 30 miles west of Horn Reef, Jutland Coast Sea. Crew saved by a Grimsby fishing smack.

WMi 30. LUTTERWORTH (1868 - 1875) Iron Ship
O.N. 60895. 883 tons. 209.2 x 33.1 x 19.9 feet.
11.1868: Launched by Denton & Gray, Hartlepool (Yard No. 78), for Watts, Milburn & Company, Newcastle.   EQUINOX (Ship WMiM 4) was taken in part exchange.   1873: Chartered to Shaw, Savill & Company, Southampton, for a period of six years.   1875: Sold together with charter agreement, to J. Grey, London. 5.1878: Re-rigged as a barque. 7.1879: Upon completion of charter, purchased by Shaw, Savill & Company, Southampton.   1882: Transferred to Shaw, Savill & Albion Company Ltd.   1906: Sold to the Colonial Sailing Ship Company (A. H. Turnbull & Company), Lyttelton.   1.10.1906: Dismasted in the Cook Straight. 1907: Sold to Union Steamship Company, Timaru, New Zealand, and hulked. 26.6.1950: Loaded with condemned cargo from the WAIPIATA, and sunk in the Cook Straight, off Wellington, by the Royal New Zealand Air Force as a training exercise.

WMi 31. SANTOS (1869 - 1871) Iron Screw Steamer
O.N. 62366. 1,016g. 641n. 224.7 x 29.2 x 17.25 feet.
Simple 2-cyl. steam engine manufactured by T. Richardson & Sons, Hartlepool. 120 nhp.
10.4.1869: Launched by C. Mitchell & Company, Newcastle (Yard No. 184), for Watts, Milburn & Company, Newcastle.   2.6.1869: Chartered to the Hamburg-Brazil Steamship Company, Hamburg. 10.1870: Released from charter. 12.1871: Sold to Hamburg South America Line. 31.10.1873: Sold to W. Zoder, Hamburg, and renamed ST. PAULI. 30.10.1877: Whilst on a voyage from Shields to Stockholm, stranded off Lys. Crew saved. NB. 1-day short of 4-years service for her owner.

WMi 32. CHARLES TENNANT (1869 - 1875) Iron Screw Steamer
O.N. 62322. 874g. 578n. 224.8 x 29.1 x 17.35 feet.
Simple 2-cyl. steam engine (E1456) manufactured by R. & W. Hawthorn & Company. 100 nhp.
1875: C. 2-cyl. steam engine manufactured by the Wallsend Slipway Company, Wallsend. 100 nhp.
30.4.1869: Launched by C. Mitchell & Company, Newcastle (Yard No. 187), for Watts, Milburn & Company, Newcastle. 8.7.1869: Completed. 3.1872: Registry transferred to London. 1875: Sold to H. Clapham & Company, Newcastle and renamed MAUD. 1884: Owners re-styled Clapham Steamship Company, Newcastle. 1887: Sold to A. Mango and D. Foscolo, Piraeus, and renamed THIRESIA. 1898: Sold to Mitovidoff & others, Odessa.   1901: Sold to E. Mouschensky & Company, Odessa.   1906: Renamed TERESIA. 1909: Sold to J. J. Kodjash, Odessa.   1912: Sold to F. E. Gladtchenock, Odessa. 1914: Sold to H. Enriiqez, Constantinople, and renamed BEATRICE. 1916: Sold to M. Nomicos, Greece, and renamed THYRA. 11.1.1916: Having arrived from Marseilles, was sunk during the bombardment of San Giovanni di Medua, Albania.

WMi 33. BRAZILIAN (1869 - 1870) & (1873 - 1874) Iron Screw Steamer
O.N. 62328. 1,359g. 880n. 240.0 x 32.4 x 24.2 feet.
Simple 2-cyl. steam engine manufactured by R. & W. Hawthorn & Company, Newcastle. 120 nhp. 1874: Compound engine manufactured by Thompson, Boyd & Company, Newcastle, 130 nhp.
11.6.1869: Launched by C. Mitchell & Company, Newcastle (Yard No. 188), for Watts, Milburn & Company, Newcastle. 4.8.1869: Completed, and chartered to the Hamburg-Brazil Steamship Company Ltd. 3.3.1870: Transferred to German registry. 9.3.1870: Sold to Hamburg-Brazil Steamship Company Ltd., and renamed BRASILIEN. 21.7.1870: Returned to British registry. 19.2.1872: Sold to Hamburg South America Line. 1873: Sold to Watts Milburn & Company, Newcastle, and renamed BRAZILIAN. 1874: Sold to H. Clapham & Company, Newcastle. 1884: Owners re-styled Clapham Steamship Company, Newcastle. 1889: Sold to H. E. Moss & Company, (Edward Asker, manager), Liverpool. 1891: Sold to Hilmi Effendi, Constantinople. 1.1892: Sold to Caramanian Shahinoglou & Company, Constantinople, and renamed MURVET. 1896: Sold to Idarei Massousieh, Constantinople. 1912: Deleted from Lloyds Register.

WMi 34. SURBITON (1) (1869 - 1873) Iron Screw Steamer
O.N. 63518. 965g. 224.5 x 29.1 x 17.5 feet.
C. 2-cyl. steam engine manufactured by Thompson, Boyd & Company, Newcastle. 110 nhp.
21.9.1869: Launched by C. Mitchell & Company, Newcastle (Yard No. 195), for Watts, Milburn & Company, Newcastle. 30.10.1869: Trials. 3.1870: Became the second, Watts, Milburn vessel to transit the Suez Canal. 3.12.1873: Whilst on a voyage from Riga to Stettin with a cargo of rye, was lost with all hands.

WMi 35. CHU KIANG (1869 - 1872) Iron Screw Steamer
O.N. 63541. 1,008g. 206.0 x 30.2 x 22.0 feet.
C. 2-cyl. steam engine manufactured by the North Eastern Marine Engineering Company, Sunderland. 120 nhp.
29.5.1869: Keel laid by C. Mitchell & Company, Newcastle (Yard No. 204), for Watts, Milburn & Company, Newcastle. 6.11.1869: Launched. 28.12.1869: Delivered. 2.1870: Became the first Watts, Milburn vessel to transit the Suez Canal. 5.2.1872: Whilst on a voyage from Shanghai to Canton, wrecked on Lamyit Island, near the entrance to the Haitan Straits. Crew saved.

WMi 36. OTTERBURN (1870 - 1872) Iron Screw Steamer
O.N. 63551. 1,342g. 855n. 238.2 x 32.1 x 23.8 feet.
C. 2-cyl. steam engine manufactured by Blair & Company, Stockton. 130 nhp.
4.12.1869: Launched by Denton, Gray & Company, West Hartlepool (Yard No. 86), for Watts, Milburn & Company, Newcastle. 1.1870: Completed. 25.2.1870: Whilst on a voyage from London to Ceylon, stranded at the entrance to Aboukir Bay, near Rosetta, Egypt. 300 tons of general cargo was discharged to aid salvage operations. 3.1870: Dry-docked and repaired at Alexandria. 4.1870: Became the third Watts, Milburn vessel to transit the Suez Canal in 3-months. 15.12.1872: Whilst on a voyage from Shields to Odessa, suffered a cargo shift in the Bay of Biscay, and was abandoned leaky and on her beam ends. Her crew were picked up by LOUISE HILLMAN and landed at Gibraltar.

WMi 37. HARE BELL (1870 - 1879) Brig
O.N. 49630. 249g. 238n. 102.2 x 26.0 x 14.6 feet.
9.1864: Launched by G. Hutchinson, Newcastle, for his own account. 29.01.1868: Whilst on a voyage from Santa Marta for Bremen, ran aground near Pigeon Island, West Indies, but was refloated. 20.5.1870: Sold to Watts, Milburn & Company, Newcastle. 9.1877: Whilst on a voyage from Cronstadt to Belfast, suffered a cargo shift and put into Inverness to rectify the problem and later proceeded on voyage using the Caledonian Canal. 9.1877: Put into Gibraltar after having collided with the barque PRESTON. 17.11.1879: Sold to T. Leighton, Newcastle. 1886: Sold to H. Andrews, Newcastle. 1886: Sold to Bessey & Palmer, Yarmouth. 1896: Owners restyled Bessey & Palmer Ltd. 1920: Sold to John. W. Robertson, Lerwick. 1925: Demolished.

WMi 38. COQUET (1870 - 1873) Iron Screw Steamer
O.N. 63608. 1,228g. 774n. 231.0 x 32.1 x 17.5 feet.
C. 2-cyl. steam engine manufactured by T. Clark & Company, Newcastle. 120 nhp.
9.10.1869: Keel Laid by C. Mitchell & Company, Newcastle (Yard No. 210), for Watts, Milburn & Company. 15.4.1870: Launched. 20.6.1870: Trials. 24.6.1870: Completed. 18.3.1873: Advertised for sale at a price not less than £24,000. 8.1873: Sold to Spanish buyers, and renamed JUAN. 16.1.1877: Sold to T. Baker, Cardiff, and reverted to COQUET. 1885: Sold to John Fry, Cardiff. 1885: Sold to W. J. Tillett, Cardiff. 24.12.1885: Whilst on a voyage in ballast, from La Rochelle to Decido, Spain, wrecked in Castro-Urdiales Bay, Spain. Crew saved.

WMi 39. BLYTHWOODE (1870 - 1879) Iron Screw Steamer
O.N. 63620. 1,214g. 770n. 230.0 x 32.0 x 17.2 feet.
C. 2-cyl. steam engine (E1479) manufactured by R. & W. Hawthorn & Company, Newcastle. 120 nhp.
14.5.1870: Launched by Denton, Gray & Company, West Hartlepool (Yard No. 95), for Watts, Milburn & Company, London. 8.1870: Completed. 7.1879: Transferred to Watts, Ward & Company, London. 1892: Sold to H. Briggs, South Shields. 1899: Sold to Aktiebolaget Gustafsbergs Fabriks Intressenter Odelberg Gustafsberg, Sweden, and renamed GUSTAFSBERG. 1911: Sold to Angfartygs Aktiebolaget Sune, (G. T. Schele, manager) Halmstad, Sweden, and renamed GUSTAF. 5.4.1915: Whilst on a voyage from Burntisland to Halmstad with a cargo of coal, wrecked on Morups Tange.

CHEVIOT (J. Dobson collection)

WMi 40. CHEVIOT (1870 - 1873) Iron Screw Steamer
O.N. 63648. 1,226g. 764n. 230.2 x 32.2 x 17.5 feet.
C. 2-cyl. steam engine manufactured by T. Clark & Company, Newcastle. 120 nhp.
15.12.1869: Keel laid by C. Mitchell & Company, Newcastle (Yard No. 228), for Watts, Milburn & Company. 29.7.1870: Launched. 15.9.1870: Completed. 24.3.1873: Stranded at Foreland Point in the Bristol Channel, taken to Cardiff with considerable bottom damage. 10.1873: Sold to J. Loughland and J. Gunn, Cardiff. 1876: Sold to Foley & Company, London. 1876: Sold to Wm. Howard Smith & Sons,

Melbourne. 19.10.1887: Having departed Melbourne at 8.00pm, on a voyage to Sydney in gale force weather, she lost her propeller and then struck rocks on the Back Beach, Port Sea and broke in two. The weather was too rough to launch the lifeboats 35 of her passengers and crew of 48 were drowned. The remains of the vessel were sold by auction and raised £62.

WMi 41. JOHN MIDDLETON (2) (1870 - 1878) Iron Screw Steamer
O.N. 63671. 1,200g. 764n. 229.1 x 31.7 x 17.3 feet.
C. 2-cyl. steam engine manufactured by the North Eastern Marine Engineering Company, Sunderland. 120 nhp.
13.9.1870: Launched by Denton, Gray & Company, West Hartlepool (Yard No. 100), for Watts, Milburn & Company, Newcastle. 6.3.1878: Whilst on a voyage from Odessa to Antwerp with a cargo of grain, foundered at Sali Bazaar, in the Bosporus, having been run into by the Turkish ironclad NEDJ-IM SHEFKET and HMS ANTELOPE.

WMi 42. RIO (1870 - 1871) Iron Screw Steamer
O.N. 62368. 1,494g. 978n. 260.8 x 33.2 x 25.5 feet.
Post 1880: 1,650g. 1,222n. 277.5 x 33.2 x 25.0 feet.
C. 2-cyl. steam engine manufactured by T. Clark & Company, Newcastle. 160 nhp.
26.1.1870: Keel laid by C. Mitchell & Company, Newcastle (Yard No. 234), for Watts Milburn & Company, Newcastle. 24.9.1870: Launched. 25.11.1870: Delivered and chartered to the Hamburg-Brasil Steamship Company. 27.12.1871: Sold to Hamburg & South America Steam Navigation Company, Hamburg. 1876: Sold to Hamburg South American Damp Gesel, Hamburg. 1880: Lengthened by the Wallsend Slipway & Engineering Company. 1891: Sold to M. Jebsen, Alpenrade. 1897: Sold to H. Diederichsen, Kiel. 1898: Sold to Rheinisch-Westalisches Kohlen-Kontor, Tsingtao. 13.12.1899: Beached at Kiau-Chau, China after her cargo of coal had caught fire and subsequently converted to a coaling hulk. 1.1901: Sold for demolition.

WMi 43. SINGAPORE (1871 - 1873) Iron Screw Steamer
O.N. 63690. 2,223g. 1,445n. 300.0 x 36.8 x 27.9 feet.
C. 2-cyl. steam engine manufactured by the North Eastern Marine Engineering Company, Sunderland. 200 nhp.
27.9.1870: Launched by C. Mitchell & Company, Newcastle (Yard No. 239), for Watts, Milburn & Company, Newcastle. 30.12.1870: Trials. 1.1.1871: Completed. 19.7.1873: Whilst on a voyage from Shanghai to London with a cargo of tea and tin wrecked off Cape Guardafudi, Somalia. 16 of her crew of 45 were lost.

WMi 44. CANTON (1871 - 1874) Iron Screw Steamer
O.N. 65558. 1,880g. 1,215n. 290.6 x 35.3 x 25.4 feet.
C. 2-cyl. steam engine (C58) manufactured by the North Eastern Marine Engineering Company, Sunderland. 200 nhp.
22.12.1870: Launched by C. Mitchell & Company, Newcastle (Yard No. 241), for Watts, Milburn & Company, Newcastle. 1.1871: Completed. 22.9.1874: Whilst on a voyage from Foo-Chow-Foo to London with a cargo of tea, wrecked on the Min Reef, Min River China.

WMi 45. HONG KONG (1) (1871 - 1875) Iron Screw Steamer
O.N. 65570. 1,881g. 1221n. 290.4 x 35.3 x 25.4 feet.
C. 2-cyl. steam engine (C59) manufactured by the North Eastern Marine Engineering Company, Sunderland. 200 nhp.
2.6.1870: Keel laid by C. Mitchell & Company, Newcastle (Yard No. 242), for Watts, Milburn & Company, Newcastle. 22.2.1871: Launched. 23.5.1871: Delivered. 24.1.1875: Departed Gravesend for Japan with 9 passengers and 2,400 tons of general cargo including 300 tons of gunpowder. 22.2.1875: Sank after striking a submerged rock near Socotra, Gulf of Aden. Six passengers and six of her crew lost their lives in a lifeboat accident.

WMi 46. RICHMOND (1871 - 1879) Iron Screw Steamer
O.N. 65561. 1,234g. 769n. 229.8 x 32.2 x 17.9 feet.
C. 2-cyl. steam engine manufactured by T. Clark & Company, Newcastle. 130 nhp.
1.1871: Launched by Schlesinger, Davis & Company, Wallsend (Yard No. 31), for Watts, Milburn & Company, Newcastle. 29.3.1871: Completed. 7.1879: Transferred to Watts, Ward & Company, London. 1894: Sold to T. S. Leinster, North Shields. 6.12.1894: Whilst on a voyage from Rotterdam to Shields, wrecked at Burniston Cliff, 3 miles North of Scarborough, Yorkshire.

WMi 47. CHISWICK (1871 - 1879) Iron Screw Steamer
O.N. 65587. 1,261g. 796n. 239.5 x 32.1 x 17.6 feet.
C. 2-cyl. steam engine manufactured by T. Clark & Company, Newcastle. 130 nhp.
28.3.1870: Keel laid by C. Mitchell & Company, Newcastle (Yard No. 237), for Watts, Milburn & Company, Newcastle. 4.4.1871: Launched. 16.6.1871: Delivered. 7.1879: Transferred to Watts, Ward & Company, London. 11.1879: Brought the master and eight of the survivors from the ROSCOMMON (see ship WM 16) from the Azores to London. 5.2.1891: Whilst on a voyage from Cardiff to St. Nazaire, with a cargo of salt, struck the Seven Stones rocks off the Isles of Scilly and sank. 8 of her crew of 19 were saved.

WMi 48. CATHERINE APCAR (1871) Iron Screw Barque
O.N. 52963. 1,019g. 230 x 32.5 x 17.2 feet.
C. 2-cyl. steam engine manufactured by Thompson, Boyd & Company, Newcastle. 100 nhp.
26.4.1865: Launched by J. Wigham Richardson & Company, Newcastle (Yard No. 34), for Gibb, Apcar & Durham, London. 1869: Registry transferred to Calcutta. 1869: Ownership transferred to S. A. Apcar. 5.1871: Sold to Watts, Milburn & Company, Newcastle. 9.8.1871: Whilst on a voyage in ballast, from London to Shields, collided in fog with the steamer DESPATCH, and sank, in a position 10 miles south of Flamborough Head. Crew saved.

WMi 49. YANGTSZE (1872 - 1879) Iron Screw Steamer
O.N. 65650. 1,218g. 783n. 244.0 x 31.1 x 22.5 feet.
C. 2-cyl. steam engine (C72) manufactured by the North Eastern Marine Engineering Company Ltd., Sunderland. 160 nhp.
24.3.1871: Keel laid by C. Mitchell, Low Walker, Newcastle (Yard No. 260), for Watts, Milburn & Company, London. 11.11.1871: Launched. 25.1.1872: Completed. 1879: Transferred to W. Milburn & Company, Newcastle. 8.10.1883: Whilst on a voyage from Shanghai to Hong Kong, collided with the Chinese steamer KIANGTEEN - bound for Ningpo, both vessels put into Shanghai. Repairs estimated at £2,500. 19.5.1888: Sold to Chinesische Kustenfahrt Gesellschaft, Hamburg. 13.6.1890: Whilst on a voyage from Singapore to Shanghai, stranded on Hieshoui Island, and abandoned.

WMi 50. COLOMBO (1872 - 1879) Iron Screw Steamer
O.N. 65664. 1,948g. 760n. 280.3 x 35.0 x 25.6 feet.
C. 2-cyl. steam engine manufactured by T. Clark & Company, Newcastle. 200 nhp.
5.1.1871: Keel laid by C. Mitchell & Company, Newcastle (Yard No. 252), for Watts, Milburn & Company, London. 13.12.1871: Launched. 13.3.1872: Delivered. 7.1879: Transferred to Watts, Ward & Company, London. 9.7.1885: Whilst on a voyage from Bull River, South Carolina to Dublin with a cargo of phosphate rock, wrecked on Scatterie Island, Cape Breton.

WMi 51. MAHARAJAH (1872 - 1890) Iron Screw Steamer
O.N. 65671. 1,571g. 994n. 259.3 x 34.0 x 18.8 feet.
C. 2-cyl. steam engine (E1515) manufactured by R. & W. Hawthorn & Company, Newcastle. 170 nhp. 1893: T.3-cyl. engine and boilers fitted by Westgarth, English & Company, Middlesbrough. 156 nhp.
19.1.1871: Keel laid by C. Mitchell & Company, Newcastle (Yard No. 253), for Watts, Milburn & Company, London. 27.12.1871: Launched. 11.4.1872: Completed. 7.1879: Transferred to W. Milburn & Company, Newcastle. 25.10.1890: Sold to Ervig, Walther and Hirsch, Xiansund, and renamed ROMSDAL. 1891: Transferred to Aetieselskabet "Romsdal" (G. C. Volckmar), Xiansund, Norway. 1901:

Sold to Acties, Romsdal (T. H. Skogland), Haugesund, Norway. 1910: Sold to Acties, Skoglands Linge (same managers), Norway. 27.8.1914: Whilst on a voyage from New York to Port Antonio with general cargo, wrecked on Long Island.

WMi 52. CONSETT (1872 - 1879) Iron Screw Steamer
O.N. 65689. 1,573g. 996n.   259.5 x 34.0 x 18.8 feet.
C. 2-cyl. steam engine (E1516) manufactured by R. & W. Hawthorn & Company, Newcastle. 170 nhp.
19.1.1871: Keel laid by C. Mitchell & Company, Newcastle (Yard No. 254), for Watts, Milburn & Company, London. 9.3.1872: Launched. 15.5.1872: Completed. 4.1876: Docked in Bombay after grounding in the Red Sea. 20.1.1877: Whilst on a voyage from Smyrna to Liverpool via Gibraltar, stranded on Pearl Rock, Gibraltar, and was subsequently salvaged. 27.3.1877: At the inquiry into the stranding the Captain was found to have been drunk and had his certificate suspended for two years. 7.1879: Transferred to W. Milburn & Company, Newcastle. 7.5.1880: Whilst on a voyage from Bassein, Burma to Port Said with a cargo of rice, wrecked on the Maldive Islands. Crew saved by the Maldive brig FUTTER FOSSEM.

WMi 53. WEST STANLEY (1872 - 1879) Iron Screw Steamer
O.N. 65704. 1,568g. 993n.   260.0 x 34.0 x 18.8 feet.
C. 2-cyl. steam engine manufactured by T. Clark & Company, Newcastle. 170 nhp.
19.1.1871: Keel laid by C. Mitchell & Company, Newcastle (Yard No. 255), for Watts, Milburn & Company, London. 23.3.1872: Launched. 13.6.1872: Completed. 7.1879: Transferred to W. Milburn & Company, Newcastle and London. 4.3.1880: Whilst on a voyage from the Tyne to Odessa, grounded in the Dardanelles. Upon payment of £600, was assisted off by local tugs. 13.1.1881: Whilst on a voyage from Norfolk, Virginia to Revel with a cargo of cotton, grounded on Oesel Reef, 60 miles off Revel, Estonia. Despite the salvage operation being seriously hampered by fog and ice, both the vessel and cargo were recovered. 9.5.1881: Towed into Farosund, Gotland by salvage steamers. 10.1881: Sold to Helsingorske Damp. Selskab, Elsinore, and renamed SVEA. 1887: Suffered heavy damage and acquired by salvors - Neptune Diving & Salvage Company, Stockholm. 22.4.1887: Sold to Bartram Haswell, shipbuilders, Sunderland, and renamed WEST STANLEY. 17.11.1887: Sold to J. F. Marshall, Sunderland. 1896: Sold to Acties. Unity, (Hjalmar Roed, manager), Tonsberg, Norway, and renamed UNITY. 1905: Owners restyled as Acties. United (Sigurd Roed, manager), Tonsberg. 1909: Acties United, Xiania, Norway, placed in liquidation, and vessel sold to A. Merveille, Dunkirk, for demolition

WMi 54. CHIN KIANG (1872 - 1879) Iron Screw Steamer
O.N. 68357. 1,249g. 799n.   243.5 x 31.2 x 22.3 feet.
C. 2-cyl. steam engine manufactured by T. Clark & Company, Newcastle. 160 nhp.
23.11.1871: Keel laid by C. Mitchell & Company, Newcastle (Yard No. 267), for Watts, Milburn & Company, London. 7.9.1872: Launched. 21.11.1872: Completed. 7.1879: Transferred to W. Milburn & Company, Newcastle and London. 29.1.1884: whilst on a voyage from Hong Kong to Shanghai with a general cargo and 50 passengers, wrecked at Hore Tow Head, Huitian Bay. 12 members of her crew and 44 passengers were lost.

WMi 55. NANKIN (1873 - 1879) Iron Screw Steamer
O.N. 68375. 2,423g. 1,830n. 330.6 x 36.8 x 25.7 feet.
C. 2-cyl. steam engine manufactured by Maudslay Sons & Field, London. 300 nhp.
25.5.1871: Keel laid by C. Mitchell & Company, Newcastle (Yard No. 263), for Watts, Milburn & Company. London. 23.7.1872: Launched. 2.1.1873: Delivered. 5.6.1879: Chartered by the Colonial Line for a voyage to Australia. 7.1879: Transferred to Watts, Ward & Company, London. 1880: Sold to G. R. Glover, Liverpool. 28.4.1882: Whilst on a voyage to Liverpool, sank after a collision with the GEORGE. W. CLYDE in New York harbour.

WMi 56. DUNRAVEN (1873 - 1876) Iron Screw Steamer
O.N. 68402. 1,613g. 1,044n. 261.2 x 32.1 x 24.2 feet.
C. 2-cyl. steam engine manufactured by Thompson, Boyd & Company, Newcastle. 140 nhp.
30.10.1871: Keel laid by C. Mitchell & Company, Newcastle (Yard No. 266), for Watts, Milburn &

Company, London. 14.12.1872: Launched. 27.3.1873: Delivered. 25.4.1876: Whilst on a voyage from Bombay to Liverpool, with a cargo of cotton valued at approximately £90,000, struck the Shaab Mahmond Reef, in the Straits of Jubal, and became a total loss.

WMi 57. NINGPO (1873 - 1879) Iron Screw Steamer
O.N. 68464. 1,173g. 762n.   245.6 x 31.1 x 22.2 feet.
C. 2-cyl. steam engine manufactured by T. Clark & Company, Newcastle. 160 nhp.
24.7.1873: Launched by J. Wigham Richardson & Company, Newcastle (Yard No. 83), for Watts, Milburn & Company, London. 9.1873: Completed. 7.1879: Transferred to W. Milburn & Company, Newcastle and London. 5.1888: Sold to Chinesische Kustenfahrt Gesellshaft, Hamburg. 1895: Sold to Okazaki Tokichi, Kobe, Japan and renamed TAIYO MARU. 1899: Sold to Takezaki Kusuma, Kobe. 2.4.1902: Whilst on a voyage from Yokohama to Moji, wrecked on Rock Island near Cape Idzu.

WMi 58. AMOY (1873 - 1879) Iron Screw Steamer
O.N. 68490. 1,250g. 814n.   249.0 x 31.6 x 22.0 feet.
C. 2-cyl. steam engine manufactured by T. Clark & Company, Newcastle. 160 nhp.
22.1.1873: Keel laid by C. Mitchell, Newcastle (Yard No. 295), for Watts, Milburn & Company, London. 10.9.1873: Launched. 19.11.1873: Completed. 7.1879: Transferred to W. Milburn & Company, Newcastle and London. 5.1888: Sold to Chinesische Kustenfahrt Gesellshaft, Hamburg. 1892: Sold to Sugano Denyemon, Fushiki Ko, Japan, and renamed KORIO MARU. 1892: Wrecked on the coast of Japan (reported 4th quarter no details).

WMi 59. PENSACOLA (1873 - 1876) Ship
O.N. 47485. 1,421g.   104.6 x 39.4 x 25.0 feet.
1863: Launched by James Nevins, St. John, New Brunswick. 1864: Sold to Crow & Company, Liverpool. 1864: Sold to Curwen & Company, Liverpool. 1873: Sold to Watts, Milburn & Company, London. 7.12.1876: Whilst on a voyage from Macabi Island, Peru to New York with a cargo of guano, foundered about 300 miles east of Bermuda Crew saved.

HANKOW (Ambrose Greenway collection)

WMi 60. HANKOW (1874 - 1879) Iron Screw Steamer
O.N. 68510. 3,594g. 2,332n.   389.0 x 42.1 x 28.8 feet.
C. 2-cyl. steam engine (E1595) manufactured by R. & W. Hawthorn & Company, Newcastle. 493 nhp. 1,320 ihp.
7.12.1872: Keel laid by C. Mitchell, Newcastle (Yard No. 290), for Watts, Milburn & Company, London. 7.10.1873: Launched. 21.2.1874: Completed. 15.12.1876: Chartered by Colonial Line. 7.1879: Transferred to W. Milburn & Company, Newcastle and London. 5.1897: Sold to Aberdeen Atlantic

Shipping Company Ltd. (John Rust & Son, managers), Aberdeen. 1898: Purchased by Wilh. Wilhelmsen, Norway, and renamed DUNNET. 6.4.1899: Sailed from Barry bound for Genoa and disappeared, believed to have foundered in the Bay of Biscay.

WHAMPOA (World Ship Society Photograph Library)

WMi 61. WHAMPOA (1874 - 1879) Iron Screw Steamer
O.N. 68517. 3,835g. 2,487n. 399.5 x 42.2 x 28.4 feet.
C. 2-cyl. steam engine manufactured by the shipbuilder. 500 nhp.
22.10.1873: Launched by Palmers' Shipbuilding & Iron Company Ltd., Jarrow on Tyne (Yard No. 300), for Watts, Milburn & Company, London. 3.2.1874: Completed. 24.12.1874: Chartered by Colonial Line until late 1878. 3.1879: Sold to R. Rubattino & Company, Genoa, and renamed MANILLA. 1881: Owners restyled Nav. Gen. Italiana, Societa Riunite Florio O. Rubattino. 1883: Owners restyled as Nav. Gen. Italiana. 1905: Sold to Italian shipbreakers and demolished at Genoa.

WMi 62. ROSEDEN (1874) Iron Screw Steamer
O.N. 70585. 1,639g. 1,063n. 265.0 x 34.0 x 24.6 feet.
C. 2-cyl. steam engine (C121) manufactured by the North Eastern Marine Engineering Company, Sunderland. 200 nhp.
1874: Built by Cole Bros, Willington Quay on Tyne (Yard No. 23), for Watts, Milburn & Company, London. 18.7.1874: Sailed from the Tyne on her maiden voyage from Newcastle to Cronstadt with a cargo of coal. 20.7.1874: Sank in the Skagerrak after a collision with ONEGA, (673g./1864) of London, 15 miles west of the Hantsholm Light. Crew saved.

WMi 63. MARCIA (1874 - 1879) Iron Screw Steamer
O.N. 70611. 1,641g. 1,060n. 265.0 x 34.0 x 24.5 feet.
C. 2-cyl. steam engine (C122) manufactured by the North Eastern Marine Engineering Company, Sunderland. 200 nhp.
7.1874: Launched by Cole Bros, Willington Quay (Yard No. 24), for Watts, Milburn & Company, London. 9.1874: Completed. 1879: Transferred to W. Milburn & Company, Newcastle and London. 10.1880: Towed the Belgian mail steamer RHYNLAND (2,366g/1879) into Falmouth, a distance of over 200 miles, after she had lost her propeller. The Belgian ship was on a voyage to New York and had on board 580 passengers. 17.7.1895: Sold to J. W. Waugh, South Shields. 10.7.1899: Whilst on a voyage from Philippeville to Aberdeen with a cargo of esparto grass, wrecked at Pern Point at the entrance to Lampaul-Ouessant,

ST OSYTH (J. Dobson Collection)

WMi 64. ST OSYTH (1874 - 1879) Iron Screw Steamer
O.N. 70617. 3,541g. 2,967n. 389.5 x 42.1 x 28.9 feet.
C. 2-cyl. steam engine (E1596) manufactured by R. & W. Hawthorn & Company, Newcastle. 450 nhp.
19.12.1872: Keel laid by C. Mitchell & Company, Newcastle (Yard No. 293), for Watts, Milburn & Company, London. 21.3.1874: Launched. 3.10.1874: Completed. 7.1879: Sold to R. Rubattino & Company, Genoa, and renamed SINGAPORE. 1882: Owners Nav. Gen. Italiana, Societa Riunite Florio O. Rubattino. 1883: Owners restyled as Nav Gen Italiana. 1910: Demolished at Palermo.

WMi 65. ACTON (1874 - 1879) Iron Screw Steamer
O.N. 70634. 1,646g. 1,066n. 279.9 x 33.3 x 24.6 feet.
C. 2-cyl. steam engine (C124) manufactured by the North Eastern Marine Engineering Company, Sunderland. 200 nhp.
1.8.1874: Launched by C. Mitchell & Company, Newcastle (Yard No. 301), for Watts, Milburn & Company. London. 7.1879: Transferred to Watts, Ward & Company, London. 12.8.1886: Whilst on a voyage from Montreal to London with a cargo of timber and copper phosphate. Wrecked 3 miles west of Cape Pine, Newfoundland.

WMi 66. GILSLAND (1874 - 1879) Iron Screw Steamer
O.N. 70641. 1,639g. 1,058n. 265.0 x 34.0 x 24.5 feet.
C. 2-cyl. steam engine (C123) manufactured by the North Eastern Marine Engineering Company, Sunderland. 200 nhp.
8.1874: Launched by Cole Bros, Willington Quay on Tyne (Yard No. 25), for Watts, Milburn & Company, London. 10.1874: Completed. 7.1879: Transferred to W. Milburn & Company, Newcastle and London. 12.12.1883: In collision with NETLEY ABBEY (1,113g./1878) off Malta. 4.11.1896: Sold to Fujimoto Yasubei, Hiojo, Japan, and renamed SHIKISHIMA MARU. 1897: Sold for demolition.

WMi 67. DEVONHURST (1874 - 1878) Iron Screw Steamer
O.N. 70650. 1,646g. 1,065n. 280.0 x 33.3 x 24.6 feet.
C. 2-cyl. steam engine (C125) manufactured by the North Eastern Marine Engineering Company, Sunderland. 200 nhp. 1882: Re-boilered by Wallsend Slipway & Engineering Company.
29.8.1874: Launched by C. Mitchell & Company, Newcastle (Yard No. 302), for Watts, Milburn & Company, London. 19.12.1878: Sold to H. Katz, Frankfurt, registered at Singapore. 1882: New boilers manufactured and fitted, by the Wallsend Slipway & Engineering Company. 1883: Sold to Atjeh

Steamship Company, London. 6.11.1884: Sold to Netherlands India Company, Batavia. 1891: Sold to T. C. Bagaardt, Singapore. 1892: Sold to Ocean Steamship Company, Liverpool. 1893: Sold to Nederlandsche Stoomvaart Maatschappij "Oceaan", Amsterdam. 1894: Sold to East Indian Ocean Steamship Company, Liverpool. 1897: Sold to Yamada Akitoro, Osaka, and renamed KIUHO MARU. 1899: Sold to Hori Rikitoro, Osaka. 1902: Sold to Tanaka Matsumosuke, Osaka. 1910: Sold to Y. Hachiuma, Tarumi. 1922: Deleted from Lloyds Register.

WMi 68. SURBITON (2) (1877 - 1879) Iron Screw Steamer
O.N. 76950. 1,373g. 883n. 240.0 x 32.0 x 22.8 feet.
C. 2-cyl. steam engine (23C) manufactured by Wallsend Slipway & Engineering Company. 130 nhp.
17.3.1877: Launched by C. Mitchell & Company, Newcastle (Yard No. 343), for Watts, Milburn & Company, London. 18.2.1879: Sailed from New York for Rotterdam, with a cargo of grain and provisions, and disappeared. All 22 of her crew were lost. 11.4.1879: REGENT (1,289g./1878), picked up a boat marked SURBITON together with a Milburn houseflag.

WMi 69. FERNWOOD (1877 - 1879) Iron Screw Steamer
O.N. 76962. 1,852g. 1,203n. 280.0 x 34.2 x 24.7 feet.
C. 2-cyl. steam engine (E1717) manufactured by R. & W. Hawthorn & Company, Newcastle. 200 nhp.
28.4.1877: Launched by C. S. Swan & Company, Wallsend (Yard No. 26), for Watts, Milburn & Company, London. 4.1877: Completed. 2.6.1877: Trials. 7.1879: Transferred to W. Milburn & Company, Newcastle and London. 30.11.1879: Rescued the crew of 14 from the Norwegian Barque OCEAN and on the following day rescued the remaining crew of the Liverpool barque FOREST BELLE, which had been dismasted and was sinking. 20.1.1885: Departed from New York on voyage from New York to Bristol and Glasgow, with a cargo of 1,200 tons of wheat and maize, 1053 tons of generals and 247 tons of bunker coal, and disappeared Her crew of 25 were lost. 28.1.1885: A severe hurricane was sweeping the North Atlantic and she is thought to have either fallen victim, as did CLANDON (see ship WMi 72) or to have struck an iceberg.

WMi 70. PLAINMELLER (1877 - 1879) Iron Screw Steamer
O.N. 76999 1,832g. 1,195n. 280.2 x 34.2 x 24.4 feet.
C. 2-cyl. steam engine manufactured by J. Shaw & Company, Newcastle. 180 nhp.
12.7.1877: Launched by J. Wigham Richardson, Newcastle (Yard No. 99), for Watts, Milburn & Company, London. 25.8.1877: Completed and ran sea trials. 7.1879: Transferred to W. Milburn & Company, Newcastle and London. 11.11.1886: Whilst on a voyage from Otaru to Yokohama with a cargo of coal, was last seen off Hakodato. 12.1886: Declared as missing.

WMi 71. COMPTON (1878 - 1879) Iron Screw Steamer
O.N. 77080. 1,804g. 1,186n. 280.0 x 34.7 x 24.4 feet.
C. 2-cyl. steam engine manufactured by J. Shaw & Company, Newcastle. 200 nhp.
19.1.1878: Launched by J. Wigham Richardson & Company, Newcastle (Yard No. 105), for Watts, Milburn & Company, London. 15.3.1878: Completed and ran sea trials. 7.1879: Transferred to W. Milburn & Company, Newcastle and London. 11.6.1886: Whilst on a voyage from Singapore to Yloilo, Panay Island, Philippines, with a cargo of rice, wrecked on an island in the Balabac Straights, Borneo. Crew saved.

WMi 72. CLANDON (1878 - 1879) Iron Screw Steamer
O.N. 77105. 1,971g. 1,286n. 285.0 x 35.0 x 24.4 feet.
C. 2-cyl. steam engine (E1749) manufactured by R. & W. Hawthorn & Company, Newcastle. 200 nhp.
8.11.1877: Keel laid by C. Mitchell & Company, Newcastle (Yard No. 358), for Watts, Milburn & Company, London. 4.4.1878: Launched. 27.5.1878: Completed. 7.1879: Transferred to W. Milburn & Company, Newcastle and London. 30.7.1879: Whilst on a voyage from Odessa to Antwerp with a cargo of grain she collided with the Norwegian barque ARGO, approximately 60 miles south west of Plymouth. Later towed ARGO into Plymouth. 9.1881: Stranded in the River Hooghly, later dry-docked at Calcutta. 6.1883: stranded at Cardenas on voyage from Montreal. 24.1.1885: Sailed from New York for Leith with a cargo of 1,239 tons of wheat and maize, 1,155 tons of generals, 104 tons of dunnage and

stores and 300 tons of bunker coal and disappeared. Her crew of 27 were lost. 28.1.1885: A severe hurricane was sweeping the North Atlantic and she is thought to have either fallen victim, as did FERNWOOD (ship WMi 69) or to have struck an iceberg.

Managed Vessels
By
Watts, Milburn & Company

WmiM 1. PERO   (1857 - 1864) see ship No. M 1. above.

WmiM 2. HALICORE (1)   (1857 - 1864) see ship No. M 2. above.

WmiM 3. WHALTON   (1857 - 1864) see ship No. M 3. above.

WmiM 4. EQUINOX   (1857 - 1864) see ship No. M 4. above.

WmiM 5. BRILLIANT   (1857 - 1864) see ship No. W 3. above.

WmiM 6. ST CLAIR   (1857 - 1864) see ship No. W 4. above.

WmiM 7. GUADIANA   (1857 - 1864) see ship No. W 5. above.

WmiM 8. CACTUS   (1857 - 1864) see ship No. W 6. above.

WmiM 9. SULTAN   (1857 - 1864) see ship No. W 7. above.

WmiM 10. HALICORE (2)   (1865 - 1868) see ship No. M 5. above.

Wm. Milburn & Company.
Newcastle And London
(1879 - 1914)

WM 1. TAUNTON   (1879 - 1881) see ship No. WMi 27 above.

WM 2. YANGTSE   (1879 - 1888) see ship No. WMi 49 above.

WM 3. MAHARAJAH   (1879 - 1890) see ship No. WMi 51 above.

WM 4. CONSETT   (1879 - 1880) see ship No. WMi 52 above.

WM 5. WEST STANLEY   (1879 - 1881) see ship No. WMi 53 above.

WM 6. CHIN KIANG   (1879 - 1884) see ship No. WMi 54 above.

WM 7. NINGPO   (1879 - 1888) see ship No. WMi 55 above.

WM 8. AMOY   (1879 - 1888) see ship No. WMi 56 above.

WM 9. HANKOW   (1879 - 1897) see ship No. WMi 60 above.

WM 10. MARCIA   (1879 - 1895) see ship No. WMi 63 above.

WM 11. GILSLAND   (1879 - 1896) see ship No. WMi 66 above.

WM 12. FERNWOOD   (1879 - 1885) see ship No. WMi 69 above.

WM 13. PLAINMELLER   (1879 - 1886) see ship No. WMi 70 above.

WM 14. COMPTON   (1879 - 1886) see ship No. WMi 71 above.

WM 15. CLANDON   (1879 - 1885) see ship No. WMi 72 above.

WM 16. ROSCOMMON (1879) Iron Screw Steamer
O.N. 79691. 1,500g. 970n. 245.0 x 33.3 x 23.0 feet.
C. 2-cyl. steam engine (464) manufactured by Black, Hawthorn & Company, Gateshead. 160 nhp.
2.1879: Launched by C. S. Swan & Company, Wallsend (Yard No. 40), for W. Milburn & Company, Newcastle. 2.1879: Completed. 20.11.1879: Whilst on a voyage from Garston to Havana, with a cargo of 1,500 tons of gas works coal, foundered in position 36.40N., 24.12W., approximately 50 miles S.E. of the Azores. 6 of her crew were lost. Her survivors were returned to London by the CHISWICK (ship WMi 47). The vessel was valued at £24,000.

WM 17. MANGERTON (1879 - 1883) Iron Screw Steamer
O.N. 81577. 2,005g. 1,317n. 285.0 x 35.3 x 24.5 feet.
C. 2-cyl. steam engine (E1779) manufactured by R. & W. Hawthorn & Company, Newcastle. 200 nhp.
22.7.1879: Launched by A. Leslie & Company, Hebburn (Yard No. 203), for W. Milburn & Company, Newcastle and London. 26.8.1879: Completed. 27.1.1883: Departed from Garston, Liverpool, bound to Havana, with a cargo of coal. 28.1.1883: Sailed from off Holyhead, and disappeared. Her crew of 26 were lost. One of her lifeboats was picked up in position 50W., 80^1/$_2$N. The Wreck Commissioner ruled that the vessel had been too deeply laden.

WM 18. TANTALLON (1879 - 1896) Iron Screw Steamer
O.N. 81594. 1,999g. 1,311n. 285.0 x 35.3 x 24.3 feet.
C. 2-cyl. steam engine (E1780) manufactured by R. & W. Hawthorn & Company, Newcastle. 200 nhp.
1.10.1879: Launched by A. Leslie & Company, Hebburn (Yard No. 204), for W. Milburn & Company, Newcastle and London. 10.1879: Completed at a cost of £27,000. 7.1896: Sold to Foscolo, Mango & Company, Piraeus, and renamed RAYMONDOS. 1898: Sold to E. J. Olivier, Rouen, France, and renamed RAYMOND. 11.1899: Sold to Watts, Watts & Company, London, and renamed ALABAMA. 1908: Sold to J. Paterson & Company, Melbourne. 1909: Transferred to James Paterson & Company Proprietary Ltd. 1924: Sold to North China Steamship Company Ltd., Tientsin, China, and renamed PEI TAI. 1935: Sold to Chinese shipbreakers.

WM 19. JOHN STRAKER (1879 - 1885) Iron Screw Steamer
O.N. 63002. 1,289g. 836n. 235.0 x 30.2 x 17.5 feet.
C. 2-cyl. steam engine (E1495) manufactured by R. & W. Hawthorn & Company, Newcastle. 130 nhp.
29.1.1871: Launched by Palmers Shipbuilding & Iron Company Ltd, Jarrow on Tyne (Yard No. 263), for Harry Smith Edwards, South Shields. 1.1871: Completed. 15.10.1879: Sold to W. Milburn & Company, Newcastle and London. 1879: New Boiler fitted. 1885: Sold to D. Jones, Cardiff, and renamed RICHARD CORY. 1886: W. Milburn the younger appointed manager. 1887: Sold to E. L. Evan-Thomas, Swansea, and renamed PROVENCAL. 3.2.1889: Whilst on a voyage from Genoa and Marseilles to Rotterdam and Antwerp, with a general cargo, wrecked at South Breakwater, New Waterway, Rotterdam,

WM 20. HARRY S. EDWARDS (1879 - 1881) Iron Screw Steamer
O.N. 63010. 1,252g. 796n. 255.5 x 33.0 x 18.8 feet.
C. 2-cyl. steam engine manufactured by Humphreys Tennant & Company, London. 140 nhp.
1875: New C. 2-cyl. steam engine manufactured by R. Steele & Company, Greenock. 180 nhp.
3.1872: Launched by Iliff, Mounsey & Company, Sunderland (Yard No. 54), for Harry Smith Edwards, South Shields. 3.1872: Completed. 10.12.1879: Sold to W. Milburn & Company, Newcastle and London. 1881: Renamed ASHINGTON. 21.4.1888: Stranded on the west point of Hong Kong Island. 6.1888: Sold, at Hong Kong, to Siemssen & Company, Hamburg. 1892: Sold to Okita Tojuro, Aikawa, Japan, and renamed SADOKUNI MARU. 1894: Sold to, owner and master, Tasaka Hatsutaro, Tokyo, Japan. 1910: Demolished at Tokyo.

WM 21. IRTHINGTON (1880 - 1896) Iron Screw Steamer
O.N. 82799. 1,961g. 1,290n. 270.0 x 36.0 x 24.7 feet.
C. 2-cyl. steam engine (505) manufactured by Black, Hawthorn & Company, Gateshead. 200 nhp.
26.7.1880: Launched by Osbourne, Graham & Company, Hylton, Sunderland (Yard No. 44), for W. Milburn & Company, Newcastle and London. 9.9.1880: Completed. 6.1.1896: Sold to the Steamship

Irthington Company Ltd. (Maclay & McIntyre, managers) Glasgow. 4.4.1901: Whilst on a voyage from Almeria to Glasgow with a cargo of iron ore, wrecked on Pearl Rock, Gibraltar

WM 22. TEDDINGTON (1880 - 1887) Iron Screw Steamer

O.N. 82817. 2,017g. 1,310n. 287.0 x 36.1 x 23.9 feet.
C. 2-cyl. steam engine manufactured by T. Clark & Company, Newcastle. 235 nhp.
16.10.1880: Launched by C. S. Swan & Hunter, Wallsend (Yard No. 49), for W. Milburn & Company, Newcastle and London. 10.1880: Completed. 9.6.1887: Whilst on a voyage from Bombay to the United Kingdom with a cargo of wheat, sank after striking a rock near Avocet Rock, Aden.

WM 23. CONISTON (1880 - 1884) Iron Screw Steamer

O.N. 82818. 2,258g. 1,491n. 300.0 x 36.4 x 25.2 feet.
C. 2-cyl. steam engine (E1799) manufactured by R. & W. Hawthorn & Company, Newcastle. 250 nhp.
20.10.1880: Launched by A. Leslie & Company, Hebburn (Yard No. 216), for W. Milburn & Company, Newcastle and London. 10.1880: Completed. 24.12.1884: Departed from Liverpool, bound in ballast to New York, and disappeared in the North Atlantic. Her crew of 27 were lost.

WM 24. BUSY BEE (1880 - 1883) Iron Screw Steamer

O.N. 51356. 770g. 202.1 x 28.2 x 17.4 feet.
Post 1870: 961g. 614n. 231.8 x 28.2 x 17.4 feet.
Simple 2-cyl. steam engine manufactured by the shipbuilder. 99 nhp.
1871: Engine rebuilt as a C. 2-cyl. steam engine by R. & W. Hawthorn, Newcastle. 150 nhp.
26.4.1865: Launched by Palmers Shipbuilding & Iron Company Ltd., Jarrow on Tyne (Yard No. 171), for W. D. Stephens, Newcastle. 1865: Completed. 1870: Lengthened by William Cleland, Willington Quay on Tyne. 1880: Sold to W. Milburn & Company, Newcastle and London. 11.10.1883: Sold for £11,000, to Tyne Steamship Company. 9.2.1896: Whilst on a voyage from Newcastle to Antwerp with a general cargo, was sunk in a collision off Wielingen Light, North Sea, with German steamer LINDENFELS (2,392g./1894).

WM 25. UNDERWRITER (1880 - 1885) Ship re-rigged 1876 as a Barque.

O.N. 56877. 1,481g. 1,440n. 183.8 x 38.8 x 30.2 feet.
Launched in a year unknown, at New York by Westervelt as a ship. 28.8.1867: Sold by the High Court of the Admiralty, England, to G. Staunton, London. 1871: Sold to J. Wilson, South Shields. 28.7.1879: Sold at a South Shields auction to P. O' Hare, Newcastle. 25.3.1880: Sold to W. Milburn & Company, Newcastle and London. 24.3.1885: Stated by the Lords Commissioners of the Admiralty, to have been dismantled and used as a hulk in the Red Sea.

WM 26. HUNTINGDON (1881 - 1897) Iron Screw Steamer

O.N. 82874. 2,224g. 1,463n. 300.0 x 36.3 x 24.7 feet.
C. 2-cyl. steam engine (E1800) manufactured by R. & W. Hawthorn & Company, Newcastle. 275 nhp.
16.3.1881: Launched by A. Leslie & Company, Hebburn (Yard No. 217), for W. Milburn & Company, Newcastle and London. 5.5.1881: Completed. 31.12.1881: Chartered by Victoria Line, (J. Potter & Company), London, for service between London and Australia until their own new vessels were delivered. 5.1897: Sold to Foscolo, Man & Company (E. J. Oliver & Company), Piraeus, Greece and renamed NORBERTOS. 1901: Sold to P. G. Foscolo, Trieste, Austro-Hungarian flag. 1902: Transferred to the executors of P. G. Foscolo (T. Cossovich) of Trieste. 1902: Sold to J. Pitts (Rougier & Company, managers), London, and renamed HUNTINGDON. 1903: Sold to Salonikli Mustapha Bey, Constantinople, Turkey, and renamed BASSORAH. 1905: Sold to S. A. Siderides, Piraeus, and renamed ALEXANDRA. 1916: Sold to Jean Carras & Sons, Greece. 1919: Owners restyled Carras Brothers. 1924: Sold to Hadji Zade Mehmed Kiazim Bey, Turkey, and renamed ISTAMBOL. 1928: Sold to Kir Zade Chevki & Company, Turkey, and renamed ISTANBUL. 1934: Sold to Italian shipbreakers at Genoa.

WM 27. DARLINGTON (1881 - 1886) Iron Screw Steamer
O.N. 82889. 1,990g. 1,293n.   285.8 x 36.0 x 24.0 feet.
C. 2-cyl. steam engine manufactured by T. Clark & Company, Newcastle. 250 nhp.
27.10.1880: Keel laid by C. S. Swan & Hunter, Wallsend (Yard No. 53), for W. Milburn & Company, Newcastle and London. 17.5.1881: Launched. 18.6.1881: Completed. 1.2.1884: Whilst on a voyage in ballast, from Antwerp to Cardiff, damaged in a collision with steamer DEVONIA off Portland. 22.2.1886: Whilst on a voyage from New Orleans to Bremen with a cargo of cotton and grain, wrecked on Western Reefs, Bermuda,

WM 28. PEKING (1881 - 1888) Iron Screw Steamer
O.N. 82896. 1,476g. 954n.   269.0 x 33.0 x 23.0 feet.
C. 2-cyl. steam engine manufactured by the shipbuilder. 200 nhp.
28.5.1881: Launched by J. Wigham Richardson & Company, Newcastle (Yard No. 132), for W. Milburn & Company, Newcastle and London.   2.7.1881: Completed.   15.5.1888: Sold to Chinesische Kustenfahrt Gessellshaft, Hamburg. 6.5.1892: Whilst on a voyage from Wuhu to Hong Kong, lost in collision with FU SHUN (2,362g./1883) of Shanghai, near Elliott Island.

WM 29. HONG KONG (2) (1881 - 1887) Iron Screw Steamer
O.N. 85077. 1,476g. 958n. 267.1 x 33.2 x 23.0 feet.
C. 2-cyl. steam engine manufactured by the shipbuilder. 200 nhp.
8.10.1881: Launched by J. Wigham Richardson & Company, Newcastle (Yard No. 135), for W. Milburn & Company, Newcastle and London. 9.1887: Wrecked and abandoned near Hong Kong in the Haiton Straights between Long Yet and Double Yet.

WM 30. ASHINGTON (1) (1881 - 1888) see ship No. WM 20 above.

WM 31. ASCALON (1882 - 1887) Iron Screw Steamer
O.N. 85178. 2,351g. 1,523n.   290.0 x 37.2 x 27.4 feet.
C. 2-cyl. steam engine (E1860) manufactured by R. & W. Hawthorn & Company, Newcastle. 300 nhp.
17.4.1882: Launched by Campbell, Mackintosh & Bowstead, Scotswood on Tyne, Newcastle (Yard No. 4), for W. Milburn & Company, Newcastle and London. 6.1882: Completed. 24.5.1884: Whilst on a voyage from Hong Kong to Calcutta ran aground off Cape Romanea, and subsequently repaired at Singapore.   13.10.1887: Whilst on a voyage Aden to Calcutta with a cargo of salt, wrecked 14 miles North of Point de Galle, S. W. Ceylon,

WM 32. FENSTANTON (1882 - 1884) Iron Screw Steamer
O.N. 87016. 2,465g. 1,606n. 300.0 x 37.0 x 27.4 feet.
C. 2-cyl. steam engine (E1871) manufactured by R. & W. Hawthorn & Company, Newcastle. 300 nhp.
14.10.1882: Launched by A. Leslie & Company, Hebburn (Yard No. 236), for W. Milburn & Company, Newcastle and London. 11.1882: Completed. 1883: Chartered by the New Zealand Shipping Company, and fitted with refrigerating machinery at Lyttelton, to enable frozen meat to be carried. 3.10.1884: Whilst on a voyage from Newcastle N.S.W., to Singapore, with a cargo of coal, wrecked off Thursday Island, Queensland.

WM 33. NORMANTON (1882 - 1886) Iron Screw Steamer
O.N. 87017. 2,367g. 1,533n. 291.2 x 37.3 x 27.4 feet.
C. 2-cyl. steam engine (E1868) manufactured by R. & W. Hawthorn & Company. 300 nhp.
11.1882: Launched by Campbell, Mackintosh & Bowstead, Scotswood on Tyne, (Yard No. 6), for W. Milburn & Company, Newcastle and London. 11.1882: Completed. 24.10.1886: Whilst on a voyage from Yokohama to Hiogo with a general cargo including tea, wrecked off Oosima, Japan. 25 passengers lost their lives. Captain subsequently convicted of manslaughter and sentenced to three months imprisonment.

WM 34. ILDERTON (1883) Iron Screw Steamer
O.N. 87048. 2,474g. 1,607n. 300.0 x 37.0 x 27.3 feet.
C. 2-cyl. steam engine (E1872) manufactured by R. & W. Hawthorn & Company, Newcastle. 300 nhp.
23.12.1882: Launched by A. Leslie & Company, Hebburn (Yard No. 237), for W. Milburn & Company, Newcastle and London. 2.1883: Completed. 23.6.1883: Whilst on a voyage from Bombay to Hull with a cargo of wheat and linseed, wrecked on the Island of Ushant.

WM 35. HAVERTON (1883 - 1894) Iron Screw Steamer
O.N. 87073. 2,531g. 1,645n. 300.0 x 37.3 x 27.5 feet.
C. 2-cyl. steam engine (E1895) manufactured by R. & W. Hawthorn & Company. 300 nhp. 10kts.
22.2.1883: Launched by the Tyne Iron Shipbuilding Company, Willington Quay on Tyne (Yard No. 45), for W. Milburn & Company, Newcastle and London. 1883: Completed, and chartered by Trinder, Anderson & Company, for a voyage from London to Australia. 31.1.1884: Sailed from London for the Anglo-Australasian Steam Navigation Company Ltd., (W. Milburn & Company, managers). 21.7.1894: Whilst on a voyage from Sydney, Cape Breton, to Montreal, with a cargo of coal, struck rocks and was run ashore at St. Croix Bay, St. Lawrence, to prevent her sinking. Subsequently refloated and condemned. 5.1895: Sold for demolition at Quebec.

WM 36. CHOLLERTON (1883 - 1896) Iron Screw Steamer
O.N. 87079. 2,650g. 1,734n. 317.2 x 37.1 x 27.2 feet.
C. 2-cyl. steam engine (144) manufactured by J. Wigham Richardson & Company, Newcastle. 300 nhp. 11kts.
22.2.1883: Launched by A. Leslie & Company, Hebburn (Yard No. 239), for W. Milburn & Company, Newcastle and London. 30.4.1883: Completed and departed on her maiden voyage, this was also to be the first sailing for the Anglo-Australasian Steam Navigation Company Ltd., (W. Milburn & Company, managers). Originally advertised to sail to Australia via the Cape of Good Hope. 11.6.1883: Whilst on a voyage from London to Sydney, lost her propeller. 7.7.1883: Arrived, under sail, at Bombay. 3.8.1883: Departed from Bombay. 29.8.1883: Arrived at Adelaide. 1894: Collided with KORNILOFF (2,079g./1869) in the Bosphorus. 1896: Sold to the Steamship Nyassa Company Ltd. (Maclay & McIntyre, managers), Glasgow. 1899: Sold to the Steamship Everilda Company Ltd. (same managers). 1902: Sold to A. Parodi fu B, Genoa, Italy, and renamed JOLANDA. 1909: Demolished at Genoa.

TIVERTON (Ambrose Greenway collection)

WM 37. TIVERTON (1883 - 1896) Iron Screw Steamer
O.N. 87168. 2,673g. 1,743n. 320.1 x 37.6 x 27.4 feet.
C. 2-cyl. steam engine manufactured by T. Clark & Company. Newcastle. 350 nhp. 10kts.

18.8.1883: Launched by Campbell, Mackintosh & Bowstead, Scotswood on Tyne, (Yard No. 11), for W. Milburn & Company, Newcastle and London. 10.1883: Completed. 5.1896: Sold to the Steamship Nyassa Company Ltd. (Maclay & McIntyre, managers), Glasgow. 1899: Sold to the Glasgow Navigation Company Ltd. (same managers). 1900: Sold to the Steamship Inverleith Company Ltd. (same managers). 1902: Sold to A. S. Vagliano, Greece, and renamed K. PASKHALIDIS. 6.6.1904: Whilst on a voyage from Shatoni to Marseilles with a cargo of ore, wrecked off Cape Leva.

PORT JACKSON (Ambrose Greenway collection)

WM 38. PORT JACKSON (1) (1883 - 1892) Iron Screw Steamer
O.N. 87170. 2,644g. 1,728n. 317.0 x 37.2 x 27.4 feet.
C. 2-cyl. steam engine manufactured by T. Clark & Company, Newcastle. 350 nhp. 1895: New Donkey boiler fitted.
5.9.1883: Launched by A. Leslie & Company, Hebburn (Yard No. 243), for the Anglo-Australasian Steam Navigation Company Ltd (W. Milburn & Company, managers), London. 10.1883: Completed. 26.10.1883: Left the Tyne for London. 12.11.1883: Sailed from Plymouth for Adelaide. 8.1.1884: Arrived Adelaide. 27.5.1892: Valued at £20,000 by A. Coote and J. H. Ridley (Directors of R. & W. Hawthorn, Leslie & Company Ltd.), and taken in part exchange for PORT MELBOURNE (see ship WM 59). Lamport & Holt & Company, Liverpool, appointed managers. 23.9.1895: Sold to A. Mancini, Genoa, Italy, and renamed AGORDAT. 1903: Sold to F. Schiaffino fu G, Genoa, Italy, and renamed BEPPE. 1905: Sold to Calame & Cortese Genoa, Italy, and renamed JEANNE MARCELLE. 1907: Sold to L. Pittaluga, Genoa. 5.1910: Demolished by L. Pittaluga at Genoa.

WM 39. PORT PHILLIP (1) (1883 - 1896) Iron Screw Steamer
O.N. 89488. 2,597g. 1,666n. 317.0 x 37.2 x 20.0 feet.
C. 2-cyl. steam engine (182C) manufactured by the Wallsend Slipway & Engineering Company Ltd. 350 nhp.
19.10.1883: Launched by A. Leslie & Company, Hebburn (Yard No. 244), for the Anglo-Australasian Steam Navigation Company Ltd. (W. Milburn & Company, managers), London. 24.11.1883: Completed and sailed on her maiden voyage to Antwerp. 15.12.1883: Departed London for Australia via Suez. Originally advertised to sail via the Cape of Good Hope. 1896: Sold to Blythe Shipping Company Ltd. (Peterson, Tate & Company), London, a very extensive engine overhaul carried out by the engine builders, and renamed BLYTH. 17.10.1897: Whilst on a voyage from Lulea to Rotterdam with a cargo of iron ore, wrecked in Gulf of Bothnia near Holmo Gadd, Umea. Wreck subsequently refloated and demolished.

PORT PHILIP (Ambrose Greenway collection)

WM 40. ANGERTON (1884 - 1896) Iron Screw Steamer
O.N. 89529. 2,794g. 1,823n. 320.0 x 38.0 x 27.4 feet.
C. 2-cyl. steam engine (190C) manufactured by the Wallsend Slipway & Engineering Company. 375 nhp. 10kts.
29.1.1884: Launched by W. Dobson & Company, Newcastle (Yard No. 2), for W. Milburn & Company, Newcastle and London. 10.3.1884: Trials. 14.3.1884: Completed and sailed on her maiden voyage on charter to Trinder, Anderson & Company. 12.1895: Stranded but refloated. 1896: She was declared as a compromised total loss. 67% of her insured value was paid. 1896: Sold by underwriters to Northumbrian Shipping Corporation Ltd. (L. Macarthy, managers), Newcastle. 9.3.1899: Whilst inbound with a cargo of coal and coke from Cardiff, wrecked on Victorieuse Shoal, 15 miles west of Alexandria,

WM 41. PORT DARWIN (1) (1884 - 1892) Iron Screw Steamer
O.N. 89546. 2,517g. 1,628n. 300.1 x 37.4 x 27.1 feet.
C. 2-cyl. steam engine (E1938) manufactured by R. & W. Hawthorn & Company, Newcastle. 350 nhp.
12.2.1884: Launched by A. Leslie & Company, Hebburn, Newcastle (Yard No. 249), for the Anglo-Australasian Steam Navigation Company Ltd., (W. Milburn & Company, managers), London. 3.1884: Completed. Sailed on her maiden voyage on charter to Trinder Anderson & Company. 19.12.1892: Valued at £20,000 by A. Coote and J. H. Ridley, Newcastle (Directors of R. & W. Hawthorn, Leslie & Company), was taken in part exchange for PORT HUNTER (see ship WM 60). 20.9.1897: Sold for £11,000, to E. Morgan & Company, London. 15.11.1905: Whilst on a voyage from Honaine, Algeria to Rotterdam, with minerals, wrecked 3 miles off La Guardea near Vigo, Spain.

WM 42. PORT ADELAIDE (1) (1884 - 1898) Iron Screw Steamer
O.N. 89560. 2,694g. 1,717n. 332.0 x 38.1 x 18.0 feet.
C. 2-cyl. steam engine (164) manufactured by Wigham Richardson & Company, Newcastle. 400 nhp. 10kts. 1893: New Donkey Boiler Fitted.
29.3.1884: Launched by A. Leslie & Company, Hebburn (Yard No. 250), for W. Milburn & Company, Newcastle. 5.1884: Completed for the Anglo-Australasian Steam Navigation Company Ltd (W. Milburn, & Company, managers). 14.11.1898: Sold to G. Brailli, Orebich, Austria, under the Austro-Hungarian flag, and renamed SOFIA BRAILLI. 11.1909: Sold to A. Merveille and demolished at Dunkirk.

WM 43. PORT VICTOR (1) (1885 - 1898)
O.N. 91872. 2,793g. 1,828n. 336.0 x 38.2 x 27.5 feet.
T.3-cyl. steam engine (191) manufactured by Wigham Richardson & Company, Newcastle. 400 nhp. 10kts. 1907: New Donkey Boiler fitted.
27.8.1885: Launched by A. Leslie & Company, Hebburn (Yard No. 261), for W. Milburn & Company, Newcastle and London. 1898: Sold to United States Army, and renamed McCLELLAN. 1918: Transferred to United States Shipping Board. 1919: Sold to Lloyd Royal Belge Soc. Anon, Antwerp, and renamed HASTIER. 3.11.1920: Caught fire at Antwerp and subsequently towed clear of her berth and settled on the bottom. 1921: Raised and laid up. 11.12.1922: Sold to Soc. Metallurgique de Merxem, Antwerp for demolition.

PORT PIRIE (Ambrose Greenway collection)

WM 44. PORT PIRIE (1) (1886 - 1897)
O.N. 91932. 3,020g. 1,929n. 353.5 x 39.4 x 19.8 feet.
T.3-cyl. steam engine (190) manufactured by Wigham Richardson & Company, Newcastle. 450 nhp. 10kts.
24.4.1886: Launched by R. & W. Hawthorn, Leslie & Company Ltd., Hebburn (Yard No. 258), for W. Milburn & Company, Newcastle and London. 1887: Transferred to the Anglo-Australasian Steam Navigation Company Ltd. (W. Milburn & Company, managers), London. 11.10.1897: Sold to Prince Steam Shipping Company Ltd. (J. Knott, managers), Newcastle, and renamed SPANISH PRINCE. 1898: Registered under Prince Line Ltd. 10.1900: Sold to Cia Cantabrica de Nav (Orbe y Gobeo, managers), Bilbao, Spain, and renamed GUERNICA. 10.2.1902: Whilst on a voyage from Cardiff to Genoa with a cargo of coal and coke, foundered in the Bay of Biscay having sprung a leak.

WM 45. PORT AUGUSTA (1) (1886 - 1891)
O.N. 91971. 2,833g. 1,856n. 347.0 x 38.7 x 19.9 feet.
T.3-cyl. steam engine (195) manufactured by Wigham Richardson & Company, Newcastle. 450 nhp. 10kts. 1894: New Donkey Boiler fitted.
29.9.1886: Launched by the Tyne Iron Shipbuilding Company Ltd., Willington Quay on Tyne (Yard No. 59), for W. Milburn & Company, Newcastle and London. 5.1891: Sold to Russian Steam Navigation & Trading Company, Odessa, and renamed CZARITZA. 10.3.1915: Commissioned into the Russian Navy as troopship N 75. 19.10.1916: Torpedoed and sunk by the German submarine UB 42, N.E. of Cape Midia, Black Sea.

PORT AUGUSTA (World Ship Society Photograph Library)

PORT DENISON (Ambrose Greenway collection)

WM 46. PORT DENISON (1) (1887 - 1892)
O.N. 94316. 3,506g. 3289n. 375.0 x 42.2 x 20.9 feet.
T.3-cyl. steam engine (216) manufactured by Wigham Richardson & Company, Newcastle. 650 nhp. 10kts. 1897: New Donkey Boiler fitted.
23.7.1887: Launched by R. & W. Hawthorn, Leslie & Company, Hebburn (Yard No. 273), for W. Milburn & Company, Newcastle and London. 29.8.1887: Completed. 1888: Transferred to the Anglo-Australasian Steam Navigation Company Ltd. (W. Milburn & Company, managers), London. 6.1892: Sold to J. Jover y Costas, Barcelona, and renamed MIGUEL JOVER. 1918: Sold for £125,000 to Hijos de Jose Taya S.en C, Barcelona, and renamed P. CLARIS. 1926: Sold for demolition in Italy.

PORT FAIRY (World Ship Society Photograph Library)

WM 47. PORT FAIRY (1) (1887 - 1893)
O.N. 94340. 2,539g. 1,645n. 330.0 x 38.3 x 18.7 feet.
T.3-cyl. steam engine manufactured by the shipbuilder. 450 nhp. 11kts.
18.10.1887: Launched by Wigham Richardson & Company, Newcastle (Yard No. 212), for W. Milburn & Company, Newcastle and London. 12.1887: Completed. 2.11.1893: Sold to J. H. Andressen, Oporto, Portugal, and renamed DONA MARIA. 1895: Transferred to the Successors of J. H. Andressen. 1907: Sold to Booth Steamship Company Ltd., Liverpool, and reverted to PORT FAIRY. 1909: Sold to shipbreakers but resold to Ellerman Lines Ltd. (F. Swift, managers), Liverpool, and renamed ITALIAN. 4.1913: Sold to T. W. Ward Ltd., Sheffield, for demolition at their Preston facility.

WM 48. WILEYSIKE (1888 - 1896) Steel Screw Steamer
O.N. 95248. 2,468g. 1,612n. 300.0 x 38.5 x 20.6 feet.
T.3-cyl. steam engine (C559) manufactured by the North Eastern Marine Engineering Company Ltd., Wallsend. 248 nhp.
12.5.1888: Launched by the Tyne Iron Shipbuilding Company Ltd., Willington Quay on Tyne (Yard No. 65), for W. Milburn & Company, Newcastle and London. 22.6.1888: Completed. 15.1.1896: Sold to Rowland and Marwood's Steamship Company Ltd. (C. Marwood), Whitby. 6.6.1906: Sold to W. S. Miller & Company, Glasgow. 1915: Transferred to the Wileysike Steamship Company Ltd. (W. S. Miller & Company, managers), Glasgow. 9.5.1918: Whilst outward bound from Glasgow to France with a cargo of coal, was torpedoed and sunk by the German submarine U 54, in the St George's Channel, 8 miles S.W. of St Ann's Head. Four of her crew were killed.

WM 49. PORT CAROLINE (1) (1888)
3,513g. 375.0 x 42.2 x 20.9 feet.
T.3-cyl. steam engine (217) manufactured by Wigham Richardson & Company, Newcastle. 600 nhp. 10kts.
28.1.1888: Launched as PORT CAROLINE by R. & W. Hawthorn, Leslie & Company, Hebburn (Yard No. 274), for W. Milburn & Company, Newcastle and London. 2.2.1888: Sold for £52,500, whilst fitting out, to Russian Volunteer Fleet Association, Odessa, and renamed KOSTROMA. 1.3.1888: Trials and delivery. 9.1913: Wrecked at Karantinskaia Kosa (Kamchatka).

WM 50. CAPE CLEAR (1889 - 1890)
O.N. 96136. 1,772g. 1,138n. 265.5 x 37.1 x 15.9 feet.
T.3-cyl. steam engine (C575) manufactured by the North Eastern Marine Engineering Company Ltd., Wallsend. 160 nhp.
5.3.1889: Completed by W. Dobson & Company, Newcastle (Yard No. 27), for W. Milburn & Company, Newcastle and London. 19.1.1890: Departed from Liverpool bound to Rosario, with a general cargo. 20.1.1890: Last reported in position 52.48N., 05.22W., and subsequently disappeared, possibly a victim of a collision in the St. George's Channel. Her crew of 34 were lost. 3.1890: Posted as missing.

WM 51. CAPE COLONNA (1889 - 1896)
O.N. 96138. 2,707g. 1,767n. 312.0 x 40.5 x 21.0 feet.
T.3-cyl. steam engine (296C) manufactured by Wallsend Slipway & Engineering Company Ltd., Wallsend. 265 nhp.
30.3.1889: Launched by the Tyne Iron Shipbuilding Company Ltd., Willington Quay on Tyne (Yard No. 70), for W. Milburn & Company, Newcastle and London. 4.1889: Completed. 8.5.1896: Sold to The International Line Steamship Company Ltd. (C. Marwood), Whitby. 9.11.1911: Sold to Northumbrian Shipping Corporation Ltd. (L. Macarthy), Newcastle. 12.9.1912: Whilst on a voyage from Smyrna to Leith she called at the Tyne to take on coal. Unfortunately she struck the Black Middens Rocks at the entrance to the River Tyne. Later pulled off by the tugs TALISMAN, HERCULES and CRUISER, she was beached between the Groyne and South pier. 12.11.1912: Registration cancelled. 30.12.1912: Refloated and upon examination was found to be so badly damaged that she was later sold to shipbreakers at South Shields.

WM 52. PORT CAROLINE (2) (1889 - 1893)
O.N. 95529. 3,528g. 2,130n. 378.5 x 44.1 x 20.8 feet.
T.3-cyl. steam engine (228) manufactured by Wigham Richardson & Company, Newcastle. 600 nhp. 10kts. 1897: New Donkey Boiler fitted.
4.12.1888: Launched by W. Dobson & Company, Newcastle (Yard No. 25), for W. Milburn & Company, Newcastle and London. 2.1889: Completed. 24.4.1890: Transferred for £70,000, to the Anglo-Australasian Steam Navigation Company Ltd. (W. Milburn & Company, managers), London. 1893: Sold to Hijo de J Jover y Serra, Barcelona, and renamed J. JOVER SERRA. 1894: Owners restyled J. Jover y Costas, Barcelona. 1918: Sold to Hijos de Jose Taya.S en C, Barcelona, and renamed ROGER DE LLURIA. 11.4.1920: Caught fire and burnt out at Santa Cruz de Teneriffe, where she had arrived from Habana (Havana) with general cargo.

WM 53. CAPE COMORIN (1891 - 1897)
O.N. 97963. 2,597g. 1,660n. 300.5 x 38.6 x 20.6 feet.
T.3-cyl. steam engine (C628) manufactured by the North Eastern Marine Engineering Company Ltd., Wallsend. 246 nhp.
25.2.1891: Launched by the Tyne Iron Shipbuilding Company Ltd., Willington Quay on Tyne (Yard No. 86), for W. Milburn & Company, Newcastle and London. 4.1891: Completed. 20.10.1897: Sold to J. Holman & Sons, London. 9.1899: Renamed YESTOR. 1.2.1900: Sold to Steamship Carisbrook Company Ltd. (Miller & Richards), Glasgow. 7.12.1900: Sold to Eldon Steamship Company Ltd. (Sinclair, Walton & Company), Newcastle. 1903: Eldon Steamship Company Ltd. (Thompson, Elliott & Company), Newcastle. 7.1904: Sold to Mawson Shipping Company Ltd. (Arthur Mawson & Company, managers), Cardiff, and renamed KIRKWALL. 5.8.1908: Whilst on a voyage from Huelva to Hamburg with a cargo of ore, sank following a collision, off Ameland, 25 miles east of the Terschelling Light.

WM 54. CAPE CORRIENTES (1891 - 1897)
O.N. 97968. 2,598g. 1,660n. 300.5 x 38.6 x 20.6 feet.
T.3-cyl. steam engine (C629) manufactured by the North Eastern Marine Engineering Company Ltd., Wallsend. 246 nhp. 1905: New Donkey Boiler fitted.
25.4.1891: Launched by the Tyne Iron Shipbuilding Company Ltd., Willington Quay on Tyne (Yard No. 87), for W. Milburn & Company, Newcastle and London. 30.5.1891: Completed. 22.11.1897: Sold to Speeding & Marshall Steam Shipping Company Ltd. (Speeding, Marshall & Company, managers), Sunderland. 6.7.1900: Sold to Golcar Steamship Company Ltd. (W. S. Allan & Company, managers), Glasgow. 16.3.1906: Re-registered in Newcastle, New South Wales, Australia. (Trading Australia). 7.1907: Sold to Golcar Steamship Company Ltd. (Shaw & Company, managers), Glasgow. 13.2.1911: Sold to W. Coupland & Company, Newcastle. 6.4.1914: Sold to G. F. Andreadis, Piraeus, and renamed VRONTADOS. 30.6.1917: Torpedoed and sunk by a German submarine in the Mediterranean Sea.

WM 55. CAPE COMINO (1891 - 1897)
O.N. 97973. 2,600g. 1,660n. 300.5 x 38.6 x 20.6 feet.
T.3-cyl. steam engine (258) manufactured by Wigham Richardson & Company, Newcastle. 250 nhp. 1892: New Donkey Boiler Fitted.
6.6.1891: Launched by the Tyne Iron Shipbuilding Company Ltd., Willington Quay on Tyne (Yard No. 88), for W. Milburn & Company, Newcastle and London. 7.1891: Completed. 1895: Whilst on a voyage from Batourn to Japan ran short of fuel and had to use cargo as fuel in order to reach destination. 26.11.1897: Sold to Speeding & Marshall Steam Shipping Company Ltd. (Speeding, Marshall & Company, managers), Sunderland. 5.1909: Sold to G. Maggiolo fu A, Genoa and renamed MADALENA. 25.10.1917: Sailed from Milford Haven on a voyage to Bagnoli and disappeared, presumed to have struck a mine later the same day after passing St Ann's Head. Mine believed to have been laid by the German submarine UC 51 on 14th October.

WM 56. PORT ALBERT (1) (1891 - 1894)
O.N. 98966. 4,140g. 2,652n. 371.4 x 46.1 x 26.1 feet.
T.3-cyl. steam engine (360C) manufactured by Wallsend Slipway & Engineering Company Ltd. 600 nhp. 10kts.
6.6.1891: Launched by W. Dobson & Company, Newcastle (Yard No. 45), for W. Milburn & Company, Newcastle and London. 10.8.1891: Completed. 29.10.1894: Sold to Japanese Government (Ministry of the Navy) and renamed KAGOSHIMA MARU. 1896: Sold to Nippon Yusen Kabushiki Kaisha, Tokyo. 1910: Sold to Goshi Shosen Kaisha Harada Shoko, Osaka, Japan. 1917: Sold to Harada Kisen Kabushiki Kaisha. 1.1918: Missing whilst on a voyage from Saigon to Port Said.

PORT ALBERT (Ambrose Greenway collection)

PORT CHALMERS as **GLACIER** (Author's Collection)

WM 57. PORT CHALMERS (1) (1891 - 1896)
O.N. 98973/224402. 4,154g. 2,667n. 371.0 x 46.1 x 27.7 feet.
T.3-cyl. steam engine manufactured by J. Dickinson, Sunderland. 600 nhp. 11kts.
22.7.1891: Launched by J. L. Thompson & Sons, Sunderland (Yard No. 277), for W. Milburn & Company, Newcastle and London. 8.1891: Completed. 27.7.1895: Whilst on a voyage from London to Sydney, seriously damaged by a collision with an iceberg in the South Indian Ocean. The bowsprit and figurehead were lost and the bow plating smashed for 20ft. 15.6.1896: Sold for £46,750 to Federal

Steam Navigation Company Ltd. (A. Hughes), London, and fitted with refrigerating machinery. 30.6.1898: Certificate of Sale empowering George Bertram Hayward, Master, to sell the ship for a sum exceeding £70,000 at any port outside the United Kingdom. 5.7.1898: Sold to United States Govt for $340,550. 6.7.1898: Commissioned at New York and renamed DELMONICO. (U.S. Navy Store Ship A.F.4.). 12.7.1898: Renamed GLACIER and served as a refrigerated supply ship during Spanish-American War. 6.3.1922: Decommissioned. 17.8.1922: Sold for $22,000 to the Barde Steel & Machinery Company, Seattle. 1924: Sold to Northern Fisheries Inc., San Francisco, U.S.A. 1938: Sold to Alaska Salmon Company, and granted a passenger certificate. 1941: Sold to Carbella Steamship Company, Panama, and renamed CARBELLA. 1944: Sold to Cia. Continental de Nav, Vera Cruz, Mexico. 1945: Renamed PRESIDENTE JUAREZ. 1949: Sold to Compania Mexicana de Navegacion, Vera Cruz. 1951: Sold to Cia. de Exportacion e Importacion Mexicana S.A. 30.11.1955: Beached north shore of Bermuda with heavy list after her cargo had shifted. 1.12.1955: Beached in Shelley Bay, Bermuda for examination. 3.3.1956: Towed by the Dutch salvage tug TYNE of Smit Tak, to Rotterdam where her cargo of coal was discharged. Subsequently sold to Thomas Young & Sons, Sunderland, for demolition but was resold to T. W. Ward Ltd., Sheffield for demolition at their Inverkeithing facility. 22.4.1956: Arrived at Inverkeithing in the tow of the Dutch tug LOIRE.

WM 58. PORT DOUGLAS (1891 - 1892)
O.N. 99000. 4,285g. 2,744n. 371.5 x 46.1 x 26.3 feet.
T.3-cyl. steam engine manufactured by G. Clark Ltd., Sunderland. 600 nhp. 10kts.
23.7.1891: Launched by Sir J. Laing, Sunderland (Yard No. 510), for W. Milburn & Company Ltd., Newcastle and London. 10.1891: Completed. 24.5.1892: Whilst on a voyage from London to Melbourne via the Cape of Good Hope, with general cargo, stranded on a reef off the Cape Verde Islands. 9.1892: Declared as being a constructive total loss, and was subsequently salvaged for scrap.

WM 59. PORT MELBOURNE (1) (1892 - 1899)
O.N. 101940. 4,670g. 3,011n. 360.4 x 48.0 x 26.2 feet.
T.3-cyl. steam engine (E2255) manufactured by R. & W. Hawthorn, Leslie & Company Ltd., Newcastle. 650 nhp. 11kts.
8.9.1892: Launched by R. & W. Hawthorn, Leslie & Company Ltd., Hebburn, (Yard No. 312), for the Anglo-Australasian Steam Navigation Company Ltd. (W. Milburn & Company, managers), London. PORT JACKSON (see ship WM 38) taken in part exchange. 30.10.1892: Completed. 27.1.1899: Last reported during a voyage New York to London with a cargo of grain and oil. 3.1899: Posted as missing.

WM 60. PORT HUNTER (1) (1892 - 1894)
O.N. 101958. 4,670g. 3,011n. 360.4 x 48.0 x 26.2 feet.
T.3-cyl. steam engine (E2256) manufactured by R. & W. Hawthorn, Leslie & Company Ltd., Newcastle. 650 nhp. 11kts.
19.11.1892: Launched by R. & W. Hawthorn, Leslie & Company Ltd., Hebburn (Yard No. 313), for the Anglo-Australasian Steam Navigation Company Ltd. (W. Milburn & Company, managers), London. PORT DARWIN (see ship WM 41) taken in part exchange. 31.12.1892: Trials. 5.1.1893: Delivered. 21.11.1894: Sold to the Japanese Government and renamed RIOJUN MARU. 1896: Sold to Nippon Yusen Kabushiki Kaisha, Tokyo. 1909: Sold to Harada & Company Ltd., Osaka. 1910: Sold to Goshi Shosen Kaisha Harada Shoko. 1916: Sold to Harada Kisen Kabushiki Kaisha. 28.5.1921: Whilst on a voyage from Dairen to Batavia with a cargo of coal, stranded on a reef and sank 45 miles North of the Gaspar Strait.

WM 61. PORT ELLIOT (1) (1894 - 1906)
O.N. 102848. 3,556g. 2,297n. 345.5 x 44.1 x 19.7 feet.
T.3-cyl. steam engine (405C) manufactured by the Wallsend Slipway & Engineering Company Ltd., Newcastle. 288 nhp. 11kts. 9.1904: New Boilers fitted.
20.1.1894: Launched by W. Dobson & Company, Newcastle (Yard No. 60), for W. Milburn & Company, Newcastle and London. 14.3.1894: Completed and after loaded sea trials left on her maiden voyage to Bombay. 8.11.1895: Transferred to the Anglo-Australasian Steam Navigation Company Ltd., (W. Milburn & Company, managers), London. 1906: Sold to Cie Royale Belgo - Argentine Soc Anon (A.

Deppe. Antwerp, managers), Belgium, and renamed REPUBLICA ARGENTINA. 1912: Managers restyled as Armement Adolf Deppe. 1922: Managers restyled as Armement Deppe. 25.7.1933: Sold for £2,500 to Orazio Rossini, Genoa for demolition. 8.1933: Resold for £2,950 to other unspecified Italian shipbreakers

WM 62. PORT STEPHENS (1) (1894 - 1906)

O.N. 102853. 3,554g. 2,278n. 345.0 x 44.1 x 18.2 feet.
T.3-cyl. steam engine manufactured by J. Dickinson, Sunderland. 287 nhp. 11kts.
20.2.1894: Launched by J. L. Thompson & Sons, Sunderland (Yard No. 310), for W. Milburn & Company, Newcastle and London. 4.1894: Completed. 8.11.1895: Transferred to the Anglo-Australasian Steam Navigation Company Ltd. (W. Milburn & Company, managers), London. 3.10.1906: Suffered a broken tailshaft off New Zealand coast. 8.10.1906: Whilst on a voyage in ballast, from Oamaru, New Zealand to Newcastle, New South Wales, was abandoned in position 49.21S., 164.48E.

NB. During the Spanish American War (1898) the ship, under the command of Capt R. Whitehead, was chartered to the United States Government as a troopship, she was also used as Transport during the Boxer Rising in China.

WM 63. PORT HUNTER (2) (1895 - 1897)

O.N. 105734. 3,552g. 2,297n. 346.0 x 44.0 x 18.3 feet.
T.3-cyl. steam engine (C695) manufactured by the North Eastern Marine Engineering Company Ltd., Wallsend. 289 nhp. 11kts.
24.4.1895: Launched by W. Dobson, Newcastle (Yard No. 64), for W. Milburn & Company, Newcastle and London. 9.1895: Completed. 5.11.1897: Sold to Gordon S. Shipping Company Ltd. (R. Gordon & Company), London, and renamed DARGAI. 8.1914: Whilst on a voyage from Hull to Montevideo with general cargo, wrecked on English Bank, River Plate.

PORT DENISON (Ambrose Greenway collection)

WM 64. PORT DENISON (2) (1896 - 1907)

O.N. 105896. 3,435g. 2,188n. 345.0 x 46.0 x 17.0 feet.
T.3-cyl. steam engine manufactured by J. Dickinson & Sons Ltd., Sunderland. 311 nhp. 11kts. 1920: New Donkey Boiler fitted.
6.10.1896: Launched by the Tyne Iron Shipbuilding Company Ltd., Willington Quay on Tyne (Yard No. 105), for W. Milburn & Company, Newcastle and London. 11.1896: Completed. 29.4.1907: Sold to Bede Steam Shipping Company Ltd. (Frew, Elder & Company, managers), Newcastle and renamed BEDEBURN. 24.6.1915: Sold to Kent Steamship Company Ltd. (S. Walton, managers), London. 11.7.1918: Sold to Britain Steamship Company Ltd. (Watts, Watts & Company Ltd, managers), for £60,000 and renamed CHISWICK. 11.1928: Sold to Sea & Land Securities Ltd., London. 30.4.1929: Sold for £11,000 to E. Jaunsems & Company, Riga, Latvia and renamed ZIGURDS. 1931: Sold to F. F. Aguardo, Santander, Spain, and renamed SANTA MARTA, under Panama register. 1934: Sold for Demolition at Ravenna, Italy and transferred to the Italian register for the delivery voyage.

WM 65. PORT ALBERT (2) (1897 - 1906)
O.N. 108207. 3,514g. 2,250n. 345.0 x 46.0 x 18.2 feet.
T.3-cyl. steam engine (C755) manufactured by the North Eastern Marine Engineering Company Ltd., Wallsend. 297 nhp. 11kts.
15.4.1897: Launched by the Tyne Iron Shipbuilding Company Ltd., Willington Quay on Tyne (Yard No. 113), for W. Milburn & Company, Newcastle and London. 14.6.1897: Completed. 1906: Sold to Aktieb, Sydafrikanska, Handels Komps (M. Wallenberg, managers), Stockholm, and renamed DELAGOA. 11.4.1910: Whilst on a voyage from Singapore and Penang to Gothenburg with general cargo, wrecked on Minicoy Island.

PORT VICTORIA (Ambrose Greenway collection)

WM 66. PORT VICTORIA (1897 - 1907)
O.N. 108266. 3,378g. 2,195n. 354.0 x 48.5 x 23.8 feet.
T.3-cyl. steam engine manufactured by J. Dickinson & Sons Ltd., Sunderland. 326 nhp. 11kts.
30.8.1897: Launched by J. L. Thompson & Sons Ltd., Sunderland (Yard No. 354), for the Anglo-Australasian Steam Navigation Company Ltd. (W. Milburn & Company, managers), London. 10.11.1897: Completed. 7.1907: Sold to P. Regier, Odessa, Russian, and renamed BELOROSSIA. 1913: Owners restyled as Russian Commercial Steamship Company (P. Regier, managers), Mariupol. 16.2.1920: E. P. Martin, Newcastle, appointed as managers. 8.1920: Sold to Anglo Commercial Shipping Company Ltd. (H.A. Brightman & Company, managers), North Shields. 7.8.1920: Renamed BALDERTON. 16.7.1921: W. S. Walton, appointed as managers. 1922: Regier Shipping Company Ltd., appointed managers. 26.4.1926: Sold to Parobrodarsko Akcionarsko Drustvo "Progres", Split and renamed POREDAK. 1933: Demolished at Savona.

WM 67. PORT PHILLIP (2) (1897 - 1900)
O.N. 108243. 3,103g. 1,971n. 324.8 x 48.5 x 22.8 feet.
T.3-cyl. steam engine (C759) manufactured by the North Eastern Marine Engineering Company Ltd., Wallsend. 279 nhp. 11kts.
17.6.1897: Launched by the Tyne Iron Shipbuilding Company Ltd., Willington Quay on Tyne (Yard No. 114), for W. Milburn & Company, Newcastle and London. 8.1897: Completed. 1900: Sold to Buenos Ayres Great Southern Railway Company Ltd. (A. Holland & Company, managers) London and renamed SOLA. 23.12.1912: Departed from Newport, Mon, bound to the River Plate, with a cargo of coal, and subsequently disappeared.

PORT PHILLIP (World Ship Society Photograph Library)

WM 68. PORT CAROLINE (3) (1905 - 1914)
O.N. 120587. 4,076g. 2,640n. 380.6 x 49.0 x 25.7 feet.
T.3-cyl. steam engine (C1616) manufactured by the North Eastern Marine Engineering Company Ltd., Wallsend. 434 nhp. 11kts.
16.12.1904: Ordered from R. & W. Hawthorn, Leslie & Company Ltd., Hebburn (Yard No. 402) by W. Milburn & Company, Newcastle and London. 5.5.1905: Launched for the Anglo-Australasian Steam Navigation Company Ltd., (W. Milburn & Company, managers), London. 29.7.1905: Completed. 1914: Sold for £41,000 to Soc Veneziana di Nav a Vap, Venice, and renamed LOREDANO. 9.1914: Stopped and searched by the German cruiser EMDEN off the entrance to the Hoogli River, but released as she was a neutral. 1932: Sold to I.N.S.A. (Industrie Navali Soc Anon), Genoa, and renamed PARISINA. 1934: Sold for demolition in Italy.

WM 69. PORT CHALMERS (2) (1905 - 1912)
O.N. 120598. 4,077g. 2,602n. 380.5 x 49.0 x 25.7 feet.
T.3-cyl. steam engine (C1617) manufactured by the North Eastern Marine Engineering Company Ltd., Wallsend. 434 nhp. 11kts.
18.7.1905: Launched by R. & W. Hawthorn, Leslie & Company Ltd., Hebburn (Yard No. 403), for the Anglo-Australasian Steam Navigation Company Ltd. (W. Milburn & Company, managers). 2.9.1905: Completed. 20.6.1912: Sold to Thomas Law & Company (W. Law, manager) Glasgow, and renamed DUNS LAW. 27.1.1913: Damaged in collision with MIRAMICHI (3,624g./12) owned by Bank Line Ltd. (Andrew Weir & Company, Glasgow, managers), off the Needles, and underwent extensive repairs at Cardiff. 8.1914: Taken and detained by Germany at Nordenheim, for the duration of the First World War. 26.1.1915: Taken over by Insurance Company, North of England Protecting & Indemnity Association (J. S. Todd, manager), Newcastle. 1918: Recovered from Germany. 29.4.1919: Sold for £95,000, to Dalgliesh S. Shipping Company Ltd. (R. S. Dalgliesh, manager), Newcastle. 2.5.1919: Renamed RAVENSWORTH. 3.1929: Sold to Metal Industries Ltd., for demolition at Rosyth. 1929: Resold and demolished at Le Havre.

WM 70. PORT HUNTER (3) (1906 - 1914)
O.N. 123689. 4,062g. 2,589n. 380.5 x 49.1 x 25.7 feet.
T.3-cyl. steam engine (E2642) manufactured by the shipbuilder. 442 nhp. 11kts.
27.10.1905: Ordered from R. & W. Hawthorn, Leslie & Company Ltd., Hebburn (Yard No. 410), for W. Milburn & Company, Newcastle and London. 21.6.1906: Launched. 13.8.1906: Completed. 13.2.1914: Transferred to The Commonwealth & Dominion Line Ltd., London. 2.11.1918: Whilst on a voyage from Boston to St. Nazaire, with general cargo and military supplies, collided with the U.S.Navy tug COVINGTON, off Vineyard Haven, Nantucket Sound, Mass., U.S.A. and was beached on Hedgefence Vineyard Shoal, later sinking in 70 feet of water. Total loss.

WM 71. PORT PHILLIP (4) (1906 - 1914)
O.N. 123708. 4,060g. 2,586n. 380.4 x 49.1 x 25.7 feet.
T.3-cyl. steam engine (E2644) manufactured by the shipbuilder. 442 nhp. 11kts.
27.10.1905: Ordered from R. & W. Hawthorn, Leslie & Company Ltd., Hebburn (Yard No. 412), for W. Milburn & Company, Newcastle and London. 6.9.1906: Launched. 6.10.1906: Completed. 13.2.1914: Transferred to The Commonwealth & Dominion Line Ltd., London. 16.10.1918: Whilst outward bound for Le Havre with a cargo of steel billets and general cargo collided with collier USS PROTEUS in Gravesend Bay, Ambrose Channel, New York and sank. 13.6.1919: Declared as derelict by United States Corp of Engineers.

PORT AUGUSTA (J. Dobson Collection)

WM 72. PORT AUGUSTA (2)   (1906 - 1914)
O.N. 123696. 4,063g. 2,587n. 380.6 x 49.1 x 25.7 feet.
T.3-cyl. steam engine (E2643) manufactured by the shipbuilder. 481 nhp. 11kts.
27.10.1905: Ordered from R. & W. Hawthorn, Leslie & Company Ltd., Hebburn (Yard No. 411), for the Anglo-Australasian Steam Navigation Company Ltd. (W. Milburn & Company, managers). 3.8.1906: Launched. 10.9.1906: Completed. 13.2.1914: Transferred to The Commonwealth & Dominion Line Ltd., London. 19-26.9.1921: Suffered a serious fire. 21.10.1925: Sold to Sir Robert John Thomas. 19.11.1925: Sold to William Thomas Shipping Company Ltd. (R. J. Thomas & Company Ltd., managers) Liverpool, and renamed CAMBRIAN COUNTESS. 6.1931: Broken up at Bo'ness by P. & W. McLellan.

PORT PIRIE (J. Dobson collection)

WM 73. PORT PIRIE (2)   (1907 - 1914)
O.N. 125615. 5,162g. 3,318n.   380.3 x 49.0 x 25.7 feet.
T.3-cyl. steam engine (C1783) manufactured by the North Eastern Marine Engineering Company Ltd., Wallsend. 435 nhp. 11kts.
17.1.1907: Ordered from R. & W. Hawthorn, Leslie & Company Ltd., Hebburn (Yard No. 420), as a joint venture between the shipbuilder and W. Milburn & Company, at a price of £52,250. 27.7.1907: Launched, for the Anglo-Australasian Steam Navigation Company Ltd. (W. Milburn & Company, managers). 18.9.1907: Completed. 13.2.1914: Transferred to The Commonwealth & Dominion Line Ltd., London. 24.4.1915: Sold to the Glasgow Steam Shipping Company Ltd. (J. Black & Company, managers), Glasgow, and renamed KELVINBRAE. 16.4.1920: Sold to the Romney Steamship Company Ltd. (Fawcett Coverdale & Company, managers), London. 1923: Renamed DARNLEY. 11.8.1925: Sold to the Britain Steamship Company Ltd. (Watts, Watts & Company Ltd.) and renamed LALEHAM. 31.3.1926: Abandoned in the North Atlantic, whilst on a voyage from Chile to the United Kingdom with a cargo of barley.

WM 74. PORT CURTIS (1)   (1910 - 1914)
O.N. 129118. 4,710g. 2,998n.   400.6 x 52.7 x 26.2 feet.
Quadruple expansion 4-cyl. steam engine (C1935) manufactured by the North Eastern Marine Engineering Company Ltd., Wallsend. 590 nhp. 11kts.
7.2.1910: Ordered from R. & W. Hawthorn, Leslie & Company Ltd., Hebburn (Yard No. 437), for W. Milburn & Company, Newcastle and London. 8.6.1910: Launched. 27.7.1910: Completed. 13.2.1914: Transferred to The Commonwealth & Dominion Line Ltd., London. 7.8.1917: Whilst on a voyage from Bahia Blanca to Cherbourg with a cargo of oats, was captured by the German submarine UC 71, and later sunk by time bombs placed aboard, in position 47.30N., 6W., 70 miles west of Penmarch, South West coast of France.

WM 75. PORT KEMBLA (1)   (1910 - 1914)
O.N. 129131. 4,700g. 2,990n.   400.6 x 52.7 x 26.2 feet.
Quadruple expansion 4-cyl. steam engine (C1962) manufactured by the North Eastern Marine Engineering Company Ltd., Wallsend. 590 nhp. 12kts.
22.7.1910: Launched by R. & W. Hawthorn, Leslie & Company Ltd., Hebburn (Yard No. 439), for the Anglo-Australasian Steam Navigation Company Ltd. (W. Milburn & Company, managers). 10.9.1910: Completed. 13.2.1914: Transferred to The Commonwealth & Dominion Line Ltd., London. 12.9.1917: Departed from Melbourne on a voyage to London with a cargo of frozen meat. 18.9.1917: Sunk by an explosion that was believed at first to have been of an internal nature, but it was later established that she had been sunk by mines laid by the German raider WOLF off Cape Farewell, New Zealand. Her crew were picked up by the steamer REGULUS.

PORT LINCOLN (World Ship Society Photograph Library)

WM 76. PORT LINCOLN (1) (1912 - 1914)
O.N. 132733. 7,243g. 4,638n. 426.0 x 53.8 x 29.3 feet.
Quadruple expansion 4-cyl. steam engine (C2043) manufactured by the North Eastern Marine Engineering Company Ltd., Wallsend. 777 nhp. 13kts. Refrigerated capacity 4,850 cu.ft.

3.4.1912: Launched by R. & W. Hawthorn, Leslie & Company Ltd., Hebburn (Yard No. 452), for W. Milburn & Company, Newcastle and London. 22.6.1912: Trials. 3.7.1912: Delivered. 13.2.1914: Transferred to The Commonwealth & Dominion Line Ltd., London. 27.7.1927: Sold to William Thomas Shipping Company Ltd. (R. J. Thomas & Company Ltd., managers), London. 3.8.1927: Renamed CAMBRIAN BARONESS. 13.12.1928: Sold to C. W. Kellock & Company Ltd. 9.5.1929: Sold to The Clan Line Steamers Ltd. (Cayzer, Irvine & Company Ltd., managers), Glasgow. 18.5.1929: Renamed CLAN GRAHAM. 4.1.1935: Transferred to the British & South American Steam Navigation Company (Houston Line (London) Ltd., managers)). 14.12.1938: Sold for £17,500 to Neill & Pandelis Ltd. (G. O. Till, managers), London, and renamed MARITIMA. 2.11.1942: Whilst on a voyage from New York and Sydney, Nova Scotia for Glasgow with 7,167 tons of general cargo including explosives, and part of convoy SC.107, was torpedoed and sunk by the German submarine U 522 (L/C Schneider), east of Belle Isle in position 52.20N., 45.40W. 29 of her crew and 3 gunners were lost.

WM 77. PORT MACQUARIE (1) (1912 - 1914)
O.N. 135132. 7,236g. 4,638n. 426.0 x 54.1 x 29.3 feet.
Quadruple expansion 4-cyl. steam engine (C2051) manufactured by the North Eastern Marine Engineering Company Ltd., Wallsend. 777 nhp. 13kts. Refrigerated capacity 4,850 cu.ft.
30.5.1912: Launched by R. & W. Hawthorn, Leslie & Company Ltd., Hebburn (Yard No. 456), for the Anglo-Australasian Steam Navigation Company Ltd. (Wm. Milburn & Company, managers). 5.9.1912: Trials. 12.9.1912: Delivered. 13.2.1914: Transferred to The Commonwealth & Dominion Line Ltd., London. 10.9.1919: Had fire on board at Victoria Dock, London, suffering damage to cargo. 25.5.1927: Sold to The William Thomas Shipping Company Ltd. (R. J. Thomas & Company Ltd., managers), Swansea. 3.6.1927: Renamed CAMBRIAN MARCHIONESS. 29.12.1928: Sold to C. W. Kellock & Company Ltd. 4.5.1929: Sold to The Clan Line Steamers Ltd. (Cayzer, Irvine & Company Ltd., managers), Glasgow. 18.5.1929: Renamed CLAN GRANT. 17.1.1935: Transferred to the British & South American Steam Navigation Company Ltd. (Houston Line (London) Ltd.). 20.1.1939: Sold to Stanhope Steamship Company Ltd. (J. A. Billmeir & Company Ltd., managers), London and renamed STANGRANT. 13.10.1940: Whilst on a voyage from Hampton Roads to Belfast with a cargo of steel and scrap metals, and part of convoy HX.77, was torpedoed and sunk by the German submarine U 37 (L/C Oehrn) N.W. of St. Kilda in position 58.27N., 12.36W. 8 of her crew of 38 were lost.

WM 78. PORT ALBANY (1)   (1914 - 1914)
O.N. 136676. 5,714g. 3,620n. 426.3 x 54.1 x 29.3 feet.
Quadruple expansion 4-cyl. steam engine (C2132) manufactured by the North Eastern Marine Engineering Company Ltd., Wallsend. 767 nhp. 13kts. Refrigerated capacity 229,870 cu.ft.
4.3.1913: Ordered from R. & W. Hawthorn, Leslie & Company Ltd., Hebburn (Yard No. 464), for W. Milburn & Company Ltd., Newcastle and London. 12.2.1914: Launched. 26.5.1914: Trials. 29.5.1914: Delivered to The Commonwealth & Dominion Line Ltd., London. 21.2.1929: Purchased for £40,000 by the Union Cold Storage Company Ltd. (Blue Star Line (1920) Ltd., managers), London. 27.9.1929: Renamed OREGONSTAR. 1930: Managers restyled as Blue Star Line Ltd. 10.1932: Laid up on the Tyne. 13.11.1932: Fire broke out in the forward holds while on the buoys off the Hebburn yard of Palmers' Shipbuilding & Iron Company Ltd., and she was extensively damaged. Her Chief Officer lost his life attempting to locate the source of the fire, which was subsequently extinguished. 24.11.1932: Dry-docked at the yard for inspection, whereupon she was declared a total loss and laid up in the River Tyne to await disposal. 12.1933: Sold to Hughes, Bolckow Ltd., for demolition at Blyth. 1.5.1934: Arrived at Blyth.

Anglo-Australasian Steam Navigation Company Ltd
(W. Milburn & Company)
London
(1883 - 1914)

This fleet has been incorporated with that of Wm. Milburn & Company above due to the complexity of vessel interchanging between the two concerns. Basically all vessels with PORT names operated on the Anglo-Australasian service.

Milburn Line Ltd
1927 - 1941
William Milburn & Company

BENWELL TOWER (World Ship Society Photograph Library)

ML 1. BENWELL TOWER (1927 - 1937)
O.N. 149438. 4,414g. 2,680n. 401.0 x 53.2 x 25.0 feet.
T. 3-cyl steam engine (C2641) manufactured by the North Eastern Marine Engineering Company Ltd., Wallsend. 2,400 ihp.
15.6.1927: Launched by R. & W. Hawthorn, Leslie & Company Ltd., Hebburn (Yard No. 545), for W. Milburn & Company Ltd., Newcastle. 2.8.1927: Trials and Delivery. 11.1937: Sold to 'Nivose' Soc di Nav. (A. Scinicariello), managers, Naples, and renamed GAETA. 10.1952: Sold to Lauro & Montella, Naples, and renamed SAGITTA. 1961: Sold for demolition.

ML 2. FOWBERRY TOWER (1929 - 1941)
O.N. 161527. 4,484g. 2,756n. 400.7 x 53.3 x 25.0 feet.
T. 3-cyl steam engine (C2704) manufactured by the North Eastern Marine Engineering Company Ltd., Wallsend. 2,400 ihp.
22.5.1929: Launched by R. & W. Hawthorn, Leslie & Company Ltd., Hebburn (Yard No. 559), for W. Milburn & Company Ltd., Newcastle. 20.6.1929: Trials and Delivery. 12.5.1941: Shortly after leaving Hull for Baltimore U.S.A, in ballast, she was bombed and sunk in position 53.34N., 0.20.25E., 1 mile S.W. by W. from the Humber Lightvessel. Four bombs were dropped, the bridge collapsed and six of her crew were killed. The remaining 40 crew were picked up by the trawler CONSORT and later transferred to the Dutch naval vessel NAUTILUS that in turn, transferred them to the tug IRISHMAN.

Milburn Family - as Mortgage Lenders

MFM 1. SAINT GEORGE (1880 - 1883) Iron Screw Steamer
O.N. 65282. 1,621g. 1,051n. 258.0 x 34.0 x 22.1 feet.
C. 2-cyl. steam engine manufactured by C. D. Holmes & Company, Hull. 145 nhp.
27.11.1871: Launched by Richardson, Duck & Company, Stockton (Yard No. 179), for G. Jinman & Company, Hull. 21.9.1881: Sold to the Jinman Steamship Company (64/64th shares mortgage to

secure account current with interest with W. Milburn, J. D. Milburn and W. Milburn the younger. All of London - joint mortgage lenders). 27.4.1883: Mortgagees restyled as the Neptune Steamship Company. 29.4.1883: The Neptune Steamship Company discharged their mortgage with the Milburns. 1886: Sold to John Chapman & Company, London. 1890: Sold to Ocean Queen Steamship Company (Wake & Saunders, managers), London. 1893: Sold to Wilson & Company (A. O. Wilson, manager), Gothenburg. 1898: Sold to Angfartygs Aktiebolaget St. George (same manager), Gothenburg. 1910: Demolished at Gothenburg.

MFM 2. SCINDIA (1880 - 1883) Iron Screw Steamer
O.N. 65259. 2,203g. 1,423n. 300.4 x 35.2 x 25.0 feet.
C. 2-cyl. steam engine manufactured by the shipbuilder, Sunderland. 250 nhp.
22.8.1871: Launched by T. R. Oswald & Company, Sunderland (Yard No. 112), for J. F. Norwood, Hull. 1871: Completed. 1876: Sold to Jinman Steamship Company Ltd., Hull. 21.9.1881: The Jinman Steamship Company. (64/64th shares mortgage to secure account current with interest with W. Milburn, J. D. Milburn and W. Milburn the younger. All of London - joint mortgag lenders). 27.4.1883: Mortgagees restyled as the Neptune Steamship Company. 29.4.1883: The Neptune Steamship Company discharged their mortgage with the Milburns. 1883: Sold to Chipchase Steamship Company (Laws, Surtees & Company), Newcastle, (later & Son). 1884: Renamed CHIPCHASE CASTLE. 1887: Sold to S. M. Kuhnle, Bergen, and renamed NORDEN. 9.1896: Demolished.

Ashington Coal Company Ltd.
(W. Milburn & Company, Managers)

A 1. ASHINGTON (2) (1892 - 1905)
O.N. 97994. 885g. 561n, 206.7 x 30.1 x 14.1 feet.
T.3-cyl. steam engine manufactured by J. Dickinson, Sunderland. 98 rhp.
1905: New Donkey Boiler fitted: 1912: New Boiler fitted.
14.3.1892: Launched by W. Dobson & Company, Newcastle (Yard No. 51), for the Ashington Coal Company, (W. Milburn & Company, managers), Newcastle. 3.1892: Completed. 29.5.1900: Sold to Ashington Coal Company Ltd. 27.10.1905: Sold to N. V. Maatschappij Totexploitatie v/h S. S. Betsy Anna (W. H. Burghuys, manager), Holland, and renamed BETSY ANNA. 17.8.1926: Whilst on a voyage in ballast, from Fleetwood to Rotterdam, stranded near Prawle Point, refloated and beached. 12.10.1926: Having been refloated, and in tow from Salcombe to Cowes foundered 12 miles off the Needles.

A 2. WOODHORN (1894 - 1911)
O.N. 104244. 1,283g. 801n. 235.0 x 34.1 x 14.7 feet.
T.3-cyl. steam engine manufactured by J. Dickinson, Sunderland. 146 rhp.
8.3.1894: Launched by J. L. Thompson & Sons, Sunderland (Yard No. 315), for the Ashington Coal Company (W. Milburn & Company, managers), Newcastle. 4.1894: Completed. 29.5.1894: Sold to Ashington Coal Company Ltd. 8.1911: Sold to B. Stolt-Nielsen, Haugesund, Norway, and renamed TENTO. 1916: Sold to D/S. A/S Kap (C. Wildhagen manager), Norway, and renamed KAPARIKA. 6.5.1917: Whilst on a voyage from Blyth to Sarpsborg with a cargo of coal, was torpedoed and sunk by the German submarine UC 77, 30 miles E of Aberdeen.

Milburn And Hawthorn, Leslie
Joint venture in ship finance / building.

MHL 1. CORNWALL (1896)
O.N. 105897. 5,490g. 3,554n. 420.0 x 54.0 x 28.7 feet.
T. 3-cyl. steam engine (E2340) manufactured by the shipbuilder. 505 nhp. 3,075 ihp.
5.4.1896: Ordered from R. & W. Hawthorn, Leslie & Company, Hebburn (Yard No. 339) by W. Milburn

& Company, Newcastle. 23.9.1896: Launched. 14.11.1896: Registered at London, by Wm. Milburn Junior. 24.11.1896: Trialed and delivered, at a cost of £67,245, and transferred, for £68,250, to Federal Steam Navigation Company, London. 2.1905: Returned to Hebburn for engine removal to renew bedplate. 29.1.1913: Sold to Atlantide Soc.Italiana di Nav., (Coe & Clerici, managers), Genoa, and renamed ATLANTIDE. 9.2.1918: Whilst on a voyage from Genoa to New Orleans, was captured and scuttled by the German submarine U 156, off Madeira.

MHL 2. DEVON (1896)
O.N. 108171. 5,488g. 3,546n. 420.0 x 54.0 x 28.7 feet.
T. 3-cyl. steam engine (E2341) manufactured by the shipbuilder. 505 nhp. 3,075 ihp.
5.4.1896: Ordered from R. & W. Hawthorn, Leslie & Company, Newcastle (Yard No. 340) by W. Milburn & Company, Newcastle. 20.11.1896: Launched. 6.2.1897: Registered at London by Wm. Milburn, jnr. 23.2.1897: Sold for £66,768, on completion to Federal Steam Navigation Company, London. 25.8.1913: Whilst on a voyage from Montreal vial Sydney and Auckland to Wellington, wrecked on Pencarrow Head, near Wellington, New Zealand.

MHL 3. KENT (1899)
O.N. 110127. 5,527g. 3,548n. 420.0 x 54.0 x 28.6 feet.
T. 3-cyl. steam engine (E2405) manufactured by the shipbuilder. 505 nhp. 3,075 ihp.
9.8.1898: Ordered from R. & W. Hawthorn, Leslie & Company, Newcastle (Yard No. 369), for W. Milburn & Company, Newcastle. 11.3.1899: Launched. 23.5.1899: Registered at London, by the Federal Steam Navigation Company. 30.5.1899: Trials and delivery. 14.10.1915: Sold to the Brodlea Steamship Company Ltd., (Blue Star Line Ltd., managers), London, and renamed BRODLEA. 14.10.1920: Transferred to Union Cold Storage Company Ltd., (Blue Star Line (1920) Ltd., managers), London. 11.11.1920: Renamed SAXONSTAR. 2.9.1929: Transferred to Blue Star Line Ltd., London. 27.9.1929: Renamed SAXON STAR. 11.1933: Laid up on the River Tyne. 8.1934: Sold for £8,000, to Soc. Anonima Ricuperi Metallici, for demolition. 17.9.1934: Arrived at Savona in Italy.

MHL 4. SURREY (1899)
O.N. 110184. 5,980g. 3,843n. 420.4 x 54.0 x 28.6 feet.
T. 3-cyl. steam engine (E2406) manufactured by the shipbuilder. 505 nhp. 3,075 ihp.
9.8.1898: Ordered from R. & W. Hawthorn, Leslie & Company, Newcastle (Yard No. 370), for W. Milburn & Company, Newcastle. 8.6.1899: Launched. 9.9.1899: Registered at London by Federal Steam Navigation Company Ltd. 10.10.1899: Trials and delivery. 25.2.1915: Whilst on a voyage from Liverpool to Dunkirk, with coal and refrigerated cargo, damaged by a mine explosion off Dunkirk, and was beached at North Deal next day. 28.5.1915: Refloated. 29.5.1916: Beached at Mucking Flats. 20.6.1915: Refloated and taken to Tilbury for examination whereupon was declared a total loss. 6.8.1915: Sold to the Brodstream Steamship Company Ltd., (Blue Star Line Ltd., managers), London. 9.8.1915: Owners restyled as Brodfield Steamship Company Ltd., (same managers), London. 15.12.1915: Following repair, was renamed BRODFIELD. 13.11.1916: Whilst on a voyage in ballast, from Le Havre to Barry, wrecked in fog, at Blue Carn, St. Mary's, Isles of Scilly.

MHL 5. SUSSEX (1) / KARAMEA (1899)
O.N. 110264. 5,564g. 3,553n. 420.0 x 54.0 x 28.6 feet.
T. 3-cyl. steam engine (E2407) manufactured by the shipbuilder. 505 nhp. 3,075 ihp.
9.8.1898: Ordered from R. & W. Hawthorn, Leslie & Company, Newcastle (Yard No. 371) by W. Milburn & Company, Newcastle. 9.4.1899: Keel laid as SUSSEX for Federal Steam Navigation Company Ltd., London. 22.8.1899: Launched as KARAMEA for Shaw, Savill & Albion Company Ltd. 13.11.1899: Trialed and delivered. 12.2.1919: Whilst outward from Montevideo, collided with HAUGLAND (3,167g./1896) off Flores Island. 1925: Sold for £30,000, to Soc. Anon. Nav. Alta Italia, Genoa, Italy, and renamed MONGIOIA. 16.4.1929: Arrived at Genoa for demolition.

MHL 6. SUSSEX (2) (1900)
O.N. 112686. 5,474g. 3,505n. 420.0 x 54.0 x 28.7 feet.
T. 3-cyl. steam engine (E2413) manufactured by the shipbuilder. 505 nhp. 3,075 ihp.
11.10.1898: Ordered from R. & W. Hawthorn, Leslie & Company, Newcastle (Yard No. 373), for W. Milburn & Company, Newcastle. 16.1.1900: Launched. 28.3.1900: Registered at London by Federal Steam Navigation Company Ltd. 29.4.1900: Trialed and delivered. 11.7.1929: Arrived at Osaka for demolition. 15.7.1929: Osaka Marine Company Ltd., commenced work.

MHL 7. PORT JACKSON (2) (1904)
O.N. 119128. 5,505g. 3,512n. 420.6 x 54.0 x 28.6 feet
T.3-cyl. steam engine (C1511) manufactured by the North Eastern Marine Engineering Company Ltd., Wallsend. 518 nhp.
19.11.1903: Launched as PORT JACKSON by R. & W. Hawthorn, Leslie & Company Ltd., Hebburn on Tyne (Yard No. 391), for the Anglo-Australasian Steam Navigation Company Ltd. (W. Milburn & Company, managers), London. 11.3.1904: Sold, whilst fitting out, to the British India Steam Navigation Company Ltd., London, and renamed WAIPARA. 21.5.1904: Completed. 1909: Refitted to carry 338 emigrants on the U.K-Australia route. 23.5.1914: Ran ashore on Hannibal Island, Great Barrier Reef. Subsequently lightened by jettisoning cargo. 27.5.1914: Successfully towed off by HMS FANTOM. 1917: Used as cadet training ship, 32 cadets carried. 23.7.1917: When south-west of Ireland, the German submarine U 46 fired a torpedo that missed. 4.8.1918: Whilst on a voyage in ballast, from Havre to Southampton, was damaged with a torpedo by the German submarine UC 71, in the English Channel, 16 miles South of Dunnose Head, and was abandoned. Later reboarded, and beached at Netley to prevent sinking. 1919: Returned to service after being refloated and repaired at Middlesbrough. 28.8.1923: Sold to shipbreakers for £10,250. 1924: Demolished in Holland by T. C. Pas.

MHL 8. PORT PHILLIP (3) / DURHAM (1904)
O.N. 118499. 5,561g. 3,550n. 420.7 x 54.0 x 28.6 feet.
T. 3-cyl. steam engine (C1512) manufactured by the North Eastern Marine Engineering Company Ltd., Wallsend. 518 nhp.
1903: Keel laid as PORT PHILLIP by R. & W. Hawthorn, Leslie & Company, Newcastle (Yard No. 392), for W.Milburn & Company, Newcastle. 18.2.1904: Launched. 3.10.1904: Registered as DURHAM, at London by A. Hughes and W. Milburn jnr, for Federal Steam Navigation service. 9.12.1904: Trialed and delivered, at a cost of £76,328. She was completed eight months late due to a decision being taken to insulate No 4 and 5 holds coupled with technical problems with the refrigeration machinery. 1.1907 until 7.1913: Both the Hughes and Milburn families sold their shares to Federal Steam Navigation Company Ltd. 15.7.1924: Sold for 35,000, to A. Zanchi, Genoa, and renamed AUGUSTA. 10.6.1940: Interned at Bahia, by the Brazilian Government 12.1941: Allocated to Lloyd Brasileiro Patrimonio Nacional, Rio de Janeiro, and renamed MINASLOIDE. 1949: Returned to Italy under the ownership of Ditta A. Zanchi, and reverted to AUGUSTA. 15.5.1950: Arrived in tow at Spezia for demolition. 6.8.1950: Soc. Anon. Cantieri di Portovenere commenced work.

TYSER LINE

G. D. Tyser & Company were well known insurance and shipping brokers and had been established by G. D. Tyser in about 1820. They also managed several sailing ships in partnership with William Haviside of T. Haviside & Company; but it was not until the early-1860's that they ordered ships for their own account for a regular trade to India. The first ship owned by G. D. Tyser & Company was the NORTHUMBERLAND built in 1838, which they acquired in 1859. The BOMBAY, built in 1861, was the first new build for the company and over the next 22 years Tysers took delivery of no fewer than 12 sailing vessels culminating with the steel ship the LUCKNOW completed in 1883. All the ships were given names associated with India and the cargoes carried were mostly building materials and railway equipment.

The opening of the Suez Canal in 1869 sounded the death knell, for sailing ships to India and the trade gradually declined. As trade to India declined, Tyser & Company looked for new opportunities and destinations. Seven years previously the BOMBAY had made several voyages to New Zealand under charter to Shaw, Savill & Company, and the HIMALAYA had undertaken a voyage to Australia. So it was to Australasia that Tyser & Company looked for new opportunities.

In 1873 George Tyser's sons joined the company and the name was changed to Tyser & Company. Later that year the HIMALAYA and her near sistership the TREVELYAN were sold to Shaw, Savill. 1874 saw the company take delivery of their largest ship to date the PLASSEY of 1,764 tons. Tyser & Company had great aspirations to operate on the Australian route, but were prevented by the Australian Associated Owners and Brokers Conference which had been founded in 1878. This organisation refused membership to Tyser & Company, but allowed them to charter their vessels to companies in the conference such as John. H. Flint's Colonial Line and others. Three years later Tyser & Company formed the short lived Alliance Line of Packets to operate both their own and chartered ships to Australia, the Conference were not impressed and in retaliation threatened to load their own ships for India. After much heated discussion, Tysers were granted a two-year moratorium but this was not to their liking and henceforth no love was lost between the two parties. Once again Tysers had been thwarted and in 1885 they formed the Merchant Line of Sailing Ships and once again an application to join the Conference was rejected. As one door closed another opened, and in 1886 Tyser agreed to transport frozen meat at $2^1/_4$d a pound from the Nelson Brothers, Tomoana, Hawkes Bay freezing works in New Zealand at a price that was a farthing lower than the previously agreed rate. This was in response to demands from the clients of the freezer works who were desperate to ship their products from Napier and not from Wellington. The Shaw Savill and Albion Line and the New Zealand Shipping Company were the main shippers of frozen meat and were loath to transport cargo from the smaller ports without surcharge. Tyser formed a company called the Colonial Union Line Ltd but again a Tyser owned company was refused membership of a conference organisation, this time the New Zealand Conference. However, Tysers chartered a number of ships equipping them for refrigerated cargo and commenced operations. Outward bound cargo to New Zealand was not restricted by the conference arrangements and the Tyser ships were free to load without restriction. The New Zealand Shipping Company appointed G. D. Tyser as their London freight brokers an appointment that lasted for four years. In 1886 George Dorman Tyser, the founder of the firm, was succeeded by his two sons - W. H. and G. W. Tyser. William Haviside Tyser (named after his father's earlier partner) took over the reins as the dominant partner in the shipping side of the business. In 1887 Tysers took over the management of the Colonial Line of Australian Packets on the death of J. H. Flint. They were eventually allowed to join the Australian Conference in 1889. Within a short period George Tyser fell out with them over rate increases that he refused to implement and resigned his membership. In May 1887 Nelson Brothers arranged for Tysers to transport frozen cargoes from Bluff, New Zealand on behalf of a number of freezing works in the area. In order to fulfil this contract a number of dry cargo ships were chartered and then fitted out with Hall's refrigerating machinery and insulated holds at Tysers expense. The first ship chartered was the BALMORAL CASTLE, (2,846g./1876) which left London for Sydney, via Cape Town, in ballast, on 23rd July 1887 and eventually arrived at Auckland on 8th October 1887. After loading some cargo at Auckland, she proceeded to Wellington, Bluff, Lyttelton and Napier before leaving for London via Cape Horn and Rio de Janeiro. This first voyage was a great success as was the second using the ASHLEIGH BROOK, (2,621g./1882), but the third cargo on board the SELEMBRIA, (2,907g./1886) was not. A fire developed in the coal bunkers on the voyage from New Zealand and she had to put into Montevideo, where 12,000 carcases were sold for $2^1/_2$d. each. More cargo had to be jettisoned at sea and when the ship arrived in London the balance of the cargo was condemned. The remaining two ships of the five originally chartered to run the service were the BAYLEY (2,392/1886) and the BALCARRES BROOK (1,874/1883). In the following years the MAORI KING, CELTIC KING, STAR OF VICTORIA and the STAR OF ENGLAND were also chartered. In addition, sailing ships were employed to transport wool and tallow, the first of these being the HERSHEL (814/1857), which first loaded at Napier in December 1887. From September 1889, Tyser & Company acquired the Colonial Union Line entirely, because the original partners were reluctant to build ships for the trade.

Tysers were also involved in other ventures, in 1882 they were associated with the International Line from London to South Africa and in 1885 Tyser started the Merchant Line of Packets to Australia.

In 1890 Tysers secured a New Zealand Government contract to transport excess grain resulting from a bumper harvest, at a much lower price than the established companies, amongst who were the New Zealand Shipping Company. The contract enabled them to fill all surplus general cargo spaces in the ships they employed in the New Zealand trade.

During his lifetime W. H. Tyser became known as "The Terror of the Rings" because of the stance he and his company took against the established conference companies. In the book "Westrays", a history of J. B. Westray & Company; the author describes him as follows. "There is little doubt that Tyser, while enjoying membership of the groups comprising respectively the Australian and New Zealand shipping companies, was despatching ships in competition, hence the stern measures taken against him. While battling with his contemporaries in one trade he was hand in glove with them in another".

In October 1890 Tysers lost their appointment as London freight brokers to the New Zealand Shipping Company when they were replaced by J. B. Westray & Company. Possibly due to the New Zealand Shipping Company appointing a new chairman, Edwin Sand Dawes, whose son was a partner in Westrays. With the change of broker Tysers lost their Australian connections and the New Zealand Shipping outbound cargoes. Ships from the fleets of J. P. Corry and William Ross were chartered to fulfil their Nelson Brothers contract. The Tyser Line Ltd was formed in 1890 and the following year the HAWKES BAY (1) a steamer of 4,500 tons gross was delivered from William Doxford, she was destined to serve the company for over 20 years. Shortly afterwards the Colonial Union Line was wound up and its interests were absorbed by G. D. Tyser & Company. In addition to chartering the Corry Line "Star" vessels, Tysers also began chartering Royden steamers in 1891 as well as some of the Milburn "Ports" which were used for the carriage of wool cargoes.

Tyser & Company were finally admitted into the New Zealand Conference in 1893, but limits were placed on the amount of cargo which could be loaded in United Kingdom as well as which discharge ports could be used in New Zealand. In spite of these restrictions Tysers found additional work for their fleet, a contract with Central Queensland Meat Exporting Company was negotiated to transport frozen meat from Rockhampton to Europe. In the same year a project in association with the London firm of Spearing & Waldron to carry frozen meat from the Falkland Islands using the chartered sailing ship the HENGIST (1,161/1860), commenced but was abandoned after six voyages. Unfortunately the meat was too tough, the wool inferior and when the ship was wrecked in the Straits of Magellan on 23rd May 1894 the project came to an end.

During 1895 the last two sailing ships in the fleet, the POONAH and the NORTH, were disposed of, both for further trading. By the following year the finances of the firm were at a very low ebb, with no depreciation having been written off the one steamer owned since her construction five years earlier. It is possible that this financial situation prevented the Tyser Line from ordering another ship until the turn of the century; the company being satisfied to use existing chartered tonnage from associated concerns.

Prior to 1898 the transport of cargoes from New York to Australia was in the hands of four American merchant firms, who also acted as agents for importers, and sailing ships were used in the trade.

In 1898 three British Lines (Bucknall, Federal and Houlder) decided to start services in this trade, but it was not until each principal was in New York making arrangements that they became aware of the plans of the other lines. They met and, instead of launching independent services, became partners in the venture, forming the American and Australasian Steam-Ship Line. Collectively, they had a considerable fleet of steamers and the service they initiated soon secured the major part of the trade, with the four American merchant firms being forced to support the new line in order to retain their merchant business. Furthermore, they in turn had to resort to steam when chartering tonnage, although sailing ships were still used to carry some of the rougher goods at lower rates of freight. The American firms eventually separated their merchant and carrying interests, and formed the United States and Australasian Steamship Company (later replaced by the Roosevelt Line).

Tyser Line decided to enter the trade in 1899, and Messrs Funch, Edye & Company was appointed agents. This was an old established firm of German origin, and was one of the leading ship-brokers in New York, representing as agents several Continental and British lines trading to various parts of the world. T. B. Royden & Sons of Liverpool, also had steamers running in the Tyser service. Sir Thomas Bland Royden was one of the directors, and it was no doubt on his recommendation that Funch, Edye

& Company were appointed. The Tyser Line was also involved in the transport of German cargoes from Hamburg, which were trans-shipped at New York. By 1901 the Line was well established, being maintained by a combination of owned and chartered tonnage. The last two sailing ships despatched were the chartered PLUS and PESTALOZZI, steam having supplanted sail at long last.

The pattern of operations of the Line remained unchanged until 1907 when Funch, Edye & Company informed Tysers that two German lines, D.A.D.G of Hamburg and the Hansa Line of Bremen, had decided to enter the trade and had invited Funch, Edye & Company Ltd., to act as agents. They subsequently declined, but suggested that some other arrangement with the Germans should be sought in the interests of preventing a freight war. The Tyser Line was still unable to avoid resorting to chartered tonnage to maintain its service and, consequently, made an agreement for a Joint Service, established as the United Tyser Line in which they had a 50% interest. A three weekly service to Australia was inaugurated, with vessels of good speed sailing on advertised dates, proving something of an innovation as, prior to this, ships were often days or even weeks late in leaving after their advertised time.

This was supported by a series of announcements that appeared in the shipping press in New York in the spring of 1907:

"Three lines unite in Australian service and will operate a regular service every 3 weeks whether or not fully loaded on advertised date. Tyser, Hansa, and German-Australian Steamship of Hamburg under management of TYSER Line of London combine to form UNITED TYSER LINES.

The New York representative will be Funch, Eyde & Company Ltd.

First to sail will be the TRAUTENFELS which will leave on 20th April for Fremantle, Adelaide Wharf, Melbourne Wharf, Sydney and Brisbane followed on the 11th May by HAWKES BAY for Melbourne, Sydney, Auckland, Wellington, Lyttelton and Dunedin and three weeks later on the 1st June by the ITZEHOE for Fremantle, Adelaide Wharf, Melbourne Wharf, Sydney and Brisbane. After discharge in Antipodes the Germans will then go east to India or China to load cargo for Europe".

In fact the first to depart was the HAWKES BAY (1) that left New York on the 20th April and arrived Fremantle direct on 2nd June. Further notices emphasising the regularity of the services appeared during the rest of 1907.

Shippers and consignees welcomed this certainty so that the Line was immediately successful with nearly all the vessels securing good cargoes. The other two lines in the trade had eventually to follow suit in the matter of despatch.

The outbreak of World War One in August 1914 threw the line into disruption, the agreement between the companies automatically coming to an end and a re-organisation of Messrs Funch, Edye & Company., who had some German management, becoming necessary if they were to represent British interests. The German element retired from the firm with the German agencies being relinquished, and an Englishman, Mr J. Ashley Sparks (later Sir Ashley), becoming head of the firm, (later Funch, Edye & Company were absorbed by Cunard and became an Incorporated Company). Naturally this reorganisation took time and it was to be about three months before a ship could be berthed under the name of Commonwealth & Dominion Line, time that had absorbed Tyser before the war. Naturally the two competing lines took full advantage of the position and it took a little time for things to settle down to something like pre-war conditions.

One incident worth recalling was that of the Hansa Lines' BIRKENFELS, which left New York a few days before the outbreak of war. Few cargo liners were equipped with wireless in those days and the captain was in ignorance that his country was involved in hostilities when he steamed his vessel into Cape Town on 20th August 1914, two weeks after the outbreak of war. His ship was seized as a prize, and placed under the management of the Federal Steam Navigation Company Ltd. In 1922 she was converted into a tanker on her sale to Anglo-Saxon Petroleum Company Ltd, and renamed PINNA. Subsequently she was sunk by Japanese aircraft off Sumatra during February 1942, whilst serving as a Royal Fleet Auxiliary.

In 1899 Tysers took delivery of the TOMOANA a single-screw steamer of nearly 6,000 tons from Sir J. Laing & Company, she was quickly followed by the MIMIRO the first of six similar vessels from the yard of Workman, Clark & Company, Belfast. Finally in 1912 the 10,600-ton MAKARINI and HAWKES BAY (2) were delivered. All except one were given Maori names in accordance with company policy.

In 1914 the Panama Canal was opened but there were teething troubles, especially with the landslides in the Culebra Cut, and it was not until 1915 that some of the sailings from New York used this route. However the Cape route was not entirely abandoned until 1922, when the Commonwealth & Dominion Line started routing ships in their Australian service via the Canal.

The Tyser Line suffered a number of shipping casualties with the TOMOANA striking an uncharted rock after dragging her anchor off Gisborne on 27th July 1901 and the NIWARU sustaining more serious damage when on her 3rd voyage to New Zealand she stranded off the Napier breakwater on 19th July 1903 after arrival from Auckland. This was her third mishap within a year. In a previous accident in September 1902 she was holed in No 2 hold after grounding at Las Palmas and over 26,000 carcasses were condemned on arrival in London. She put to sea again to jettison the condemned cargo in the North Sea where some of it was promptly requisitioned by local fishermen for their own use. Previous to this she had struck wreckage which caused her slight damage.

After discharging all her cargo and coal, she left Napier on 8th August for Auckland in company of the steamer TANGAROA. Water was now being kept down to the level of the shaft tunnel. Arriving in Auckland on 14th August she was promptly drydocked, where it was found that 32 plates on both sides were damaged, the hull was badly dented, all this together with a large hole in the starboard side resulted in repairs which lasted 42 days and cost over £6,000. Her Captain was censured in having not stopped the steamer sooner. His certificate was returned to him and an order made that he should pay the costs of the inquiry. The court added that the port was improperly lighted and something should be done about it. Shortly afterwards her Captain resigned his position.

A serious fire broke out on the WHAKARUA on 16th February 1908 whilst on passage from London to Australia and the vessel had to divert to Cape Town for repairs.

In April the MIMIRO, after 52 days at sea, ran short of fuel and put into Albany to take on 205 tons of coal which should have been sufficient fuel to reach Melbourne. After three days the fuel ran out, due to the poor quality of the coal taken onboard at Albany. The coal was worse than useless and was carried up the funnel as if it was shavings. After the coal ran out, fittings were burnt, including a large boom (as big as a large tree). In desperation the contents of nearly 1,000 cases of kerosene were mixed with the remaining fittings and lastly the cases were burnt, the kerosene being sprayed over the fittings by means of a piece of equipment made up by the ship's engineers. So fierce was the heat that the funnel became red hot and cabins in that part of the ship became uninhabitable. The MIMIRO eventually reached Portland after a trip of seven days from Albany. After taking on more coal from the railway depot she finally reached Melbourne three days later.

Further casualties occurred with some of the chartered tonnage. The three year old STAR OF CANADA owned by J. P. Corry, while lying in the Gisborne roadstead, was blown ashore on Kaiti beach on 23rd June 1912 and broke her back and became a total loss.

The INDRABARAH (2) owned by T. B. Royden & Company, was more fortunate. She was waiting to load at Wanganui and was blown ashore on 10th May 1913 and remained stuck fast in the sand until early July even though extensive efforts were made to pull her off. Eventually she was refloated, and repairs were carried at Port Chalmers, which took over seven weeks to complete.

The loss of the WARATAH off South Africa in 1909 resulted in an extensive search being carried out for wreckage and survivors. On the 8th January 1910 a lookout on the TOMOANA two days before the vessel rounded Cape of Good Hope and about 500 miles from the Cape, sighted a large lifeboat painted white which had been in the water for a considerable time. The TOMOANA did not turn back because Chief Officer thought that seaman had sighted a large dead fish.

From 1909 onwards it was apparent that emigration to Australia was on the increase. Accordingly, Tysers' ordered two large steamers with provision in the 'tween decks for the carriage of up to a 1,000 migrants. These ships entered service in 1912 and operated under a Victorian Government contract and were the last ships delivered to the company before the amalgamation took place. The other partners, in the soon to be formed Commonwealth & Dominion Line also ordered similar ships. Tyser & Company were directly concerned with the management of most of these other ships and negotiations started in late 1913 which eventually resulted in an amalgamation of interests.

Tyser & Company were the principal force in the formation of the Commonwealth & Dominion Line. Three of the eight directors of the new company came from Tysers and their existing fleet of eight vessels all went into the new company.

The insurance section was not absorbed during the amalgamation but continued to operate as a flourishing brokerage business in London under the name Tyser & Company, which it still does today. W. H. Tyser died in 1908, having retired the previous year, and was later succeeded by a son of G. W. Tyser, Walter P. Tyser (who had joined the board of the Tyser Line in 1896) as head of the shipping side of the business. Subsequently W. P. Tyser became the first Chairman of the Commonwealth & Dominion Line serving in that capacity from 1914 to 1939. Designated President in 1939, he finally retired from the Company's service in 1940. He was the largest individual shareholder in the Cunard Steam Ship Company for about fourteen years after Cunard purchased the Commonwealth & Dominion Line, and he died in May 1944.

The Tyser Fleet

T 1. NORTHUMBERLAND (1859 - 1868) Wooden Ship
812 tons. 126.11 x 29.11 x 22.0 feet.
2.8.1837: Keel laid by R. & H. Green, Natmo, Moulmein, Burma. 4.10.1838: Launched for R. & H. Green, London. 1859: Purchased by G. D. Tyser, London. 1868: Sold to W. Pile, London. 1878: Sold to Aga Syed Abdool Hossain, Moulmein, Burma. 1879: Demolished.

T 2. BOMBAY (1861 - 1872) Wooden Ship
O.N. 29383. 937 tons. 186.0 x 33.4 x 20.9 feet.
1.1861: Launched by Vaux, Harwich, for G. D. Tyser, London. 6.3.1872: Whilst on a voyage from Yloilo to Singapore, wrecked on a coral reef N.N.E of the Mangsee Islands, Balabac Straights. Crew saved.

T 3. TREVELYAN (1863-1873) Iron Ship
O.N. 47368. 1,042 tons. 203.6 x 33.4 x 21.2 feet.
2.5.1863: Launched by Pile, Hay & Company, Sunderland (Yard No. 15), for G. D. Tyser, London. 28.5.1863: Completed. 1873: Sold to Shaw, Savill, London. 17.5.1876: Registration transferred to Southampton. 1882: Transferred to Shaw, Savill & Albion. 1885: Reduced to a barque. 23.3.1888: Departed from Glasgow bound to Otago, Dunedin. 31.3.1888: Last sighting. 3.10.1888: Lifebuoy washed ashore at Knysna, South Africa.

T 4. BERAR (1863 - 1883) Iron Ship
O.N. 48529. 902 tons. 188.5 x 32.4 x 20.3 feet.
16.6.1863: Launched by Pile, Hay & Company, Sunderland (Yard No. 19), for G. D. Tyser, London. 3.10.1863: Completed. 7.1883: Sold to Foley & Company, London. 1895: Reduced to a barque. 1895: Sold to G. Bertolotto, Genoa. 7.10.1896: Whilst on a voyage from Borga to Seville with a cargo of deals and planks, wrecked off Charton Bay, near Seaton, Devon, and later broke in two.

T 5. HIMALAYA (1863 - 1873) Iron Ship
O.N. 48594. 1,008 tons. 201.6 x 33.0 x 20.5 feet.
26.11.1863: Launched by Pile, Hay & Company, Sunderland (Yard No. 20), for G. D. Tyser, London. 1873: Sold to Shaw, Savill. 1879: Reduced to a barque. 1882: Transferred to Shaw, Savill & Albion. 1897: Sold to J. J. Moore & Company, Valparaiso, Chile. 1903: Sold to Alaska Packers Association, San Francisco, and renamed STAR OF PERU. 1926: Sold to Burns, Philip Company (San Francisco) Inc. 1927: Sold to Comptoirs Francais des Nouvelles Hebrides, Port Vila, and renamed BOUGAINVILLE. Used as coal hulk and later sold for demolition.

T 6. HOWRAH (1864 - 1890) Iron Ship
O.N. 50033.1,098 tons. 207.7 x 33.6 x 21.2 feet.
4.6.1864: Launched by Pile, Hay & Company, Sunderland (Yard No. 124), for G. D. Tyser, London. 5.7.1864: Completed. 28.5.1890: Sold to A. & L. Verdeau Freres & Company, Bordeaux, France, and renamed TOURNY. 1892: Sold to Verdeau et Cie., Bordeaux. 1899: Sold to G. Dor, Marseilles. 1903: Sold to L. Mortola fu A. Genoa, and renamed AGOSTINO M. 1911: Demolished at Genoa.

T 7. POONAH (1867 - 1895) Iron Ship
O.N. 56889. 1,199 tons. 223.5 x 34.9 x 21.8 feet.
28.10.1867: Launched by William Pile & Company, Sunderland (Yard No. 157), for G. D. Tyser, London. 5.3.1895: Sold to H. Janentzky, Rostock. 1902: Sold to Th. Nordaas, Egersund, Norway, and renamed LEIF. 5.12.1905: Whilst on a voyage from Cork to Bridgwater stranded in the River Parret, Bridgwater.

T 8. ARCOT (1868 - 1871) Iron Ship
O.N. 60864. 1,191 tons. 223.3 x 34.8 x 21.8 feet.
8.7.1868: Launched by William Pile & Company, Sunderland (Yard No. 165), for G. D. Tyser, London. 24.7.1868: Completed. 10.4.1871: Sailed from Calcutta for London with general cargo. 4.6.1871: Last sighted in position 36S., 24E., off the Cape of Good Hope.

T 9. NORTH (1868 - 1895) Iron Ship
O.N. 58907. 1,333 tons. 220.4 x 37.1 x 22.6 feet.
8.1868: Launched by G. R. Clover & Company, Birkenhead (Yard No.18), for G. D. Tyser, London. 24.6.1895: Sold to G. Casabona & Company, Genoa, and renamed CASABONA. 3.1906: Sold for demolition.

T 10. LIGHTNING (1872 - 1881) Iron Ship
O.N. 48506. 1,194 tons. 210.8 x 35.0 x 23.0 feet.
29.10.1863: Launched by M. Samuelson, Hull, for Kendall Bros, Liverpool. 1868: Sold to Guion Line, Liverpool. 1868: Sold to J. Morrison, London. 1872: Sold to G. D. Tyser, London. 1878: Reduced to a barque. 6.11.1881: Departed from New York bound for London with general cargo and disappeared.

T 11. PLASSEY (1874 - 1883) Iron Ship
O.N. 70579. 1,764 tons. 258.5 x 40.1 x 23.7 feet.
14.5.1874: Launched by Assignees of William Pile & Company (Bankrupt), Sunderland (Yard No. 236), for G. D. Tyser, London. 23.12.1882: Departed from Demerara bound for London with a cargo of sugar and rum. 29.1.1883: At 1 a.m, stranded at Sandgate, near Dover, Kent, with very little damage. 2.2.1883: During a very heavy gale the vessel broke up. Of the seven people who were aboard at the time, four were rescued, three including a customs officer were drowned. 15.2.1883: The hull was sold for £800 and sundry items disposed of, for £550.

T 12. LUCKNOW (1883 - 1889) Steel Ship
O.N. 87113. 1,494 tons. 245.3 x 37.1 x 22.4 feet.
10.4.1883: Launched by William Doxford & Company, Sunderland (Yard No. 146), for G. D. Tyser, London. 22.2.1889: Departed from Newcastle, New South Wales bound for San Francisco with a cargo of coal. 12.3.1889: Last sighted in position 33S., 179E.

T 13. ROUEN (1888 - 1894) Twin Screw Iron Lighter converted from being non-powered.
O.N. 91946. 221g. 147.0 x 21.0 x 7.7 feet.
Post 1886: Two T.3-cyl. steam engines manufactured by Koninklijke Maatschappij De Schelde, Flushing. 40 hp.
1872: Completed as VLISSINGEN by J. & K. Smit, Kinderdyk, for unspecified Dutch owners. 1886: New engine and boiler fitted. 1888: Sold to G. W & W. H. Tyser, London, and renamed ROUEN, for use between London and Rouen. 1889: Sold to Colonial Union Company, London, (Tyser managers). 1890: Sold to the Tyser Line Ltd., (Tyser & Company, managers), London. 1894: Sold to W. Reid & Company Ltd., Rockhampton, Australia. 1895: Owners restyled Hunter Reid & Company Ltd. 13.6.1898: Whilst on a voyage from Keppel Bay to Rockhampton, in ballast, was sunk in a collision at Rockhampton.

T 14. HAWKES BAY (1) (1891 - 1912)
O.N. 98893. 4,583g. 2,960n. 383.1 x 48.0 x 22.2 feet.
T.3-cyl. steam engine manufactured by the shipbuilder. 495 nhp. 12kts.
27.11.1890: Launched by William Doxford & Sons, Sunderland (Yard No. 201), for the Tyser Line Ltd. (Tyser & Company, managers), London. 2.1891: Completed. 18.3.1912: Sold to the Chasehill Steamship Company Ltd. (Kaye, Son & Company Ltd, managers), London. 27.3.1912: Renamed CHASEHILL. 22.2.1915: Whilst on a voyage from Newport, Mon., to Zarate, Argentine Republic, with a cargo of coal, was captured by the German armed merchant cruiser KRONPRINZ WILHELM in a position 06.15S., 28.15W. 9.3.1915: Heavily damaged, was released, after her cargo had been removed,

in a position 06.57S. 26.05W. Prisoners previously captured by the raider were transferred and despatched in this vessel. 12.3.1915: Arrived at Pernambuco. 8.6.1915: Sold to Essex Chase Steamship Company Ltd. (Meldrum & Swinson, managers), London. 18.1.1916: Whilst on a voyage from New York to Le Havre with general cargo, foundered in North Atlantic in position approximately 40N., 63W. Her crew of 32 were saved.

HAWKES BAY (Ambrose Greenway collection)

T 15. TOMOANA (1899 - 1912)

O.N. 110136. 6,837g. 4,428n. 440.0 x 54.3 x 29.6 feet.
T.3-cyl. steam engine manufactured by G. Clark Ltd., Sunderland. 515 nhp. 12kts.
11.3.1899: Launched by Sir J. Laing & Sons Ltd., Sunderland (Yard No. 540), for the Tomoana Steamship Company Ltd. (Tyser & Company, managers), London. 6.1899: Completed. 14.1.1903: Transferred to Tyser Line Ltd., (same managers). 24.6.1912: Sold to the Brodvale Steamship Company Ltd. (The Blue Star Line Ltd., managers), London. 13.9.1912: Renamed BRODVALE. 15.4.1920: Transferred to the Union Cold Storage Company Ltd. (Blue Star Line (1920) Ltd., managers), London. 7.6.1920: Renamed TUDORSTAR. 3.9.1929: Transferred to Blue Star Line (1920) Ltd., London. 27.9.1929: Renamed TUDOR STAR. 20.5.1930: Owners restyled as Blue Star Line Ltd. 8.1934: Sold for £8.000, to S.A. Ricuperi Metallici, Italy, for demolition. 6.10.1934: Arrived at Savona, Italy.

MIMIRO (Copied by Tom Rayner)

T 16. MIMIRO (1900 - 1914)
O.N. 112681. 6,225g. 4,025n. 440.0 x 55.1 x 29.9 feet.
T.3-cyl. steam engine manufactured by the shipbuilder. 570 nhp. 12kts. Refrigerated capacity 237,000 cu.ft.
30.1.1900: Launched by Workman, Clark & Company Ltd., Belfast (Yard No. 162), for the Tyser Line Ltd. (Tyser & Company, managers), London. 22.3.1900: Sold to the Mimiro Steamship Company Ltd. (same managers), London. 8.1902: Whilst on a voyage from Auckland to Wellington, towed the steamer TAVIUNI into Gisborne after she had broken her tail shaft. 7.5.1903: Sold to Tyser Line Ltd. (same managers). 13.2.1914: Transferred to The Commonwealth & Dominion Line Ltd., London. 30.8.1916: Renamed PORT HACKING. 18.9.1916: In collision off Dover with VIRGINIA 1.1928: Sold for £13,150 to unspecified Italian buyers. 3.1928: Sold for £16,000, to Andrea Zanchi, Genoa, Italy, and renamed CAPO NORD. 1933: Sold for demolition in Italy.

NIWARU (A. Duncan)

T 17. NIWARU (1902 - 1914)
O.N. 114854. 6,444g. 4,170n. 450.0 x 55.2 x 30.2 feet.
Two T.3-cyl. steam engines manufactured by the shipbuilder. Twin screw. 583 nhp. 12kts. Refrigerated capacity 252,000 cu.ft.
24.12.1901: Launched by Workman, Clark & Company Ltd., Belfast (Yard No. 183), for the Tyser Line Ltd. (Tyser & Company, managers), London. 15.3.1902: Completed. 19.7.1903: Struck rocks near the breakwater at Napier, when inbound from Auckland. 14.8.1903: Arrived at Auckland to dry-dock and undergo repair. 13.2.1914: Transferred to The Commonwealth & Dominion Line Ltd., London 25.7.1916: Renamed PORT LYTTELTON. 23.1.1924: Stranded at Tamar Heads, Tasmania. Subsequently salvaged. 23.10.1924: Sold to L. E. Conti, Italy, for demolition.

T 18. MARERE (1902 - 1914)
O.N. 115941. 6,443g. 4,160n. 450.0 x 55.2 x 30.4 feet.
Two T.3-cyl. steam engines manufactured by the shipbuilder. Twin screw. 583 nhp. 12kts. Refrigerated capacity 252,000 cu.ft.
17.11.1902: Launched by Workman, Clark & Company Ltd., Belfast (Yard No. 194), for the Tyser Line Ltd. (Tyser & Company, managers), London. 12.1902: Completed. 5.1906: In collision off Gravesend with AIREDALE. 1914: Transferred to The Commonwealth & Dominion Line Ltd., London. 18.1.1916: Whilst on a voyage from Fremantle and Mudros to Gibraltar with general cargo, was sunk with gunfire by the German submarine U 35, in position 35.51N., 19.70E. Her crew were picked by HM Hospital ship NEURALIA and landed at Alexandria.

MARERE (Ambrose Greenway collection)

WHAKARUA (Ambrose Greenway collection)

T 19. WHAKARUA (1907 - 1914)

O.N. 125591. 6,534g. 4,198n. 450.3 x 55.3 x 30.4 feet.
Two T.3-cyl. steam engines manufactured by the shipbuilder. Twin screw. 650 nhp. 12kts. Refrigerated capacity: 256,000 cu.ft.
30.5.1907: Launched by Workman, Clark & Company Ltd., Belfast (Yard No. 247), for the Tyser Line Ltd. (Tyser & Company, managers), London. 10.7.1907: Completed. 16.2.1908: Whilst on a voyage from London to Australia, suffered a serious fire and put into Cape Town for repairs. 13.2.1914: Transferred to The Commonwealth & Dominion Line Ltd., London. 30.8.1916: Renamed PORT CHALMERS. 12.3.1917: Chased by a submarine off South West Ireland. Her gunfire drove the submarine off and she reached port safely. 1922 until June 1925: Suffered various machinery problems. 1926: Sold for £30.000 to Italian shipbreakers. 24.6.1926: Resold to Andrea Zanchi, Genoa, and renamed NORGE. 21.12.1940: Whilst on a voyage from Palermo to Tripoli, was sunk by air attack 35 miles south of Kerkenna, Tunisia, in position 34.39N., 10.48E.

NEREHANA (Ambrose Greenway collection)

T 20. NEREHANA   (1907 - 1914)

O.N. 125633. 6,533g. 4,196n. 450.3 x 55.3 x 30.4 feet.
Two T.3-cyl. steam engines manufactured by the shipbuilder.   Twin screw. 650 nhp. 12kts. Refrigerated capacity 252,000 cu.ft.
27.8.1907: Launched by Workman, Clark & Company Ltd., Belfast (Yard No. 248), for the Tyser Line Ltd. (Tyser & Company, managers), London.   30.10.1907: Completed.   1914: Transferred to The Commonwealth & Dominion Line Ltd., London.   3.4.1916: Renamed PORT HARDY.   6.7.1918: Whilst on a voyage from Buenos Ayres to Genoa with a cargo of oats, wheat and frozen meat, was torpedoed and sunk by the German submarine U 91, 78 miles W. by N. of Cape Spartel, Morocco.   7 members of her crew were lost.

T 21. MURITAI   (1910 - 1914)

O.N. 129099. 7,280g. 4,645n. 470.0 x 58.2 x 31.7 feet.
Two T.3-cyl. steam engines manufactured by the shipbuilder. Twin screw. 727 nhp. 12kts. Refrigerated capacity 295,000 cu.ft.
28.4.1910: Launched by Workman, Clark & Company Ltd., Belfast (Yard No. 291), for the Tyser Line Ltd. (Tyser & Company, managers), London.   8.6.1910: Completed.   13.2.1914: Transferred to The Commonwealth & Dominion Line Ltd., London.   28.9.1916: Renamed PORT VICTOR. 26.9.1917: Torpedoed by submarine 30 miles south of St. Catherine's Point, reached Southampton under her own power where her cargo was discharged and temporary repairs undertaken. Subsequently returned to Belfast for permanent repairs by her builders. 11.1935: Sold to P. & W. McLellan, Bo'ness for demolition. 10.11.1935: Arrived at Bo'ness in tow of the tug QUEENS CROSS (286g./21).

T 22. MAKARINI (1912 - 1914)

O.N. 132703. 10,624g. 6,943n. 10,024d. 490.2 x 61.4 x 32.9 feet.
Two T.3-cyl. steam engines manufactured by the shipbuilder.   Twin screw. 804 nhp. 13kts. Refrigerated capacity 330,000 cu.ft.
3.12.1912: Launched by Workman, Clark & Company Ltd., Belfast (Yard No. 310), for the Tyser Line Ltd. (Tyser & Company, managers), London.   25.4.1912: Completed.   13.2.1914: Transferred to The Commonwealth & Dominion Line Ltd., London. 22.5.1916: Renamed PORT NICHOLSON. 15.1.1917: Whilst on a voyage from Sydney to Dunkirk with meat and general cargo, exploded a mine laid by the German submarine UC 1, and sank in position 51.02N., 01.58E., 15 miles W. ½ N. from Dunkirk.   2 members of her crew were lost.

MAKARINI (Ambrose Greenway collection)

HAWKES BAY (R. A. Snook)

T 23. HAWKES BAY (2) (1912 - 1914)

O.N. 135175. 10,641g. 6841n. 490.2 x 61.4 x 32.9 feet.
Two T.3-cyl. steam engines manufactured the shipbuilder. Twin screw. 804 nhp. 13kts. Refrigerated capacity 330,000 cu.ft.
27.9.1912: Launched by Workman, Clark & Company Ltd., Belfast (Yard No. 313), for the Tyser Line Ltd. (Tyser & Company, managers), London. 19.12.1912: Completed. 12.2.1914: Transferred to The Commonwealth & Dominion Line Ltd., London. 20.6.1916: Renamed PORT NAPIER. 24.8.1928: On fire 106 miles from Pago Pago, where she was later docked and the fire extinguished by members of the ships crew and personnel of the US Navy. 16.12.1936: Sold for £28,000 free of commission, to T. & J. Brocklebank Ltd., Liverpool. 29.12.1936: Renamed MARTAND at Middlesbrough. 20.4.1938: Sold to Andrea Zanchi, Genoa, and renamed MARTANO. 7.1938: Fitted for oil fuel. 1938: Renamed MAR BIANCO, same owners. 9.1943: Taken over by Germany at Venice. 7.12.1943: While under the German flag, was bombed and sunk at Zara, Dalmatia, Yugoslavia.

PART No. 2

Post Amalgamation.

1. The Commonwealth & Dominion Line Ltd.

The Commonwealth & Dominion Line Ltd. was an amalgamation of four family concerns: Tyser & Company, part of the Star Line of James P. Corry & Company, part of the Indra Line of T. B. Royden & Company, and William Milburn and their Anglo-Australasian Steam Navigation Company. All these shipping companies were already well established in trade with Australia and New Zealand, the group at its formation owned 23 steamers afloat with two more about to be completed.

Established with a capital of £2,000,000, its objectives were:- to acquire and carry on the business of shipowners; shipbuilders; shipbrokers; insurance brokers; managers of shipping property; importers; exporters; freight contractors; carriers by land and sea; barge owners; lightermen; forwarding agents; and, also to enter into agreements with:-

The Tyser Line Ltd. and Tyser & Company of 9 & 11, Fenchurch Street, London,
The Anglo-Australasian Steam Navigation Company Ltd. and William Milburn & Company, of 130, Fenchurch Street, London,
The Indra Line Ltd., T. B. Royden of 20, Brown's Buildings, Liverpool,
The Star Line Ltd., and James P. Corry & Company of 9 & 11, Fenchurch Street, London.

The first directors appointed were:
W. P. Tyser, P. K. F. Foot and Sir E. Montague Nelson K.C.M.G., from Tyser & Company.
Sir William Corry Bt. and R. Corry from the Star Line of James P. Corry & Company.
T. Royden from T. B. Royden & Company.
C. T. Milburn and W. H. Moore of William Milburn & Company.

Their remuneration was set at £500 each per annum. Qualifications (other than first directors), 1,000 shares. The Registered Office of the "Private Company" was situated at 9 & 11, Fenchurch Street, London.

At the initial meeting of the Board of Directors on 28th January 1914 it was decided "to leave the question of the appointment of the first Chairman in abeyance for the present". Mr W. P. Tyser was unanimously requested to act as Chairman at the meeting and he also did so at the following three subsequent monthly meetings.

When the board met on 14th May 1914 Mr W. P. Tyser was elected first Chairman of the Company and Mr C. T. Milburn Vice-Chairman. The following were elected managing directors: W. P. Tyser, C. T. Milburn, P. K. F. Foot (Tyser), W. H. Moore (Milburn), R. Corry and Sir William Corry, Bt.

At the amalgamation in 1914 the whole of the shipping office staff from Tyser's, Corry's and Milburn's were taken over but only one man came over from the Royden office. He was Mr J. R. Rooper (grandson of Sir Thomas B. Royden and nephew of Mr Thomas Royden, later Lord Royden), and he was to play a prominent part in the affairs of the company on both sides of the world and eventually to become a managing director in London and his son, David Royden Rooper, subsequently became a director of Port Line.

A re-arrangement of the Tyser and Corry offices at 9 & 11, Fenchurch Avenue, was made to cope with the influx of Milburn staff.

A notice appeared in 'Lloyds List' on Wednesday 28th January 1914 under New Companies Registered. Newspaper accounts at first stated that all the fleet of the Indra Line were being taken over which was not the case, as only three ships were transferred. The first advert for the new company appeared in 'Lloyds List' on Friday 30th January 1914 and a Bill of Sale for 23 steamers was signed on the 12th March 1914

At the time the Commonwealth & Dominion Line was formed the funnels of the ships of the different companies were: buff with a black top for the Tyser and Corry steamers; red with a black top for Royden; and black for Milburn. It was now decided, however, to adopt the Tyser Line colours - buff with a black top and grey hull. A minute of the first board meeting on 28th January 1914 reads: "The Board decided to adopt the present House Flag of the Tyser Line Ltd. as the House Flag of the Commonwealth & Dominion Line Ltd.".

At the time of the amalgamation the Tyser Line, the Indra Line and the Star Line had been running a joint service for many years and all wore the Tyser Flag at the fore and their own at the mainmast. The fourth company, William Milburn & Company, had two house flags, one was blue with W.M. & Co.

or just W.M. in white, and the other a pennant of blue with more white letters. All were unsuitable so the Tyser Flag was adopted.

Tyser were the dominant party of the amalgamation and their flag and ship colouring (grey hull, white deck houses) was adopted. In the event to make it not appear as a Tyser takeover Milburn's naming prefix "PORT" and the Star Line red funnels with black tops were adopted.

Mid-way through the First World War, on the 5th May 1916, the directors entered into an agreement with the Cunard Steamship Company Ltd. whereby they took over all the shares of the Commonwealth & Dominion Line Ltd. in exchange for Cunard shares and debentures and some War Loan and cash. One of the results of this was that C. T. Milburn and W. P. Tyser became the two largest shareholders in the Cunard Company.

Sir Alfred Booth Bt. and Sir Percy Bates Bt, Cunard directors, joined the Board of the Commonwealth & Dominion Line, whilst its Chairman (Mr W. P. Tyser), Vice-Chairman (Mr C. T. Milburn) and Sir William Corry Bt. became directors of Cunard. Mr T. Royden was already a member of the board of both companies and eventually followed Sir Alfred Booth and preceded Sir Percy Bates as Chairman of Cunard.

For a time the subsidiary title of "Cunard Line Australasian Service, Commonwealth & Dominion Line Ltd." was adopted, but this proved unwieldy and fell into disuse. It was not until 1937 that the name was formally changed to Port Line.

Although better known as the pre-eminent operator on the North Atlantic, the Cunard Steamship Company made a significant contribution to the development of the Australian and New Zealand trades through Port Line.

Hardly had this new company started operating when it was beset with the problems of World War One. Of the 25 ships in service on 4th August 1914 seven were lost through enemy action and two through collision.

Throughout the war years the building of new ships went on, as circumstances and Government licences permitted.

On the 3rd December 1914 a report in the 'Shipbuilding and Shipping Record' stated that the Commonwealth & Dominion Line had ordered a steamer of 9,000 tons from Workman, Clark & Company, Belfast. This was the first new tonnage ordered by the company since the amalgamation. Over the course of the next few months three further ships were ordered.

The war delayed the agreed delivery of these vessels that should have started from June 1916 but actually commenced in January 1918 with Yard No. 351, PORT DARWIN (2).

In mid-1916 the Board had decided to name all its ships with the prefix "Port", a style adopted by Wm. Milburn since 1883 and PORT DARWIN (2) was the name chosen for this the first new ship completed for the company. She was followed in April by Yard No. 352, PORT DENISON (3), that had also been delayed by the War.

The third and fourth vessels, Yard No. 356, PORT BOWEN and Yard No. 358, PORT CAROLINE (4) had also been due for delivery in late 1916 but were not completed until after the war had ended.
During 1915 the PORT PIRIE (2) was sold for £38,078 to other British owners after first being reported sold to Italian buyers. The directors did not deem her suitable for the trading pattern envisaged for the new company.

On the 11th May 1916 an order for three ships, Yard No. 487, PORT NICHOLSON (2), Yard No. 488, PORT ADELAIDE (3) and Yard No. 489, PORT KEMBLA (2) was placed with Hawthorn, Leslie. Further orders were placed on 17th August 1917 for another two twin-screw turbine vessels from the same builders, Yard No. 502, PORT HUNTER (4) and Yard No. 503, PORT HARDY (2).

PORT MACQUARIE
Displaying wartime
Pennant No. A39

(World Ship Society
Photograph Library)

PORT MELBOURNE Displaying wartime Pennant No. A16 (World Ship Society Photograph Library)

PORT PIRIE In wartime grey. HMNZT No.8. on her stern (World Ship Society Photograph Library)

    Meanwhile some of the company's ships had been requisitioned early in the war by the Governments of Australia and New Zealand as well as Britain for transporting large numbers of troops. In 1917 the situation at sea had become very serious and the British Government commandeered all the company's remaining ships employed in the Australian and New Zealand trade. The ships continued, however, to be managed by their owners but were subject to the directions of the Shipping Controller.

    First to be requisitioned, by the Admiralty in September 1914, was the MURITAI, followed by HAWKES BAY (2) and the STAR OF INDIA requisitioned by New Zealand Government at 20/- a gross ton, closely followed by the STAR OF ENGLAND, STAR OF VICTORIA, PORT LINCOLN and the MARERE all requisitioned by Australian Government at prices to be agreed.

    In September of 1914, the STAR OF ENGLAND (2) was fitted out in Australia for the carriage of 530 officers and men and 500 hundred horses. As HMT "A15" she left Brisbane on 24th September for Liverpool with 32 officers and 1,557 troops. Joining a convoy at Albany, Western Australia which consisted of 38 transports and four warships including her sister, the STAR OF VICTORIA (2), they sailed for Europe together with other ships of the Commonwealth & Dominion Line, the PORT LINCOLN (1), MARERE, HAWKES BAY (2) and the STAR OF INDIA.

On 5th November 1914 the convoy conveying the 2nd Division, Australian Imperial Force received a wireless message from the Cocos Islands stating that they were being shelled by the German cruiser EMDEN. The Australian cruiser SYDNEY left the convoy and disposed of the EMDEN. In January 1915, the STAR OF ENGLAND (2) and the PORT LINCOLN (1) were again required by the Australian Government for second voyages with troops. For the rest of the war the STAR OF ENGLAND (2) was employed carrying troops from Australia to England and France, but also made one voyage to the Greek port of Salonika. In June 1916, her name was changed to PORT SYDNEY (1) and later in December, she left London and made six voyages from Australia and New Zealand to Suez. PORT SYDNEY (1) resumed peace-time trading after being reconditioned by the Cockatoo Dockyard, Sydney following her return to Australia in July 1919. As a memento of her trooping service the 2nd Light Horse (Queensland) A.I.F. 1914 presented the ship with a gangway bell as a token of appreciation.

The MURITAI, which had been requisitioned in September 1914, was redelivered to the company at Chatham after one voyage and then sailed for New Zealand in ballast, the Government paying £5,000 in consideration.

During June 1915 the PORT LINCOLN (1) sailed from Tilbury under the Australian Blue Ensign as HMT. "A 17". Fitted out with accommodation for 1,000 men and 22 officers, her only armament consisted of half a dozen rifles and a 12-pounder gun. Arriving at Devonport she embarked 250 troopers of the Warwickshire Yeomanry and 500 horses for Alexandria. After discharge in Alexandria she continued on to the Dardanelles with a water distilling plant that was unloaded using the heavy lifting gear of the 'Duncan' class battleship HMS CORNWALLIS. Refitted to carry sick and walking wounded, the PORT LINCOLN (1) sailed for Sydney, where the 12-pounder gun was removed and a 4.7in gun of Japanese origin was fitted. Arriving back in the United Kingdom in early 1917, she later sailed from Swansea, trooping for a further year. Transferred to North Atlantic from May - September 1918, she was employed transporting United States troops from Montreal to Liverpool, sailing outward in ballast.

The first casualty of the war was the MARERE sunk by submarine gunfire from U35 in position 35.51N., 19.70E., 236 miles east of Malta on 18th January 1916 whilst on a voyage from Fremantle via Mudros to Gibraltar with general cargo. Her crew were picked by HM Hospital ship NEURALIA and landed at Alexandria. The company received a sum from the government of £105,000 in respect of her loss.

During April 1916 the PORT CURTIS (1) one of only four-non refrigerated ships operated by the company, was requisitioned by the Admiralty, but during the same month was released to enable her to carry coal to South America. Later, in September the PORT HACKING was involved in a collision off Dover with the VIRGINIA owned by the Texas Steamship Company.

The year 1917 was an unfortunate one for the company starting on the 15th January when the PORT NICHOLSON (1) was sunk by a mine laid by UC 1 fifteen miles from Dunkirk, whilst on a voyage from Sydney to Dunkirk with meat and general cargo. Two members of her crew were lost. During February the PORT ADELAIDE (2) was ordered by the Shipping Controller to load meat in New Zealand for London and whilst outward bound to Sydney she was sunk by U 81 in the North Atlantic 180 miles west-south-west of Fastnet, with her master was taken prisoner. In March the PORT CHALMERS (2) was chased by a submarine off the south-west coast of Ireland. After a fierce gun battle, she out ran the submarine and reached port safely.

Later in May the PORT CAMPBELL (1) and PORT VICTOR (2) were chartered to carry coal, and in the same month the PORT CAMPBELL (1), PORT VICTOR (2), PORT PIRIE (3), and the PORT HACKING were ordered by the Government to make return voyages to the River Plate.

On 7th August the PORT CURTIS (1) was captured by UC 71 whilst on a voyage from Bahia Blanca to Cherbourg with a cargo of oats and later sunk by a delayed charge 70 miles west of Penmarch, off the south-west coast of France. The company claimed £184,000 for her loss from the Ministry. The following month the loss of the PORT KEMBLA (1) off Cape Farewell, New Zealand was reported, whilst on passage from Melbourne to London with a cargo of meat. At first it was thought that she had been sunk by an internal explosion, but it later transpired that she had hit a mine laid by the German raider WOLF. Later, on the 26th of the same month, the PORT VICTOR (2) was torpedoed by a submarine 30 miles south of St. Catherine's Point, Isle of Wight, however, she reached Southampton under her own power where her cargo was discharged. Temporary repairs were undertaken there before proceeding to Belfast where her builders Workman, Clark & Company, carried out permanent repairs.

During November 1917 the Ministry of Shipping ordered the PORT CHALMERS (2) to make a round trip to the River Plate and the PORT NAPIER (1) to proceed to Cape Town with returned contract workers and coal and afterwards proceed to the River Plate to load frozen meat for the United Kingdom.

From December and through to February 1918 the PORT AUGUSTA (2), PORT PHILLIP (4), PORT HARDY (1) and the PORT ELLIOT (2) made several return voyages to the United States, whilst the PORT ALBANY (1) was ordered to the River Plate in early 1918 to load a cargo of frozen meat for the United Kingdom.

It was not until the 7th April 1918 that another ship was lost. This was the PORT CAMPBELL (1) that was torpedoed by U 53, 115 miles west-south-west of Bishop Rock whilst on a voyage from London to New York. The company claimed £230,000 from the Ministry in respect of her loss.

During April all the company's steamers, with the exception of the PORT DARWIN (2), PORT SYDNEY (1), PORT ALMA (1), PORT HACKING and the PORT LYTTELTON (1) were working the River Plate trade.

The last World War One loss through enemy action was on 6th July 1918 when the PORT HARDY (1) was torpedoed and sunk by U 91 with the loss of seven crew members, 78 miles west by north of Cape Spartel, Morocco whilst on a voyage from Buenos Ayres to Genoa with a cargo of frozen meat, wheat and oats. £135,000 was claimed from Ministry for her loss.

On the first day of August 1918 the PORT STEPHENS (2) was in collision with and sank the steamer NORTH CAMBRIA approx 70-80 miles west of Ushant. The last losses in World War One were not caused by enemy action but by collision. In October the PORT PHILLIP (4) sank after colliding with the large collier USS PROTEUS (AC 9) in Gravesend Bay, Ambrose Channel, New York, whilst outward bound for Le Havre with a cargo of steel billets and general cargo. Two weeks later, the PORT HUNTER (3) was beached on Hedgefence, Vineyard Shoal, Nantucket, after a collision with the U.S. Navy tug COVINGTON and became a total loss.

Release from wartime requisition started in April 1919 with the PORT LINCOLN (1), PORT MELBOURNE (2), PORT DENISON (3), PORT PIRIE (2), PORT CHALMERS (2) and the PORT NAPIER (1). It took until September for the board to report that all the company's steamers had been released. Previous to this the WAR HECUBA a standard war built ship and the VALENCIA, late of the Hamburg America Line had been placed under management.

On the 9th October 1919, the Cunard funnel colours were adopted: i.e. black top and red below with the addition of two narrow black bands. The hulls, however, remained Tyser grey but later changed to the more stable Pacific grey.

In the same month the board discussed the great shortage of outward cargo to Australia and considered the advisability of carrying Third Class passengers in any of the company's steamers that were suitable. It was decided, as an experiment, to book Third Class passengers onto PORT NAPIER (1), for her next outward voyage. If the response proved satisfactory the experiment would be continued, with the PORT DARWIN (2) that would follow her outwards shortly afterwards. In the event, the British Government requisitioned the whole of the space for passengers in the PORT NAPIER (1) to accommodate returning Australian families and it was then decided not to adapt the PORT DARWIN (2), for passenger traffic, due largely to the difficulty and expense in converting cargo ships to comply with Board of Trade regulations.

2. Post-War Reconstruction.

The loss of seven ships by enemy action and two by collision in World War One together with the need to replace obsolete tonnage resulted in an extensive replacement programme that although started in 1916, was delayed due to Admiralty commitments. Over six years, 11 steamers were delivered; six by Workman, Clark & Company (later part of the Harland & Wolff Ltd.) Belfast, and five by Hawthorn, Leslie & Company of Hebburn-on-Tyne. With one exception, these steamers were all 480 feet long, twin-screw, with five holds and a speed of some $12^1/_2$ knots. The exception was the PORT WELLINGTON (1), completed in 1924 and the last coal burner built for the company. Also purchased at this time was the PORT CURTIS (2) a standard G class ship (proposed as WAR THALIA) built by Workman, Clark & Company, Belfast and delivered in 1920.

The 11 new steamers were all to have been driven by steam turbine engines, the steam being supplied from coal-fired boilers. The turbine blades in some of the first six ships suffered damage which took over six months to repair. As a result of this trouble, the decision was taken not to fit steam turbines to the remaining five ships but to revert to the well-proven steam reciprocating triple-expansion engine. Even though the reciprocating engines, developed less power than the turbine installations. To recover the knot lost in speed, modifications were carried out in the late 1920's with a turbine being fitted to the propeller shafting which was driven by exhaust steam from the reciprocating engine. Thus extra horsepower needed to increase the speed was obtained without increasing the size of the boilers. This was the Bauer-Wach system, the invention of two German engineers. A low-pressure turbine with double reduction gearing driving through a hydraulic clutch was fitted. The exhaust steam from the low-pressure cylinder had previously gone directly into the condenser but it now went via the exhaust turbine to the condenser. This resulted in an increase in power of about 15% on the same fuel consumption. An automatic coupling threw this turbine out of gear the moment the engines were manoeuvred and it was the difficulty of inventing this which did much to delay the application of the principle.

The advantages of the motorship were well known in the early 1920s. The main benefit was a smaller engine room squad, plus the ability to convey fuel in the double bottom tanks and thereby make available what would have been coal bunker space for cargo. The motorship was examined very closely by the Commonwealth & Dominion Line in the post-war period, other leading shipping companies such as Furness, Withy and the Silver Line had already seen the advantages.

Herbert W. Corry and J. R. Rooper, had been impressed at how successful Scandinavian motor ships trading to Australia and New Zealand were and urged that this method of propulsion should be adopted. They found H. G. Dearden a willing ally and in this he had the encouragement of his chief Alexander MacDonald. During the post-war re-building programme the company took the bold decision to build motor ships. Two motor ships, the PORT HOBART (1) and the PORT DUNEDIN, were ordered and both were launched in the same week in March 1925, one at Wallsend-on-Tyne (Swan, Hunter & Wigham Richardson Ltd.) and the other at Belfast (Workman, Clark & Company). These were the first British twin-screw refrigerated motor ships to trade regularly between the United Kingdom and Australia and New Zealand. Their construction was the most far-reaching decision taken by any British line in this trade up to that time. The engine chosen was the patented two-stroke opposed piston oil engine designed and made by William Doxford & Sons, Sunderland.

This major decision was very successful as all subsequent vessels built for the company were motorships and it must have been a great relief to all concerned as the previous decision to try turbines was not far short of a disaster.

The PORT DUNEDIN and the PORT HOBART (1), when completed had a total insulated cargo space of 297,000 cu ft and an uninsulated capacity of 307,000 cu ft., and were the first twin-screw vessels ever fitted with Doxford main engines. The PORT DUNEDIN's main engines developed 5,680 horsepower to give a service speed of 13 knots and it is worthy of note that the same engine at the end of 37 years' service gave this ship the same average speed on her last voyage in 1962.

The period immediately after World War One saw prices of labour and materials increase dramatically and the Commonwealth & Dominion Line entered into negotiations with Hawthorn, Leslie in an effort to keep down costs. Abstracts from the minute books of the Commonwealth & Dominion Line give a good idea of the problems faced by both shipowner and shipbuilder. Between April 1920 and February 1923 a considerable amount of correspondence flowed between the two parties.

On the 8th April 1920, due to the high cost of labour and the increased cost of steel, Hawthorn, Leslie informed the Commonwealth & Dominion Line that they were prepared to accept a £35,000 fixed sum profit in respect of the five ships the PORT NICHOLSON (2), PORT ADELAIDE (3), PORT KEMBLA (2), PORT HUNTER (4) and the PORT HARDY (2). This was instead of 10% on cost which they were entitled under agreements of 11th May 1916 and the 17th August 1917, when the ships were originally ordered. This was agreed by the Commonwealth & Dominion Line.

On the 4th May 1921 a letter was received by Hawthorn, Leslie from the Commonwealth & Dominion Line requesting suspension of work on Yard No. 502, PORT HUNTER (4) and Yard No. 503, PORT HARDY (2).

On the 30th August a letter was again received from the Commonwealth & Dominion Line requesting a coat of paint to the steelwork of these two vessels.

On the 7th October Hawthorn, Leslie received permission from the Commonwealth & Dominion Line to proceed on the machinery of the PORT HUNTER (4) using apprentices at a cost of £170 a week.

On the 21st October the necessary preparatory work to launching the PORT HUNTER (4) was completed and all men were taken off the ship. The launch was postponed indefinitely although the work on the machinery proceeded at £170 a week.

On the 9th February 1922 work was restarted on the PORT HUNTER (4) and the PORT HARDY (2), with the launch of the former being set for 14th or 15th March. It was decided to despatch the two Low Pressure port and starboard rotors, together with their split diaphragms, to the PORT KEMBLA in substitution for the defective rotors that were now being removed from this vessel. This would necessarily delay the ultimate completion of the machinery for the PORT HUNTER (4). On the 9th June 1922 Hawthorn, Leslie received instructions from Commonwealth & Dominion for twin-screw triple-expansion engines to be fitted to the PORT HUNTER (4) instead of the double-geared turbine machinery originally ordered and at this time partially constructed.

A couple months later the decision was taken to change the engines of the PORT HARDY (2) from a turbine installation to triple-expansion. However it was only the PORT HARDY (2) that had triples fitted instead of the intended turbine installation as the following letter explains.

To The Commonwealth & Dominion Line,
9 & 11, Fenchurch Avenue
London E.C.3

From Hawthorn, Leslie & Company Ltd
Hebburn Shipbuilding Yard
Hebburn on Tyne
1st August 1922

Dear Sirs

No. 503 SHIP - PORT HARDY

We have pleasure to confirm arrangement made with you respecting the conversion from Twin-screw Turbines to Twin-screw Reciprocating Machinery at our interview in London on the 27th and 28th July.
Each engine to have cylinders $28^1/_2$", 38" and $63^1/_2$" Diameter by 48" stroke, working with superheated steam at 200 lbs pressure and fitted with MacTaggart, Scott's reversing engine.
Each engine will be provided with the following: Edwards Air Pump, Feed Pump, Bilge Pump, Sanitary Pump, all worked off the Main Engines by levers, together with two special Regulator Valves and Aspinall's Governors.
The Boilers, Condensers, Thrust Blocks and shafting as made for the Turbines will be utilized for the Reciprocating Machinery.
Spares will be supplied in accordance with Lloyds and Board of Trade requirements.
Modifications will require to be made to the following: Steam, exhaust and other pipes, cocks and valves, lifting gear, ladders and platforms, exhaust pieces to Condenser, adjustment of propellers, engine room Ventilators and 6 Plumber blocks.
With various other minor details, and generally in accordance with the specification handed to us by Mr. MacDonald in June 1922, in so far as it affects the Reciprocating Machinery.
The present turbine seating to be removed from the ship and new Reciprocating Engines eats to be built in accordance with the revised plan submitted and approved by Mr. Macdonald.
The present thrust seating as built in Vessel to remain, but to be modified in height to suit the new shaft centre. This seating to be extended one frame space further aft in accordance with the plan submitted to and approved by Mr. Macdonald.
TUNNELS. The two tunnels between frames Nos.36 to 62 to be lowered bodily about 15", also the tunnel stools to be reduced in height to suit the new centre.
HOLD PILLARS. These will require to be lengthened.
CASINGS. Casing between Main and Upper Deck will be recessed in the way of L.P.cylinder. Platforms and Entrance Doors modified to suit new arrangement.
MAIN DISCHARGE. Doubling to be fitted on shell, port and starboard, to suit new position of Discharge Valve.
The agreed price to carry out all the above alterations and additions is £21,000 : say Twenty-one Thousand Pounds). With regard to the values of the fittings made for the turbine machinery which will not be required for the Reciprocating outfit, also the prices for completing the sets of gearing, gear case and rotors, all as stated in our letter of the 20th June 1922, we shall be glad to hear from you hereon.

Yours faithfully,
JOHN T. BATEY
R. & W. HAWTHORN, LESLIE & COMPANY LTD.

Launched on the 9th October 1922, PORT HARDY (2) was the fifth of a series of similar vessels built and engined by Hawthorn, Leslie for the Commonwealth & Dominion Line Ltd. Gold bracelets were presented as a memento of the occasion to Miss Nellie Corry who performed the naming ceremony and to Miss Evelyn Corry, her sister who released the lever. Shortly after the launch a further delay to her completion occurred when a serious fire broke out causing considerable damage to the insulated holds. PORT HARDY (2) was finally delivered in February 1923 after being fitted with deck houses to provide washing, cooking and toilet facilities and her upper tween decks pierced for port-holes, in anticipation of her use as an emigrant carrier. However she was never used for this purpose.

In 1923 a policy to dispose of the older and obsolete vessels began and continued until 1928.

Shortly before midnight on the 12th January 1924 the PORT ELLIOT (2), bound from Auckland to Wellington in thick weather, stranded near Horoera Point between Te Araroa and East Cape and 80 miles north of Gisborne, New Zealand. The crew of 70, who had taken to the boats at about 3.30a.m., remained near the ship until the arrival of the steamer TUTANEKAI responding to a wireless message from the PORT ELLIOT (2). The PORT VICTOR (2) and other steamers in the vicinity also went to rescue the crew. The small steamers KURU and the KOUTUNUI were despatched from Napier and Tolga Bay respectively to assist in salvage operations. The TUTANEKAI rescued the crew from the boats and transferred them to the PORT VICTOR (2) that then proceeded to Wellington. The following day the ship was lying upright and half broadside on to the sea, on a reef about 300 yards from the shore, with her bow slightly dipped and her stern out of the water.

At an enquiry into the loss of the PORT ELLIOT (2) the Court held that there was a set inshore of which the Master was unaware, and therefore could not provide against, that the course set at 10.05p.m, would have cleared the East Cape, but owing to the third officer reporting a light in the direction and corresponding to that at East Cape the Master altered the course at 10.25p.m. which the Court held he was justified in doing. He was also justified in assuming that the light reported to him was the East Cape Light although, in fact, it was a bush fire showing at intervals. The Court was of the opinion that the set and alteration of the course combined resulted in the casualty but that under the circumstances and existing weather conditions it was not caused by the wrongful act or default of the master, officers or crew and the certificates of the Master and third officer were returned to them. Another casualty occurred in October 1924 when the PORT NICHOLSON (2) struck a rock off Las Palmas. Considerable damage was caused and she had to be towed back to her builders for repairs that took over four months.

The unofficial seaman's strike in 1925 was one of the last episodes to be dealt with by old time methods, running the gauntlet, dodging the pickets, completing the crew and sailing the vessel, by ruse and stratagem. This unfortunate dispute occurred towards the end of June 1925. At first there were informal negotiations between the Shipping Federation and the Union, followed by formal ones with the National Maritime Board for a reduction in wages for both seamen and firemen. Agreement was reached both with officers and representatives that the reduction, corresponding to the amount of increases granted the previous year would come into effect on 1st August. Towards the end of the month there was trouble with crews in Australian ports and this spread to New Zealand and South Africa and subsequently, though to a lesser extent to the United Kingdom.

During the strike the PORT CURTIS (2), under the command of Captain George Hearn and loading at Cairns, was caught up in the strike and remained there for ten weeks. Captain Hearn refused to supply the seaman on strike with food; the men retaliated by refusing to maintain steam for the refrigeration plant. The ship was eventually moved using a crew consisting of the Captain, four Deck Officers, the Chief Engineer, four engineers, two refrigeration engineers, the Chief Steward and a few catering staff, not forgetting the pilot. After a voyage of 1,000 miles, with stops each night, with only the pilot on the bridge, and everyone else below acting as firemen and coal trimmers, the ship reached Brisbane. A rendezvous was made enroute with the PORT HARDY (2), which had broken away from Townsville, for an exchange of water and coal. Other vessels of the fleet were affected including PORT BRISBANE, PORT WELLINGTON, PORT ADELAIDE and the PORT NAPIER. The strike ended towards the end of the year, after the strikers resumed work.

With the onset of the Australian depression, emigrant trade came to an end, ships were withdrawn from the Cape route and sent out via the Panama Canal. The Cape route was not used again until the end of 1931 when ships were sent out via South Africa, the Cape route at this time being the most economical.

When the PORT KEMBLA (2), outward bound for Lyttelton went ashore on a reef on the north side of San Salvador (Watling) Island, Bahamas in July 1926 some remarkable native behaviour was witnessed. A piano, jettisoned overboard is said to have been propelled ashore by dozens of Bahamians who dragged it up on to the beach and then played a song of thanksgiving while others swam close to the vessel calling out to the crew to throw wines and spirits into the sea. She was eventually declared a Constructive Total Loss.

The year 1925 was a depressed one with competition amongst shipbuilders very keen indeed, and may have prompted the Commonwealth & Dominion Line to order a number of motorships of which the PORT GISBORNE was one.

The launch of the PORT GISBORNE on the last day of April 1927 was especially interesting in that it was the first time, at least in the United Kingdom, that a launching ceremony had been broadcast. Immediately before the launch a description of the vessel was broadcast by N. M. Hunter, General Manager of the Wallsend Shipyard. Mrs John Royden Rooper performed the ceremony. The PORT GISBORNE was the first in a series of four similar ships to be delivered from Swan, Hunter & Wigham Richardson Ltd., in the late 1920s. Three were powered by Doxford engines and one, the PORT HUON (2) by Sulzer engines. A similar vessel, the PORT FREMANTLE, had been delivered by Workman, Clark & Company, Belfast, in April of the same year and was also fitted with Doxford engines.

In 'THE TIMES' of the 24th November 1961 an interesting account of a voyage around Cape Horn during June 1927 in the PORT PIRIE (3) was published. In those days, engineers, whose main interest was speed, used to welcome a voyage home from New Zealand via the Horn, a distance of approximately 12,000 miles. There were several reasons for this, the fundamental one being cold sea water. This made it possible to maintain an almost perfect vacuum in the main condensers, thereby increasing the performance of the engines beyond belief. It was really something for nothing. Then again, these cold conditions made the lot of the 'black squad' much easier, there was no difficulty keeping the 'steam on the blood'. (This was a red line on the pressure gauge). Most shipmasters got down to the latitude of the Horn as soon as practicable after leaving New Zealand, thus shortening the distances and having the benefit of wind and sea behind them across the Southern Ocean.

Unlike the engineers, the navigators on the draughty and unprotected bridges of those days did not appreciate this route, as apart from the cold and the weather, there were the additional hazards of fog, snow and ice, all of which were commonplace. Traffic was non-existent, as were weather reports. With the advent of the internal combustion engine and the favourable price of oil fuel at Curacao compared with Montevideo, the Cape Horn route has become a thing of the past.

In August 1928 a fire and explosions on board the PORT NAPIER (1) approximately 106 miles off Pago Pago, (Tutuila Island), one of the Samoan Group, caused the ship to put into port and the fire was extinguished with the help of U.S. Navy personnel under the command of Lt John P. Dix. U.S.N. who was later awarded a Navy Silver Cross in recognition of his services.

Speaking at the launch of the PORT ALMA (1) in September 1928, Robert Corry said that the Commonwealth & Dominion Line did not intend to build more motorships at present but instead were sending eight or nine steamships to Swan, Hunter & Wigham Richardson Ltd to have Bauer-Wach turbines fitted. The ships which were modified were as follows:- the PORT AUCKLAND (1) and the PORT HARDY (2), in 1928, followed by the PORT SYDNEY(1), PORT DENISON (2), PORT MELBOURNE (2), PORT DARWIN (2), PORT CAMPBELL (2) in 1929 and finally, in October 1930, the PORT WELLINGTON (1). Some years previous to this announcement the PORT CAROLINE (3) had been returned to her builders for extensive modifications to her engines.

3. Port Line Ltd.

During the erection of the Sydney Harbour Bridge, which was opened on 19th March 1932, a total of 19,000 tons of material was shipped from the United Kingdom to Sydney by three lines, the Commonwealth & Dominion Line, Aberdeen Line, and the P & O Branch Service.

Several of the company's ships carried on behalf of the contractors, Dorman, Long & Company, the major proportion of the steelwork, including girders, plates and holding cables.

The bridge was eight years in construction and is the largest single arch span bridge in the world. The combined length of the arch span and the steel approach spans is 3,770 feet and it has a height of over 400 feet. On the occasion of it's opening the Commonwealth & Dominion Line was represented in a pageant of maritime activities associated with the development of Australia by the PORT AUCKLAND (1) (Captain. C. A. Robinson) which headed a convoy of about a dozen overseas cargo vessels.

During the 1930s an annual event reminiscent of the clippership era took place - The Wool Race. As a memo to the Directors in Australia points out they were not without incident -

'Holland Australia Lines TANIMBAR we understand averaged 15.8 knots on the homeward run and as we advised you in our cable regarding the PORT BOWEN, the two vessels came into collision while proceeding at full speed in charge of pilots up the four-mile wide channel off the mouth of the Schelde. The PORT BOWEN has been seriously damaged amidships, and it is anticipated that the repairs will run to about £5,000. Despite the collision, the TANIMBAR covered the direct passage from Adelaide with new season's wool in 29 days 16^1/$_2$ hours (allowing for the time difference), a fast voyage. The Norwegian motorship the TRICOLOR which reached Antwerp five hours before the TANIMBAR after creating a new record from Sydney to Dunkirk direct, took 31 days 11^1/$_2$ hours on the voyage from Sydney to Antwerp. The PORT BOWEN, which made the direct passage from Sydney to Hull was the first vessel to reach the other side of the world with new season's wool from the first Sydney sales'.

The PORT CHALMERS (4), delivered in December 1933, was the first of a group of fast refrigerated ships ordered from British yards in the 1930s for the Australian/New Zealand food trade with the United Kingdom. In 1931 the British Government adopted the economic doctrine of Imperial Preference brought about by the world depression. By this policy the British Dominions and Colonies were to be become a self-contained economic partnership. One of the benefits of this policy was that ten fast refrigerated ships which became known as Empire Food Ships were ordered from United Kingdom yards. Trade between the Dominions flourished and each of the companies engaged in it - New Zealand Shipping, Shaw, Savill and Albion, Blue Star and Port Line - placed orders for new tonnage. The ships although different in design, were similar in capacity and propulsion.

Launched in October 1933 the PORT CHALMERS (4) was only the second vessel to be launched on the Tyne that year and the only vessel of any consequence. Built on the same berth as the liner MAURETANIA, a feature of her construction was the extensive use of electric welding. The fact that she was the only major vessel built that year on the Tyne meant that Swan, Hunter & Wigham Richardson Ltd, were able to put their very best workmen on her, and the riveting and general finish of the vessel was of the highest standard. In common with her running mates and rivals, committed to the longest and loneliest deep water run on earth, she was provided with twin-screw propulsion to avoid disablement in mid ocean through mechanical breakdown. In their provision for ratings the Port Line at that time were less enlightened than others, in as much that seamen were berthed in the forecastle and greasers in a deckhouse at the after end of the weather deck.

The PORT CHALMERS (4) was the first ship in the fleet to be fitted for the carriage of chilled beef. Even though for many years previously experiments had been carried out into better ways of transporting frozen meat. In early 1933 the PORT FAIRY (2) carried the first experimental consignment of chilled beef from New Zealand, having been fitted the previous year with gas lockers. Other ships on the Australian routes participated in similar trials.

Before she sailed on her maiden voyage her master, Captain S. W. Hayter, was presented by Mr R. S. Forsyth, manager of the New Zealand Meat Producers Board with a "Tiki", a semi-precious greenstone miniature of a Maori tribal god. The Maoris, according to legend, initiated this ceremony when the giant canoes led by TE ARAWA departed from the fabled Hawaiki (believed to be Rarotonga) to colonise Ao-Tearoa (New Zealand). As later events were to prove, the luck of the PORT CHALMERS

(4) was phenomenal. A note sent to the directors in Australia on 11th January 1934 asked them to join in a publicity effort in conjunction the Meat and Dairy Boards. "As you are probably aware, the PORT CHALMERS was the largest British Ship to be built last year, and as she is in commission some six months before any of the new ships ordered by the other lines for the New Zealand trade, we think this would benefit us tremendously".

Shortly after the completion of the PORT CHALMERS (4) the Commonwealth & Dominion Line placed orders for a further two ships, one to be built on the Clyde and the other on Tyneside. Near sister ships, they differed in one major respect in that one was fitted with twin eight-cylinder Sulzer engines and other with twin four-cylinder Doxford engines. This was in order to evaluate the merits of both types of propulsion. Initially the names chosen for the new-buildings were the PORT WYNDHAM and the PORT JACKSON and application was made to the Register of Shipping advising them of this choice, but, as the following series of letters shows all was not plain sailing.

11.5.1934: Letter to

Register of Shipping,
Custom House,
London E.C.3

Sir,
We beg to make application for proposed names for two vessels we have building, as follows:
   No. 541 at Clydebank by Messrs. John Brown & Company.
   No.1495 at Wallsend by Messrs. Swan. Hunter & Wigham Richardson.

The names we propose are mv. PORT WYNDHAM and PORT JACKSON respectively.

These vessels will be registered in London.

The Commonwealth & Dominion Line

12.5.1934. Reply to above:

Gentlemen.
Forms of application are enclosed. It is observed however that "Port Jackson" is already the name of a registered vessel, and may not be available. 197 tons gross, built 1904 at Aberdeen.

15.5.1934: Letter to
The Commonwealth & Dominion Line

 We are in receipt of your letter of yesterday's date regarding our Steam Trawler "Port Jackson".
In reply thereto we have to inform you that there is no likelihood of this vessel disappearing from the Register in the near future, and we would not be willing to change her name.

KELSALL & BLACKBURN
FLEETWOOD

16.5.1934: Letter to
Kelsall & Blackburn

We are very disappointed to receive your letter of the 15th May regarding the name "PORT JACKSON".
As your vessel of this name appears from Lloyds Register to be older and smaller than the other members of your fleet, we had hoped that, on condition of our paying all expenses and a small premium, you might have been willing to consent to a change.
yours faithfully

C & D

21.6.1934:

Further refusal to accept remunerative offer received.

The directors had a rethink and provisionally decided that the vessel would be called PORT TOWNSVILLE (1). There were several old names which they would have liked to revive, such as PORT LINCOLN, PORT MACQUARRIE, and PORT LYTTELTON, but they felt that the important thing at that time was to obtain all the political capital possible from naming the vessel after a port in which they were endeavouring to increase their business.

In July 1934 contracts were placed with J. & E. Hall & Company Ltd for refrigerating machinery for both ships, the costs being as follows - PORT TOWNSVILLE £30,800 and PORT WYNDHAM £32,000. The increased price of £1,200 was due to higher labour costs on the Clyde. In September it was decided to fit both ships with Silent Super Sonic Echo Sounders manufactured by Henry Hughes & Sons Ltd., at a cost of £405 per ship.

Guests on the launching platform for PORT TOWNSVILLE - 21st May 1935. (Liverpool University Archives)

Launched on 21st May 1935, at 5.30pm, by Mrs Joseph Lyons, wife of the Prime Minister of Australia, PORT TOWNSVILLE (1) ran her trials on 24th August of that year. She was specially constructed for the carriage of chilled beef in gas tight compartments which were electrically welded instead of riveted, she was fitted with electric winches, and her hatchways had steel covers resting on rubber joints. The final cost of the PORT TOWNSVILLE (1) was:- Hull £141,958, Machinery £125,642 and Refrigeration and Insulation £72,849, Total Cost £340,449. She was the tenth motor ship built for the company, and brought the number of ships owned to 27.

The cost of PORT WYNDHAM, which was built on the slipway alongside the QUEEN MARY, in comparison were:- Hull £158,575, Machinery £106,600, Refrigeration Machinery and insulation £68,871, Total Cost £335,046.

At the conclusion of the return leg of her maiden voyage the PORT WYNDHAM arrived off Dunkirk, after a passage from Sydney of less than 30 days, her average speed being 16.74 knots on a daily consumption of 38.28 tons of oil.

During July 1935 the shipping press reported that the Commonwealth & Dominion Line was negotiating the sale of three ships and in October both the PORT PIRIE (4) and the PORT VICTOR (3) were sold to shipbreakers T. W. Ward for a total of £25,000, handover to be in early November. The third ship, the PORT CURTIS (2), was sold to the Downs Steamship Company for £17,750 less 4% brokerage and this sale was completed on 13th November 1935.

Possibly as a result of these sales, the company chartered the ADLINGTON COURT, ANGLO-CANADIAN and the ANGLO-COLUMBIAN for voyages to Australia via the United States.

It was reported at the October 1935 board meeting that agreement had been reached for participation in Blue Star Line Australian Trade both outwards and homewards and that a long term agreement had consequently been concluded between British lines on a pooling basis both for fine cargo and wool. Also reported was the renewal of the British and Continental Wool Pool. Mention was also made of another newbuilding for completion in late 1936.

Shortly after this, at the December 1935 board meeting the directors agreed that for popular use the company should be known as 'PORT LINE'. Considerable publicity was given in the press to the adoption of PORT LINE as a popular designation for the company and during the February 1936 board meeting the directors agreed to consider taking steps to alter the name to PORT LINE LTD. During this meeting it was also reported that the pay cuts made to sea-going staff during the depression had been restored.

It was duly announced in the press that the Commonwealth & Dominion Line Ltd., on and after 1st February 1936, would be known as PORT LINE and that Commonwealth & Dominion Line Ltd would remain the registered title of the company. This was given considerable newspaper publicity at the time, but it was not until the following year that this title, with the addition of the word "Limited" was officially adopted. At an Extraordinary General Meeting held on the 11th November 1937 at the registered offices of the Cunard Line, 88, Leadenhall Street, with W. P. Tyser in the chair, the following Resolution was passed unanimously: "That the name of the Company be changed to Port Line Ltd."

At the next meeting of the board on 9th December, it was reported that the alteration of the registered name of the company to "Port Line Ltd." had received the approval of the Board of Trade and that the Certificate of the entry of the new name was dated 18th November 1937. The change of name emanated from a suggestion made to the directors by Mr W. D. Watson, who at that time was working in the Inward Freight Department (later he became Head of the Claims Department after being Continental Representative in Antwerp) and was frequently on the Continent visiting the wool trade clientele. During his travels he had noticed that the Commonwealth & Dominion Line was known among Continental shippers as "Zee Port Line".

The new name was much more compact than the original. Commonwealth and Dominion and Cunard Line Australasian Service, Commonwealth & Dominion Line Ltd. (the title adopted after the company was taken over by the Cunard Steamship Company Ltd. in 1916) was certainly not among the shortest of titles for a shipping line and the contraction to "C & D" by which the line was commonly known, bore a striking similarity to a term familiar in the retail trade! There was also, an "Aberdeen & Commonwealth Line" serving Australia and confusion between the two titles was accordingly excusable. The renamed line had long paid the Commonwealth of Australia and the Dominion of New Zealand the compliment of naming each vessel in its Fleet after a port in one of those countries so there was everything to be said in favour of the change. The transfer of the existing Commonwealth & Dominion Line share certificates to Cunard Steamship Company who shortly afterwards exchanged them for certificates in the name of PORT LINE LTD was authorised.

THE COMPANIES ACT, 1929.

Special Resolution

OF

COMMONWEALTH AND DOMINION LINE LIMITED.

Passed 11th November, 1937.

At an EXTRAORDINARY GENERAL MEETING of the Company, held at Cunard House, Leadenhall Street, in the City of London, on Thursday, the 11th day of November, 1937, the SPECIAL RESOLUTION hereunder was passed:—

"THAT the name of the Company be changed to PORT LINE LIMITED."

I Certify the above to be a true copy of the Resolution.

Chairman of the Meeting.

Facsimile of the Special Resolution to change name.

(Liverpool University Archives)

Certificate of the Incorporation of a Company.

I hereby Certify that

PORT LINE LIMITED

(originally called COMMONWEALTH AND DOMINION LINE, LIMITED which name was changed by Special Resolution and with the Authority of the Board of Trade on the eighteenth day of November One thousand nine hundred and thirty-seven)

was **Incorporated** under the Companies Acts, 1908 and 1913

as a **Limited** Company, on the twenty-third day of January One thousand nine hundred and fourteen.

Given under my hand at London, this twentieth day of January One thousand nine hundred and thirty-eight.

Registrar of Companies.

Facsimile of the Certificate of Incorporation of Port Line.

(Liverpool University Archives)

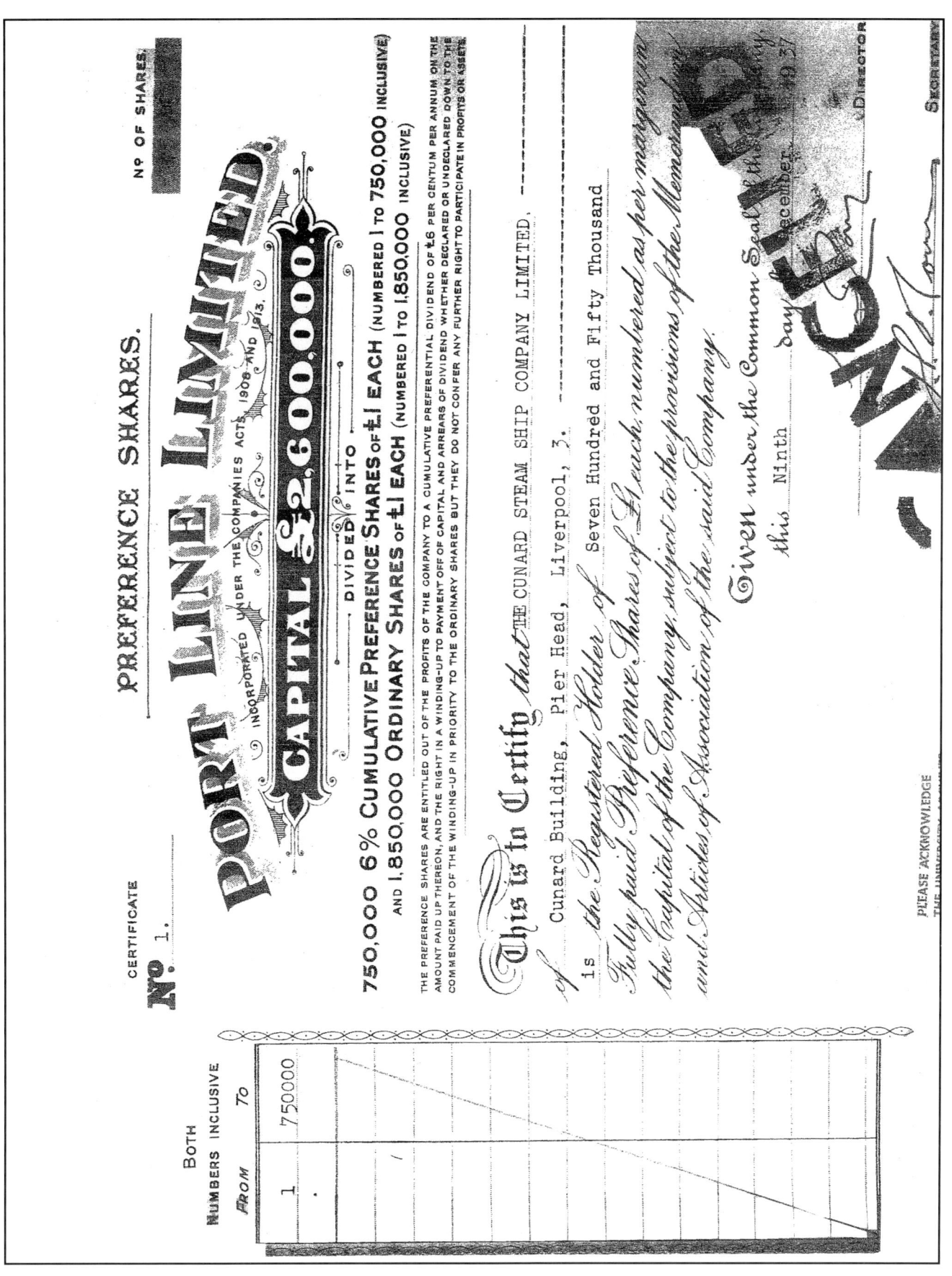

Facsimile of Cunard's Preferential Share Certificate for Port Line.

(Liverpool University Archives)

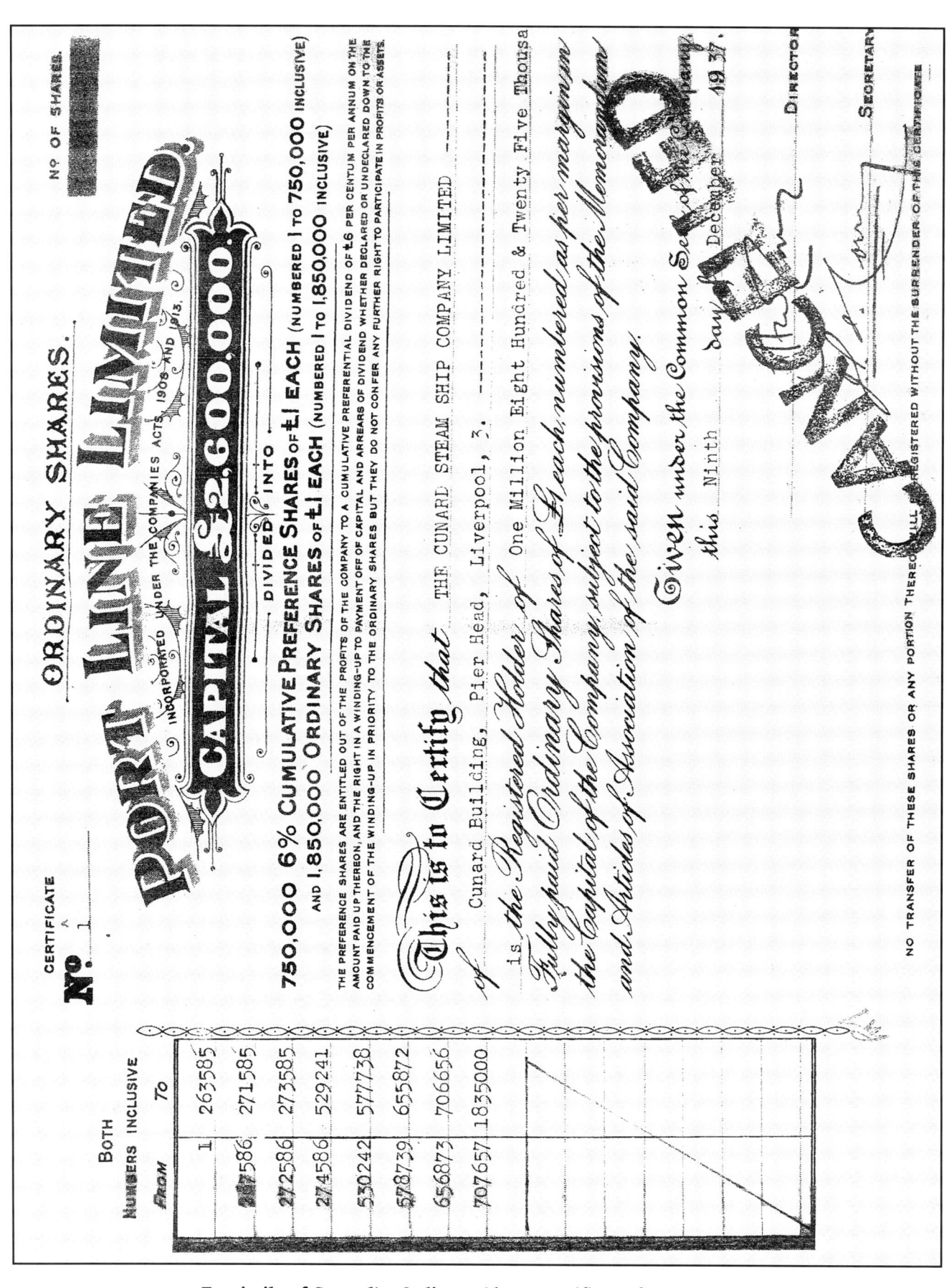

Facsimile of Cunard's Ordinary Share Certificate for Port Line.

(Liverpool University Archives)

Previously, in October 1935, the directors had authorised the construction of a further vessel, and once again Swan, Hunter & Wigham Richardson Ltd, were the preferred builders. In an effort to spread the work between the principal shipbuilding areas, the Doxford type engines of the new ship were be constructed by Barclay Curle & Company on the Clyde.

Launched on the 26th November 1936 by Lady Hankey, the PORT JACKSON (3) was the first Port Line vessel to be fitted with a forced air cooling system in her refrigerated compartments, a system later adopted for all the ships in the fleet. PORT JACKSON (3) caused quite a stir in the shipping world when she appeared. With her long bridge above the upper deck over No 3 hatch considered to add greatly to the beauty of the ship. By avoiding the break in the line between the two deck houses, this added to the utility value of the design giving more space for cargo. As previously mentioned, a Fleetwood trawler built in 1917 named Port Jackson precluded the use of that name by the Port Line for an ocean-going vessel. They had long wished to revive this famous name in their fleet and when Lady Hankey named their new motor vessel, on 26th November 1936 the wish was fulfilled.

The PORT JACKSON (3), when commissioned, had an overall length of 495 feet, a beam of 68 feet and a gross tonnage of 9,720 tons. Her capacity totalled over 690,000 cubic feet of which over 460,000 cubic feet was specially insulated and adapted for the carriage of refrigerated and chilled produce. Her Doxford type engines, developing well over 10,000 brake horse power, gave a sea speed of about 16 knots. The PORT JACKSON (3), in common with all the new tonnage for the line completed during the 1930s was fully equipped with all the latest navigation aids including Sperry Gyro compass equipment. Final cost of the PORT JACKSON (3) was £376,202. On her maiden voyage she averaged 14.84 knots at 27.9 tons of fuel per day.

Four single and four double cabins with luxurious fittings accommodated twelve saloon passengers who also had four bathrooms and two public rooms for their use. It is interesting to note the progress in the design of passenger accommodation, during the 50 years or so since the completion of the original PORT JACKSON (1), in that the twelve saloon passengers in that ship were berthed in two cabins, each measuring about 11feet by 7feet 6in, giving twelve of them about half the space devoted to the Captain's luxury flat in the new motor vessel.

An article appeared in the shipping press comparing the new ship with the original of the same name entitled 'A New Motor Vessel With A Famous Old Name'.

> When Captain Cook discovered the greatest harbour in Australia, he named it Port Jackson in honour of the Secretary of the Admiralty of that time. Since then the fine township of Sydney, capital of New South Wales, with a rapidly growing population has grown out of the original settlement and is one of the principal ports of call for the company.
>
> In 1883 the firm of William Milburn & Company, long established as sailing ship owners, founded the Anglo-Australasian Steam Navigation Company Ltd and named the ships that they built for this service with the prefix "Port". The first of these, an iron steamship rigged as a brig with four yards on each of her two masts and a compound steam engine rated at 350 nominal horse power, was named PORT JACKSON (1) when launched from the Hebburn yard of A. Leslie & Company on 4th September 1883.
>
> The PORT JACKSON (1) was a fine specimen of the type then required by the trade in which she was engaged. Her length was 316 feet and beam 37 feet. With a capacity of just under 200,000 cubic feet, she could carry 3,670 tons of general cargo in addition to twelve saloon passengers. During the greater part of her service emigration from the United Kingdom to Australia was at its peak and she accommodated about 100 passengers in portable cabins in the upper 'tween decks. She had a very useful and comparatively long life before being broken up in 1910.

At the April 1937 board meeting the managing directors agreed to proposals for the modernisation of the PORT MELBOURNE (2) and the PORT SYDNEY (1), which was carried out towards the end of the year at a cost of £3,300 for insulation and £1,700 for refrigeration.

It was also reported that six ships had already been fitted with echo sounders and arrangements to fit 18 others were in hand, so that eventually 24 out of the fleet of 28 would be fitted, the exceptions being the PORT SYDNEY (1), PORT MELBOURNE (2), PORT DARWIN (2) and the PORT DENISON (3).

On the 7th July 1937 the PORT HALIFAX, the first single screw vessel the company had ever ordered and the first of a series of three ships for the M.A.N.Z. Line, the Canada - New Zealand service of the Port Line, was launched by Swan, Hunter & Wigham Richardson Ltd and named by Miss Nelly Corry.

PORT HALIFAX enters the waters of the River Tyne. (Authors collection)

The following month two further vessels of this new fleet were launched, the PORT SAINT JOHN and the PORT MONTREAL (1) which was originally to have been named the PORT QUEBEC.

In mid-January 1938 the PORT SAINT JOHN, on her maiden voyage, ran aground twice, most seriously on a reef near Lady Elliott Island off the Queensland coast, where Lloyds took a pessimistic view of her chances by quoting a high re-insurance rate; their prediction was wrong and she finally came off. Earlier on the same voyage she had run aground on the rocks of Petries Ledge, Sydney, Cape Breton. Her captain was dismissed from his employment as a result of these incidents.

PORT SAINT JOHN leaves the water off Queensland.

(Liverpool University Archives)

As consequence of these and other incidents J. R. Roper (Director) circulated a memo to Captain H. E. Higgs (Marine Superintendent) on 9th August 1939:-

> "Captain W. G. Higgs of the PORT CHALMERS has made a suggestion which I think is an admirable one. He points out that our recent disasters have occurred to ships commanded by recently promoted Captains.
>
> As Chief Officers they have always been on the forecastle head approaching port, and in fact have not seen the operation from the bridge for perhaps 10 or 12 years. Captain Higgs' suggestion is that all the senior Chief Officers - say the top half dozen - should be on the bridge, the second officer on the focastle head, the third down aft and the fourth who has a certificate on the bridge in place of the third.
>
> It appears to me an eminently sound suggestion, and I think you should get Mr Robert Corry's approval to institute it, at any rate as a trial forthwith".
>
> JRR

Previously in June 1938 an astonishing incident occurred at the time of the second Test Match for the ashes, nearing Fremantle, all radio sets on the PORT HUON (1) were tuned to the Test broadcasts. When suddenly, from stem to stern, the cry was taken up of 'Bradmans out for 51'. Captain W. Hearn an Englishman, literally jumped for joy, and broke his toe against a table. When his ship reached Melbourne Captain Hearn was still limping, but even though his toe was well on the mend he limped ashore none too happy.

Discussions must have been taking place amongst the directors whether to order new tonnage for some time as the following letter depicts

> Sir Percy Bates
> Cunard White Star Ltd
> C/o Hotel Regina
> Wengen
> Switzerland,
>
> 13.1.1939
>
> 'I am afraid the shipbuilders' price may be a little higher as our people do not altogether like the PORT JACKSON's engines. We propose in the new ship to have five-cylinder engines instead of four, thus reducing the size of the cylinders. She will be generally similar to No 1515, PORT JACKSON but will be 2 feet 9 ins longer and have additional chilled meat spaces in No 3 'tween decks'.
>
> W. P. Tyser.

At the February 1939 board meeting it was reported that, on 27th January 1939, an order for a new ship had been placed with Swan, Hunter & Wigham Richardson Ltd with an estimated completion date of 26th April 1940. Her estimated cost was likely to be £380,000, plus Gregson's insulation at £35,400, J. & E. Hall & Company to supply the refrigeration at £46,000, extras £3,000, Total estimated cost £464,500. This costing was 24% greater than the PORT JACKSON (3).

Extras, that had already been agreed, were, fresh water-cooling for the generators, a derrick to lift 60 tons, pumps of increased capacity, solid bronze propellers and spares and automatic steering. Some savings were being made by a reduction in the number of CO2 bottles, together with smaller derricks and winches at the after ends of hatches 2, 3 and 4 and by fitting a composition instead of wood on steel decks in the passenger and crew accommodation. The main difference was that her engines were five-cylinder instead of four and the funnel was a little further forward to give a better uptake for the exhausts. The extra cylinders did not necessarily mean a faster ship, but there was a little reserve, which might be useful under pressure. The board were also informed that unsuccessful tenders had been received from J. L. Thompson; Cammell, Laird; William Doxford; William Hamilton; John Brown; Barclay, Curle, and Harland & Wolff.

The board meeting at which Percy Bates, Thomas Royden and Sir Alfred Booth were present greeted the announcement of the order placed with Swan, Hunter & Wigham Richardson Ltd without criticism. At the same time the opportunity was taken to point out that orders would have to be placed for two or three more ships before long, seeing that eight of the fleet would soon reach the age of 20 years. Such were the demands for chilled beef space that Australia was bereft of modern ships during the height of the present season. This announcement also was greeted without adverse comment.

The contract was sealed for the new ship on the 6th March 1939 and the directors agreed on 10th

March 1939 that the name PORT LAUNCESTON would be best from a policy point of view, but PORT NAPIER was chosen as it was shorter, sounded good, and it belonged to the original stronghold of the company and also commemorated a fine old ship. The final price for the never to be delivered PORT NAPIER (2) was builders cost: £380,697, Insulation £7,915, Sundries £1,141, and interest on progress payments £7,828. A grand total of £397,581 (which excluded the planned refrigeration equipment that was in the end, never fitted).

A contingency plan in the event of war was implemented as early as April 1939. Negotiations to purchase a house in the country were commenced and in June the purchase of "OAKLAWN" a large country house at Leatherhead in Surrey, suitable as a headquarters was confirmed at a cost of £10,250.

The winter of 1939 in New Zealand was particularly severe, strong southerly gales with snow and particularly cold weather prevailed throughout the country. Dockers refused to work vessels located in exposed positions due to extreme cold and this resulted in delays with loading vessels.

Shortly after midnight on 19th July 1939 the PORT BOWEN, under the command of Captain F. W. Bailey, whilst steaming to the anchorage off Wanganui stranded about a quarter of a mile off the Castlecliff Beach and a mile north of the harbour entrance. The PORT BOWEN's cargo comprised 2,075 carcasses of mutton, 27,227 carcasses of lamb, 400 boxes of butter, 850 crates of cheese, a large quantity of wool, tallow, bags of wheatmeal, whey powder and sacks of peas. She also had about 3,000 tons of bunker coal aboard and was to have loaded a further 20,000 carcasses of meat at Wanganui. After several unsuccessful attempts at refloating, it was decided to remove the cargo of frozen meat, butter and wool from the holds and to achieve this a road and ramp was built over which lorries were able to reach the ship's side. She was subsequently abandoned as a total loss and this same ramp was utilised when the ship was broken up.

At the July 1939 board meeting the directors were greatly concerned to hear that the PORT JACKSON (3) was still suffering from severe vibration problems. Previously, the directors had sent Mr Arrowsmith to Stockholm in her, and they engaged experts to test the degree of vibration under different conditions on the way to Antwerp. So far, no one had found a solution, and in the meantime rivets around hatch combings forward and aft had worked loose, and there were other signs of the effect of the snake like movement which she made when going through the water at full speed. They devoutly hoped that the five-cylinder engine in the PORT NAPIER (2) would show an improvement.

As well as the PORT JACKSON (3), the PORT TOWNSVILLE was suffering engine problems and the PORT FREMANTLE had been operating on one engine for the last few days of her last voyage, due apparently, to the oil in the sump being allowed to get too low. The PORT SAINT JOHN also had her problems and, on top of this, the PORT MONTREAL (1) had leaky oil tanks, due it was thought, to unsatisfactory workmanship in Doxford's shipyard.

At the board meeting held on 13th August 1939 it was confirmed that the cost of repairs to the PORT MONTREAL (1) would be expensive. The directors came to the conclusion that Doxfords' shipyard work was not comparable with their engine work, and was far below the standard of Swan, Hunter & Wigham Richardson Ltd or even J. L.Thompson & Company, who had built the other two M.A.N.Z. Line ships.

A report in the 'MOTOR SHIP' of August 1939 attested to the reliability of the diesel engine.

> *'The PORT HUON in her first twelve years of operation has covered approx 840,000 miles without any engine or auxiliary breakdowns. The Chief Engineer, Mr A.G.Neall, has been with her the whole time. In July 1927 the 'MOTOR SHIP' estimated that fuel consumption would not exceed 27 tons per day for all purposes. In fact the highest consumption per day has been 25.9 tons per day. The first voyage to Australia and back represented 29,430 miles, the second 30,281. One of the New Zealand voyages amounted to 25,897 miles. Bunkers were taken on at Panama or Curacao on the Australian run and Tenerife or Las Palmas when on the New Zealand run. Her present voyage (28th) included Halifax and New York to Australia, and amounts to 32,237 miles for the complete trip. She differs from all the other motor vessels in the fleet except one in that she is a twin-screw Sulzer engined ship'.*

A similar report on the 'PORT GISBORNE, powered by a Doxford installation was later published in

PORT HUON passing Dover. (Ambrose Greenway collection)

the 'MOTOR SHIP' of January 1940.

At the outbreak of the Second World War in September 1939 the company had 14 motor ships and 14 steamers in commission. Two motor ships had Wallsend Slipway Sulzer two-stroke engines and the remainder all had Doxford engines.

The outbreak of the war caused immediate interruptions to the expansion programme and in October 1939 construction of the PORT NAPIER (2) was delayed due to the late delivery of her crankshaft. The following month Swan, Hunter & Wigham Richardson Ltd advised the company that due to government restrictions they were unable to obtain a licence to build a second ship similar to the PORT NAPIER (2). About this time, the decision taken at an earlier board meeting to sell both the PORT MELBOURNE (2) and the PORT SYDNEY (1), for breaking up was cancelled.

PORT SYDNEY fitted and armed for war. (Ambrose Greenway collection)

4. Another War.

Measures brought into effect by the British Government almost as soon as war was declared showed that as far as shipping was concerned the lessons of the World War One had not been forgotten. The formation of a Ministry of Shipping was announced within one month of the declaration of war and by the end of January 1940 all shipping was under Government control. Day to day management remained in the hands of the owners, outward commercial voyages when made were "fixed" through brokers at market rates, with inward cargoes carried to Government account. Early in 1941 the formation of the Ministry of War Transport brought all aspects of land, sea and air transport under one banner.

The first vessel of the fleet to be requisitioned was the PORT ADELAIDE (3) handed over at 3.00 p.m. on 4th January 1940 and the last vessel to leave with cargo on the company's account was the PORT HOBART (1), which left London on 22nd January 1940 bound for Australia. All vessels were then requisitioned after the conclusion of their voyages on 31st of that month.

During January 1940 the Admiralty expressed a great interest in the PORT NAPIER (2). The following month she was requisitioned on a T 98 agreement. Port Line made a great protest during early March 1940 but to no avail.

As from February 1940 some ships were routed home via Suez and in April it was agreed all future ships would have their tonnage openings closed to increase safety.

Some time before the war commenced the Government had agreed on certain standard designs of merchant ships that included fast refrigerated ships, but it was considered that these designs were ill suited for the business of the company.

In March 1940 an order was placed with Swan, Hunter & Wigham Richardson Ltd, for a ship similar to the PORT NAPIER (2) to cost a maximum of £525,000, plus £975 for an extra 6in in depth.

On 23rd April the PORT NAPIER (2) was launched without ceremony by Mrs Arrowsmith, wife of the Superintendent Engineer and as the ship was now under the control of the Admiralty her timber and cork insulation was put into store.

In May the directors were informed that John Brown had been given leave to lay down a cargo ship on a slip which would be free in August and they were applying for permission to build a sister ship to the one which was being built for the company by Swan, Hunter & Wigham Richardson Ltd. Authority was given to seal a contract with John Brown at a cost of £35,000 more than the Swan, Hunter & Wigham Richardson Ltd ship ordered in March.

In the same month a shortage of certificated marine engineers was reported and the company arranged to accommodate supernumerary engineers by utilising unwanted passenger accommodation. This was to enable them to put in the required sea time in order that they could obtain their certificates. On 7th July the PORT NAPIER (2) was registered in the name of the company. Her intended refrigeration plant was installed in Yard No. 1609 and subsequently in August 1940 the price of Yard no 1609, which became the PORT PHILLIP (5), was reduced by £17,456 because of use of these materials.

Port Line suffered their first loss of the war when, on the 26th September 1940, the PORT DENISON (3), whilst on a voyage from London to New Zealand and the flagship of a 44 vessel convoy, was attacked by a single aircraft off the Aberdeen coast and disabled by a bomb which penetrated the lower 'tweendeck. A gaping hole was blown in the ship's side and 16 lives were lost in the explosion. The ship sank the following day.

Less than a month later, on the 11th October, the PORT GISBORNE was torpedoed by U 48 (Kapitanleutnant Heinrich Bielchrodt) in position 56.38N., 16.40W., south-west of Rockall. The vessel was on a voyage from New Zealand to Belfast and Cardiff. Unfortunately 26 of her crew of 63 were lost when No. 3 lifeboat capsized shortly after leaving the ship.

In the spring of 1940 Germany despatched surface raiders with the intention of disrupting trade and one of these, the PINGUIN was assigned the Indian Ocean as her operating area, which proved unfortunate for the Port Line. The month of November 1940 became a black month for the company as in just over a week four ships were lost, one by internal explosion and three sunk by surface raider. The PORT BRISBANE (1) was captured by the PINGUIN and sunk off Cape Leeuwin on 21st November 1940. One crew member was lost, 27 eluded capture and their lifeboat, under the command of Second Officer Dingle, was later picked up by an Australian cruiser, but the remaining crew became prisoners of war. On the same day south-east of Bermuda, the PORT HOBART (1) outward bound from Liverpool to New Zealand was captured by the pocket battleship ADMIRAL SCHEER and later sunk. All the crew and passengers were taken prisoner. Less than a week later the PORT NAPIER (2), never delivered to the company and now converted to a minelayer, blew up and sank, thankfully without loss of life at her base in Scotland.

PORT DENISON in wartime grey. (Ambrose Greenway collection)

The PORT WELLINGTON (1) homeward bound from Sydney was captured on the 30th November by the raider PINGUIN in the southern Indian Ocean in position 32.10S., 75.00E. Her crew and passengers were taken prisoner and later transferred to the STORSTAD, a German supply ship. The Chief Radio Officer died in the attack and Captain Thomas received serious wounds and later died. The Chief Officer who then took command was Captain F. W. Bailey late of the PORT BOWEN that had run aground in 1939.

The Royal Canadian Navy's rush to the aid of the mother country was most cruelly rewarded. HMCS FRASER, after helping with post Dunkirk evacuations, went to the estuary of the French river Gironde to join up with other Canadian and British ships. During a manoeuvre the FRASER (Commander W. B. Creery, RCN), was cut in half by the cruiser HMS CALCUTTA and sank with the loss of 47 of her crew of 187 officers and men on 25th June 1940. The blame for the first naval disaster in Canadian history was eventually divided evenly between the two ships' captains. The postscript to this sad story was even worse. The Canadians bought the British destroyer HMS DIANA and had her refitted and recommissioned as HMCS MARGAREE under the command of Lt Cdr J. W. R. Roy, RCN., to replace the FRASER, with most of the surviving crew transferring to the substitute. On 20th October 1940 she left Londonderry, Northern Ireland, as the sole escort of a small convoy that was to join a larger one bound for Halifax, Nova Scotia out at sea. Falling back on 22nd October, from her position ahead of the sub convoy in squally weather, the MARGAREE was cut in two in her turn, this time by the PORT FAIRY. In the collision, some 300 miles west of Ireland, the captain, four officers and 136 ratings - four-fifths of the crew were lost. The stern containing all the confidential books remained afloat even though the PORT FAIRY (2) used up all the ammunition of her single gun trying to sink it, and it was eventually abandoned. The MARGAREE was blamed for making a sudden and unexplained turn to port, which put her in the path of the merchantman. No replacement was sought this time by the grief-stricken Canadians after one of the most extraordinary double catastrophes on record, in which the enemy played no part.

In January 1941 the directors investigated the cost of building a similar ship to the PORT JACKSON (3), and in the same month both the PORT FREMANTLE and the PORT JACKSON (3) were ordered to make voyages to South America to load meat for the United Kingdom.

PORT VICTOR - 23rd October 1942. (Authors collection)

In February 1941, Yard No. 1659, PORT VICTOR (3) was ordered from Swan, Hunter & Wigham Richardson Ltd, she was a duplicate of Yard No. 1609, PORT PHILLIP (5) and was scheduled to be laid down in May 1941 for delivery in August 1942.

On the 3rd February, Captain Cottell was appointed to the PORT TOWNSVILLE (1) but he did not take up the appointment. That proved to be fortunate, as the next casualty in the fleet was the PORT TOWNSVILLE (1). On 4th March, outward bound from Newport, Monmouthshire to Australia, she was bombed and sunk in the St Georges Channel whilst travelling independently. The coaster HARPTREE COMBE picked up two boatloads of survivors and transferred them to the Free French Sloop LA MOQUETTE, which had previously rescued the remainder of her crew. Unfortunately two passengers lost their lives in this attack.

At the end of April the PORT HARDY (2), homeward bound in convoy HX 121, was torpedoed and sunk by U 96 north of Rockall. One member of the crew was lost and luckily the rescue ship ZAAFARAN picked up the remaining 97 passengers and crew.

In September an order for a new ship whose plans and specifications had been agreed by the Admiralty, was placed with Swan, Hunter & Wigham Richardson Ltd for completion in June 1943. On 7th October Mrs H. E. Higgs, wife of the Marine Superintendent, launched the PORT PHILLIP (5).

At the March 1942 board meeting it was reported that a licence had been granted to Swan, Hunter & Wigham Richardson Ltd, build a single screw refrigerated motor ship for the company and the following month it was reported that a model of her was being tested at the William Froude Laboratory. Known as Yard No. 1685, her plans and hull specification were being submitted to the Admiralty and her keel was due to be laid in August 1942 for completion in August 1943. The cost was estimated at £385,000 exclusive of refrigeration, insulation, defence measures and war risks insurances.

During May 1942, Captain W. Gilling, was appointed as Marine Superintendent following the death of Captain H. E. Higgs.

In June the PORT MONTREAL (1), en route for the Panama Canal was torpedoed and sunk in the Caribbean Sea by U 68. Her crew were picked the following day by a Colombian schooner and landed at Cristobal. Less than a week later the PORT NICHOLSON (2) was torpedoed south of Portland, Maine by U 87. She was later reboarded but sank suddenly taking six people including Captain Jeffery to their deaths.

PORT LINERS AT WAR.

PORT FREMANTLE (World Ship Society Photograph Library)

EMPIRE TREASURE wallowing disabled awaiting the rescue tug. (Vic Young collection)

PORT MACQUARIE - 22nd February 1944. (Source unknown)

PORT CHALMERS arriving at Malta. (Liverpool University Archives)

Three weeks later, on the 11th July, the PORT HUNTER (4), outward bound to New Zealand had just left convoy OS.33 when she was struck by torpedoes fired by U 582. There were only three survivors from her crew of 85, this being the most serious loss of life from any of the company's fleet.

Two days earlier on the 9th July Yard No. 577 building at John Brown Ltd, Clydebank was taken up by the Admiralty as a chattel and the directors thought it would be preferable to pursue the question of building another ship at the same price in preference to a cash settlement.

In August 1942, the prospect of building further ships was again considered, and it was decided to ask Swan, Hunter & Wigham Richardson Ltd, to give the company the first refusal of the slipway that they expected to be vacant in December 1943 at their Neptune Yard.

The PORT JACKSON (3) on the day after being involved in a gun battle with U 516 picked up 27 survivors of the SYLVIA De LARRRINAGA that had been sunk on the 14th August 1942.

Convoy SC 122 has often been described as a turning point in the war at sea. One of the vessels sunk in this convoy was the PORT AUCKLAND (1) homeward bound from New Zealand to Avonmouth with a full cargo of frozen produce and general cargo. On St Patrick's Day 17th March 1943 when S. E. of Cape Farewell in position 52.25N., 30.15W., a torpedo fired from U 305 struck her and she sank with the loss of eight of her crew.

During March 1943, it was agreed that application should be made for licences to build two ships similar in design to the PORT MACQUARIE (2) with Swan, Hunter & Wigham Richardson Ltd.

In the same month the crew of the PORT CHALMERS (4) were awarded £1,000 in recognition of their efforts when the steering gear was disabled during exceptionally heavy weather in the North Atlantic. The cost of this award was split equally between the underwriters and the company.

The nearly new PORT VICTOR (3), which was similar to the PORT JACKSON (3) but had no rake to her funnel or masts and making only her second voyage, was torpedoed and sunk 600 miles west of Ireland on 30th April 1943 whilst homeward bound from South America by U 107 with the loss of 17 passengers and crew. Thankfully this was the last of the company's own vessels to be lost. The navigator of HMS WREN Lt. J. Robson, 'charged' the Chief Officer of the PORT VICTOR (3), for a lifebelt after rescuing him from a watery grave after his sinking by U 107. The lifebelt is at present on display at the Langford Wartime Centre in Northern Ireland. Disaster struck the managed FORT STIKINE when she blew up in Bombay docks on the afternoon of Friday, 14th April 1944 causing great loss of life.

On 11th April 1945 the PORT WYNDHAM was shaken by a terrific underwater explosion when off Dungeness and her Nos. 2 and 3 holds became swiftly flooded. The 24 passengers were quickly transferred to a naval vessel and were landed safely and unhurt. After tremendous efforts by the ship's crew under Captain. E. J. Syvret and the Admiralty Salvage Department the vessel was towed stern-first to Southampton and drydocked there, despite the fact that she was well "down by the head". The huge extent of the damage could then be seen, caused, so it was thought, by two torpedoes from a

German "midget" submarine, but was later found to be caused by a mine. It was to be over eighteen months before she returned to service and was afterwards known throughout the company as the 'WOBBLY WYNDHAM'.

During May 1945 Port Line returned to Cunard House, 88 Leadenhall Street, London from their wartime address at Leatherhead, Surrey.

Before the war ended the Port Line had prepared their policy for replacement of the heavy losses they had sustained of very valuable refrigerated cargo ships, and designs were so far advanced that it was possible to place orders for no fewer than five big vessels in the summer of 1945. One, the PORT NAPIER (3), was of 12,100 tons gross, and there were two ships of 10,600 gross tons and two single-screw 9,200 gross ships. In addition, a 12,000 ton refrigerated motor cargo vessel laid down for the Merchant Shipbuilding Department of the Admiralty was purchased and renamed PORT HOBART (2). All the new tonnage was built under the supervision of Mr. B. P. Arrowsmith O.B.E, who, despite the differences in machinery power required in the various ships, excluding the PORT HOBART (2), arranged that such a degree of standardisation should be employed that in all vessels the cylinder size should be the same, resulting in a very substantial degree of uniformity in the new fleet. The PORT NAPIER (3) had two six-cylinder engines, the PORT WELLINGTON (2) and the PORT PIRIE (4) two five cylinder units, and each of the smaller ships a six cylinder engine. In every case the engines were of the Doxford type, with a cylinder bore of 670 mm. and a combined piston stroke of 2,320 mm. The output per cylinder was in the neighbourhood of 1,100 b.h.p. at 110 r.p.m.

When the Ministry ordered the fast meat ship the EMPIRE GRACE from Messrs Harland & Wolff, a somewhat simplified adaptation of the WAIMARAMA design of Shaw, Savill & Albion Line designed shortly before the war and placed under the management of that firm, they put accommodation of 112 tourist class passengers in the midships island, giving the minimum amount of space in the cabins but providing quite a comfortable dining saloon and combined lounge and smoke room.

When Port Line was allowed to build its next ship under licence they contrived to get Admiralty approval for considerable improvements in the comfort of the passengers although the accommodation was arranged on the same principle.

In the Port Line's new motorship the PORT HOBART (2), originally laid down for the Ministry as the EMPIRE WESSEX, the principle was again modified. She had accommodation for 36 saloon passengers in a house under the bridge in cabins fitted with two, three or four berths. Below the cabins on the bridge deck was a lounge on the port side, the dining saloon which the passengers shared with the officers on the centre line and a smokeroom on the starboard side. A total of 92 tourist class passengers were accommodated on shelter-deck level in the midship house. The cabins were fitted with six or eight berths and ran along the starboard side from the break of the house to the after side of the funnel. There was also a smokeroom, lounge and dining saloon, the first on the centre line under the saloon passenger's dining room, the lounge on the portside of the dining saloon abaft that.

Handed over in January 1947, the PORT PIRIE (4), a similar ship to the earlier PORT WELLINGTON (2) that had been launched by Lady Freyberg in February 1946, was designed for the carriage of 12 passengers, but was initially completed with accommodation for 24 in view of the shortage of passenger space at that time. Completed at the Wallsend shipyard of Swan, Hunter & Wigham Richardson Ltd she was a twin-screw motor vessel fitted with Swan, Hunter-Doxford machinery giving a service speed of 16 knots.

In June 1947 the ceremony of unveiling a memorial to the staff and ships of the Port Line lost during the war took place in the main hall at Cunard House, Leadenhall Street, London, E.C.3. The unveiling was undertaken by Lord Royden, the senior Director of Port Line. He gave an outline of the casualties that the memorial recorded. A total of 14 ships were lost, one of these being a vessel managed on behalf of the Government. Altogether 166 lives were lost and 219 officers and men were taken prisoners of war. The memorial gave the names of each vessel and crew, and also recorded the decorations awarded to the numerous members of the sea and shore staffs of the Port Line.

One of the most interesting developments in connection with the PORT NAPIER (3) completed in September 1947 was the adoption for the first time of Birmabright, a form of stainless steel which was used for lining some of the refrigerated cargo spaces. These spaces comprised No 2 lower hold and 'tween decks and two meat lockers. The owners were convinced that this represented a step forward and they decided that the next two ships to be delivered, which were already under construction, would have holds wholly lined with Birmabright which would represent a saving in weight of approximately 250 tons in each vessel. Mr B. P. Arrowsmith (Superintendent Engineer) made the maiden voyage in the PORT NAPIER (3) that was described by many as the ideal cargo ship.

When the PORT AUCKLAND (2) and the PORT BRISBANE (2) were delivered they created a huge interest because of their modern design that was a complete contrast to most other cargo liners of the day. With their long forecastle, streamlined bridge front and funnel, they created a unique image for

Port Line and looked like small passenger liners even though they carried only 12 passengers. Cargo was carried in six holds, five of which were insulated, and they were among the first British ships to be fitted with a deck crane that was situated aft between Nos 4 and 5 hatches.

The PORT BRISBANE (2) was launched in June 1948. Her streamlined design was developed by the shipbuilders at the request of the directors of Port Line who wanted some distinguishing feature to be introduced since their new ship was destined to be the flagship of the line. Built by Swan, Hunter & Wigham Richardson Ltd, she was the seventeenth completion by that firm for the Port Line since 1925. She was propelled by twin-screw Wallsend Doxford balanced type opposed piston, reversible engines constructed by the Wallsend Slipway and Engineering Company. Each engine had six cylinders of 670 mm bore and 2,320 mm combined stroke, working on the single acting two-stroke cycle principle. The machinery was designed to develop an aggregate of 13,200 bhp at about 115 revolutions a minute on regular service, giving a cruising speed of 17 knots on a consumption of 38 tons of fuel per day. Built with three complete steel decks, her most striking feature was a completely enclosed, curved bridge structure containing the navigating bridge, the Master's and officers' accommodation, the passengers' lounge, smoke room and writing room and the dining saloon. Much thought and planning were devoted to the design of these features and when their general characteristics had been settled, a model to a scale of three inches to one foot was erected in the mould loft of the shipyard, so that a perfect construction would result. The hull form below the load water-line was identical with that of the PORT NAPIER (3) completed the previous year and for which extensive model tests were completed at Ship Division of the National Physical Laboratory, Teddington.

The PORT BRISBANE (2) had accommodation for 12 passengers. Their staterooms were single and double berth, panelled in Australian maple and luxuriously furnished with en-suite facilities. The dining saloon was panelled in silver birch. Good use was made throughout of weathered sycamore, Australian walnut, Indian laurel, white ash burr and Australian pear tree veneer. Attractive effects were also obtained by the use of glass screens, brilliantly cut and acid etched in various designs, the main feature in the principal entrance being a dolphin design, while screens featured Australian and New Zealand birds and animals. An embossed coat of arms of the City of Brisbane dominated the main stairway.

She was one of the most expensive cargo liners ever built up to that time. The accommodation for the Master and officers was above that of the passengers in the main bridge structure and was spacious and extremely well furnished.

PORT BRISBANE (Author's collection)

Members of the crew were berthed in well-furnished, two-berth cabins in the bridge 'tween decks, amidships. Food was served on the cafeteria principle, separate messes being provided for seamen and engine room ratings. Her cargo capacity consisted of 561,470 cu ft insulated for the carriage of frozen and chilled cargo, and 239,540 cu ft of uninsulated space in six holds, five of which, with the lower 'tween decks and No. 1 upper 'tween deck, were insulated. Compartments at the sides of the four remaining upper 'tween decks were provided to carry chilled cargo. Numbers 1 and 2 hatchways together with the after hatch were fitted with steel hatches sliding horizontally; the rest of the hatches were fitted with orthodox beams and wooden hatches. 16 motor-driven winches, together with a deck crane serviced them. The engine room crew, together with the stewards, were mostly from the London area, but her deck crew hailed from Stornoway. With a Master and four deck officers, the Chief Officer - following the Port Line custom, did not keep watch; the Fourth kept the eight to twelve, the Third the twelve to four, and the Second the four to eight

---

PORT BRISBANE - No. 1763 Ship.

PRELIMINARY SEA TRIALS

Thursday 24th February 1949.

High water 01.21 - 13.31

Leave Wallsend Shipyard Wharf	08.00
Out through Tyne Piers	09.00
Compasses and D. F. adjusted	12.00
Anchor trials completed	12.30

Proceed to Newbiggin Mile

Start first run North	13.30
Complete two double runs on Mile	15.30
Steering trials, start	15.45
Complete	16.15
Engineers' Stops and Starts	17.00
In through Piers	18.00
Berth at Wallsend Shipyard, Head Down	19.30

PORT BRISBANE - No. 1763 Ship.

OFFICIAL SEA TRIALS

Monday 28th February 1949.

High Water 04.06 - 16.03

Leave Wallsend Shipyard Wharf	08.30
Out through Tyne Piers	09.30

Proceed to Newbiggin Mile

Start first run North	10.30
Complete two double runs	12.30

Proceed to Tyne Entrance and disembark trials Party by ship	14.00
Proceed to London	14.30

Prior to her completion, plans had long been laid to have a Royal reception aboard PORT BRISBANE, in London. Invites were sent for consideration at Buckingham Palace.

> **BUCKINGHAM PALACE**
>
> February 26th. 1949.
>
> Dear Mr Rooper,
>
> This is to confirm my thanks for your letter of February 21st. and for the enclosures, as well as the specially bound copies of Notes on the Ship.
>
> I have ascertained that Princess Margaret is definitely accompanying The Queen.
>
> A Standard is being despatched to you to-day, and I will look forward to seeing you on Tuesday.
>
> Private Secretary to The Queen.

HM Queen Elizabeth (later Queen Mother) accompanied by HRH Princess Margaret visited the ship on 3rd March 1949. When the Queen's personal standard was broken from the masthead as she boarded the vessel it was the first time for at least a century that a Queen's standard had been flown from a merchant ship in the Port of London. It was also believed to be the first time that a Queen of England had boarded a cargo vessel in the Thames since the reign of Elizabeth 1.

After a two-hour tour of the ship, Her Majesty Queen Elizabeth and Princess Margaret and over forty other guests including Mr and the Hon. Mrs R. H. Senior, Lord and Lady Royden and other prominent members of the Port Line Board of Directors, as well as local politicians attended a reception and lunch on board the PORT BRISBANE.

>
> T. S. M. V. "PORT BRISBANE"
>
> March 3rd, 1949
>
> Menu
>
> Fried Fillets of Sole - Hollandaise Sauce
>
> Duchess Potatoes
>
> ———
>
> Lamb Cutlets Green Peas
>
> Creamed and French Fried Potatoes
>
> ———
>
> Strawberry Melba
>
> ———
>
> Cheese Biscuits
>
> ———
>
> Coffee
>
> Chateau Nairac Haut Barsac 1937
>
> Kummel (Wolfschmidt)
>
> Bisquit Dubouche (V.S.O.P.)

The menu for the **PORT BRISBANE** reception.

On an occasion such as this, there were, inevitably, a number of amusing incidents that obviously did not receive publicity, but with the passage of time make interesting reading.

The first occurred as the ship was rounding up in the Thames to enter King George V lock on her way from the Tyne where she was built. A hopper barge going down river struck her and the result was a small hole in the hull about 20 ft abaft the stem. As the Queen was due to visit the vessel within two days there was insufficient time to carry out a repair. Ship repair work was as uncertain then as it is today and the chance of the Queen arriving alongside with staging rigged overside and a plate off was too great a chance to take. The solution was to paste brown paper over the hole and then paint over the brown paper. None of the distinguished guests who boarded the ship that day realised she had a hole in her bow. Once the Royal visit was over the brown paper plate was removed and a more permanent repair put in hand.

Perhaps the most hair-raising incident of the visit nearly cost the Chief Officer serious injury. Incorporated in the design of the PORT BRISBANE (2) was a new idea. Instead of the usual varnished wood panels lining the refrigerated holds and forming the shuttering in the 'tween decks Birmabright was used. Straight from the shipyard with its brand new shine it was a most impressive sight, particularly in the large No. 3 hold.

It was felt that the Queen would wish to see a hold, but as she obviously could not be expected to clamber down the access ladder, the ship's accommodation ladder was rigged into No. 3 so that she could descend to the upper 'tween deck and then view the hold from this vantage point.

The Chief Officer was stationed in the upper 'tween-deck as were various members of the ship's company in different parts of the vessel to answer any questions that might be asked. When the Queen reached the bottom of the accommodation ladder she did not take the route which had been arranged, but turned towards the Chief Officer who, shaken by this change of plan, stepped back to let her pass and nearly fell down the hold. The Queen caught hold of the lapels of his jacket, steadied him and indicated that he should be more careful next time.

A signal was later sent to all the ships in the fleet instructing them to splice the mainbrace. Letters were received by the directors from many of the captains including one from Captain Thomas Kippins of the PORT HOBART (4).

PORT HOBART (Author's collection)

> Gentlemen,
>
> It gives me great pleasure to be able to report that your instructions to Splice the Mainbrace in honour of the visit of Her Majesty the Queen and Princess Margaret to the PORT BRISBANE were carried out in Sydney as soon as possible after receipt of Instructions on the 4th March. All officers were assembled in the Lounge and the splice was tucked in a seamanlike manner by all on board. It was considered that we were making history in Australian waters for the Port Line in as much as the Instructions were unique and we were very proud to know we had a ship in the fleet worthy to be honoured by a Royal visit.
>
> A toast was drunk to the Royal Family, Port Line Directors, the good ship PORT BRISBANE and all who sail in her. All on board wish to thank you for the opportunity they were given for sharing the honour attached to a visit of Her Majesty the Queen and the Princess Margaret to a Port Line vessel, at a distance of twelve thousand miles away.
>
> Thos Kippins,
> Master.
> PORT HOBART.

A similar letter was received from Captain Pedrick of the PORT CAROLINE (4), at that time at Istanbul.

BUCKINGHAM PALACE

March 4th. 1949.

My dear Brigadier,

By command of Her Majesty The Queen I am writing to say how greatly Her Majesty enjoyed her visit to "Port Brisbane" yesterday.

The Queen was most appreciative of the arrangements made for her welcome, and would like you to convey to Mr. Rooper, and to Commodore Higgs, her warm gratitude for all that they did to make her visit such a pleasant one. Her Majesty was much struck by the excellence of the Ship, and by the happy atmosphere in evidence on all sides.

I am also desired by Princess Margaret to say how much she enjoyed herself, and Her Royal Highness joins with Her Majesty in sending to the Captain and Ship's Company of "Port Brisbane" every good wish for the future.

Yours sincerely,

Private Secretary to The Queen.

Brigadier R. H. Senior, D.S.O., T.D.

Lord Royden wrote to the Deputy Chairman after the visit:-

> "I cannot allow so great an occasion to pass without writing to offer my personal congratulations on the amazingly successful show that the Port Line put up yesterday.
> I have attended a good many ceremonies of this sort and have never yet seen one better organised or where and this is the most important part there was such a wonderful spirit of happiness and loyalty as characterised the whole of yesterday's proceedings. The smoothness with which Her Majesty's visit passed off was the best evidence of the marvellous planning and execution of the programme".

Two sister-ships subsequently constructed for the fleet were commanded by the two Senior Masters in the Company's Service

---

Capt. W G Higgs OBE
Commodore of the Fleet

Captain W G Higgs O.B.E Commodore, first went to sea in 1902, at the age of 16, in the full-rigged ship CELTIC MONARCH and served 4½ years in her. He gained his Second Mate's certificate in 1906 and joined the Tyser Line (one of the constituents of Port Line) in September 1907. After promotions he attained his first command in 1919 - the PORT MACQUARIE (1), after which he commanded the following ships in the Port Line fleet:- the PORT STEPHENS (2), PORT PIRIE (3), PORT SYDNEY (1), PORT HUNTER (4), PORT GISBORNE , PORT CHALMERS (4), PORT JACKSON (3), PORT VICTOR (4), EMPIRE TREASURE, PORT CAROLINE (4) and the PORT WELLINGTON (2). It was for his part in getting his ship the PORT CHALMERS (4) safely through to Malta in convoy with urgently needed supplies in July 1941 that Captain Higgs was awarded the OBE. Captain Higgs retired after taking the PORT BRISBANE (2) on her maiden voyage and after a short period of retirement died in 1953.

Capt. W. J. Enright OBE RD

Captain W J Enright O.B.E R.D in command of the PORT AUCKLAND (2) joined Royden's Indra Line in July 1909 as a Third Officer. From 1914 until 1919 he served in the Royal Naval Reserve, rising to the rank of Lt. Commander when in command of a Monitor in the Dover Patrol. After World War One he returned to the Merchant Navy and became Chief Officer of the PORT PIRIE (3) and his first command was the PORT CHALMERS (3) in 1925. He was awarded the O.B.E for long and devoted service. In December 1947 when he and his crew joined the new PORT PIRIE (4) he flew the Blue Ensign. This was permissible as seven of his crew in addition to himself were members of the R.N.R. It is believed that the PORT PIRIE (4) was one of the first, if not the first, merchant vessel entitled to fly the Blue Ensign since the termination of the war.

Somewhat overshadowed by the intense publicity which greeted the entry into service of their streamlined consorts, the PORT VINDEX and the PORT VICTOR (4), converted from escort carriers back to cargo ships, nevertheless represented a tremendous British shipbuilding achievement. In the PORT VINDEX the crew's recreation room was in direct contrast to the rest of the ship since it was furnished and panelled with material taken from the PORT MELBOURNE (2) that had been broken up the previous year. This was purchased by Mr Rooper, one of the Port Line directors and installed in the ship as a memorial to his son who had lost his life in the Second World War. Under the command of Captain H. H. Smith O.B.E. the ship sailed on her maiden voyage without her refrigerating machinery, which was then installed before the commencement of her second voyage.

Her near sister-ship the PORT VICTOR (4), converted at Belfast left on her maiden voyage shortly afterwards.

At the close of 1949 Mr Herbert W. Corry retired as a director. He was Vice Chairman from 1927 to 1939, and Chairman from 1939 to 1947.

5. New For Old.

As the year 1950 dawned the PORT ADELAIDE (3), dating from 1919, was sold to breakers. Her name was perpetuated in the vessel completed in May 1951 which was the first new ship in the Port Line's fleet to use heavy fuel oil in her engine, but the necessary arrangements to this end were made in the PORT VINDEX some time before. Launched by Mrs B. P. Arrowsmith, wife of a Port Line director, the PORT ADELAIDE (4) was the third ship of that name to be launched by Hawthorn, Leslie. The first of three similar vessels, her refrigerated holds were entirely sheathed in aluminium-alloy (on the Gregson system) which had previously been fitted in the PORT BRISBANE (2) after tests had been made in one hold in the PORT VINDEX. The results in service were successful and all the refrigerated holds of the PORT ADELAIDE (4) were similarly treated.

PORT TOWNSVILLE (2), building at Wallsend, was successfully launched on the 21st June by the Hon. Mrs Geoffrey Gibbs. This was the first occasion when a Port Line ship had been sponsored by a lady whose connection with the firm had been through an agent of the company rather than directly with the company itself. The ship had a bridge structure and funnel which had been streamlined similar to that of the PORT BRISBANE (2). The machinery was designed to develop 7,500 bhp at about 114 revolutions per minute in regular service, and its construction was supervised by R. W. Cromarty, representing the owners.

The builders delivered the PORT TOWNSVILLE (2) well before the end of the year, despite the difficulties they encountered during construction, such as the ban on overtime and piecework, and also delays in the supply of steel which had begun to make itself felt in the last three or four months of construction. The PORT TOWNSVILLE (2) named after a port in North Queensland, Australia completed her trials on the 22nd October 1951 and sailed for London via Hamburg to load her first cargo for Australia.

When the PORT TOWNSVILLE (2) was launched by Swan, Hunter & Wigham Richardson Ltd, Wallsend, a hint was given that another vessel would be ordered by Port Line. Brigadier R. H. Senior, deputy-chairman of the Port Line Ltd, said his company had reserved another berth at Swan, Hunters and conversations between the owners and Swan, Hunters were going on very well and were rapidly reaching the stage when an order could be placed. Mr J. W. Elliott, chairman of Swan, Hunters, said that since 1925 they had been almost continuously employed with orders for the Port Line Ltd. PORT TOWNSVILLE (2) was a smaller version of the 1949 pair but with a shorter forecastle and an extended bridge front that became a feature of most of the subsequent ships. The idea of having the midships superstructure extended forward of the bridge front, as introduced in the PORT TOWNSVILLE (2) and developed in the PORT NELSON, was taken further with the PORT MELBOURNE (2) and the PORT SYDNEY (3) when the forward section was raised to the height of two decks. This was continued in subsequent ships and in some cases resulted in some distinctly odd appearances.

Launched on the 28th June 1951, the PORT NELSON was the 45th ship to be built at Belfast for the Port Line Ltd and its forerunners. She was named by Lady Corry, wife of Sir James Corry, a director and secretary of Port Line Ltd, who was the third baron and grandson of the Star Line's founder. Not as streamlined as the ships which had been recently completed on the North East Coast of England, she was nevertheless the first of five similar ships on order.

Speaking after the launch, W. Donald, chairman of the Port Line, announced that the company had reserved two berths, one at Belfast and one at the Govan yard of Harland & Wolff. He added that discussions about specifications for the new ships were proceeding.

PORT CAMPBELL (2) the last coal burner in the fleet, was sold to the shipbreakers in May 1953.

Between the years 1954 and 1966, Port Line Ltd took on long term charter, seven medium sized cargo vessels for periods of one to seven years, all of which were given PORT names. One of these the THISTLEDOWNE was renamed PORT CURTIS (3) in 1955 and had to run continually at full power to meet the charter speed of 14 knots in fair weather. She was dry-docked twice a year for cleaning and painting to help her maintain this.

PORT SYDNEY (3) was launched on 29th October 1954 by the Hon Mrs R. H. Senior wife of the Deputy Chairman of Port Line Ltd. She was christened with a bottle of Australian champagne specially presented to Mr Senior by a South Australian winery for use at the launching. She was completed on the 3rd March 1955 somewhat later than expected due to the difficulties being experienced at that time through the shortage of steel. With a service speed of $17^1/2$ knots she was the twentieth ship to be built at the Wallsend shipyard for the Port Line.

Running trials on the 4th February 1954 the PORT MONTREAL (2), a one-off ship designed for the

M.A.N.Z. Line, was powered by a 7,500 bhp, Harland B&W opposed piston engine giving her a speed of 17 knots. In 1957 she was transferred to the Crusader Shipping Company and was destined to become the most popular ship in the fleet for crew and was known as the "yacht".

Both the PORT MELBOURNE (3) and PORT SYDNEY (3), delivered in 1955, were smaller versions of the 1949 built PORT BRISBANE (2) and PORT AUCKLAND (2) but with less streamlining. Their design included a shorter forecastle, an extended bridge deck, and a tripod signal mast above the bridge. They were the first Port Line ships with anchors that fitted into a recess and were also fitted with a heavy lift derrick as well as a deck crane. The Belfast built PORT MELBOURNE (3) differed in the design of the signal mast and the design of the promenade deck. Considered by some to be superior vessels to their streamlined sisters, they were both sold in 1972 to Italian owners and are still in service today under a completely different guise. Their accommodation was designed to give better drop-stow access to No. 3 hold.

CRUSADER SHIPPING COMPANY

Formed in 1957, jointly by Port Line, the New Zealand Shipping Company Ltd., Shaw, Savill & Albion Company Ltd, and the Blue Star Line Ltd., with the aim to provide a service from New Zealand to Japan, primarily to cater for the diversification of meat from the traditional markets. Japan had rapidly become "Westernised" after World War Two, resulting in a large increase in the consumption of meat. The Japanese had looked towards the Dominions for their meat resources.

For this purpose two new motor ships were purchased from Swedish builders and named CRUSADER and SARACEN. KNIGHT TEMPLAR was also purchased second-hand. The new service was inaugurated by CRUSADER (3,338g./57) that left New Zealand in February 1958 with her first cargo of meat for Yokohama and Kobe. At first monthly sailings were maintained from the main New Zealand Ports to Kobe, Tagoshima, Yokkaichi, and Nagoya, with Tokyo in the summer season.

A service was also maintained between New Zealand and the West Coast of America with either CRUSADER and SARACEN.

The Shaw, Savill & Albion Company operated the ships as managing agents for Crusader Shipping

---

With the intention of providing suitable tonnage for the expansion of the Japanese and West Coast of North America meat trades, and with the search for new markets in mind, New Zealand Conference Lines ordered three new refrigerated ships in 1960 and converted a fourth, each of its ships were about 7,500 tons. Shaw, Savill's ALMERIC and Blue Star's CANTERBURY STAR opened up a service between New Zealand, the West Indies and South American ports and Port Line's PORT MONTREAL (2) and New Zealand Shipping Company's TURAKINI operated on the Crusader's service to Japan.

On the 3rd June 1958 the PORT INVERCARGILL arrived in the port of Bluff. A festive occasion was held on board the ship when the new coat of arms for the City of Invercargill was unveiled by the Mayor, A. L. Adamson. She was scheduled for launching in 1957 but industrial troubles again delayed her launch until 1958.

An unusual incident occurred in 1958 when the PORT FAIRY (2) lost a propeller on arrival at Port Said and returned to Southampton on one engine, to obtain a spare from her sister the PORT ALMA (2).

During 1959, on their outward voyages, the PORT NELSON and the PORT HOBART (2) were fixed to load oranges at Famagusta in Cyprus, the PORT HUON (1) loaded phosphates at Lisbon and the PORT FAIRY went to Bone in Algeria for a cargo of bagged phosphates. All these cargoes were destined for New Zealand. Unusual discharge ports on the outward voyage included Lautoka and Nukualofa in the South Seas and several vessels went to Noumea.

Homewards, vessels were making regular calls at Trinidad, Jamaica, Barbados and Aruba. Occasional calls were also made at La Guaira in the Caribbean, Houston in the Mexican Gulf, Callao in Peru and Bermuda. PORT LAUNCESTON visited Matarani and Mollendo in Peru and ships on the Crusader berth called at Los Angeles and San Francisco, besides Seattle and Vancouver. PORT MONTREAL (2) also called at Honolulu to discharge whilst on Crusader service.

In the Mediterranean Piraeus was a regular port of call and also, occasionally, Barcelona and Rijeka, Odessa and Novorossisk in the Black Sea were also visited.

Quite a number of vessels were employed in Brocklebank service and they found themselves in many harbours off their normal tracks. The Hooghly River to Calcutta was navigated in the course of voyages to Indian, Singalese and Pakistani ports that included Chalna, Chittiagong, Madras, Colombo, Trincomalee and Visakhapatnam. Cargo from the PORT LAUNCESTON was landed at Gan in the Maldive Islands where Messrs Richard Costains' were building an airstrip and Brocklebank cargo was also taken to the Red Sea ports of Assab, Massawa, Berbera Djibouti and Jeddah while the PORT CHALMERS (4) had the distinction of serving Mahe in the Seychelles.

Baie Comeau, close to Father Point on the north side of the St Lawrence River, became a new port on the M.A.N.Z. Line run and the PORT HALIFAX as well as the PORT CURTIS visited there. On this berth regular visits were made to Montreal, Three Rivers, Port Alfred, St John, Liverpool and Sydney in Nova Scotia. Gothenburg, Stockholm and Oslo were also regular ports of call.

6. Port Line Railway Locomotive.

In the 1950's British Railways operated a class of steam locomotive that was defined as "Merchant Navy Class". Each unit was named after a famous British shipping company, including Port Line.

> Letter from
>
> Southern Railway Company,
> General Manager's Office,
> Waterloo Station.
> 22nd December 1947
>
> Dear Mr Corry,
> As you may know, we have in service a powerful class of locomotive designed for both passenger and heavy goods service, known as the "Merchant Navy" Class. The engines bear the names of famous Shipping Companies and the original idea was conceived as a tribute to the part played by the Merchant Ships, their officers and crews during the war, and to cement the bond that exists between the various Shipping Interests and the Southern Railway.
> The first engines of the class came out in 1941. A further series is now "on the stocks " and we feel greatly honoured and delighted if one of these could bear the name "PORT LINE".
> I am, therefore, writing to ask if you would be good enough to agree to this suggestion; if you do, our Public Relations and Advertising Officer, whose office is at Waterloo Station, will get in touch with his opposite number in your Company for the exact details of your house flag etc. for reproduction on the name plate of the engine.
>
> GENERAL MANAGER

On 24th April 1950 a 'Merchant Navy' Class express locomotive No. 35027 designed for passenger and freight service on the Southern Region of British Railways and capable of a speed of 80 miles an hour was named "PORT LINE" at Southampton Docks.

Mr R. F. Biddle C.B.E, Southern Region Docks and Marine Manager, presided over the "PORT LINE" naming ceremony which was performed by Mr W. Donald (Chairman) who subsequently drove the new locomotive a short distance along the quay.

At the luncheon, which followed the naming ceremony held aboard the cross channel steamer FALAISE, Mr Biddle presented Mr Donald with a coffee table which had the company's flag on a sea-green background painted on its top.

The 'Merchant Navy' Class of steam locomotives were the largest and most powerful steam locomotives built by the Southern Railway for express passenger duties. Designed by O. V. S. Bulleid, they were introduced in 1941. All thirty members of the class were named after merchant shipping lines sailing from Southampton at that time.

"PORT LINE" was built at Eastleigh and entered service on the 11th December 1948, having been built to the original Bulleid design with an airsmoothed casing. Initially allocated to

Bournemouth shed, 35027 was used to haul the prestigious express trains of that era such as the "Bournemouth Belle" and the "Royal Wessex".

Soon afterwards it was transferred to Stewarts Lane Depot, Battersea, London after which it could frequently be seen hauling Channel boat trains including the famous "Golden Arrow" between London Victoria and Dover.

All of the 'Merchant Navy' Class locomotives were extensively rebuilt between 1956 and 1959. Whilst many of the more troublesome features were removed, the modified locomotives retained many of the excellent qualities of the original design. "PORT LINE" emerged from Eastleigh Works in May 1957 looking the more conventional locomotive it is today and, once again, returned to Bournemouth shed. It soon became a favourite there and was unofficially known as "Bournemouth's best engine".

In April 1959 "PORT LINE" saw Royal duty hauling the Queen and Prince Charles from Southampton to Windsor. By the mid 1960s steam traction was in decline and despite receiving a major overhaul in 1963, 35027 was declared "surplus to requirements" and withdrawn from service in September 1966 having steamed a total of 872,290 miles.

In 1967, 35027 was taken, along with many other redundant locomotives, to the now famous scrap yard of Woodham Brothers at Barry Dock, South Wales to bleakly await the cutter's torch. However, by a quirk of fate few of the locomotives were scrapped and a large number continued to stand in sidings for many years, as at this time the scrap yard had a contract to cut up redundant wagons which was far more profitable than cutting up old railway locomotives. The non-ferrous parts were removed and as the years passed by sea air took its toll and many remaining parts became seriously corroded. Indeed, by the end of the 1970's, in reality, only the frames, wheels and the boiler remained, many other parts having been removed by souvenir hunters.

Locomotive No. 35027 - PORT LINE - seen at Swanage. (Mrs C. A. Spong)

The nameplate and houseflag on the locomotive. (H. C. Spong)

In January 1982 "PORT LINE" was acquired by the Port Line Locomotive Project at a cost of £6,500 and later that year moved by road to the Swindon and Cricklade Railway, north of Swindon, Wiltshire. Restoration work began on the 17th January 1983 and continued at a pace previously unseen in locomotive preservation. The locomotive was in the open in a field and engineering facilities were non-existent. The locomotive was dismantled down to its component basic parts prior to the rebuilding.

Many missing parts had to be located or manufactured. The work was undertaken mostly by volunteers, many of whom had little previous experience of locomotive restoration. As time progressed the team gained experience and its success became the envy of many.

In the Autumn of 1987 with the restoration nearing completion, the locomotive was moved from the Swindon and Cricklade Railway to covered accommodation at the former railway works in central Swindon by kind courtesy of the new owners of this site, Tarmac Properties Ltd.. Restoration work continued in the shadow of the former massive "A" shop and steam was finally raised, for the first time in preservation, early in 1988. The restoration was completed during May of that year, the speed of restoration being a record for a locomotive of that size.

35027 made its restored public debut, albeit as a static exhibit, at a celebration to mark the 150th anniversary of the railway reaching Woking in 1838.

Immediately after the Woking event "PORT LINE" was transferred to the Bluebell Railway in Sussex where, in June 1988, it hauled its first public train since withdrawal by British Railways in 1966. For many years it became a regular performer on the Bluebell Line and became a firm favourite with both train crews and visitors alike. Eventually withdrawn for boiler repairs, it was moved to the Swanage Railway in Dorset for the work to be carried out, arriving there on 24th February 2004 "PORT LINE" remains in service on this restored line today.

7. Rationalisation And Co-operation.

Launched on 29th March 1960 by Lady Brocklebank, the PORT NEW PLYMOUTH was the largest ship completed for the company to date and also regarded by many as the ugliest, having a funnel far too small. She was the first of the larger ships to have no deck cranes and had a raised poop that included No 6 hatch. Named after a very pleasant town on the west coast of the North Island of New Zealand, she was designed for a service speed of 18 knots and completed her trials on 11th October 1960. In 1967 she took a single container to Melbourne as an experiment that was successful and marked the beginning of the end for the conventional meat trade.

During 1960 the PORT MACQUARIE (2) carried the following animals on deck from Durban to Adelaide: - two jaguars, five ring-tailed lemurs and a panther. Every precaution was taken to ensure the safety of the crew, and when the two docile beasts and timid fox-faced lemurs were shipped some of the senior staff felt that precautions had been overdone. Within twelve hours the male jaguar developed the habit of ripping the bars from the front of his cage, while the female ate through the expanded metal grills outside the bars of her cage. The captain said he had never known so many of his ship's company sleep behind closed doors and firmly secured ports.

PORT ST LAWRENCE, launched on 31st May 1961, and named by Mrs D. R. Rooper, was delivered in October and the PORT ALFRED, delivered the previous March, both intended for the M.A.N.Z Line service. With a service speed of 17 knots, they carried ten passengers and were similar to the PORT LAUNCESTON and the PORT INVERCARGILL except for a pair of kingposts forward of No 3 hatch.

PORT LAUNCESTON Showing her spare propeller to good vantage. (World Ship Society Photograph Library)

Some of the more unusual cargoes carried during 1961 were two Euclid dump trucks, each weighing 19 tons which were shipped to Melbourne in the PORT NAPIER (3). Shortly afterwards the PORT AUCKLAND (2) carried 7 tons of pencil leads to Sydney. That worked out at three million leads.

At the launch of the PORT NICHOLSON (3) Dr Rebbeck, Chairman of Harland & Wolff, referred to the strike in 1956, that caused the postponement of the launch of the PORT LAUNCESTON, and said, "As those men pace the streets of Belfast today unemployed I wonder if they remember the day we could not launch that ship. I sincerely hope they do". At the same time he pointed out this was the eighth ship that Harland & Wolff had built for the company.

In 1962 a small zoo was brought into Liverpool in the PORT LAUNCESTON from Adelaide for the Dudley Zoological Society in Worcestershire. It included two female kangaroos, two wallabies, six pairs of galahs, one pair of cockatoos, four keas (natives of New Zealand) and one pair of kookaburras (the laughing jackass).

In 1960, for the first time in the history of the company, a father and Son both captains served together at the same time, Captain J. A. Fairbairn on the PORT SYDNEY (3) and Captain T. A. Fairbairn relieving Captain based in Australia. In December 1961, Captain Fairbairn the elder died aged 60, he had first joined the company in 1921 and his first command was the PORT SYDNEY (2) in 1945. In 1940, when the PORT BRISBANE (1) was sunk, he was the Chief Officer and became a P.O.W. for five years.

In late 1961 the PORT HUON (1) (the first ship in the fleet with Sulzer engines) commenced her last voyage from Avonmouth to the Spanish port of Valencia where she loaded a full cargo of rice in bags for the Philippines, after discharge she proceeded to Japan for breaking up. At about the same time the PORT SAINT JOHN was sold for further trading, she was renamed REDESTOS after a village on a Greek island where the principal of the new owners lived.

In 1962 company ties were sold at twelve shillings and sixpence for silk and ten shillings for terylene. The design, on a dark blue background illustrated the company flag interspersed with letters P. L. in small italics.

A St. Bernard dog was shipped in the PORT NEW PLYMOUTH and landed at Melbourne where it was used to publicise Hennessy Brandy. Both the ship and the dog featured on television. Part of the cargo of the PORT MONTREAL (2) on a voyage in 1962 was old newspapers which were used by the natives at Port Moresby as cigarette papers.

Delivered on 9th November 1962 by Harland & Wolff, the PORT NICHOLSON (3) was the largest vessel yet built for the company. She was named after the expanse of water on which the city of Wellington stands and had a capacity of 603,000 cu ft insulated and 220,000 cu ft general, or 400,000 carcasses of lamb and 11,000 bales of wool and was the first ship to be fitted with, 'ships head up - true motion' Marconi Argus Radar. The PORT NICHOLSON (3) averaged 20.9 knots on trials, against a service speed of $18^{1}/_{2}$ knots and had a crew of 82. Sailing on her maiden voyage from London on 29th November 1962, her first cargo included three Rolls-Royce cars which were to be used by the Queen on her visit to New Zealand as well as a Formula One racing car which was used by Graham Hill and Innes Ireland in the New Zealand Grand Prix held at Auckland.

During 1962 a second cargo of meat was taken to Guam by the PORT MONTREAL (2), the first cargo having been taken by the TURAKINA of New Zealand Shipping on the Crusader Shipping Company service. This was due to a relaxation of security by America as, before 1962, New Zealand meat was taken to Japan and then transhipped to American vessels for onward transportation to Guam.

On 11th May 1963 a unique occasion was witnessed in Sydney Harbour when three vessels of the company, the PORT BRISBANE (2), PORT LAUNCESTON and the PORT ST LAWRENCE all sailed within an hour of each other.

PORT LYTTELTON (Liverpool University Archives / Skyfotos)

Cargo carried during 1963 included 400 tons of explosives shipped in the PORT LYTTELTON (2) from London, together with nine Whippy ice-cream vans painted in pink and cream and 16 squirrels destined for Adelaide Zoo. Shortly afterwards a further shipment of ice-cream vans left in the PORT MELBOURNE (3).

In the same year the racehorse Bonnie Mac with Peter Scudamore in the saddle won the Hereford Hugh Summer Challenge Bowl. On 3rd January 1964 he won again, at Windsor. On both occasions he rode in the Port Line colours.

On a more sombre note in October 1963 the last apprentice was indentured.

On 4th February 1964 the PORT LAUNCESTON locked out of Avonmouth into the Bristol Channel for the short passage to Cardiff, having cast off the tugs. Tragically, one tug, the KINGSGARTH, came into contact with her. Having crossed her bow, the tug was pushed over on to her beam ends from where she rolled over and passed beneath the PORT LAUNCESTON, scraping the hull as she went. A lifeboat was launched and one survivor was picked up, a further crewman was picked by another tug, the remaining three crew were drowned.

A book celebrating 50 years of the Port line written by A. S. McMillan was published in 1964 and a Golden Jubilee dance held on 15th April 1964 at the Connaught Rooms, London was attended by over 420 people.

Some significant events occurred in 1964:-

> The first consignment of chilled veal was shipped to Genoa from New Zealand in the PORT INVERCARGILL.
>
> Donald Campbell's world record-breaking car "BLUEBIRD" was loaded at Sydney, in the PORT MELBOURNE (3) to take part in the Lord Mayor's Show in London on the 14th November.
>
> PORT NELSON transited the St. Lawrence Seaway in June becoming the first Port Line ship to do so.

Notable events celebrated during 1965 included the distinction of being the shipping company having the longest association with the Meteorological Office (for weather reporting) through Corry & Company.

On a personal note, Thomas Hargreaves retired after having been Radio Officer in the PORT NAPIER (3) since her maiden voyage. He had completed 36 deep-sea voyages.

In 1965 the company placed an order worth approximately £6 million with Alexander Stephen & Sons Ltd. for two twin-screw refrigerated motor ships, one for delivery in December 1967, and the other in June 1968. Each vessel had approximately 600,000 cu.ft of refrigerated space and approximately 200,000 cu.ft of general cargo space. There was also tank space to enable 450 tons of bulk liquids to be carried. The cargo holds were designed to facilitate the carriage of palletised and unitised cargo, both refrigerated and general, to the maximum extent.

In 1965 the PORT HUON (2), named after an anchorage at the mouth of the Huon River in Tasmania, was delivered and a sister ship, PORT ALBANY (3), followed shortly afterwards. Each had a speed of 19 knots and a refrigerated capacity of 350,000 cu ft and 19,000 cu ft of general cargo. They were designed for the carriage of meat from Australia to the East Coast of the United States and fruit from Australia to the United Kingdom and the Continent of Europe, and were also suitable for the increasing New Zealand/Pacific trade. It was intended that these small-type vessels, with their speed of 19 knots, would be able to make two quick voyages with fruit in each Australian season, and that during the rest of the year would be free for other trades requiring ships with totally insulated space and able to give speedy delivery. The ships were powered by a single Wallsend Sulzer 8-cylinder turbo-charged engine using 1500-second fuel oil. Designed to operate with a much smaller crew, totalling 52, they had no passenger accommodation. Additional features were nearly 8,000 cu ft of space for tallow in bulk, a 70-ton derrick and hydraulic hatches throughout. A third ship, the PORT BURNIE with very similar specifications, both in size, cargo spaces and machinery was ordered from Swan, Hunter & Wigham Richardson Ltd and was launched by Mrs J. H. Cook on the 17th April 1965 at their Barclay Curle shipyard on the Clyde.

On the 12th January 1966 A.C.T. Ltd., (Associated Container Transportation Ltd.) was formed jointly by Ellerman Lines, T. & J. Harrison Ltd, Blue Star Line Ltd, Ben Line, and Cunard Line Ltd. This company was formed for the purpose of carrying out research into the development of containerisation, unitisation and other new methods of cargo handling and carriage by sea. It was clear that the carriage of goods by and in containers was revolutionary and would involve changes in the pattern of services provided.

On a lighter note, in September 1966, a ship spotting competition was held on board the PORT ST. LAWRENCE in order to induce night signalling (by Morse lamp). Additional points were given for ascertaining the vessel's name, destination and last port of call, making a maximum of four.

PORT ST LAWRENCE (World Ship Society Photograph Library)

The competition ran from the 9th to 22nd September from Cape Guardafui Passage to Le Havre and the following statistics were compiled, giving a general indication of shipping at that time.

Total number of ships observed	42
Total number of points awarded	1101
Percentage of cargo ships	55%
Percentage of tankers	40%
Passenger ships and miscellaneous	5%

The miscellaneous section included
1 tank landing task force ship (HMS FEARLESS)
3 coastal minesweepers (2 British and 1 Italian)
1 submarine (British)
1 ocean cable layer (Italian)
1 oceanographic survey (German)
2 cross straits ferries.

Percentage in Nationalities

British	20%
German	15%
Greek	10%
Norwegian and Liberian	7%
Spanish and Danish	6%
French and American	5%

The remaining 37% comprised a mix of Russian, Dutch, Polish, Indian and Italian shipping.

It is worth noting that the exercise took place on passage time only - thus excluding the Canal transit and also the last two days were spent in fog with moderate and at times very poor visibility. Amazing how many ships can pass in fourteen days.

The seaman's strike of 1966 had disastrous consequences for the Port Line and British shipping in general and the company declared a loss of £160,000 for that year.

The chairman in his annual address delivered in December stated that 1966 had been a difficult year for the industry and Port Line's interests, in common with others, had been adversely affected by the seamen's strike in the middle of the year. In addition, the severe and long-lasting drought in Australia, now mercifully broken, had obvious repercussions on the flow of exports from the Commonwealth with consequently smaller carryings. The strike was now over and Australia's recuperative powers would no doubt be equal to the task of building up her stock population to a normal level. 1967, like any other year, would bring its crop of problems and difficulties. The company must face it without repining over the past, but with a cheerful determination to continue giving the service and efficiency our customers require and deserve to get. The longer term future, with the advent of different methods of cargo carriage, presented a challenging problem which had to be tackled resolutely. The changes both in operation and "make up" of cargo liner fleets were likely to be considerable, and it was no exaggeration to say that the late sixties and early seventies would see a revolutionary alteration of the present pattern within which we have worked for many years. He was certain in this context that "change" should be regarded as "progress", and he was confident it would be so looked at by all hands.

PORT JACKSON (Author's collection)

The PORT JACKSON (3) on her way to the breakers and under her new name LEGATION, was recognised in the Red Sea in March 1967 by the smoke from her generators by the crew of the PORT ST LAWRENCE under the command of Captain A. Kinsett.

The PORT INVERCARGILL had the misfortune to be trapped in the Suez Canal during the Arab Israeli war in June 1967. After being declared a constructive total loss in 1970, she was not towed out of the Suez Canal until May 1975. Sold to Greek owners, she was renamed KAVO KOLONES and was finally sold to the breakers in 1979.

In September, Atlas Line commenced trading between Australia and Japan and comprised Port Line, Blue Star Line and the Ellerman and Bucknall Steamship Company. The first voyage in this new fortnightly service was taken by the ROCKHAMPTON STAR that commenced loading at Adelaide on the 1st September. The first Port Line vessel to depart was the PORT MONTREAL (2) that loaded at Adelaide at the end of September.

PORT CHALMERS (5) was launched, on 9th October 1967, by Lady Porritt, wife of the Governor General designate of New Zealand. She brought the fleet up to 29 and was the twenty fourth ship built for the company since the war. Delivered in April 1968, the PORT CHALMERS (5) was the largest refrigerated ship in the world, and her deadweight tonnage of 19,710 tons far outstripped that of any other refrigerated cargo liner afloat or building. The cargo capacity has probably only been topped by a few conventional ships, (the Atlantic Transport Line's MINNEWASKA, which was built in 1923, carried just over 19,800 tons).

Cargo was carried in seven main holds, of which five were fully refrigerated. In addition, there was extensive tank capacity for the carriage of liquid cargo. The refrigerating equipment held temperatures between 0 degrees F to minus 10 degrees F. Cargo equipment consisted of four 10 ton and two 15-ton derricks, all of which were operated by independent topping and slewing winches. There were three 5-ton travelling cranes and one fixed crane of similar capacity. In addition there was a 25-ton Thompson swinging derrick. In order to stow palletised cargo and unitised cargo more economically the ship was built without sheer for the greater part of her length. There was no camber and 'tween decks were flush with the deck.

All of this type of cargo could be handled with fork-lift trucks. An interesting feature of the holds was the employment of permanent corrugated steel dunnage supplied by Gregson & Company Ltd., the main contractors for the insulation. This system was estimated to save £10,000 a year on loose dunnage charges. It was developed to provide sufficient area for air flow in the cooled holds and was carefully investigated in collaboration with the Shipowners Refrigerated Cargo Association using model tests and full scale trials held in an existing Port Line ship. Previously when cargo was stowed it was laid on wooden planks and timber, called "dunnage" and a ship used enormous quantities of it on every voyage.

PORT CHALMERS (5) was also designed to carry two tiers of containers on the bridge deck. The Alexander Stephen technique of using a 10% scale model was employed to develop the engine-room design and the result was notably successful in providing a high degree of accessibility, store and workshop space despite the fact that the overall length of the engine room was only 64 feet. Bridge control was provided by a "Mahout" system developed by Alexander Stephen and an extension provided remote control from a well instrumented console in the engine-room. It was not intended to operate her with an unmanned engine-room and, therefore, the range of alarms and the extent of automation was limited.

12 passengers were carried in single and double berth cabins. There was a lounge, smoke room and a dining room which was shared with the ship's officers. Officers also had their own lounge and recreation room.

The 1967 Message from the Chairman started with the words:

"Tempora mutantur nos et mutamur in illis" (Horace 8 B.C.)
"Times are changing and we must change with them"
"The next two or three years will see Port Line's image changing to conform with the pattern of things to come in a container ship era. We must face the challenge of the future with the same resolution we have displayed in the past, adapting ourselves to the new techniques, both in ships and in management which are the inevitable partners of change. This is no time for regret over the passing of the "good old days"; but a time for looking forward to the "brave new days" ahead which we can help to create. The future is in your hands, I could not wish for it to be in better keeping".

The latter years of the conventional service were far from happy. In the interests of economy in adverse trading conditions and with containerisation around the corner it was decided that the Port Line and Blue Star fleets should be brought under the single management of Blue Star Port Lines (Management). An agreement between Port line Ltd. and Blue Star Line Ltd was signed by the Chairman, Sir Basil Smallpiece, and Mr R. A. Vestey on 9th February 1968. As from 15th March 1968, this new management company operated and managed between them 56 ships in the trades from Australia, New Zealand and South Africa. The company was formed in order to rationalise the two companies Australasian services.

The Board of Directors of the joint company were as follows:
    Mr R. A. Vestey (Chairman)
    Mr P. E. Bates
    Mr D. G. Hollebone (General Manager)
    Mr J. G. Payne (General Manager)
    Mr P. H. Shirley.
    Mr E. H. Vestey.
The Board of Port Line as at 1st April 1968
    Chairman   Sir Basil Smallpiece, K.C.V.O.
    Managing Director   D. G. Hollebone, M.B.E, M.C, T.D.
    Directors   P. E. Bates, V.R.D.
                        P. J. Fuller, T.D.
                        Capt W. S. Jenks, O.B.E, R. N. Retd.
                        J. D. M. Hearth
                        P. H. Shirley
                        Sir Geoffrey Gibbs, K.C.M.G.
                        Capt A. G. Russell
                        E. C. Sutton

This management company was formed to manage both companies' fleets in those trades common to both lines. Principally these were in the UK/Continent - Australasia and, East Coast USA/Canada - Australasia services, these routes were operated with refrigerated cargo liners serving Australian and New Zealand meat and fruit shippers on north-bound services and European general cargo shippers south-bound. Although the arrangement was modestly successful in finding alternative work for the declining fleet it was terminated from March 1973. The overall management of Port Line was assumed by Cunard Brocklebank, virtually marking the end of Port Line as an operational shipping company.

The traditions, however, lived on through Associated Container Transportation (Australia) that was financed by Cunard through its Port Line subsidiary, together with Blue Star and Ellerman Lines. Prior to the launch of the container service in March 1969 Port Line vessels took part in many of the trial shipments of containerised cargoes, north and south bound. With Trafalgar House's acquisition of Ellerman, Cunard-Ellerman now had a $57^1/2$% shareholding in A.C.T. (A) that traded between Europe and Australasia and from Australasia and the Pacific to the USA and Canada which, in effect, was a regular round the world service.

Mr Derek Hollebone, managing director of Port Line, stated on the 16th April 1968 after the launching at the Linthouse yard, Glasgow, of the 18,000 tons dwt., 21-knot, refrigerated cargo ship PORT CAROLINE (5), that four British shipping lines intend to start a container service to New Zealand in 1972. He had just returned from New Zealand with a delegation representing the New Zealand Shipping Company; Shaw, Savill; Port Line and Blue Star Line. All were members of either A.C.T. or O.C.L. , the two container consortia which were due to start operations on the Australian run early next year.

The New Zealand lines' announcement that the need for a year of further studies, delaying the start of a service until 1972, had been "received with great interest and not without comment", he added. Disappointment in some quarters had been balanced by strong support in others for the lines' approach.

Mr Hollebone had also said it was the Port Line's intention that initially the PORT CAROLINE (5) would be engaged in the Australian and New Zealand trades. It was probable that, with the introduction of the container era into the Australian trade in 1969, she would subsequently be engaged almost entirely in the New Zealand trade. The PORT CAROLINE (5) might well be the last of that class of vessel that the Port Line would require to be built to maintain the existing services and whilst she was capable of carrying up to 100 containers, if required, she was a conventional vessel. Alluding to the recent delegation to New Zealand, Mr Hollebone said the purpose of the visit was to inform the New Zealand Government, the authorities concerned and clients, of their intentions regarding containers.

Although Mr Molyneaux's inquiry (excerpts were published in "Shipbuilding and Shipping Record" on 25th May 1967) that was sponsored by the British lines, considered that a limited introduction of container ships would be a practical and economic proposition in 1971, the subsequent studies made by the lines themselves indicated that even further studies were required. It was one thing to keep up with the Joneses in the Australian trade where the trade was reasonably balanced but, where there was an imbalance, as in New Zealand, everyone concerned with New Zealand's interests should be satisfied that a new concept would incorporate the most efficient and economic methods of operation. The difference could be summed up in one word "refrigeration". New Zealand was the world's largest exporter of refrigerated cargo and, over the years, the British lines had built up four of the largest fleets of refrigerated cargo liners in the world to meet New Zealand's special requirements. It would be madness for the same lines to rush into a new venture and a new era without first taking all reasonable precautions to ensure its success.

With the advent of containerisation the whole pattern of Europe-Australasia trade underwent a radical change, one of which the Port Line actively participated in through its membership of the Associated Container Transportation consortium (A.C.T). The Port Line vessels PORT CHALMERS (5) and PORT CAROLINE (5) operated jointly by the Blue Star/Port Line management company were the last of their class to be built.

Like her sistership, the PORT CAROLINE (5) was contracted at Alexander Stephen & Sons Ltd Linthouse, before the builder became part of Upper Clyde Shipbuilders Ltd and which under a rationalization programme later closed down the famous Linthouse yard. Thus the PORT CAROLINE (5) was the last of a long line of Stephen-built ships.

In 1969 Compass Line services were inaugurated between Australia and South Africa. The service was an extension of the Blue Star/Port Line partnership, and it had originally been proposed to register the participating ships under the South African flag. However, since the South African Government proposed levying import duty on any ships so registered, British registry was retained. The PORT MELBOURNE (3) opened the service in October 1969. Unfortunately as a result of poor cargoes from South Africa and intense competition Compass Line services ceased in March 1971.

In March 1969 the Actanz Line was started to operate all the non-container conventional cargo services in the fleet and PACE Line was formed to replace the M.A.N.Z Line service.

Developments in shipbuilding and refrigerating equipment

TSS **PORT NICHOLSON** (1)		TSMS **PORT NICHOLSON** (3)
Built, 1912 (Workman, Clark & Company)		1962 Harland & Wolff
Particulars 490ft x 61ft x 29ft 7½in		573½ft x 75¾ft x 30¾ft
Capacities:		
Insulated	266,380 cu. ft.	594,310 cu ft
General Cargo	277,920 cu. ft	214,891 cu ft
Total	544,300 cu. ft.	809,201 cu ft
Horsepower	3,500	15,950
Speed	12 knots	19 knots
Daily fuel consumption	75 tons (coal)	71 tons (heavy fuel oil)

Comparative statistics are interesting and the following particulars give some indication of the trends.

	PORT LINE FLEET in November 1922	PORT LINE FLEET in November 1962
Number of ships	26 steamers	30 motor ships
Average ship Dimensions	464ft 3in x 59ft x 29ft	485ft 7in x 67ft x 29ft
Deadweight	10,812 tons	11,067 tons
Speed	12 knots	16½ knots
Insulated Capacity	288,225 cu. ft	435,114 cu. ft
Main engine Horsepower	4,270	11,280
Generator output	37 kilowatts	1,070 kilowatts
Average age of ships	9 years 8 months	14 years 7 months
Total serving Engineer officers	205	439

Shipbuilders	Numbers constructed	
	1922	1962
Workman, Clark	16	
Hawthorn, Leslie	8	3
Swan, Hunter	1	14
Charles Connell	1	
Joseph Thompson	1	
John Brown		3
Harland & Wolff		9
Total	26	30

8. Under Pressure.

The Blue Star Line influence in the Port Line was so strong in the early 1970s through the Blue Star-Port Lines (Management) Ltd that the shipping press wondered if it was still a Cunard group company. A replacement to Port Lines' Company Magazine "G.W.Z.C" which ceased publication in April 1968 was launched in April 1970, entitled Blue Star Port Line Journal, it was short lived and lasted for only two years. Shortly after this a new house magazine ' The Cunarder' took its place in the winter of 1972.

Typical voyages undertaken during the period July 1970 - July 1972
Dates are usually arrival/departure, unless otherwise stated

PORT VINDEX (July 1970 - Jan 1971)

London - July 13
Falmouth - July 16
Cape Town - August 2/3
Fremantle - August 17/21
Adelaide - August 25/31
Melbourne - September 2/5
Sydney - September 7/12
Brisbane - September 14/17
Townsville - September 20/20
Port Alma - September 27/29
Portland (Vic) - October 4/7
Melbourne - October 7/18
Fremantle - October 23/30
Cape Town - November 12/13
London - November 30/Jan 7
Liverpool - January 9/9
Hamburg - January 22/26
Bremen - January 27

PORT HUON (Jan 1972 - July 1972)

Falmouth - January 3-Laid Up
Falmouth - Sailed January 19
Agadir - January 23/30
Klaipeda - February 5/13
Copenhagen - February 15/16
Panama - March 2
Guayaquil - March 4/6
Valparaiso - March 11/25
Panama - March 31
Rotterdam - April 12/15
Hamburg - April 16/21
Southampton - April 23/25
Gibraltar - April 27/28
Ashdod - May 2/8
Rotterdam - May 16/20
London - May 21/25
Rio Grande - June 8/12
Buenos Aires - June 13
Rio Grande - June 18/21
Lisbon - July 4/14
Rotterdam - July 17/19
Hamburg - July 19.

Sailing from Bremen on the 28th January 1971, the PORT VINDEX completed one more voyage to New Zealand returning to London on the 24th June 1971. After discharge she sailed to Kaohsiung via Durban for breaking up, arriving there on 23rd August 1971.

After arriving in Hamburg the PORT HUON (2) was sold to Greek owners and renamed JULIETTA.

In the period April 1970 and December 1972 no less than 19 vessels were disposed of - 13 to shipbreakers and 6 for further trading. Unfortunately, there was practically no future use for ships with large refrigerated capacity designed for specific trades, when they had outlived their owner's usefulness. The shipbreakers were the only people who would buy them.
In August 1971 Cunard was taken over by Trafalgar House Investments and in January 1972 W. Slater of Cunard Brocklebank became Chairman of Port Line.
In 1972 the Crusader services were split between the constituent companies and the passenger accommodation on the PORT CHALMERS (5) was used only for company employees travelling between postings.
Blue Star Port Line (Management) Ltd ceased operating in 1973 and shortly afterwards Cunard Brocklebank took over the management of the remaining conventional ships
By 1974 the fleet was reduced to just nine ships and during 1975 the PORT ST LAWRENCE and PORT ALFRED were transferred to Cunard - Brocklebank.
In his yearly report the Chairman of Port Line Mr W. Slater said that the Australian/New Zealand

trades were somewhat depressed at present and he doubted if the boom conditions of twelve months ago would ever return. Port Line's conventional service had had an exceptionally good year he added, but it was probably the last year of its type.

With further containerisation planned for 1977/78, including the South Island of New Zealand, rationalisation of the fleet still continued and Mr Slater warned that unless there was a very considerable change in the freight market the PORT AUCKLAND's (2) fate would be the same as that of the PORT BRISBANE (2) when at the end of 1976 the vessel was due for survey.

PORT AUCKLAND (2) was duly sold at the end of 1976 to a Kuwait company Gulf Fisheries WLL and then converted over a period of three months at the Keppel shipyard in Singapore, with the aid of Cunard, into a sheep carrier. Cunard Brocklebank managed the vessel, now named MASHAALLAH, (In Arabic the name means "God is wonderful") on behalf of the venture, and after several voyages had gained considerable experience in a what was a comparatively new trade.

Mr W. B. Slater speaking at a Junior Officers seminar held in May 1977 said of Port Line "It has had a very good year, having taken advantage of the reefer market generally. The future depended greatly on what Australia and New Zealand could do to find new markets to compensate for the effect of the European Economic Community. In due course a new use must be found for the PORT CHALMERS (5) and the PORT CAROLINE (5). By 1979 requirements in Australia and to some degree New Zealand might be very limited for this class of vessel. PORT NICHOLSON (3) would probably be the second ship to be converted into a sheep carrier, but with additional refrigerated space to cope with the growing trade from Australia to the Gulf ports. The decision may be taken in the next two to three months. Mr Slater commented "If we don't do it someone else will. The problem of keeping the sheep alive is the major issue on which we have to concentrate".

By 1978 Port Line had ceased to exist as a separate entity in the Cunard Group. With the sale of the PORT NICHOLSON (3) to Taiwan shipbreakers in October 1979 and the disposal of the PORT NEW PLYMOUTH to Panamanian-flag operators, the fleet of conventional cargo ships had dwindled away to only two and both were laid up.

The two remaining ships, the PORT CHALMERS (5) and the PORT CAROLINE (5), spent their last years in and out of lay up and finally, in January 1982 although remaining registered to Port Line, were renamed MATRA and MANAAR respectively for operation by Brocklebank but still suffered periods of lay-up.

MATRA 6th July 1983 laid up on the R. Fal. (P. White)

Proposals were considered to convert them into either container ships or 800 capacity passenger cruise liners but both were dismissed as being unsuitable and too expensive respectively. Disposed of to Greek owners in 1983, both were broken up in 1985. A sad end for two fine ships and a company that had been overtaken by the container revolution.

PORT LINERS IN DISGUISE

PORT MONTREAL in Compass Line funnel markings. (World Ship Society Photograph Library)

PORT MONTREAL in Atlas Line colours. (Alex Duncan)

PORT ALFRED in Crusader Line funnel markings. (World Ship Society Photograph Library)

PORT ST LAWRENCE in Atlas Line colours. (Ambrose Greenway collection)

DANAE above was converted from PORT MELBOURNE (Selim San)

DAPHNE below from PORT SYDNEY   (Alex Duncan)

PORT HOBART wearing Brocklebank funnel markings. (A. Duncan)

PORT NELSON wearing Clan Line funnel markings. (A. Duncan)

The Commonwealth & Dominion Line Ltd. / Port Line Ltd., Fleet

NB.
The numbers contained in brackets immediately after and relating to the use of the ship name have been continued from the Ancestoral fleets contained in Part No.1, hence Port Hunter (3) etc.

1. PORT HUNTER (3) (1914 - 1918) see ship No. WM.70 in the Milburn fleet.

PORT AUGUSTA (Ambrose Greenway collection)

2. PORT AUGUSTA (2) (1914 - 1925) see ship No. WM 72 in the Milburn fleet.

PORT PHILLIP (World Ship Society Photograph Library)

3. PORT PHILLIP (4) (1914 - 1918) see ship No. WM 71 in the Milburn fleet.

PORT PIRIE (J. Dobson collection)

4. PORT PIRIE (2) (1914 - 1915) see ship No. M 73 in the Milburn fleet.

PORT CURTIS (World Ship Society Photograph Library)

5. PORT CURTIS (1) (1914 - 1917) see ship No. WM 74 in the Milburn fleet.

PORT KEMBLA (Ambrose Greenway collection)

6. PORT KEMBLA (1) (1914 - 1917) see ship No. WM 75 in the Milburn fleet.

PORT LINCOLN (World Ship Society Photograph Library)

7. PORT LINCOLN (1) (1914 - 1927) see ship No. WM 76 in the Milburn fleet.

PORT MACQUARIE (Ambrose Greenway collection)

8. PORT MACQUARIE (1) (1914 - 1927) see ship No. WM 77 in the Milburn fleet.

PORT ALBANY (Ambrose Greenway collection)

9. PORT ALBANY (1) (1914-1929) see ship No. WM 78 in the Milburn fleet.

INDRALEMA (Ambrose Greenway collection)

10. INDRALEMA (2) (1914 - 1916)
PORT ALMA (1) (1916 - 1923) see ship No. R 32 in the Royden fleet.

PORT ALMA (Ambrose Greenway collection)

PORT ELLIOT (World Ship Society Photograph Library)

11. INDRABARAH (2) (1914 - 1916)
PORT ELLIOT (2) (1916 - 1924) see ship No. R 38 in the Royden fleet.

12. INDRAPURA (3) (1914 - 1916)
PORT ADELAIDE (2) (1916 - 1917) see ship No. R 39 in the Royden fleet.

PORT STEPHENS (Ambrose Greenway collection)

13. STAR OF AUSTRALIA (1914 - 1916)
PORT STEPHENS (2) (1916 - 1924) see ship No. C 32 in the Corry fleet.

14. STAR OF SCOTLAND (1914 - 1916)
PORT CAMPBELL (1) (1916 - 1918) see ship No. C 34 in the Corry fleet.

PORT PIRIE (World Ship Society Photograph Library)

15. STAR OF INDIA (1914 - 1916)
PORT PIRIE (3) (1916 - 1935) see ship No. C37 in the Corry fleet.

PORT MELBOURNE (World Ship Society Photograph Library)

16. STAR OF VICTORIA (2) (1914-1916)
PORT MELBOURNE (2) (1916 - 1948) see ship No. C 38 in the Corry fleet.

PORT SYDNEY (World Ship Society Photograph Library)

17. STAR OF ENGLAND (2) (1914 - 1916)
PORT SYDNEY (1) (1916 - 1948) see ship No. C 39 in the Corry fleet.

PORT HACKING (Ambrose Greenway collection)

18. MIMIRO   (1914 - 1916)
PORT HACKING (1916 - 1928) see ship No T 16 in the Tyser fleet.

PORT LYTTELTON (Ambrose Greenway collection)

19. NIWARU   (1914 - 1916)
PORT LYTTELTON (1) (1916 - 1924) see ship No T 17 in the Tyser fleet.

20. MARERE (1914 - 1916) see ship No. T 18 in the Tyser fleet.

PORT CHALMERS (World Ship Society Photograph Library)

21. WHAKARUA   (1914 - 1916)
   PORT CHALMERS (3) (1916 - 1926) see ship No. T 19 in the Tyser fleet.

PORT HARDY (Ambrose Greenway collection)

22. NEREHANA (1914 - 1916)
   PORT HARDY (1) (1916 - 1918) see ship No. T 20 in the Tyser fleet.

23. MURITAI   (1914-1916)
   PORT VICTOR (1) (1916 - 1935) see ship No. T 21 in the Tyser fleet.

PORT VICTOR (Alex Duncan)

24. MAKARINI   (1914 - 1916)
PORT NICHOLSON (1) (1916 - 1917) see ship No. T 22 in the Tyser fleet.

PORT NAPIER (World Ship Society Photograph Library)

25. HAWKES BAY (2) (1914 - 1916)
PORT NAPIER (1) (1916 - 1936) see ship No. T 23 in the Tyser fleet.

PORT DARWIN (Warwick Foote)

26. PORT DARWIN (2) (1918 - 1949)
O.N. 140446. 8,179g. 5,137n. 480.4 x 60.3 x 40.8 feet.
Two T.3-cyl. steam engines manufactured by the shipbuilder. Twin screw. 809 nhp. 13kts. Refrigerated capacity 351,772 cu.ft.
1929: Additionally fitted with two low-pressure turbines with reduction gearing and hydraulic couplings. Now 986 nhp.
9.7.1917: Launched by Workman, Clark & Company Ltd., Belfast (Yard No. 351), for The Commonwealth & Dominion Line Ltd., London. 1.1918: Completed. 28.8.1940: Whilst on a voyage in convoy, from Methil to Newcastle, collided with and sank DRIEBERGEN (5,231g./1923), in position 55.25N., 1.22W., north of the Tyne. Subsequent repairs delayed her for three weeks. 11.1941: Whilst west bound in the Atlantic, suffered serious fire damage. Subsequent repairs undertaken at New York also took three weeks. 8.1949: Sold via the British Iron & Steel Corporation to T. W. Ward Ltd, Sheffield, for demolition at their Barrow in Furness facility. 5.8.1949: Arrived at Barrow in tow from Liverpool.

PORT DENISON (Warwick Foote)

27. PORT DENISON (3) (1918 - 1940)
O.N. 142397. 8,191g. 5,152n. 480.4 x 60.3 x 32.3 feet.
Two T.3-cyl. steam engines manufactured by the shipbuilder. Twin screw. 809 nhp. 13kts. Refrigerated capacity 352,656 cu.ft.
5.1929: Additionally fitted with two low-pressure turbines with reduction gearing and hydraulic couplings. Now 984 nhp.
18.9.1917: Launched by Workman, Clark & Company Ltd., Belfast (Yard No. 352), for The Commonwealth & Dominion Line Ltd., London. 30.4.1918: Completed. 26.9.1940: Whilst on a voyage

from London to Auckland and Lyttleton with 1,500 tons of general cargo, was bombed and damaged in position 6 miles N.E. of Peterhead, Scotland. 27.9.1940: Sank. 16 of her crew were lost.

PORT NICHOLSON (Warwick Foote)

28. PORT NICHOLSON (2) (1919 - 1942)
O.N. 143058. 8,402g. 5,338n. 481.2 x 62.3 x 33.0 feet.
Four steam turbines (E3191) manufactured by the shipbuilder, reduction geared to twin screw shafts. 967 nhp. 13kts. Refrigerated capacity 386,997 cu.ft.
3.11.1918: Launched by R. & W. Hawthorn, Leslie & Company Ltd., Newcastle (Yard No. 487), for The Commonwealth & Dominion Line Ltd., London. 13.5.1919: Completed. 23.10.1924: Struck a rock off Isleta Point, Las Palmas and sustained considerable bottom damage. 22.12.1924: Left Las Palmas in tow of the Dutch tug ROODE ZEE (573g./08), enroute to her builders yard. 1.1925: Arrived at Hawthorn, Leslie, Newcastle for repairs that lasted approximately 4 months, and included extensive work on the rudder and starboard propeller shaft that had been broken. 4.6.1938: In collision with the tug OCEAN COCK (182g./32), off Gravesend. 3 members of the tug crew were lost, plus an employee of Shaw, Savill & Albion Line who was on his way to join the steamer TAIROA which the tug was due to meet. 10.11.1938: PORT NICHOLSON was found 60% to blame for this incident. 10.4.1940: In collision with NELA at Glasgow. Subsequent repairs took 8 days. 16.6.1942: Whilst on a voyage from Avonmouth, Barry and Halifax for New York and Wellington, with a cargo of 1,600 tons of automotive parts and 4,000 tons of military stores, and part of convoy XB.25, was damaged with a torpedo by the German submarine U 87 (Kapitan L Joachim Berger), south of Portland Maine, in position 42.11N., 62.95W., and although abandoned, remained afloat. Subsequently she was reboarded by the Master and 3 crew, accompanied by 6 members of the crew of a corvette. Unfortunately she sank suddenly and all but 4 crew from the corvette were lost.

PORT BOWEN (Warwick Foote)

29. PORT BOWEN (1919 - 1939)
O.N. 143202. 8,267g. 5,110n. 480.7 x 62.4 x 32.9 feet.
Four steam turbines manufactured by the shipbuilder, reduction geared to twin screw shafts. 1,060 nhp. 14kts. Refrigerated capacity 375,225 cu.ft. 10.1926: Unspecified modifications carried out to her engines.
17.12.1918: Launched by Workman, Clark & Company Ltd., Belfast (Yard No. 356), for The Commonwealth & Dominion Line Ltd., London. 20.5.1919: Completed. 10:1933: Seriously damaged amidships in collision with TANIMBAR off the River Schelde. 19.7.1939: Whilst on a voyage Picton to Wanganui, went ashore off Castlecliff Beach, 1/2 a mile north of Wanganui, New Zealand, and became a total Loss.

PORT CAROLINE (World Ship Society Photograph Library)

30. PORT CAROLINE (4) (1919 - 1950)
O.N. 143790. 8,263g. 5,108n. 480.7 x 62.4 x 32.9 feet.
Four steam turbines manufactured by the shipbuilder reduction geared to twin screw shafts. 1,001 nhp. 13 1/2 kts. Refrigerated capacity 378,483 cu.ft. 5.1922: Returned to builders for extensive modifications to machinery.
28.6.1919: Launched by Workman, Clark & Company Ltd., Belfast (Yard No. 358), for The Commonwealth & Dominion Line Ltd., London. 11.1919: Completed. 7.1942: Extensive repairs to one set of gear wheels, which took 3 1/2 months to complete. 1949 until 1950: Chartered to the Ministry of Food and used as a meat storage ship. 1950: Sold via the British Iron & Steel Corporation to Smith & Houston, Port Glasgow, for demolition, but was subsequently re-allocated to Hughes, Bolckow Ltd., Blyth. 18.2.1950: Left Gravesend in tow for Blyth. 21.2.1950: Arrived and demolition commenced.

PORT ADELAIDE (World Ship Society Photograph Library)

31. PORT ADELAIDE (3) (1919 - 1949)
O.N. 143949. 8,422g. 5,350n. 481.2 x 62.3 x 33.0 feet.

Four steam turbines (E3192) manufactured by the shipbuilder, reduction geared to twin screw shafts. 967 nhp. 13kts. Refrigerated capacity 377,217 cu.ft.
27.8.1919: Launched by R. & W. Hawthorn, Leslie & Company Ltd., Newcastle (Yard No. 488), for The Commonwealth & Dominion Line Ltd., London. 23.12.1919: Completed. 1949: Sold via the British Iron & Steel Corporation to T. W. Ward Ltd., Sheffield, for demolition. 21.8.1949: Arrived at their Inverkeithing facility from Avonmouth. 14.10.1949: Demolition commenced.

PORT CURTIS as built (World Ship Society Photograph Library)

PORT CURTIS in later life - rebuilt as **KRONSTADT** (World Ship Society Photograph Library)

32. PORT CURTIS (2) (1920 - 1936)
O.N. 144533. 8,287g. 5,155n. 450.2 x 58.4 x 37.1 feet.
Post 1936: 6,475g. 3,981n.
As built: Two steam turbines manufactured by the shipbuilder, reduction geared to a single screw shaft. 892 nhp. 13kts. Refrigerated capacity 215,561 cu.ft.

Post 1936: T.3-cyl. steam engine manufactured in 1922 by Palmers Company Ltd., Newcastle, 729 nhp. 10¹/₂kts

Proposed as WAR THALIA for the Shipping Controller. 9.10.1919: Launched by Workman, Clark & Company Ltd., Belfast (Yard No. 447), for The Commonwealth & Dominion Line Ltd., London. 4.1920: Completed. 14.5.1920: Trials. 15.5.1920: Delivered. 13.11.1935: Sold for £17,750, to Downs Steamship Company Ltd., London (Counties Ship Management Company Ltd., managers), and renamed TOWER DALE. 1936: Re-engined at Amsterdam. 1937: Sold to J. A. Zachariassen & Company, Nystad, Finland, renamed KRONOBORG. 6.1945: Taken as prize by Russia as war reparations. 1946: Renamed KRONSTADT. Owners U.S.S.R. Vladivostok. Subsequently underwent extensive rebuilding. 1965: Renamed KRONSHTADT. 1970: Sold to Navigation Maritime Bulgare. Renamed ALGENEB. 25.4.1970: Arrived Bilbao, Spain for demolition by Eduardo Varela. 26.5.1970: Work commenced.

PORT KEMBLA (World Ship Society Photograph Library)

33. PORT KEMBLA (2) (1920 - 1926)

O.N. 144631. 8,435g. 5,345n. 481.2 x 62.3 x 33.0 feet.

Six steam turbines (E3193) manufactured by the shipbuilder, reduction geared to twin screw shafts. 967 nhp. 13kts. Refrigerated capacity 326,553 cu.ft.

20.3.1920: Launched by R. & W. Hawthorn, Leslie & Company Ltd., Newcastle (Yard No. 489), for The Commonwealth & Dominion Line Ltd., London. 6.7.1920: Completed. 8.7.1926: Whilst on a voyage from London to New Zealand via Norfolk, Virginia, wrecked on a reef at San Salvador Island, West Indies.

PORT CAMPBELL on the Thames. (World Ship Society Photograph Library)

34. PORT CAMPBELL (2) (1922 - 1953)

O.N. 146580. 8,308g. 5,123n. 480.8 x 62.4 x 32.9 feet.
Two T.3-cyl. steam engines manufactured by the shipbuilder. Twin screw. 859 nhp. 13½kts. Refrigerated capacity 401,869 cu.ft.
10.1929: Additionally fitted with two low-pressure turbines with reduction gearing and hydraulic couplings. Now 1,040 nhp.
15.3.1922: Launched by Workman, Clark & Company Ltd., Belfast (Yard No. 383), for The Commonwealth & Dominion Line Ltd., London. 6.1922: Completed. 1953: Sold via the British Iron & Steel Corporation to T. W. Ward Ltd., Sheffield, for demolition. 2.5.1953: Arrived at their Briton Ferry facility. 2.1.1954: Demolition commenced.

PORT AUCKLAND (World Ship Society Photograph Library)

35. PORT AUCKLAND (1) (1922 - 1943)

O.N. 146606. 8,308g. 5,123n. 480.8 x 62.4 x 32.9 feet.
Two T.3-cyl. steam engines manufactured by the shipbuilder. Twin screw. 859 nhp. 13kts. Refrigerated capacity 403,653 cu.ft.
1928: Additionally fitted with two low-pressure turbines with reduction gearing and hydraulic couplings. Now 1,070 nhp.
11.5.1922: Launched by Workman, Clark & Company Ltd., Belfast (Yard No. 382), for The Commonwealth & Dominion Line Ltd., London. 13.8.1922: Completed. 22.11.1937: Whilst at Antwerp, collided with a raft of lighters of which two sank. 15.9.1940: Credited with shooting down a German aircraft during an air attack on London. 7.6.1942: In collision with the British vessel HISTORIAN, (5,074g./24). 10.6.1942: Put into Falmouth for repairs to damage to No 2 hold. 17.3.1943: Whilst on a voyage from Auckland, Brisbane, Cristobal and Halifax to Belfast Lough and Avonmouth, with 7,000 tons of frozen produce, 1,000 tons of general cargo and mails and in convoy SC.122, was torpedoed and sunk by the German submarine U 305 (Kapitan L Bahr), in North Atlantic S.E. of Cape Farewell, Greenland, in position 52.25N., 30.15W. 8 of her crew of 86 were lost.

36. PORT HUNTER (4) (1922 - 1942)

O.N. 146641. 8,437g. 5,296n. 481.2 x 62.3 x 33.0 feet.
Six steam turbines (E3322) manufactured by the shipbuilder, reduction geared to twin screw shafts. 967 nhp. 13kts. Refrigerated capacity 390,597 cu.ft.
14.3.1922: Launched by R. & W. Hawthorn, Leslie & Company Ltd., Newcastle (Yard No. 502), for The Commonwealth & Dominion Line Ltd., London. 10.1922: Completed. 15.4.1940: Whilst sailing in convoy sustained damage in collision with QUEEN MAUD and was subsequently repaired at Southampton. 11.7.1942: Whilst on a voyage from Liverpool to Durban and New Zealand, and in convoy OS.33, was torpedoed and sunk by the German submarine U 582 (Kapitan L Werner Schulte), in the North Atlantic in position 31N., 24W. There were only 3 survivors from her crew of 85.

PORT HUNTER (World Ship Society Photograph Library)

PORT HARDY (World Ship Society Photograph Library)

37. PORT HARDY (2) (1923-1941)
O.N. 146697. 8,705g. 5,43ln.   481.2 x 62.3 x 33.0 feet.
Two T.3-cyl. steam engines (E3323) manufactured by the shipbuilder. Twin screw. 856 nhp. 13½kts. Refrigerated capacity 380,453 cu.ft.
1928: Additionally fitted with two low-pressure turbines with reduction gearing and hydraulic couplings. Now 1,038 nhp.
Had accommodation for about 650 emigrants in the midship shelter tween decks.
19.10.1922: Launched by R. & W. Hawthorn, Leslie & Company Ltd., Newcastle (Yard No. 503), for The Commonwealth & Dominion Line Ltd., London. 10.1922: Sustained considerable fire damage in her insulated holds during fit-out. 2.1923: Completed. 6.3.1923: Departed on her maiden voyage. 22.4.1940: Suffered damage in a collision with NEW SEVILLA (ex RUNIC). Repairs lasting 18 days were subsequently undertaken at Cardiff. 28.4.1941: Whilst on a voyage from Wellington, New Zealand to Ellesmere Port and Avonmouth, with 700 tons of zinc, 3,000 tons of cheese, 4,000 tons of mutton and general cargo and in convoy HX 121, was torpedoed and sunk by the German submarine U 96 (L/c Lehmann Willenbrock), North of Rockall in position 60.14N., 15.20W. She was apparently hit by chance, the torpedo being intended for another target. 1 of her crew of 84 was lost.

PORT BRISBANE (Warwick Foote)

38. PORT BRISBANE (1) (1923 - 1940)
O.N. 147563. 8,315g. 5,077n.   480.7 x 62.4 x 32.9 feet.
Two T.3-cyl. steam engines manufactured by the shipbuilder.   Twin screw. 860 nhp. 13^1/$_2$kts. Refrigerated capacity 401,715 cu.ft.
8.1930: Additionally fitted with two low-pressure turbines with reduction gearing and hydraulic couplings. Now 1,067 nhp
11.10.1923: Launched by Workman, Clark & Company Ltd., Belfast (Yard No. 462), for The Commonwealth & Dominion Line Ltd., London. 12.1923: Completed. 21.11.1940: Whilst on a voyage from Newcastle, New South Wales and Port Adelaide to the United Kingdom via Durban with refrigerated cargo and generals including 6,079 tons of food stuffs, 500 tons of lead and 44 tons of wolffram ore, was captured by the German raider PINGUIN, in a position 29.22S., 95.36E., some miles N. E., from Cape Leeuwin. 22.11.1940: Sunk with bombs placed aboard. Of the crew, 1 was lost, 27 picked up by an Australian cruiser, the remainder having been taken prisoner.

PORT WELLINGTON (World Ship Society Photograph Library)

39. PORT WELLINGTON (1) (1924 - 1940)
O.N. l47589. 7,868g. 4,784n.   470.l x 60.4 x 32.3 feet.
Two T.3-cyl. steam engines manufactured by the shipbuilder. Twin screw. 860 nhp. 14kts. Refrigerated capacity 372,557 cu.ft.
10.1930: Additionally fitted with two low-pressure turbines with reduction gearing and hydraulic couplings. Now 1,067 nhp.

8.1.1924: Launched by Workman, Clark & Company Ltd., Belfast (Yard No. 463), for The Commonwealth & Dominion Line Ltd., London. 2.1924: Completed. 30.11.1940: Whilst on a voyage from Sydney and Port Adelaide to the United Kingdom via Durban, with a cargo of 10, 000 tons of refrigerated and general cargo, was captured by the German raider PINGUIN, in South Indian Ocean in position 32.10S., 75.00E. 1.12.1940: Sunk by bombs placed aboard. The Chief Radio Officer was killed in the attack and the Captain later died from his wounds aboard the raider. The remainder of the crew were taken prisoner and later transferred to the supply ship STORSTAD.

PORT DUNEDIN at Cape Town. Note the Carley float aft. (World Ship Society Photograph Library)

40. PORT DUNEDIN (1925 - 1962)

O.N. 148599. 7,463g. 4,453n. 466.9 x 59.8 x 31.3 feet.
Two 4-cyl. 2 S. C. S. A., oil engines manufactured by William Doxford & Sons Ltd., Sunderland. Twin screw. 1,112 nhp. 14kts. Refrigerated capacity 442,151 cu.ft.
12.3.1925: Launched by Workman, Clark & Company Ltd., Belfast (Yard No. 477), for The Commonwealth & Dominion Line Ltd., London. 5.1925: Completed. 1949: Funnel shortened and appeared for a time with black top and only one black band. 1962: Sold for £80,000, to Italian shipbreakers. 31.8.1962: Arrived at Genoa. 25.9.1962: Arrived La Spezia, Italy for demolition by S.P.A. Cantieri Nav Del Golfo. 12.1962: Work commenced.

PORT HOBART (World Ship Society Photograph Library)

41. PORT HOBART (1) (1925-1940)

O.N. 148631. 7,448g. 4,493n. 466.9 x 59.7 x 31.3 feet.
Two 4-cyl. 2 S. C. S. A., oil engines manufactured by William Doxford & Sons Ltd., Sunderland. Twin screw. 1,112 nhp. 14kts. Refrigerated capacity 442,151 cu. Ft.
10.3.1925: Launched by Swan, Hunter & Wigham Richardson Ltd., Newcastle (Yard No. 1257), for The Commonwealth & Dominion Line Ltd., London. 2.7.1925: Completed. 6.1940: Taken out of service for 2 months with a cracked crank-shaft. 8.1940: Return to service delayed for a further 2 months as the casting made for her proved to be defective. 21.11.1940: Whilst on a voyage from Liverpool to Auckland with 8,000 tons of general cargo, was captured and sunk by the German pocket battleship ADMIRAL SCHEER, in position 24.44N., 58.21W., South East of Bermuda. All crew and passengers were taken prisoner, and the vessel sunk.

PORT FREMANTLE (World Ship Society Photograph Library)

42. PORT FREMANTLE (1927 - 1960)

O.N. 149807. 8,072g. 4,960n. 477.4 x 63.4 x 31.0 feet.
Two 4-cyl. 2 S. C. S. A., oil engines (154) manufactured by William Doxford & Sons Ltd., Sunderland. Twin screw. 1,281 nhp. 14¹/₂kts. Refrigerated capacity 401,761 cu.ft.
6.1.1927: Launched by Workman, Clark & Company Ltd., Belfast (Yard No. 489), for The Commonwealth & Dominion Line Ltd., London. 4.1927: Completed. 1932: Suffered fire damage at Wanganui. 8.1940: Suffered fire damage at New York. 21.12.1940: Upper works damaged by blast and splinters from incendiary bombs. 1.9.1960: Arrived Osaka, Japan for Demolition. 15.10.1960: Work commenced.

43. PORT GISBORNE (1927 - 1940)

O.N. 149874. 8,00lg. 4,952n. 477.2 x 63.3 x 31.0 feet.
Two 4-cyl. 2 S. C. S. A., oil engines (155) manufactured by William Doxford & Sons Ltd., Sunderland. Twin screw. 1,281 nhp. 14¹/₂kts. Refrigerated capacity 330,000 cu.ft.
30.4.1927: Launched by Swan, Hunter & Wigham Richardson Ltd., Newcastle (Yard No. 1295), for The Commonwealth & Dominion Line Ltd., London. 8.1927: Completed.11.10.1940: Whilst on a voyage from New Zealand to Belfast and Cardiff with refrigerated and general cargo including 2,475 bales of wool and 200 bales of sheepskin, and in convoy HX77, was torpedoed and sunk by the German submarine U 48 (K/L Heinrich Bielchrodt), in position 56.38N., 16.40W., South West of Rockall. 26 of her crew of 63 were lost. 25.10.1940: 10 survivors were landed from the tug SALVONIA. 26.10.1940: Twenty-seven survivors were landed from the ALPERA.

PORT GISBORNE (World Ship Society Photograph Library)

PORT HUON (Warwick Foote)

44. PORT HUON (1) (1927 - 1961)
O.N. 149842. 8,02lg. 4,956n.   477.2 x 63.3 x 31.0 feet.
Two 6-cyl. 2 S. C. S. A., Sulzer type oil engines (864C) manufactured by the Wallsend Slipway Company Ltd., Newcastle. Twin screw. 1,495 nhp. 14^1/$_2$kts. Refrigerated capacity 403,266 cu.ft.
4.3.1927: Launched by Swan, Hunter & Wigham Richardson Ltd., Newcastle (Yard No. 1293), for The Commonwealth & Dominion Line Ltd., London. 7.6.1927: Completed. 10.11.1961: Arrived Yokosuka, Japan for demolition. 20.11.1961: Togo Menka K.K. commenced work.

45. PORT FAIRY (2) (1928-1965)
O.N. 160590. 7,980g. 4,927n.   477.3 x 63.2 x 31.0 feet.
Two 4-cyl. 2 S. C. S. A., oil engines (169) manufactured by William Doxford & Sons Ltd., Sunderland. Twin screw. 1,374 nhp. 14^1/$_2$kts. Refrigerated capacity 408,014 cu.ft.
18.7.1928: Launched by Swan, Hunter & Wigham Richardson Ltd., Newcastle (Yard No. 1339), for The Commonwealth & Dominion Line Ltd., London. 19.10.1928: Completed. 5.2.1940: Had serious fire in engine room at Wellington. 28.2.1940: Whilst part of Convoy H.X.23, collided with LOCH DEE striking her on her starboard quarter, resulting in both ships being ordered to Halifax for repairs. 22.10.1940: Whilst part of Convoy OL.8 collided with and sank the Canadian destroyer MARGAREE ex HMS DIANA,

in position 53.47N., 23.01W. Only 31 crew survived from the destroyers total complement of 171. 29.10.1940 until 2.11.1940: At Bermuda for temporary repairs to bow and stern. 28.11.1940 until 3.12.1940: Further repairs at Auckland. 12.7.1943: Whilst on a voyage from the Clyde to Buenos Aires was bombed and damaged by aircraft in position 37.18.N 14.37.W. Temporary repairs were carried at Casablanca. After reaching Buenos Aires further repairs were carried out at the Argentine Naval drydock at Puerto Belgrano. 1954: Major refit carried out by Swan, Hunter & Wigham Richardson Ltd. 11.1962: Towed PORT TOWNSVILLE 160 miles into Auckland, after the latter had broken down whilst on a voyage from Lautoka, Fiji Islands to Dunedin. 7.4.1965: Sold to Embajada Cia. Nav. S.A. Panama. (Greek Flag), and renamed TAISHIKAN for her delivery voyage to the breakers. 4.6.1965: Arrived Hong Kong for demolition by Cheoy Lee Shipyard, Ngautaukok, but was resold. 7.7.1965: Demolition commenced by Mollers Ltd. 23.7.1965: Caught fire at breakers and sustained serious damage. 27.7.1965: Fire extinguished. 1.9.1965: Completely gutted.

PORT FAIRY at Hull. (World Ship Society Photograph Library)

PORT ALMA (World Ship Society Photograph Library)

46. PORT ALMA (2) (1928 - 1964)
O.N. 160615. 7,983g. 4,926n. 477.3 x 63.2 x 31.0 feet.
Two 4-cyl. 2 S. C. S. A., oil engines (170) manufactured by William Doxford & Sons Ltd., Sunderland. Twin screw. 1,374 nhp. 14$^{1}/_{2}$kts. Refrigerated capacity 407,441 cu.ft.

17.9.1928: Launched by Swan, Hunter & Wigham Richardson Ltd., Newcastle (Yard No. 1341), for The Commonwealth & Dominion Line Ltd., London. 13.12.1928: Completed. 20.12.1940: Badly shaken by two near misses during an air-raid at Liverpool. 30.8.1964: Arrived Onomichi, Japan from Auckland via Kobe for demolition. 14.9.1964: Work commenced.

PORT CHALMERS at Swansea (World Ship Society Photograph Library)

47. PORT CHALMERS (4) (1933 - 1965)

O.N. 163429. 8,535g. 5,204n. 488.8 x 65.3 x 31.6 feet.
Two 4-cyl. 2 S. C. S. A., Doxford type oil engines manufactured by Barclay Curle & Company Ltd., Glasgow. Twin screw. 1,570 nhp. 15kts. Refrigerated capacity 442,151 cu.ft.
13.3.1933: Keel Laid by Swan, Hunter & Wigham Richardson Ltd., Newcastle (Yard No. 1483), for The Commonwealth & Dominion Line Ltd., London. 4.10.1933: Launched. 10.12.1933: Completed. 20.12.1933: Unsuccessfully trialed. 28.12.1933: Trials. 3.9.1937: Collided with CITY OF ORAN in dense fog in about position 42N., 10W., and returned to Falmouth for repair. 23.9.1937: Left Falmouth after repair. 15.11.1965: Arrived Kaohsiung for demolition by Nam Feng Steel Enterprises Company, Taipei. 17.11.1965: Work commenced.

PORT TOWNSVILLE (Warwick Foote)

174

48. PORT TOWNSVILLE (1) (1935 - 1941)
O.N. 164519. 8,661g. 5,228n. 496.4 x 65.2 x 31.0 feet.
Two 8-cyl. 2 S. C. S. A., Sulzer type oil engines (913C) manufactured by the Wallsend Slipway & Engineering Company Ltd. Twin screw. 2,237 nhp. 16½kts. Refrigerated capacity 408,802 cu.ft.
16.6.1934: Keel laid by Swan, Hunter & Wigham Richardson Ltd., Newcastle (Yard No. 1495), for The Commonwealth & Dominion Line Ltd., London. 21.5.1935: Launched. 22.8.1935: Completed. 22.8.1935: Unsuccessfully trialed. 24.8.1935: Trials. 12.1.1941: Ran ashore in Jamaican waters, being refloated with slight damage. 3.3.1941: Whilst on a voyage from Newport, Mon. to Townsville, Australia with general and approximately 3,000 tons of tinplate, was bombed and set on fire. 4.3.1941: Sank in St George's Channel in position 52.05N., 05.24W

PORT WYNDHAM (World Ship Society Photograph Library)

49. PORT WYNDHAM (1935 - 1967)
O.N. 163561. 8,580g. 5,233n. 494.5 x 65.3 x 30.6 feet.
Two 4-cyl. 2 S. C. S. A., oil engines manufactured by William Doxford & Sons Ltd., Sunderland. Twin screw. 1,882 nhp. 16½kts. Refrigerated capacity 454,710 cu.ft.
23.10.1934: Launched by John Brown & Company Ltd., Clydebank (Yard No. 541), for The Commonwealth & Dominion Line Ltd., London. 24.1.1935: Completed. 8.9.1937: Ran aground at Townsville, and was refloated after two days, with damage to propeller blades. 2.1942: Had extensive repairs to her engines which took over 8 weeks to complete. 3.1943: Attacked by Focke-Wolf bomber, 700 miles from Ireland and during four 'run-ins', two of the ship's gunners were wounded by machine gun fire. 11.4.1945: Damaged by mine explosion off Dungeness. 12.1946: Returned to service after very extensive repairs and modernisation at Southampton. 5.1956: Whilst on a voyage from Dunedin to London and Glasgow, collided in thick fog off Dover with the tanker ESSO CHEYENNE. 25.11.1959: Ran aground River Scheldt. 12.5.1966: Whilst at New Plymouth suffered a blow back in a furnace, that ignited a fire in the engine room, which was subsequently flooded. With a dredger standing-by to tow the ship out to sea, most of the crew were evacuated whilst the port area was sealed off. The fire was extinguished. 9.1.1967: At 4.30pm, and the end of her seventieth voyage she left New Plymouth for demolition in Japan. 23.1.1967: Arrived Osaka. 24.1.1967: Delivered to Japanese Brokers, Okadagumi Ltd., Osaka at 05.30 hours G.M.T. (coincidentally - her 32nd birthday). 1.2.1967: Demolition commenced at Funamachi, Osaka.

50. PORT JACKSON (3) (1937 - 1967)
O.N. 165383. 9,687g. 5,826n. 500.6 x 68.2 x 29.8 feet.
Two 4-cyl. 2 S. C. S. A., Doxford type oil engines manufactured by Barclay Curle & Company Ltd., Glasgow. Twin screw. 2,025 nhp. 16½kts. Refrigerated capacity 494,751 cu.ft.
15.2.1936: Keel laid by Swan, Hunter & Wigham Richardson Ltd., Newcastle (Yard No. 1515), for The Commonwealth & Dominion Line Ltd., London. (Port Line). 26.11.1936: Launched. 19.1.1937: Completed. 19-20.1.1937: Trials. 27.8.1942: 900 miles west of Ireland she was attacked by the

German submarine U 516 that fired four torpedoes at her all of which missed. Surfacing, U 516 engaged PORT JACKSON with her deck gun scoring two hits. The action was however quickly broken-off after the U boat was hit by accurate gunfire from the ship. 28.8.1942: Picked up survivors of SYLVIA DE LARRINAGA that had been sunk two weeks earlier by the Italian submarine REGINALDO GIULIANI. 26.8.1952: On fire off South Africa, her cargo included 8 tons of explosives. The fire burned for 8 days eventually being extinguished with the assistance of the Cape Town Fire Brigade, after the explosives had been transferred to a lighter. 12.3.1959: Involved in collision with the Indian vessel JALAVIKRAM (4573g./58), at Pagan Sound in the River Elbe. Both vessels sustained heavy damage, and PORT JACKSON was beached. Later the same day, refloated with aid of four Bugsier owned tugs and docked for repair at Deutsche Werft, Hamburg. 10.2.1967: Sold to Embajada Cia. Nav. S. A., Greece, delivered at London, and renamed LEGATION for the delivery voyage to the shipbreakers. 13.4.1967: Arrived Kure, Japan for demolition. 26.4.1967: Iwai & Company Ltd., commenced work at Etajima Island, near Kure.

PORT JACKSON (World Ship Society Photograph Library)

PORT MONTREAL 8th October 1938 (Warwick Foote)

51. PORT MONTREAL (1) (1937 - 1942)
O.N. 165587. 5,882g. 3,458n. 438.9 x 58.9 x 25.7 feet.
4-cyl. 2 S. C. S. A., oil engine manufactured by the shipbuilder. 861 nhp. 13kts. Refrigerated capacity 18,598 cu.ft.
10.8.1937: Launched by William Doxford & Sons Ltd., Sunderland (Yard No. 633), for The Commonwealth & Dominion Line Ltd., London. (Port Line) 7.10.1937: Completed. 10.6.1942: Whilst on a voyage from Halifax and Hampton Roads for Cristobal and Melbourne with a cargo of 7,500 tons of ammunition and a deck cargo of 14 aircraft, was torpedoed and sunk by the German submarine U 68 (F.K. Merten), in the Caribbean Sea, in a position 12.17N., 80.20W. Her crew was picked up the following day by a Colombian schooner and landed at Cristobal.

52. PORT HALIFAX (1937 - 1962)
O.N. 165611. 5,820g. 3,350n. 440.1 x 59.0 x 25.8 feet.
4-cyl. 2 S. C. S. A., oil engine (1544) manufactured by the shipbuilder. 861 nhp. 13kts. Refrigerated capacity 18,598 cu.ft.
7.12.1936: Keel laid by Swan, Hunter & Wigham Richardson Ltd., Newcastle (Yard No. 1539), for Port Line Ltd. 7.7.1937: Launched. 9.11.1937: Completed. 29.11.1937: Trials. 6.1941: Damaged by

aircraft bombs. 1962: Sold to Olistim Navigation Company Ltd., Lebanon, and renamed ILENA. 1969: Transferred to Cypriot Flag. 1973: Sold to Turkish shipbreakers. 10.2.1973: Left Alexandria bound for Istanbul.   15.2.1973: Arrived at Istanbul. 4.5.1973: Detel Malatya Demir Sanayu Ltd. commenced demolition.

PORT HALIFAX with superstructure as built. (World Ship Society Photograph Library)

PORT HALIFAX with modified superstructure. (Warwick Foote)

53. PORT SAINT JOHN (1938 - 1961)
O.N. 166332. 5,668g, 3,306n,   448.4 x 59.0 x 25.2 feet.
4-cyl. 2 S. C. S. A., Doxford type oil engine manufactured by Richardsons, Westgarth & Company Ltd., Hartlepool. 861 nhp. 14kts. Refrigerated capacity 37,319 cu.ft.
9.8.1937: Launched by J. L. Thompson & Sons Ltd., Sunderland (Yard No. 579), for Port Line Ltd., London. 3.1.1938: Completed. 17.1.1938: Grounded near Sydney, Cape Breton and refloated after 8 hours. The extensive bottom damage sustained was repaired at Halifax at a cost of about £20,000. 2.3.1938: Repairs complete, she departed Halifax, but had to return the following day with a defective thruster block, which was relined. 4.5.1938: Grounded on a coral reef off Lady Elliot Island,

Queensland. 12.5.1938: Refloated and temporary repairs were then carried out at Sydney. Captain's employment terminated and 3rd 0fficer demoted to 4th. 12.1944: Rescued the crew of the MICHAEL J. GOULANDRIS after the vessel had foundered after striking rocks off D'Entrecasteaux Point, on the South Coast of Australia. 1961: Sold to Cia. Lamia de Nav. S. A., Greece, and renamed REDESTOS. 10.3.1962 until 20.6.1962: Under repair at Cobh, Ireland. 8.7.1969: Arrived Hsinkang for breaking up by Chinese Mainland Shipbreakers. 9.8.1969: Delivered to the shipbreakers.

PORT SAINT JOHN with superstructure as built. (Alex Duncan)

PORT SAINT JOHN with modified superstructure. (World Ship Society Photograph Library)

PORT QUEBEC (Warwick Foote)

54. PORT QUEBEC (1939 - 1944)
DEER SOUND (1944 - 1947)
PORT QUEBEC (1947 - 1968)

O.N. 167532. 5,936g. 3,453n. 451.0 x 59.7 x 25.2 feet.
5-cyl. 2 S. C. S. A., Doxford type oil engine (212) manufactured by William Doxford & Sons Ltd., Sunderland. 14½kts. Refrigerated capacity 19,084 cu.ft.
17.8.1939: Launched by J. L. Thompson & Sons Ltd., Sunderland (Yard No. 593), for Port Line Ltd., London. 11.1939: Completed. 10.11.1939: Hired by The Admiralty. 18.12.1939: Returned by The Admiralty. 27.12.1939: Rehired by The Admiralty. 12.6.1940: At Rosyth. 1944: Converted to an aircraft component repair ship, and renamed DEER SOUND. 1.1.1945: Purchased by The Admiralty as a repair ship. 24.10.1947: Sold to Port Line Ltd. Machinery subsequently damaged by fire whilst fitting out at Jarrow. 20.12.1947: Post conversion trials. 7.6.1968: Left Albany, Western Australia. 23.6.1968: Arrived at Kaohsiung for demolition but was resold to Chons Iron & Steel Company for demolition at Keelung. 12.1968: Demolition Commenced.

55. PORT NAPIER (2) (1940)

Proposed to be 9,847g. 450.0 x 60.0 x 25.0 feet.
Two 5-cyl. 2 S. C. S. A., Doxford type oil engine (1624) manufactured by William Doxford & Sons Ltd., Sunderland. Twin screw 16kts.
10.5.1939: Keel laid by Swan, Hunter & Wigham Richardson Ltd., Newcastle (Yard No. 1569), for Port Line Ltd., London. 23.4.1940: Launched and requisitiond by the Admiralty 12.6.1940: Completed as a minelayer, armed with two 4" guns and four 20mm cannons. 16.6.1940: Trials and sailed to Rosyth. 26.6.1940: Rosyth to Port Z.A. (Lochalsh). 28.6.1940: Arrived at Port Z.A., and joined the 1st Minelaying Squadron. 27.8.1940: Voyaged from Port Z.A. to Greenock for repairs and alterations to LD sponsons. 8.9.1940: Repairs completed. 26.11.1940: Whilst at Kyle of Lochalsh, collided in heavy weather with the collier BALMAHA (1428g./24). 27.11.1940: Around 13:40 hrs, whilst completing bunkering from the tanker RUDDERMAN (290g./34), caught fire in the vicinity of the donkey boiler. RUDDERMAN hastily departed. PORT NAPIER subsequently exploded, capsized and sank in the shallows. No loss of life. Loss very confidential and no details of the vessel reported in Lloyds Register.

PORT PHILLIP (World Ship Society Photograph Library)

56. PORT PHILLIP (5) (1942 - 1971)

O.N. 168257. 12,439g. 7,587n. 503.5 x 68.2 x 38.3 feet.
Two 5-cyl. 2 S. C. S. A., Doxford type oil engines (1692) manufactured by the shipbuilder. Twin screw. 10,700 bhp. 16kts. 11 passengers. Refrigerated capacity 522,633 cu.ft.
14.5.1940: Keel laid by Swan, Hunter & Wigham Richardson Ltd., Newcastle (Yard No. 1609), for Port Line Ltd., London. 7.10.1941: Launched. 20.3.1942: Completed. 9.1942: In an accident during gun practice, which resulted in the deaths of the 3rd Officer, a D.E.M.S rating and caused injury to 7 others, the vessel was also damaged. 26.1.1971: Arrived at Hong Kong en route to Shanghai for demolition. 30.1.1971: Arrived Shanghai. 10.2.1971: Chinese Mainland Shipbreakers had already commenced demolition.

57. PORT VICTOR (2) (1942 - 1943)

O.N. 168324. 12,411g. 7,433n. 503.5 x 68.2 x 38.3 feet.
Two 5-cyl. 2 S. C. S. A., Doxford type oil engines (1720) manufactured by the shipbuilder. Twin screw. 10,700 bhp. 16kts. Refrigerated capacity 522,633 cu.ft.
15.5.1941: Keel laid by Swan, Hunter & Wigham Richardson Ltd., Newcastle (Yard No. 1659), for Port Line Ltd., London. 27.6.1942: Launched. 12.10.1942: Completed. 11.4.1943: Sailed from Buenos Aires. 14.4.1943: Sailed from Montevideo bound to Liverpool with 7,600 tons of refrigerated cargo and 2,000 tons of general. 30.4.1943: Torpedoed and sunk by the German submarine U 107 (K/L Gelhaus), 600 miles west of Ireland in position 47.48N., 22.02W. 10 crew, 2 gunners and 5 passengers were lost out of a total complement of 164.

PORT MACQUARIE (World Ship Society Photograph Library)

58. PORT MACQUARIE (2) (1944 - 1968)

O.N. 169750. 9,072g. 5,485n. 8,395d. 470.9 x 62.2 x 37.2 feet.
6-cyl. 2 S. C. S. A., Doxford type oil engine (1760) manufactured by the shipbuilder. 6,600 bhp. 14kts. Refrigerated capacity 391,487 cu. ft.
30.9.1942: Keel laid by Swan, Hunter & Wigham Richardson Ltd., Newcastle (Yard No. 1685), for Port Line Ltd., London. 19.8.1943: Launched. 22.2.1944: Trials and completed. 11.6.1957: Towed the disabled CAPTAIN HOBSON to Auckland. 26.1.1953: At 8.35 a.m., grounded off Crosby, River Mersey. 26.1.1953: At 8.16pm, successfully refloated and placed to anchor. 27.1.1953: At 8.45am, arrived at Sandon Half-Tide Dock, having sustained no damage. Coincidentally, this was the same day as the burning EMPRESS OF CANADA turned over in Gladstone Dock. 13.9.1968: Arrived Kaohsiung for demolition and was then laid up to wait the breaker's torch. 12.1968: Tai Kien Industries Ltd., finally commenced work.

PORT LINCOLN 2nd June 1959 (World Ship Society Photograph Library)

59. PORT LINCOLN (2) (1946 - 1971)
O.N. 180808. 7,250g. 4,255n. 487.11 x 62.2 x 28.4 feet.
6-cyl. 2 S. C. S. A., Doxford type oil engine (1774) manufactured by Swan, Hunter & Wigham Richardson Ltd., Newcastle. 6,600 bhp. 15kts. 2 passengers. Refrigerated capacity 372,455 cu.ft.
23.8.1945: Launched by Swan, Hunter & Wigham Richardson Ltd., Wallsend (Yard No. 1707), for Port Line Ltd., London. 24.1.1946: No full power trials due to fog. 25.1.1946: Completed. 27.10.1971: Arrived Castellon for demolition by I. M. Varela Davalillo. 2.1972: Work commenced.

PORT HOBART (Alex Duncan)

60. PORT HOBART (2) (1946 - 1970)
O.N. 180937. 11,138g. 6,542n. 540.6 x 70.5 x 29.8 feet.
Two 8-cyl. 2 S. C. D. A., Burmeister & Wain type oil engines manufactured by Harland & Wolff Ltd., Glasgow. Twin screw. 11,500 bhp. $16^1/2$ kts. 12 passengers. Refrigerated capacity 497,189 cu.ft.
5.12.1945: Launched as EMPIRE WESSEX by Harland & Wolff Ltd., Belfast (Yard No. 1188), for the Ministry of War Transport, London, and subsequently sold to Port Line Ltd., London. 29.8.1946: Completed as PORT HOBART, with accommodation for 124 passengers, and delivered to Port Line Ltd., London. 1950: Arrived at Belfast for conversion work to reduce her accommodation to that for only 12 passengers. 28.7.1970: Sold to China National Machinery Import & Export Corporation, Peking for demolition. 27.8.1970: Left Colombo en route to Shanghai. 17.9.1970: Delivered to shipbreakers at Shanghai.

PORT WELLINGTON (World Ship Society Photograph Library)

61. PORT WELLINGTON (2) (1946 - 1971)
O.N. 180911. 10,585g. 6,347n. 528.10 x 68.5 x 28.11 feet.
Two 5-cyl. 2 S. C. S. A., Doxford type oil engines manufactured by the shipbuilder. Twin screws. 10,700 bhp. 16kts. 12 passengers. Refrigerated capacity 532,000 cu.ft.
4.2.1946: Launched by John Brown & Company Ltd., Clydebank (Yard No. 628), for Port Line Ltd., London. 26.9.1946: Completed. 1971: Sold to Spanish shipbreakers. 16.7.1971: Left Southampton under her own power. 21.7.1971: Arrived at Castellon. 15.9.1971: I. M. Varela Davalillo commenced work.

PORT PIRIE (M. R. Dippy)

62. PORT PIRIE (5) (1947 - 1972)
O.N. 181562. 10,535g. 6,163n. 529.0 x 68.4 x 30.2 feet.
Two 5-cyl. 2 S. C. S. A., Doxford type oil engines manufactured by the shipbuilder. Twin screw. 10,700 bhp. 16kts. 12 passengers. Refrigerated capacity 536,616 cu.ft.
14.6.1945: Keel laid by Swan, Hunter & Wigham Richardson Ltd., Wallsend (Yard No. 1741), for Port Line Ltd., London. . 29.5.1946: Launched. 30.1.1947: No trial due to rough weather. 30.1.1947: Completed. 2.7.1972: Arrived Castellon from London for demolition. 10.1972: I. M. Varela Davalillo commenced work.

63. PORT ALBANY (2) (1947 - 1951)
O.N. 169933. 7,229g. 4,423n. 441.8 x 57.0 x 27.9 feet.
Triple-expansion 3-cyl steam engine manufactured by Iron Fireman Manufacturing Company, Portland, Oregon. 2,500ihp. 10kts.
13.7.1943: Launched as WILLIAM C. LANE by Oregon Shipbuilding Corp., Portland, Oregon (Yard No. 724), for the United States War Shipping Administration and bareboat chartered to the Ministry of War Transport, London, (Port Line Ltd., London, managers). 7.1943: Completed as SAMPLER. 1947: Sold for £135,197 "as is" through Funch, Edye, (who took 1% commission) to Port Line Ltd., London, and renamed PORT ALBANY. 1951: Sold to Cia. Nav. Vista Dorada, Panama, and renamed TENI. 1953: Sold to Mid-Atlantic Shipping Company Ltd., Monrovia, Liberia, and renamed GLORIANNA. 1959: Transferred to Greek registry. 1968: Sold for £58,000, to Chinese mainland shipbreakers. 3.6.1968: Arrived at Shanghai. 9.1968: Demolished at Shanghai.

PORT ALBANY at Cape Town. (World Ship Society Photograph Library)

PORT LYTTELTON (World Ship Society Photograph Library)

64. PORT LYTTELTON (2) (1947 - 1972)

O.N. 181590. 7,413g. 4,310n. 11,040d. 487.10 x 63.8 x 28.4 feet.
6-cyl. 2 S. C. S. A., Doxford type oil engine (E4027) manufactured by the shipbuilder. 6600 bhp. 15kts. 5 passengers. Refrigerated capacity 380,937 cu.ft.
10.9.1946: Launched by R. & W. Hawthorn, Leslie & Company Ltd., Newcastle (Yard No. 685), for Port Line Ltd., London. 3.1947: Completed. 19.12.1953: Went aground when leaving Fernandina, Florida, and, although refloated the same day, suffered extensive damage. Her cargo was transferred to the PORT MACQUARIE and she was repaired at Savannah. 11.4.1959: Suffered a fire and explosion at Brisbane. 7.6.1972: Arrived at Faslane for demolition. 8.6.1972: Shipbreaking Industries Ltd. commenced work.

PORT NAPIER (Warwick Foote)

65. PORT NAPIER (3) (1947 - 1970)
O.N. 181707. 11,834g. 6,824n. 11,930d. 559.6 x 70.4 x 29.4 feet.
Two 6-cyl. 2 S. C. S. A., Doxford type oil engines (992C) manufactured by the Wallsend Slipway & Engineering Company Ltd., Wallsend. Twin screw. 13,200 bhp. 17kts. 12 passengers. Refrigerated capacity 568,886 cu.ft.
20.9.1945: Keel laid by Swan, Hunter & Wigham Richardson Ltd., Wallsend (Yard No. 1749), for Port Line Ltd., London. 12.11.1946: Launched. 1.9.1947: Completed. 15.9.1947: Trials. 10.2.1970: Arrived at Kaohsiung for demolition. 1.4.1970: Nan Feng Steel Enterprise Company Ltd., commenced work.

PORT BRISBANE (World Ship Society Photograph Library)

66. PORT BRISBANE (2) (1949 - 1975)
O.N. 182957. 11,942g. 6,836n. 11,950d. 559.11 x 70.3 x 29.4 feet.
Two 6-cyl. 2 S. C. S. A., Doxford type oil engines (1006C) manufactured by the Wallsend Slipway & Engineering Company Ltd., Wallsend. Twin screw. 13,200 bhp. 17kts. 12 passengers. Refrigerated capacity 568,886 cu.ft.
6.1946: Ordered. 8.5.1947: Keel laid by Swan, Hunter & Wigham Richardson Ltd., Wallsend (Yard No. 1763), for Port Line Ltd., London. 6.7.1948: Launched. 28.2.1949: Trials and completed. 19.3.1949 Maiden Voyage. She was the Flagship of the Company. 2.11.1975: Arrived at Hong Kong for demolition. 23.12.1975: Loy Kee Shipbreaking & Transportation Company commenced work.

PORT AUCKLAND at Cape Town. (World Ship Society Photograph Library)

67. PORT AUCKLAND (2) (1949 - 1976)
O.N. 183007. 11,945g. 6,817n. 12,017d. 559.9 x 70.3 x 29.4 feet.
Two 6-cyl. 2 S. C. S. A., Doxford type oil engines (E4046) manufactured by the shipbuilder. Twin screw. 13,200 bhp. 17kts. 12 passengers. Refrigerated capacity 571,250 cu.ft.
4.10.1948: Launched by R. & W. Hawthorn, Leslie & Company Ltd., Newcastle (Yard No. 693), for Port Line Ltd., London. 26.4.1949: Trials and completed. 1976: Sold to Gulf Fisheries Company W. L. L., Kuwait, converted into a live sheep carrier by Keppel Shipyard, Singapore, and renamed MASHAALLAH. 30.9.1979: Arrived at Kaoshiung for demolition. 25.10.1979: Chien Cheng Iron & Steel Company Ltd., commenced work.

PORT VICTOR (World Ship Society Photograph Library)

68. PORT VICTOR (3) (1949 - 1971)
O.N. 181935. 10,390g. 5,863n. 11,290d. 524.0 x 68.4 x 28.1 feet.
Two 5-cyl. 2 S. C. S. A., Doxford type oil engines manufactured by the shipbuilder. Twin screw. 10,700 bhp. 16kts. 12 passengers. Refrigerated capacity 520,520 cu.ft.

1941: Under construction as PORT PIRIE (4) by John Brown & Company Ltd., Clydebank (Yard No. 577), for Port Line Ltd., London. 2.11.1941: Purchased on the stocks by the Admiralty. 20.5.1943: Launched as the escort carrier HMS NAIRANA. 12.12.1943: Completed. 3.1946 until 1948: Loaned to the Royal Netherlands Navy as KAREL DOORMAN. 1948: Returned to the Admiralty. 6.1948: Re-purchased by Port Line Ltd., and sent to Belfast for reconversion to a merchant ship. 10.1949: Departed on maiden voyage. 21.7.1971: Arrived Faslane for demolition. 7.8.1971: Shipbreaking Industries Ltd., commenced work.

PORT VINDEX (World Ship Society Photograph Library)

69. PORT VINDEX (1949-1971)

O.N. 183031. 10480g, 5884n, 11080d. 523.9 x 68.4 x 28.9 feet.
Two 5-cyl. 2 S. C. S. A., Doxford type oil engines (1738) manufactured by the the shipbuilder. Twin screw. 10,700 bhp. 16kts. 12 passengers. Refrigerated capacity 528,360 cu.ft.
1941: Building as PORT SYDNEY (2) by Swan, Hunter & Wigham Richardson Ltd., Wallsend (Yard No. 1667), for Port Line Ltd., London, when purchased on the stocks by The Admiralty. 4.5.1943: Launched the escort carrier HMS VINDEX. 3.12.1943 Completed. 8.1947: Purchased by Port Line Ltd., and sent to her builders for re-conversion. 31.5.1949: Trials.1.6.1949: Trials.30.3.1950: Trials. 22.6.1949: First commercial voyage as PORT VINDEX. 23.8.1971: Arrived at Kaohsiung for demolition. 15.9.1971: Zui Fat Steel & Iron Works commenced work.

70. PORT ADELAIDE (4) (1951 - 1972)

O.N. 184435. 8,114g. 4,565n. 10,650d. 490.0 x 64, 8 x 28.9 feet
6-cyl. 2 S. C. S. A., Doxford type oil engine (E4085) manufactured by the shipbuilder. 7,500 bhp. 15½ kts. 10 passengers. Refrigerated capacity 354,760 cu.ft.
24.2.1950: Keel Laid by R. & W. Hawthorn, Leslie & Company Ltd., Newcastle (Yard No. 705), for Port Line Ltd., London. 8.12.50: Launched. 30.5.1951: Trials. 30.5.1951: Completed. 19.12.1966: Rescued crew of fishing vessel "BELL OF PORTUGAL" which had caught fire and sunk, landed survivors at Balboa. 1972: Sold to Chinese shipbreakers. 26.7.1972: Called at Cape Town for bunkers. 19.8.1972: Arrived Kaohsiung for demolition 23.11.1972: Jui Fat Steel & Iron Company Ltd., commenced work. 23.12.1972: Work completed.

PORT ADELAIDE in the Suez Canal. (World Ship Society Photograph Library)

PORT TOWNSVILLE (World Ship Society Photograph Library)

71. PORT TOWNSVILLE (2) (1951-1972)
O.N. 184519. 8,681g. 4,479n. 10,360d. 489.1 x 64.8 x 28.9 feet
6-cyl. 2 S. C. S. A., Doxford type oil engine (1030C) manufactured by the Wallsend Slipway & Engineering Company Ltd., Wallsend. 7,500 bhp. 15^1/$_2$ kts. 10 passengers. Refrigerated capacity 350,730 cu.ft.
21.5.1951: Launched by Swan, Hunter & Wigham Richardson Ltd., Newcastle (Yard No. 1809), for Port Line Ltd., London. 2.10.1951: Trials and completed. 26.6.1962: Had fire in engine room at Avonmouth. 29.10.1962: Whilst on a voyage from Lautoka, Fiji Islands to Dunedin, suffered main engine failure and was taken in tow by PORT FAIRY to Auckland over 600 miles distant. 10.11.1962: Following repairs, sailed from Auckland for the U.K via Fremantle and Suez. 21.11.1965: Having suffered another main engine failure, in Chesapeake Bay, was towed to port by PORT ALFRED. 1972: Sold to Spanish shipbreakers. 27.6.1972: Passed Gibraltar enroute to Castellon. 8.1972: Isaac Manuel Varela Davalillo commenced work.

PORT NELSON (World Ship Society Photograph Library)

72. PORT NELSON (1951 - 1972)
O.N. 184526. 8,950g. 4,667n. 10,260d. 490.0 x 64.10 x 28.9 feet.
7-cyl. 2 S. C. S. A., Burmeister & Wain type oil engine manufactured by the shipbuilder. 7,500 bhp. 15^1/$_2$ kts. 10 passengers. Refrigerated capacity 348,060 cu.ft.
19.6.1951: Launched by Harland & Wolff Ltd., Belfast (Yard No. 1437), for Port Line Ltd., London. 31.10.1951: Completed and delivered. 11.5.1972: Arrived Castellon for demolition. 6.1972: I. M. Varela Davalillo commenced work.

PORT MONTREAL at Cape Town. (Alex Duncan)

73. PORT MONTREAL (2) (1954 - 1972)
O.N. 186004. 7,179g. 3,794n. 8,251d. 468.11 x 64.4 x 26.9 feet.
7-cyl. 2 S. C. S. A., Burmeister & Wain type oil engine manufactured by Harland & Wolff Ltd., Belfast. 7,700 bhp. 17kts. 4 passengers. Refrigerated capacity 271,960 cu.ft.
22.9.1953: Launched by Harland & Wolff Ltd., Govan, Glasgow (Yard No. 1482 G), for Port Line Ltd., London. 4.2.1954: Completed and Delivered. 1959: Refitted by Silley Cox & Company Ltd. Falmouth, including refrigerated cargo space being increased to 290,000 cu.ft. 14.9.1972: Arrived Falmouth for pre-sale inspection. 20.9.1972: Sold to Maritime Company Overseas Inc. Liberia. 25.9.1972: Renamed PUERTO PRINCESA at Falmouth. 1978: Sold to Maritime Company of the Philippines Inc., Philippines.

9.1978: Whilst at anchor in Manila South Harbour, was struck by Typhoon 'Lola' causing her to drag her anchors and collide with the Singapore registered FIDES ORIENT (4,850g. /58). Both ships sustained considerable damage that resulted in her sale to Taiwan shipbreakers. 27.11.1978: Arrived at Kaohsiung for demolition 17.12.1978: Nan Long Steel & Iron Company Ltd., commenced work.

PORT SYDNEY (World Ship Society Photograph Library)

74. PORT SYDNEY (3) (1955 - 1972)

O.N. 186201. 10,166g. 5,585n. 10,950d. 532' 9" x 70' 3" x 28' 11^1/$_2$" oa.
Two 6-cyl. 2 S. C. S. A., Doxford type oil engines (1048C) manufactured by the Wallsend Slipway & Engineering Company Ltd., Wallsend. Twin screw. 13,200 bhp. 17^3/$_4$kts. 12 passengers. Refrigerated capacity 413,741 cu.ft.
29.10.1954: Launched by Swan, Hunter & Wigham Richardson Ltd., Wallsend (Yard No. 1827), for Port Line Ltd., London. 28.2.1955: Trials. 3.3.1955: Completed. 1972: Sold to Chion Shipping Company Ltd., Greece. Renamed AKROTIRI EXPRESS. 1973: Owners restyled as Akrotiri Express Shipping Company, (Carras Liner Services S.A., managers). 1974: Renamed DAPHNE and converted into a cruise liner. 1976: Sold to Delian Athena Cruises S.A. 1978: Chartered by Flotta Lauro. 1979: Chartered by Costa Armatori for 3 years. 1985: Transoceania Armec S.p.A. Genoa, appointed as managers. 2.7.1986: Whilst at the entrance to Frederick Sound, about 80 miles S.W. of Juneau, during a cruise from Skagway to Ketchikan, suffered a fire in her generator room. The fire was extinguished and there were no casualties, and she arrived at Juneau under her own power. 1986: Sold to Independent Cruise Lines Ltd. (Transoceania Armec S.p.A., managers), Panama. 1992: Prestige Cruises Management S.A.M. Monrovia. 1996: Sold to Leisure Cruises S.A. Switzerland, and renamed SWITZERLAND. 1999: Sold to Dreamline Cruises. 2001: Laid up at Marseilles after the collapse of her Swiss charterer that was owned by the near bankrupt Swiss Air. 27.2.2002: Sold to Majestic Cruises, Greece. Handed over at Piraeus and renamed OCEAN ODYSSEY. 2002: Sold to Ocean Cruise Corp., Panama, and renamed OCEAN MONARCH.

PORT MELBOURNE (World Ship Society Photograph Library)

75. PORT MELBOURNE (3) (1955 - 1972)

O.N. 186263. 10,470g. 5,657n. 13,864d. 532' 6" x 70' 4" x 28' 11^1/$_2$" oa.

Two 6-cyl. 2 S. C. S. A., Burmeister & Wain type oil engines manufactured by the shipbuilder. Twin screw. 13,200 bhp. 17^3/$_4$kts. 12 passengers. Refrigerated capacity 412,180 cu.ft.
10.3.1955: Launched by Harland & Wolff Ltd., Belfast (Yard No. 1483), for Port Line Ltd., London. 7.7.1955: Completed and delivered. 1972: Sold to Chion Shipping Company Ltd., Greece, and renamed THERISOS EXPRESS. 1974: Sold to Therisos Express Shipping Company, Greece. 1974: Renamed CHLOE, but did not trade under this name. 1974: Renamed DANAE, (Carras Liner Services S.A. appointed as managers), and converted into a cruise liner. 1979: Sold to Delian Artemis Cruises Inc. (Carras Shipping Company Ltd., Piraeus, managers). 1985: Sold to Independent Continental Lines Ltd. (Transoceania S.p.A., Piraeus, managers). 1985: Registered under the ownership of Prestige Cruises Management S.A.M., Monrovia, Liberia, (Transoceania Armec S.p.A. Genoa, managers). 1986: Transferred to Panama registry. 10.12.1991: While undergoing repairs in dry-dock at Genoa, prior to undertaking a three month cruise, a fire broke out in a children's playroom, causing major damage. 5.1992: Declared a constructive loss. 5.1992: Sold to Greek shipbreakers. 6.1992: Resold to Harbour Maritime Ltd., Liberia, and renamed ANAR. 9.7.1992: Departed from Genoa, in tow for Piraeus, and during the course of the voyage was renamed STARLIGHT PRINCESS. 20.7.1992: Arrived at Piraeus, in the ownership of Capricorn Maritime Inc., St. Vincent. 1.9.1992: Having been renamed DANAE, she arrived and sailed from Gythion, apparently under her own power, enroute to Venice. 1994: Renamed BALTICA. 5.1994: Sold to Flax Maritime (Ellis Marine, Piraeus, managers). 1994: Sold to Waybell Cruises Inc., Panama, and renamed PRINCESS DANAE.

PORT LAUNCESTON 25th May 1977 (M. R. Dippy)

76. PORT LAUNCESTON (1957 - 1977)
O.N. 187546. 8,957g. 5,006n. 10391d. 490' 6" x 65' 9" x 28' 11^3/$_4$" oa.
7-cyl. 2 S. C. S. A., Burmeister & Wain motor type oil engine manufactured by the shipbuilder. 7,700 bhp. 15^1/$_2$kts. 10 passengers. Refrigerated capacity 417,640 cu.ft.
21.11.1956: Launched by Harland & Wolff Ltd., Belfast (Yard No. 1534), for Port Line Ltd., London. 12.3.1957: Completed and delivered. 1964: In collision with tug KINGSGARTH (181g./38), at Avonmouth. 2 of the crew of the tug were saved the rest were killed. 1977: Sold to Woburn Shipping Company Ltd., Singapore, and renamed UNITED VANTAGE. 1980: Sold to Taiwan shipbreakers. 23.1.1980: Arrived at Kaohsiung for demolition. 20.2.1980: Nan Long Iron & Steel Company Ltd., commenced work.

77. PORT INVERCARGILL (1958 - 1970)
O.N. 187753. 8,847g. 4,924n. 10,391d. 490' 5" x 65' 9" x 31' 6^1/$_2$" oa.
7-cyl. 2 S. C. S. A., Burmeister & Wain type oil engine manufactured by the shipbuilder. 7,700 bhp. 15^1/$_2$kts. 10 passengers. Refrigerated capacity 401,690 cu.ft.
22.11.1957: Launched by Harland & Wolff Ltd., Belfast (Yard No. 1565), for Port Line Ltd. 26.3.1958: Completed and delivered. 5.6.1967: Whilst on a voyage from New Zealand to the United Kingdom became trapped in Great Bitter Lake, Suez Canal, a victim of the Arab-Israeli War. 6.1970: Taken over by the ("P. & I. Club")-London Steam Shipowners Mutual Insurance Association Ltd., Subsequently sold to Invercargill Shipping Company Ltd. 30.5.1975: Left the Great Bitter Lake in tow for Port Said and arrived there later the same day. 1975: Sold to Defteron Corp., Greece, renamed KAVO KOLONES. 6.9.1975: Arrived in tow at Piraeus from Suez, to undergo repair. 22.8.1979: Arrived at Kaohsiung for demolition. 12.9.1979: Shyeh Sheng Huat Steel & Iron Works & Enterprise Ltd., commenced work.

PORT INVERCARGILL 14th July 1960 (World Ship Society Photograph Library)

PORT NEW PLYMOUTH (World Ship Society Photograph Library)

78. PORT NEW PLYMOUTH (1960 - 1979)
O.N. 301251. 13,085g. 7,218n. 13,620d. 561' 4" x 73' 11" x 31' 2¹/₂"oa.
Two 6-cyl. 2 S. C. S. A., Sulzer type oil engines (1104C) manufactured by the Wallsend Slipway & Engineering Company Ltd., Wallsend.   Twin screw. 15,600 bhp. 18kts. 12 passengers.   Refrigerated capacity 575,960 cu.ft.
29.3.1960: Launched by Swan, Hunter & Wigham Richardson Ltd., Wallsend (Yard No. 1899), for Port Line Ltd., London.   11.10.1960: Trials.   15.10.1960: Completed. 1979: Sold to Tex Dilan Shipping Company Inc, Panama, and renamed PLYMOUTH.   3.10.1979: Arrived Kaohsiung for breaking up by Chi Yeung Steel Enterprises Company. She made only one voyage as PLYMOUTH.

79. PORT ALFRED (1961 - 1975)
O.N. 302596. 10,534g. 6,075n. 12,150d.   500' 2" x 67' 9" x 28' 6" oa.
7-cyl. 2 S. C. S. A., Burmeister & Wain type oil engine manufactured by the shipbuilder. 11,500 bhp. 17kts. 10 passengers. Refrigerated capacity 430,910 cu.ft.
8.9.1960: Launched by Harland & Wolff Ltd., Belfast (Yard No. 1630), for Port Line Ltd., London. 1.3.1961: Completed and delivered. 21.11.1965: Towed PORT TOWNSVILLE into Chesapeake Bay after she had broken down.   1975: Transferred to Cunard Steamship Company Ltd., Liverpool.   1978: Renamed MASIRAH, (Cunard Brocklebank Bulkers Ltd., London, managers). 7.1982: Sold to Orpheus Ltd., Gibraltar, and renamed MASIR. 22.7.1982 until 8.3.1986: In lay-up at Piraeus. 3.1986: Sold to

Indian shipbreakers and sailed via Rotterdam and the Philippines to India. 24.7.1986: Arrived at Siracha.

PORT ALFRED on the Tyne (W. J. Harvey)

80. PORT ST LAWRENCE (1961 - 1975)
O.N. 302814. 10,627g. 6,075n. 12,221d. 500' 2" x 67' 8" x 28' 5³/₄" oa.
7-cyl. 2 S. C. S. A., Burmeister & Wain type oil engine manufactured by the shipbuilder. 11,500 bhp. 17kts. 10 passengers. Refrigerated capacity 441,490 cu.ft.
31.5.1961: Launched by Harland & Wolff Ltd., Belfast (Yard No. 1631), for Port Line Ltd., London. 20.10.1961: Completed and Delivered. 1975: Transferred to Cunard Steamship Company Ltd., Liverpool. 1975: Renamed MATANGI, (Cunard Brocklebank Bulkers Ltd., London, managers). 9.1982: Sold to Armier Shipping Company Ltd., Malta, and renamed NORDAVE. 30.4.1983: Arrived at Gadani Beach for demolition by Pakistani shipbreakers.

PORT NICHOLSON at Sydney (B. S. Nicol)

81. PORT NICHOLSON (3) (1962 - 1979)
O.N. 304378. 14,942g. 8,536n. 19,127d. 573' 6" x 76' 2" x 35.1¹/₂" oa.

Two 6-cyl. 2 S. C. S. A., Burmeister & Wain type oil engines manufactured by the shipbuilder. Twin screw. 17,000 bhp. 18½kts. 12 passengers. Refrigerated capacity 603,810 cu.ft.
4.5.1962: Launched by Harland & Wolff Ltd., Belfast (Yard No. 1646), for Port Line Ltd., London. 9.11.1962: Completed and delivered. 9.10.1979: Arrived Kaohsiung for demolition. 5.11.1979: Dah Yung Steel Manufacturing Company Ltd., commenced work

PORT BURNIE (World Ship Society Photograph Library)

82. PORT BURNIE (1966 - 1972)
O.N. 308012. 8,374g. 4,682n. 9,650d. 489' 4" x 67' 10" x 30' 7½" oa.
8-cyl. 2 S. C. S. A., Sulzer type oil engine manufactured by the Wallsend Slipway & Engineering Company Ltd., Wallsend. 13,100 bhp. 19kts. Refrigerated capacity 350,780 cu.ft.
7.8.1965: Launched by Barclay Curle & Company Ltd., Whiteinch, Glasgow (Yard No. 2015), for Port Line Ltd., London. 1.1966: Completed. 1972: Sold en-bloc for $5,000,000, with PORT ALBANY and PORT HUON to Afromar Inc., (Societe de Gestion Evge S.A., managers), Greece, and renamed ANGELIKI. 1992: Sold to Niverco Inc, Greece, and renamed SKOPELOS. 1993: Sold to Emerald Navigation Ltd., (Incom Ltd., managers), St.Vincent & The Grenadines, and renamed SKOPELO. 21.8.1993: Arrived at Alang for demolition by Indian shipbreakers.

PORT HUON (M. R. Dippy)

83. PORT HUON (2) (1968 - 1972)
O.N. 306501. 8,493g. 4,663n. 9,775d. 489' 3" x 67' 10" x 30' 7¾" oa.
8-cyl. 2 S. C. S. A., Sulzer type oil engine manufactured by the Wallsend Slipway & Engineering Company Ltd., Wallsend. 13,100 bhp. 19kts. Refrigerated capacity 361,060 cu.ft.

21.10.1964: Launched by Caledon Shipbuilding & Engineering Company Ltd., Dundee (Yard No. 541), for Cunard Steamship Company Ltd. 27.1.1965: On fire at fitting out berth. 3.1965: Completed. 1968: Transferred to Port Line Ltd., London. 1972: Sold en-bloc for $5,000,000, with PORT ALBANY and PORT BURNIE to Afromar Inc., Greece. 19.7.1972: Renamed JULIETTA at Hamburg. (Societe de Gestion Evge S.A, managers). 1984: Sold to Egyptian Reefer & General Cargo Shipping Company SAS. "AMANA", Egypt, and renamed AMANA. 1993: Sold to Universal Ltd., (Incom Shipping Ltd, managers), St Vincent & The Grenadines, and renamed MANA. 31.1.1994: Anchored off Alang, having been sold to Indian shipbreakers. 10.2.1994: Beached at Alang.

PORT ALBANY 24th December 1970 (M. R. Dippy)

84. PORT ALBANY (3) (1968 - 1972)

O.N. 308652. 8,493g. 4,663n. 9,775d. 489' 3" x 67' 10" x 30' 7³/₄" oa.
8-cyl. 2 S. C. S. A., Sulzer type oil engine manufactured by the Wallsend Slipway & Engineering Company Ltd., Wallsend. 13,100 bhp. 19kts. Refrigerated capacity 361,060 cu.ft.
18.5.1965: Launched by Caledon Shipbuilding and Engineering Company Ltd., Dundee (Yard No. 542), for Cunard Steamship Company Ltd., Liverpool. 10.1965: Completed. 1968: Transferred to Port Line Ltd., London. 1972: Sold en-bloc for $5,000,000 with PORT BURNIE and PORT HUON to Afromar Inc., (Societe de Gestion Evge S.A., managers), Greece, and renamed MARIETTA. 1990: Sold to Greek Regular Lines Special Shipping Company Inc., Greece, and renamed ARTEMON. 5.1992: Sold to Indian shipbreakers. 15.5.1992: Arrived at Alang for demolition. 15.6.1992: Khanbai Esoofbhai commenced work.

PORT CHALMERS (World Ship Society Photograph Library)

85. PORT CHALMERS (5) (1968 - 1981)
MANAAR (1981 - 1983)

O.N. 335667. 16,283g. 9,217n. 19,710d. 612' 2" (BB) x 81' 5" x 29' 0" oa.

Two 6-cyl. 2 S. C. S. A., Sulzer type oil engines manufactured by G. Clark & N.E.M. Ltd., Wallsend. 26,000 bhp. 19¹/₂kts. 12 passengers. Refrigerated capacity 606,940 cu.ft.
9.10.1967: Launched by A. Stephen & Sons Ltd., Glasgow (Yard No. 700), for Port Line Ltd., London. 4.1968: Completed. 1979: Cunard Shipping Services, appointed as managers. 3.7.1981: Arrived at Falmouth on last Port Line voyage. 1981: Renamed MANAAR. 1982: Laid up at Opua New Zealand. 5.1983: Sold to Mint Crown Shipping Corp, Greece (Kappa Maritime Company Ltd., London, "as agents only") and laid up at Piraeus. Renamed GOLDEN GLORY. 1985: Sold to Vincor Shipping Ltd., Hong Kong. 1985: Sold to Chinese shipbreakers. 13.6.1985: Arrived at Shanghai for demolition.

MANAAR (Ambrose Greenway collection)

PORT CAROLINE (World Ship Society Photograph Library)

86. PORT CAROLINE (5) (1968 - 1981)
MATRA (1981 - 1983)
O.N. 335944. 16,283g. 9,217n. 19,710d.   612' 2" (BB) x 81' 5" x 32' 11" oa.
Two 6-cyl. 2 S. C. S. A., Sulzer type oil engines manufactured by G. Clark & N.E.M. Ltd., Wallsend. 26,000 bhp. 19¹/₂kts. 12 passengers. Refrigerated capacity 606,940 cu.ft.
16.4.1968: Launched by Upper Clyde Shipbuilders Ltd. (Linthouse Division) Linthouse, Glasgow (Yard No. 701), for Port Line Ltd., London. 10.1968: Completed. 13.2.1978: Whilst on a voyage from Napier to Avonmouth, struck a bank whilst transiting the Panama Canal, damaging a propeller but proceeded to Avonmouth on one engine. 1979: Cunard Shipping Services appointed as managers. 1979: Laid up at Falmouth. 8.1981: Laid up at Rabual. 1981: Renamed MATRA. 19.7.1982: Laid up at Falmouth. 1983: Sold to Golden Crown Marinera S.A., Greece, (Zephyros Agentia de Vapores S.A. Piraeus "as

Agents only"), and renamed GOLDEN DOLPHIN. 17.10.1984: Sailed from Falmouth to Cherbourg to load for Iran. 1985: Sold to Chinese shipbreakers. 31.1.1985: Departed from Fujairah Anchorage. Prior to 1.4.1985: Arrived at Shanghai for demolition.

The Commonwealth & Dominion Line - Managed Vessels.

CDM 1. VALENCIA (1919 - 1920)
O.N. 143225. 5,232g. 3,164n. 356.6 x 50.9 x 29.7 feet.
T.3-cyl. steam engine manufactured by the shipbuilder.
7.1913: Completed by A. G. Neptun Schiffswerft und Maschinenfabrik, Rostock (Yard No. 330), for Hamburg-Amerikanische Packetfaht A. G., Germany. 21.5.1919: Surrendered to Great Britain as a prize and allocated to the Shipping Controller (The Commonwealth & Dominion Line Ltd., managers), London. 1920: Sold to James Nourse Ltd., London, and renamed HUGHLI. 1927: Purchased for £27.000 by Bank Line Ltd. (Andrew Weir & Company, managers), Glasgow and renamed TINHOW. 11.5.1943: Whilst on a voyage from Durban to Calcutta via Beira with general cargo, and having dispersed from convoy DN-37, was torpedoed and sunk by the German submarine U 181 in position 25.15S., 33.30E. Of the 78 crew, 5 gunners and 124 passengers on board, 25 crew and fifty passengers were lost.

CDM 2. WAR HECUBA (1919)
O.N. 143286. 7,920g. 4,908n. 450.0 x 58.5 x 37.1 feet.
Two T.3-cyl. steam engines manufactured by the shipbuilder. Twin screw.
6.3.1919: Launched by Workman, Clark & Company Ltd., Belfast, (Yard No. 439), for The Shipping Controller (The Commonwealth & Dominion Line Ltd., managers), London. 6.1919: Completed as ALBIONSTAR for Albionstar Steamship Company Ltd. (The Blue Star Line Ltd., managers), London. 1920: Transferred to Union Cold Storage Company Ltd., (Blue Star Line (1920) Ltd., managers), London. 1929: Renamed ALBION STAR. 1930: Managers restyled as Blue Star Line Ltd. 1948: Sold via the British Iron & Steel Corporation, to T. W. Ward Ltd., Sheffield, for demolition. 23.4.1948: Delivered at their Briton Ferry facility.

Port Line - Managed Vessels.

LOWLANDER as **LEME** (Alex Duncan)

PM 1. LOWLANDER (1941 - 1947)
O.N. 168281. 8,059g. 4,977n. 6,712n. 467.6 x 57.2 x 32.3 feet.
As built: Two 6-cyl. 4 S. C. S. A., oil engines manufactured by Soc. Anon. Franco Tosi, Legano. 694 nhp.

Post 1938: Two 6-cyl. 2 S. C. S. A., oil engines manufactured by Soc an 'Fiat' S.G.M., Turin. 1,500 nhp. 12kts. 57passengers. Refrigerated capacity unspecified.
31.12.1924: Launched as LEME by Stabilmento Techico, Trieste (Yard No. 743), for Nav. Libera Triestina S.A., Venice. 10.1925: Completed. 1936: Sold to 'Italia' Soc. Anon. di Nav. Converted to Passenger Ship. 10.1941: Seized by the United States Maritime Commission at Astoria, Oregon, and renamed LOWLANDER under the Panamanian Flag. 10.1941: Placed under the control of the Ministry of War Transport, London (Port Line Ltd., London, managers). 10.9.1947: Returned to United States Maritime Commission and laid up. 1948: Handed back to 'Italia' Soc. Anon. Di Nav., Genoa, and renamed LEME for employment on an Italy to South America -passenger, cargo service. 1954: Recorded as having accomodation for 63 passengers. 15.9.1960: Arrived at Trieste for demolition by Sidemar. 4.1961: Demolition commenced.

FORT CHAMBLY (World Ship Society Photograph Library)

PM 2. FORT CHAMBLY (1942 - 1947)

O.N. 168820. 7,130g. 4,256n. 441.10 x 57.2 x 27.0 feet.
T.3-cyl. steam engine manufactured by Dominion Engineering Works Ltd., Montreal. 505 nhp. 2,500 ihp.
22.11.1941: Launched by Davie Shipbuilding & Repairing Company Ltd., Lauzon P.Q (Yard No. 533), for the United States War Shipping Administration. 28.4.1942: Completed and bareboat-chartered to the Ministry of War Transport, London, (Port Line Ltd., London, appointed as managers). 1947: Returned to the United States Maritime Commission and laid up pending survey. 3.1957: Class suspended, survey overdue. 10.12.1958: Sold at Dallas, Texas for demolition. 1959: Demolished at Mobile.

FORT STIKINE (World Ship Society Photograph Library)

PM 3. FORT STIKINE (1942 - 1944)

O.N. 168351. 7,142g. 4,261n. 420.6 x 57.2 x 34.9 feet.
T.3-cyl. steam engine manufactured by Dominion Engineering Works Ltd., Montreal. 505 nhp. 2,500 ihp.

15.4.1942: Launched by Prince Rupert Dry Dock. & Shipyard, Prince Rupert, British Columbia, Canada (Yard No. 43), for the United States War Shipping Administration. 31.7.1942: Completed and bareboat chartered to Ministry of War Transport (Port line Ltd., London, appointed as managers). Collided with another ship only hours after completion, repairs took about 6 weeks to complete. 14.4.1944: Exploded violently whilst discharging military stores at Bombay. The explosion devastated a large area of Bombay and caused the loss of no less than 10 allied ships in the port at the time.

EMPIRE TREASURE (World Ship Society Photograph Library)

PM 4. EMPIRE TREASURE (1943 - 1946)
O.N. 168992. 7,040g. 4,973n. 447.7 x 56.2 x 34.2 feet.
T.3-cyl. steam engine manufactured by J. G. Kincaid & Company Ltd., Greenock. 558 nhp. Refrigerated capacity unspecified.
28.12.1942: Launched by Lithgows Ltd., Port Glasgow (Yard No. 977), for the Ministry of War Transport. (Port Line Ltd., appointed managers), London. 3.1943: Completed. 15.1.1944: Whilst on a voyage in convoy, from Liverpool to Halifax and New York, her stern frame fractured, she lost a propeller blade and also the use of her rudder, causing her to drop out of the convoy. The rescue/ salvage tug BUSTLER (1,110g./1942) was despatched by the Admiralty and EMPIRE TREASURE was taken in tow. 29.1.1944: Arrived in the Bristol Channel at the end of a tow of over 1,000 miles. 5.1946: Sold to Donaldson Line Ltd. (Donaldson Brothers & Black Ltd., managers), Glasgow, and renamed GRACIA. 10.1946: Fitted for oil fuel. 3.1954: Purchased by Blue Star Line Ltd., London, and renamed OREGON STAR. 5.1955: Sold to Williamson & Company Ltd., Hong Kong, and renamed INCHLEANA. 1966: Sold to National Shipping Corporation, Pakistan, and renamed TETULIA. 21.7.1968: Arrived at Chittagong and used for lighterage work. 18.9.1969: Mohamadi Iron Traders commenced demolition at Chittagong.

SAMPLER as **GLORIANA** (World Ship Society Photograph Library)

PM 5. SAMPLER (1943 - 1947) See ship No. 63 in main fleet.

PM 6. SAMBLADE (1943 - 1948)
O.N. 169670. 7,219g. 4,380n.   441.8 x 57.0 x 34.8 feet.
T. 3-cyl steam engine manufactured by Joshua Hendy Iron Works, Sunnyvale, California. 2,500 ihp.
8.1943: Launched as AUGUSTUS H. GARLAND by California Shipbuilding Corp., Los Angeles, California (Yard No. 230), for the United States War Shipping Administration. 1943: Completed as SAMBLADE for bareboat charter to the Ministry of War Transport, London (Port Line Ltd., London, appointed as managers).   1948: Returned to United States Maritime Commission, and renamed AUGUSTUS H. GARLAND.   Laid up James River Reserve Fleet, owners U.S. Dept of Commerce. 15.10.1959: Sold to Bethlehem Steel Corp. 29.10.1959:Arrived at Baltimore for demolition by the Patapsco Scrap Company.

PM 7. SAMLEVEN (1944 - 1947)
O.N. 169817. 7,248g. 4,417n.   441.8 x 57.0 x 34.8 feet.
T.3-cyl. steam engine manufactured by General Machinery Corp., Hamilton, Ontario. 2,500 ihp.
31.1.1944: Launched by Bethlehem Fairfield Shipyard Inc., Baltimore, Maryland (Yard No. 2319), for United States War Shipping Administration. 2.1944: Completed, and bareboat chartered to the Ministry of War Transport (Port Line Ltd., London, managers).   1947: Counties Ship Management appointed, managers.   18.4.1947: Sold to Tramp Shipping Development Company Ltd. (Counties Ship Management Company Ltd., managers), London, and renamed BISHAM HILL. 31.7.1947: Delivered. 10.1951: Transferred to London & Overseas Freighters Ltd. (same managers). 1.1952: Sold to Global Carriers Inc., (N. K. Venizelos, manager), Monrovia, Liberia, and renamed NAUSICA.   2.1952: Class withdrawn at owners request.   1956: Sold to Panormitana Navl. S.P.A., (Leonardo Arrivabene Cia. Di Nav. S.P.A., managers), Palermo, Italy, and renamed PRAGLIA.   1959: Sold to Olisman Cia. Naviera Ltda., Lebanon, and renamed VASSILIKI. 1967: Owners Vassiliki Shipping Ltd., Cyprus. 1968: Owners restyled as Franco Shipping & Managing Company Ltd., Cyprus.   31.3.1970: Whilst on a voyage from Augusta to Havana with fertiliser, grounded I mile north of Mayaguana Island, Bahamas, in position 22.28N., 73.08W.   Holed, and part flooded, was abandoned by her crew.

SAMEDEN as **KANARIS** (Alex Duncan)

PM 8. SAMEDEN (1944 - 1947)
O.N. 169851. 7,245g. 4,428n.   441.8 x 57.1 x 34.8 feet.
T.3-cyl. steam engine manufactured by Filer & Stowell Company, Milwaukee, Wisconsin. 450 nhp.
3.3.1944: Launched by Bethlehem Fairfield Shipyard Inc., Baltimore, Maryland (Yard No. 2334), for United States War Shipping Administration. 3.1944: Completed and bareboat chartered to the Ministry of War Transport. (Port Line Ltd., London, appointed managers). 1947: Counties Ship Management appointed managers.   1947: Sold to Mill Hill Steamship Company Ltd., (Counties Ship Management Company Ltd., managers), London, and renamed MILL HILL.   19.8.1950: Abandoned in the Australian

Bight, when her cargo of pig iron shifted. 25.8.1950: Having been salvaged, was towed into Port Lincoln and subsequently repaired. 8.1951: Transferred to London & Overseas Freighters Ltd. (same managers). 9.1951: Sold to Costa de Marfil Cia. Nav. S.A. (Diamantis Pateras Ltd., London, managers), Monrovia, Liberia, and renamed EDUCATOR. 8.1955: Class withdrawn owners request. 1960: Transferred to Greek registry. 1961: Renamed KANARIS. 1964: Transferred to Cia. Nav. Kanaris S.A., Greece. 1966: Sold to Active Steamship Company Ltd., Panama, and renamed SPLENDID SKY. 4.10.1969: Whilst on a voyage from Antwerp to Spezia and Split with a cargo of silversand. Grounded off Bats, River Schelde. 6.10.1969: Refloated, but was found to be cracked and buckled amidships and leaking. Towed to Antwerp. Repairs deemed uneconomic. 2.1969: Sold to Jos de Smedt, Antwerp for breaking up. 8.1.1970: Demolition commenced at Antwerp.

EMPIRE MOULMEIN as **VILLE DE DIEGO SUAREZ** (World Ship Society Photograph Library)

PM 9. EMPIRE MOULMEIN (1944 - 1945)

O.N. 180219. 7,047g. 6,546n. 430.9 x 56.2 x 27.0 446.5 x 56.1 x 27.0 feet.
T.3-cyl. steam engine with low pressure turbine manufactured by the shipbuilder. 2,500 ihp. Refrigerated capacity unspecified.
8.6.1944: Launched by John Redhead & Sons Ltd., West Docks, South Shields (Yard No. 540), for the Ministry of War Transport. 2.8.1944: Port Line Ltd., London, appointed as managers. 24.8.1945: Sold to the French Government (Ministere De La Marine Marchande)(Nouvelle Cie Havraise Peninsulaire De Nav., managers), and renamed COLONEL VIELJEUX. 1948: Sold to Nouvelle Compagnie Havraise Peninsulaire de Nav, Havre, and renamed VILLE DE DIEGO SUAREZ. 1962: Sold to Soc. Anon Monegasque d'Armement et de Nav, Monaco, and renamed VIMY. 1962: Sold to Riza Ve Aslan Sadikoglu Ortaklari Komandit Sirketi, Istanbul, and renamed DEMIRHAN. 1966: Sold to Manizade Vapuru Donatma Istiraki, renamed MANIZADI. Owners subsequently restyled Manioglu Gemi Isletmeciligi A.S.Turkey and later as Sevket Manioglu Denizcilik Isletmesi Donatmi Istiriki, Istanbul. 3.1976: Sold for demolition. 20.3.1976: Zeki Venen commenced demolition at Aliaga, Turkey.

Port Line - Chartered vessels.

PORT HARDY (World Ship Society Photograph Library)

PC 1. PORT HARDY (3) (1954 - 1961)
O.N. 168872. 8,311g. 4,870n. 10,950d. 492.6 x 64.4 x 29.11 feet.
Two 4-cyl. 2 S. C. S. A., Doxford type oil engines manufactured by Barclay Curle & Company Ltd, Glasgow. Twin screw. 9,000 bhp. 15^1/$_2$kts.
1.10.1943: Launched as HEREFORDSHIRE by Barclay Curle & Company Ltd., Whiteinch (Yard No. 693), for Bibby Line Ltd., Liverpool. 28.12.1943: Completed. 1954: Renamed PORT HARDY for duration of time charter to Port Line Ltd., London. 1961: Renamed HEREFORDSHIRE on completion of charter. 1969: Sold for about £130,000, to Troodos Shipping & Trading Ltd., Cyprus, and renamed MERRYLAND. 1970: Sold to Meritath Cia. Nav. S.A., Cyprus. 1973: Sold to Taiwan shipbreakers. 7.2.1973: Arrived at Kaohsiung for demolition. 9.3.1973: Chia Tai Steel & Iron Works commenced work.

PORT CURTIS (World Ship Society Photograph Library)

PC 2. PORT CURTIS (3) (1955 - 1961)
O.N. 181155. 5,635g. 3,071n. 10,200d. 449.8 x 59.7 x 26.0 feet.
4-cyl. 2 S. C. S. A., oil engine manufactured by Wm. Doxford & Sons Ltd., Sunderland. 4,400 bhp. 14kts.
22.10.1952: Launched as THISTLEDOWNE by J. L. Thompson & Sons Ltd., Sunderland (Yard No. 675), for Albyn Line Ltd (Allan, Black & Company Ltd, managers), Sunderland. 3.1953: Completed. 1955: Renamed PORT CURTIS for duration of a time charter to Port Line Ltd. 22.3.1961: Reverted to THISTLEDOWNE on completion of charter. 31.1.1966: Sold for £285,000 to The Somerston Shipping Company Ltd (Chapman & Willan Ltd. managers). 18.2.1966: Handed over at Cardiff. 12.4.1966: Transferred to the Carlton Steamship Company Ltd (same managers). 1966: Sold for £392,500 to Ratnaker Shipping Company Ltd, India. 16.5.1966: Handed over in the River Tyne and renamed RATNA JYOTI. 15.11.1972: Sold to the Great Steel Corporation, Mazagan, India. 30.11.1972: Arrived at Bombay for demolition. 1.1.1973: Work commenced.

PORT STEPHENS at Cape Town. (World Ship Society Photograph Library)

PC 3. PORT STEPHENS (3) (1955 - 1956)
O.N. 169879. 6,597g. 3,861n. 10,376d. 490.4 x 63.6 x 26.1 feet.
Two 4-cyl. 2 S. C. S. A., oil engines manufactured by Wm. Doxford & Sons Ltd., Sunderland. 6,800 bhp. 15kts.
14.10.1943: Launched as SILVEROAK by J. L. Thompson & Sons Ltd., Sunderland (Yard No. 629), for Silver Line Ltd., London. 6.1944: Completed. 1955: Renamed PORT STEPHENS for duration of charter to Port Line Ltd., London. 1956: Returned to Silver Line Ltd. 9.1956: Sold to the Ben Line Steamers Ltd., (Wm. Thomson & Company, managers), Leith, and renamed BENVANNOCH. 11.1.1969: Arrived at Kaohsiung for demolition. 4.1969: Chin Ho Fa Steel & Iron Company Ltd., commenced work, at Onahama.

PORT WANSTEAD (World Ship Society Photograph Library)

PC 4. PORT WANSTEAD (1957 - 1960)
O.N. 183130. 5,664g. 2,745n. 8,526d. 475.10 x 64.4 x 25.1 feet.
5-cyl. 2 S. C. S. A., Doxford type oil engine manufactured by Scotts Shipbuilding & Engineering Company Ltd., Greenock. 5,500 bhp. 14kts.
10.5.1949: Launched as WANSTEAD by Caledon Shipbuilding & Engineering Company Ltd., Dundee (Yard No. 469), for Britain Steamship Company Ltd. (Watts, Watts & Company Ltd., managers), London. 29.10.1949: Completed. 1957: Renamed PORT WANSTEAD for duration of a time-charter to Port Line Ltd., London. 1960: Renamed WANSTEAD. 1963: Renamed RAEBURN for duration of a time-charter to Lamport & Holt. Ltd., Liverpool. 1964: Renamed WANSTEAD. 1964: Renamed WANLIU for a charter to John Swire & Sons Ltd. (China Navigation Company Ltd.), London. 1969: Sold to China Navigation Company Ltd. 1975: Sold to Maldives Shipping Ltd., Maldive Islands, and renamed MALDIVE EXPLORER. 1978: Sold to Pakistani shipbreakers. 11.6.1978: Arrived at Gadani Beach for demolition.

PORT DENISON (World Ship Society Photograph Library)

PC 5. PORT DENISON (4) (1960 - 1965)
O.N. 301402. 6,227g. 3,294n. 10,830d. 485' 0" x 61' 7" x 26' 10" feet.
7-cyl. 2 S. C. S. A., oil engine manufactured by Akt. Burmeister & Wains Maskin-og-Skibsbyggeri, Copenhagen. 6,300 bhp. 15kts.
3.6.1959: Launched as FAIR LADY by Ab Ekensbergs Varv, Stockholm (Yard No. 215), for unspecified owners. Contract sold for £750.000. 11.1959: Completed as VIMEIRA for the Dornoch Shipping Company Ltd., (Harrisons (Clyde) Ltd., managers), Glasgow. 1960: Renamed PORT DENISON for duration of charter to Port Line Ltd. 1965: Renamed VIMEIRA. 1965: Sold to Rederi Ab Nordstjernan (A. A. Johnson, manager), Sweden, and renamed STAR ALTAIR. 1965: Sold to A. Johnson & Company HAb., (same manager). 1978: Sold to Laertis Shipping Corp, Greece, (A. Bacolitsas Compania Naviera S.A., managers), renamed LAERTIS. 1983: Sold to Genesis Shipping Corp. Ltd. (same managers), Valetta. 1985: Sold to Contessa Shipping Company, Valetta, and renamed TESSA. 23.2.1986: Arrived at Gadani Beach for demolition.

PORT WIMBLEDON (World Ship Society Photograph Library)

PC 6. PORT WIMBLEDON (1960 - 1965)
O.N. 300765. 9,223g. 5,126n. 10,000d. 487' 6" x 63' 5" x 27' 9" feet.
6-cyl. 2 S. C. S. A., Doxford type oil engine manufactured by the shipbuilder. 6,700 bhp. 15kts.
17.4.1958: Launched as WIMBLEDON by Barclay, Curle & Company Ltd., Glasgow (Yard No. 742), for Britain Steamship Company Ltd (Watts, Watts & Company Ltd., managers), London. 8.9.1958: Completed. 1960: Renamed PORT WIMBLEDON for duration of charter to Port Line Ltd., London. 1965: Renamed WIMBLEDON. 1967: Sold to National Shipping Corporation, Pakistan, and renamed SWAT, retaining British registry. 1979: Taken over by Pakistan National Shipping Corporation, Pakistan. 27.9.1982: Arrived at Karachi for demolition.

PC 7. PORT CAMPBELL (3) (1961 - 1966)
O.N. 301408. 7,683g. 3,949n. 505' 0" x 66' 0" x 27' 7" oa.

6-cyl. 2 S. C. S. A., Burmeister & Wain type oil engine manufactured by J. G. Kincaid & Company Ltd., Greenock. 5,800 bhp. 14kts.

3.12.1959: Launched as CLARKSPEY by Lithgows Ltd., Port Glasgow (Yard No. 1124), for H. Clarkson & Company Ltd (J. & J. Denholm (Management) Ltd., managers), Glasgow. 3.1960: Completed. 1961: Renamed PORT CAMPBELL for duration of a 5 year time charter to Port Line Ltd., London. 1966: Reverted to her owners and then sold to Counties Steam Navigation Company Ltd., London, and renamed KINGS REACH. 1970: Sold for about £650,000 to Alderminster Shipping Company Ltd., London, and renamed ALDERMINSTER. 1975: Sold to Joli Shipping Inc., Liberia, and renamed JOLI. 1976: Sold to Kyklops Cia. Nav.S.A., Panama, and renamed FLORA C. 1976: Transferred to Greek registry. 24.9.1982: Sailed from Kakinda bound for Calcutta but was sold to Pakistani shipbreakers. Prior to 22.10.1982: Arrived at Chittagong for demolition by Burhani Metal Works, Bhatiau Beach, Chittagong.

PORT CAMPBELL (World Ship Society Photograph Library)

APPENDIX No. 1 - Ships Machinery

Engine power is now defined in kilowatts, but until recently it was horsepower, a term that was devised by James Watt to give him a basis to describe his new steam engines to his potential customers. In Watt's day steam engines in most cases would be replacing the work done by horses. Watt's horsepower was 33,000 foot pounds per minute.

For commercial reasons nominal horsepower was preferred to the actual power of the machinery, as a rule of thumb the N.H.P. is about a fifth of the I.H.P. The N.H.P continued in use for many years since it was claimed it gave a good estimate of the physical size of engines and hence a useful basis for costing. It was also used as a basis for manning levels in merchant ships, e.g. for engines of 600 N.H.P. and above the manning level was 7-Engineers, 1-Storekeeper, 1-Donkeyman, 4-Greasers and 1-Fireman per 18-foot of boiler grate.

I.H.P: indicated horsepower usually associated with the reciprocating steam engine

B.H.P: brake horsepower is the power measured on an engine test bed using a water brake and is usually associated with oil engines

S.H.P: shaft horsepower usually associated with steam turbine machinery and is obtained using a torsion meter on the output shaft.

The early marine engines were used with paddle wheels and on this type of ship or tug the engine cylinders were below the paddle shaft and turned this shaft from below and could be described as driving upwards. With the success of the propeller (or screw) the machinery installation became a crankshaft coupled to propeller shafting at low level with the engine cylinders above driving upwards. This type of installation was at first described as inverted, but as these type of installations became the norm, inverted ceased to be used when describing this type of installation even though the layout had not changed.

Steam engines convert the energy in the steam to mechanical power by moving the piston and hence the crankshaft which turns the screw. The machinery fitted to merchant ships usually had two cylinders until about 1885 and the steam was used to drive the piston up and down (i.e.- double acting).

Up to about 1869 most steam engines worked as simple engines. In this type of engine steam works in the cylinder and is then exhausted to a condenser, the boiler pressure was of the order 10 to 50 p.s.i. The first 13 iron screw steamships built for Watts, Milburn were propelled by two-cylinder simple engines. Commencing in 1864 with the SHEARWATER the last simple engined ship owned was the BRAZILIAN, in 1869. Also in 1869 the compound engines were fitted commencing with the SURBITON, CHU KIANG and the OTTERBURN. In these engines higher pressure (90 to 100 p.s.i.) steam was first used in the high pressure (h.p.) cylinder (the smallest diameter) and on being exhausted was then exhausted to the condenser, where the steam was converted back into water for re-use in the boiler. The important advantage of the compound engine was the improvement in fuel consumption and the range of steamships was dramatically increased.

The next important development was the triple expansion engine generally adopted from about 1885 when steel became readily available. Among the benefits to engineers was the use of this material to build stronger boilers that in turn led to higher steam pressures (from 150 p.s.i and upwards). This higher pressure steam was used to work in three different sized cylinders in turn h.p, intermediate pressure i.p. and l.p. A further development was the quadruple expansion engines with four cylinders all of different diameters. The merger in 1914 brought together a fleet of 25 ships, five had quadruple engines and the remainder were fitted with the ubiquitous triple expansion engine.

The dramatic demonstration by Charles Parsons at the Spithead Review in 1897 did not effect ordinary (low powered) merchant ships for some time. It was not until 1910 that Parsons installed geared turbine machinery in the EASTERN PRINCE built in 1887 and later renamed VESPASIAN. Commonwealth & Dominion Line Ltd ordered a series of twin- screw ships in the early part of World War One, merchant ships were given low priority and delivery did not commence until 1918 the last ship ordered at that time being delivered in 1924. Workman, Clark built nine of these ships at Belfast of which three were fitted with turbine machinery. Hawthorn, Leslie built five ships on the Tyne all with turbines, unfortunately the turbines developed problems and to maintain the ships in service the vessel being fitted out was used as a source of spare parts. The last of the Tyne ships the PORT HARDY (2) was finally delivered in 1923 with triple expansion engines and not the turbines as originally intended.

After the unhappy trial of steam turbine machinery Commonwealth & Dominion embarked on the beginning of a motorship programme. The choice of engine for their first ship was fundamental in the success of the motorship (as had been the unfortunate choice of turbine machinery). In the 1920s there were about ten designs of oil engine available. The success of the Doxford prototype in the Swedish cargo ship YNGAREN, which made a successful maiden voyage from Europe to Australia in 1921, must have been an influence in the decision to specify Doxford machinery for the first two motorships the PORT DUNEDIN and the PORT HOBART (1).

The Doxford engine, designed and built at Sunderland by William Doxford & Sons was one of the most successful of the ten or so oil engine types that Commonwealth and Dominion had to choose from. It was a two-stroke opposed piston engine and from the beginning used a solid injection fuel system. With the exception of the four-stroke Vickers engine, all the remaining designs needed high pressure air for their "blast injection" fuel systems. This system was phased out in the 1930s much to the relief of the ships' engine room staff. The Doxford had a unique self-aligning design for all the crankshaft bearings which was achieved by these bearings having a spherical component in their make-up. The Sunderland engine builders were pioneers in the use of welded prefabrications to replace large castings for such items as the bedplate, crankcases etc. This engine's popularity can be judged by the number of successful licence agreements taken up. Fifteen engine builders in the United Kingdom and another ten around the world in the U.S.A, France, Italy, Norway, Hong Kong, Australia, Holland and Sweden. In general the emergence of the motorship was somewhat hampered by such factors as the dominant position of coal in the first quarter of the twentieth century. Other factors being the obvious limited progress to technical development during World War One and the trade depression of the 1920s. The latter factor would have contributed to Commonwealth and Dominion's decision to upgrade several of their twin-screw steam ships by having them fitted with Bauer-Wach exhaust turbines. This item of equipment used the exhaust steam from the low pressure cylinder of the main engine and provided additional power to the propeller via a hydraulic clutch and reduction gearing. The option was that for a similar fuel consumption the vessel would gain $1/2$ knot or to maintain the design speed with a reduced fuel consumption.

The Doxford engine proved to be a preferred choice by the company for many years, but Sulzer machinery was tried in 1927 in the PORT HUON (1) and again in 1935 when the PORT TOWNVILLE (1) was delivered. For the benefit of the uninitiated, it should be explained that the Sulzer type of motor engine resembles more nearly that of a motor car; the explosions take place in the top of the eight cylinders in each engine, and the pistons are driven downwards to act on the crankshaft. In the Doxford engine the explosion takes place in the middle of each of the four cylinders, and two pistons are driven, one up and one down, both acting through connecting rods on the crank shafting.

In 1946 the double-acting two-stroke engined PORT HOBART (2) joined the fleet, built at Harland & Wolff, Belfast to a Shaw Savill design. The Doxford engine continued to be installed in the company's new tonnage with few exceptions until the PORT SYDNEY (3) in 1955. The Burmiester and Wain engines built at Belfast were installed in several ships and the last five Port ships were fitted with Sulzer engines. The end of the conventional refrigerated ships was brought about by the container revolution. The new container ships were bigger and faster and the power needed made the steam turbine the obvious choice. The machinery installed in the ACT container ships was supplied with superheated steam of 1,055p.s.i, an interesting comparison with the SHEARWATER whose engine was using steam of 20p.s.i.

When the Commonwealth & Dominion Line came into existence in 1914, the engineering departments of the four companies amalgamating were supervised by William Esplen & Swainston Ltd. of London, in the case of Tyser & Company by William Esplen & Son; Goodwin, Hamilton and Adamson, of Liverpool for the Indra Line of T B Royden & Company; and by Dudgeon and Gray Ltd. of London for William Milburn & Company. The Star Line of James P. Corry & Company had as their Chief Engineer Mr Alexander MacDonald who became Superintendent Engineer of the combined fleets - a total of 25 steamers. Alexander MacDonald (1857-1930) had been born in Perthshire and after serving as an engineering apprentice joined Clan Line. He had proved himself to be a man of exceptional ability and soon progressed to become a Chief Engineer.

In 1886 he was engaged by James P. Corry & Company as Chief Engineer of their first steamer, the STAR OF VICTORIA(1), then building in the Belfast yard of Workman, Clark & Company. The ship was completed in 1887. In 1889 he was appointed to the newly built steamer STAR OF ENGLAND (1), which with the STAR OF VICTORIA (1), was chartered for a series of voyages to New Zealand. Both ships were fitted with refrigeration equipment by the charterers and this was subsequently purchased by the owners. With the introduction of more steamships Corry decided that Alexander MacDonald should remain ashore as their Superintendent Engineer. Prior to the merger in 1914 he was largely responsible for the development of the refrigerating ships, not only of the Star Line but also of the Indra Line. After the takeover by Cunard in 1916, he became an active member of the Cunard Technical Committee. In 1923 ill-health caused him to retire at the age of 67.

In comparison with the complex engineering problems which have to be grappled with today, matters in those days were comparatively simple. At the time of the amalgamation every ship in the fleet was propelled by reciprocating steam engines, steam being supplied from coal-fired boilers. The older ships were single screw and the new ships twin-screw. The steam-driven refrigerating machinery for the carriage of frozen meat in the older ships was either the type that used cold air as the refrigerating medium or ammonia. In the newer ships Messrs J. & E. Hall's carbonic acid gas (carbon dioxide) steam -driven machines were installed.

lexander Macdonald's successor, H. G. Dearden, a native of Sunderland, was born in 1876. He served an apprenticeship with North Eastern Marine Engineering Company, which was followed by two years in the drawing office and a further five years at sea. He came ashore in 1904 as a Ship and Engine Surveyor to Lloyds Register of Shipping at Newcastle-upon-Tyne. In 1908 he was transferred to their head office in London. He left Lloyds in 1914 to join the newly formed Commonwealth and Dominion Line as assistant to Alexander MacDonald. During his time in the Superintendent's chair in 1925 the company's first motor ships were built, being the PORT DUNEDIN and the PORT HOBART (1) which were fitted with twin-screw Doxford engines.

H G Dearden made a considerable contribution to resolving the problems with the carriage of apples, pears, cheese and chilled beef from Australia and New Zealand. Working with Dr A. J. M. Smith (Shipowners Refrigerated Cargo Research Council) and J. & E. Hall Ltd they were responsible for the change over from the system of cooling cargo holds by means of cold brine circulating through grids arranged on the roof and sides of the hold to the system of circulating cold air around the hold by a fan after it had been forced through a battery of brine cooled pipes. The first ship to be fitted with the cooled air system was the PORT JACKSON (3) built in 1937.

H G Dearden was followed by B. P. Arrowsmith who had been born in 1891 in Petone, New Zealand where he had served an engineering apprenticeship. Prior to joining the INDRAPURA (2) in 1913 he was a keen rugby player. He served in a number of the company's vessels and came ashore in 1926 as Dearden's assistant. During World War Two the company were allocated nine ships to manage for the Government and suffered the loss of thirteen ships. For his outstanding services during this period Mr Arrowsmith was awarded an O.B.E. The pioneering use of aluminium linings for the insulation in refrigerated cargo spaces and the introduction of streamlined superstructure on the sister ships PORT BRISBANE (2) and PORT AUCKLAND (2) completed in 1949 were among his contributions. In 1947 he was appointed a Director of Port Line Ltd and retired in 1958.

B. P. Arrowsmith was succeeded by R. W. Cromarty as Superintendent Engineer in 1947. He was born in Northumberland in 1901 and served an engineering apprenticeship on the Tyne. After four years at sea in oil tankers he joined the company in 1927 and was appointed to the PORT HUON (1), then being built on the Tyne. She was the company's first Sulzer-engined vessel. Between 1933 and 1939 R. W. Cromarty went to Lloyds Register of Shipping as a Ship and Engine Surveyor serving in London, Barry, Swansea and Antwerp. When he rejoined the company in 1939 he became B. P. Arrowsmith's assistant. He was greatly interest in the training of young engineers and engine room ratings, taking an active interest in the development and implementation of the Alternative Training Scheme for Marine Engineers and the Leith Course for Engine Room Ratings. During his term in office he saw the change of the fleet from steamers to all motorships, the introduction of alternating current for ships' electrical equipment, hydraulically-operated cargo hatch covers, high speed automatic running freon refrigerating machinery and data logging of essential pressures and temperatures in engine rooms and cargo holds, plus other innovations designed to give increased efficiency with less staff and lower costs. He was appointed a director in 1960 and retired in 1964.

Captain W. S. Jenks took over as Superintendent Engineer in 1964. He had been born in 1908 and joined the Royal Navy in 1921. After engineering training at the Royal Naval Colleges at Dartmouth, Keyham and Greenwich he spent many years at sea before taking up a shore appointment and finally becoming Manager of the Engineering Departments HM Dockyards. In 1958 he retired from the Royal Navy with the rank of Captain to join Thos. & Jno. Brocklebank Ltd and was responsible for the modernisation and increased efficiency of their fleet. He was elected a director of Brocklebank and in 1964 transferred to Port Line where he became a director the following year. With the introduction of containerisation he was responsible for co-ordinating the design of new tonnage specially arranged for the carriage of both refrigerated and general cargo containers. These ships required high powered machinery to provide service speeds of 24 knots and steam turbines were fitted which used steam pressure at 1,055p.s.i.

In 1968 when Port Line and Blue Star Line Ltd formed the management company, Blue Star Port Line (Management) Ltd, known as Blueport. Captain Jenks was appointed General Manager of the newly formed Cunard International Technical Services but retained his responsibility for the Port Line new tonnage. With his retirement in May 1970 ended an era during which the directors of Port Line always encouraged their Superintendents to keep ahead of technical progress. The company was very fortunate in their choice of Superintendent Engineers.

APPENDIX No. 2 - M.A.N.Z. Line

(**M**ontreal, **A**ustralia, **N**ew **Z**ealand **Line Ltd.**).

MANZ LINE JOINT SERVICE

REGULAR SAILINGS TO AND FROM

EASTERN CANADA-AUSTRALIA
and NEW ZEALAND

Separate Services

AUSTRALIAN PORTS	NEW ZEALAND PORTS
BRISBANE	AUCKLAND
SYDNEY	WELLINGTON
MELBOURNE	LYTTLETON
ADELAIDE	DUNEDIN

Service to other Australian and New Zealand ports and also to Tasmania can be arranged.

Full information on application to Agents

Montreal Australia New Zealand Line Ltd.
(Incorporated in Canada)

The company was first registered in August 1936, when it took over the existing services of the Canadian Government Line. Prior to World War One, there were only occasional direct sailing's from Canada to Australia and New Zealand and most of these were handled by New Zealand Shipping Company vessels. During World War One the Canadian Government embarked on an extensive shipbuilding programme and, being left with many surplus ships after the war, they decided to follow the example of the Australian Government and form a national flag line. In 1919 the Canadian Government Merchant Marine ships began a regular run to Auckland and Australian ports, with warbuilt ships whose name all began with the prefix "Canadian". Initially they ran from the west coast, offering through Bills of Lading to Montreal via Canadian National Railways. In 1921 they commenced their direct service from the east coast via the Panama Canal. In 1925 they extended their service to all main New Zealand ports and returned to Canada via New York and Boston. Base ports in Canada were usually Montreal or Halifax.

In 1928 the company became known as Canadian National Steamships and became well supported and ran on a monthly basis. In that year the New Zealand Shipping Company decided to operate a regular direct service as well and commenced a vigorous freight war with the Canadian company. Freights which averaged $25 dropped as low as $5 and after three months, in which eight ships were despatched by both parties. New Zealand Shipping withdrew. Slump conditions in 1931 caused the Canadian National Steamships to rationalise its services and at the end of that year it was estimated that the line had lost $16,000,000 since it was formed. The position improved somewhat in 1932 but although they were obtaining good freights from New Zealand and Australia the high wages of the Canadian seamen cut into their profits and from owning 70 ships totalling 425,000 tons at the end of the war they were down to ten in 1936. In the period 1921-1934 the line lost $11,000,000 and it was obvious in Canadian business circles that the sooner their "white elephant" was disposed the better. The main British companies in the United States-Australian trade could foresee the trends and were therefore interested in picking up the pieces. In November 1934, representatives of the Commonwealth and Dominion Line left for Montreal, but on arrival later in New York found that the Ellerman and Bucknall Line, through their agents McLean, Kennedy & Company, were already putting out feelers for a take-over. A message also arrived from London indicating that New Zealand Shipping Company were also interested, and as a result the three parties joined and made a joint approach for the purchase of the line. Early in 1936 the 10 ships were purchased for $320,000. In addition the three companies agreed to maintain the Canadian National services for five years and undertook to take over the crews of the remaining ships.

In August 1936, the M.A.N.Z. Line was formed and the CITY OF BATAVIA left Canada on 22nd May 1936, for Auckland, Wellington, Sydney, Melbourne and Adelaide and inaugurated the first voyage of the new company.

Sir Thomas Royden presented the old Royden Line houseflag to the new concern and this, with the addition of a maple leaf in the centre diamond became the M.A.N.Z. Line houseflag.

The Canadian Government ships were not suitable for the trade and both Port Line and New Zealand Shipping Company each initially ordered three ships, while Ellermans employed some of their existing fleet. The Port Line tonnage comprised the PORT MONTREAL (1) and the PORT HALIFAX, completed in 1937, as well as the PORT SAINT JOHN, delivered in 1938. PORT QUEBEC was laid down for the service but was requisitioned after the outbreak of World War Two and didn't come into M.A.N.Z. Line service until 1948. All these ships and the New Zealand Shipping Company's KAIMATA, KAIKOURA and KAIPARA, and the later ships KAIPAKI and KAITUNA (both 1939), were operated by the parent companies and no vessels were registered to the direct ownership of the new company.

At the October 1936 Board Meeting it was reported that the Managing Directors had placed orders on 23rd September 1936 for three single screw ships to be fitted with Doxford type engines of four-cylinders 620mm x 2320mm to give an estimated speed of 12^1/$_2$ knots. To be built to the design and under the supervision of Mr H.G. Dearden.

Builder	Wm. Doxford	Swan, Hunter	J.L. Thompson
Yard No	633	1539	579
Length	424.6 ft	425.0 ft	430.0 ft
Breadth	58.0 ft	58.0 ft	58.2 ft
Depth	38.11 ft	38.3 ft	38.5 ft
Bale Space	541,300 cu.ft.	529,000 cu.ft.	549,950 cu.ft.
Cost	£142,390	£143,500	£144,140
Delivery	August 1937	September 1937	October 1937

After much discussion the Managing Directors were authorised to arrange for larger engines to give an increased of speed of ^{3}/$_4$ of a knot if this could be done at reasonable cost. The question of fitting these ships with refrigeration was deferred, and it was suggested that, should this be advisable, tenders should be obtained from Messrs L. Sterne & Company as well as from Messrs J and E Hall Ltd.

At the following meeting in November 1936 the Board approved of the Managing Directors having given orders for three ships for the M.A.N.Z. Line service of increased size to take Doxford type engines 670 mm x 2320 mm giving a speed of 13^1/$_2$ knots.

Builder	Wm. Doxford	Swan Hunter	J.L. Thompson
Yard No	633	1539	579
Length	432.0 ft	433.0 ft	435.0 ft
Breadth	59.0 ft	59.0 ft	58.10 ft
Depth	29.8 ft	29.8 ft	29.8 ft
Bale Space	558,780 cu.ft.	556,300 cu.ft.	559,430 cu.ft.
Deadweight	9,800 tons	9,800 tons	9,800 tons
Cost	£157,457	£159,078	£159,493

Finally at the December 1936 meeting it was reported that the contracts for the building the three vessels for the M.A.N.Z. Line services was sealed on 1st December, and that in comparison with what was reported at the October meeting, the Joseph L. Thompson ship was to be greater by 2 ins in beam, namely 59.0 ft, and less in depth by 2 ins, namely 29.6 ft, and the final contract prices differ as follows: -

	Original Price	Contract Price
William Doxford & Sons Ltd	£157,457	£156,925
Swan, Hunter & Wigham Richardson Ltd	£159,078	£159,168
Joseph L. Thompson & Sons Ltd	£159,493	£159,518

Making the final cost of the 3 M.A.N.Z. Line ships as follows.

Final Cost	Port Montreal	Port Halifax	Port Saint John
Yard No	633	1539	579
Builder	Wm. Doxford	Swan, Hunter	J.L. Thompson
Hull	£93,198	£87,674	£97,712
Machinery	£65,959	£74,959	£64,284
Sub Total	£159,157	£162,633	£161,996
Refrig + Insul	£9,053	£9,059	£9,921
Grand Total	£168,210	£171,692	£171,917
Delivered	October 1937	November 1937	January 1938

The PORT MONTREAL (1), PORT SAINT JOHN and the PORT HALIFAX were powered by 4-cylinder Doxford engines with steam auxiliaries and steam driven cargo winches and the proposed engine room personnel of 13 was made up of 6-Engineers, 3-Donkeyman Greasers, 3-Firemen, 1-Storekeeper.

The first of the new ships the PORT HALIFAX was launched on the 7th July 1937, after being named by Miss Nelly Corry, daughter of Robert Corry.

Her father said in reply to the toast "As the PORT HALIFAX was the first vessel to be launched in the United Kingdom for the M.A.N.Z. Line, he must take the opportunity of saying something about the origin of the comparatively new Imperial service. The new company was formed last year to take over the business which has been carried on for the last ten years by the Canadian National Steamships, a government owned Line. The existing vessels and the business were purchased by New Zealand Shipping Company, Ellerman Lines and the Port Line from the Canadian Government. The Head Office of the new Company is in Montreal. The three partners have accepted under contract with the Canadian Government the liability of carrying on the trade.

We hope the service will be improved by the provision of vessels of greater speed and of a more uniform type. The Line serves the port of Montreal during the St. Lawrence season, and Halifax during the winter.

PORT HALIFAX (J. Dobson collection)

Five new vessels, including the PORT HALIFAX, were now under construction; two for the New Zealand Shipping Company, and three for Port Line. These vessels were practically identical, being 9,800 deadweight, cargo capacity 550,000 cubic feet, with Doxford engines of 4,250 horse-power, and capable of a speed of 13^1/$_2$ knots.

With the approval of the Canadian Government it has been recently agreed with the Canadian Pacific Railway that St. John, New Brunswick, should also be a port of call during the winter season. The homeward service is from New Zealand and Australia to New York, Boston and Canadian ports.

The new ships had been designed especially for the trade in which they will be engaged. For instance, they will have deep 'tween decks suitable for the carriage of newsprint and automobiles, which constitute the bulk of the outward cargo from Canada. The new vessels are fitted with Refrigerating Machinery supplied by Messrs. J. & E. Hall, being to a small extent insulated for the carriage of insulated cargo. No 4 lower ' tween deck space is insulated for the carriage of refrigerated cargo, the capacity being 18,789 cu.ft. grain or 17,891 cu.ft. bales. If necessary the insulated space can be increased. Ellerman's are not building new ships for this service as they can supply suitable tonnage from their existing fleet. The trade is rather one sided at present as the volume of cargo leaving Canada largely exceeds that from the sister Dominions."

Appointment Letter To Captains Of The New M.A.N.Z. Vessels

Letter to Captain E. J. Syvret: M.A.N.Z.

Dear Sir,

We confirm our conversation on the 27th ultimo when we appointed you to the command of our PORT MONTREAL in the M.A.N.Z. service, to take effect from the 6th September.
Your commencing salary will be £550 per annum, rising by annual amounts of £25.
In addition, you will receive a special allowance of £50 per annum on account of the extra living expenses which no doubt you will incur by trading abroad.
It is our present intention that Masters appointed to M.A.N.Z. ships must be prepared to serve continuously for two years.
If there is then a vacancy for a Master in our U.K. fleet they would receive special consideration in the appointment.
If you join the U.K. Service after two years, your commencing salary would be the minimum in that service (at present this is £600 per annum) but if this appointment to U.K. vessels is longer delayed, then your salary would be based on our U.K. scale.
The effect of this is that the first two years in M.AN.Z. vessels brings you level with a junior Captain of our U.K. vessels, so that if you were appointed Master of a U.K. vessel at the end of three years with M.A.N.Z. your commencing salary would be £625 per annum.
It is possible that we may on occasions load your vessel from Australia or New Zealand to U.K. either via Canada or direct or in the reverse direction, but this will not alter your scale of salary.
We also agreed that if Mrs Syvret and your daughter visit Canada during next year, we will provide them with a free return passage, provided they travel at the off-season for passengers.

Yours faithfully,

for Commonwealth & Dominion Line Ltd.
(Port Line)

Similar letters were also sent to Captain Cooper PORT HALIFAX and Captain Lynd PORT SAINT JOHN.

PORT MONTREAL (1) launched by Miss Eyelyn Corry daughter of Mr R. Corry on 10th August 1937 was delivered in November 1937 and became the twelfth motor ship to enter service with the Port Line (Commonwealth and Dominion Line) and the first with single screw machinery. She was the first of three oil-engined cargo vessels for her owners' Canada-New Zealand service. All were fitted with Doxford-type opposed-piston engines, and, in the case of the PORT MONTREAL (1), both the ship and her machinery were constructed by Messrs. Wm. Doxford & Sons at Pallion, Sunderland. PORT MONTREAL (1) was of the open shelter deck type, with a raked stem, a conical stern and a Tutin balanced reaction rudder. There were five hatchways and 12 steam cargo winches, also a steam warping winch aft. Steam auxiliary machinery was fitted, with minor exceptions throughout the ship. No oil firing, however, was needed at sea, as a generator, the steering gear and the refrigerating machinery were run by steam raised through the medium of the exhaust from the main engine, which was a two-stroke opposed-piston unit of the standard Doxford airless-injection design.

PORT MONTREAL (1) completed her maiden voyage, a non-stop crossing to Montreal, at 12.32 knots using 12.22 tons of oil per day.

PORT SAINT JOHN originally to have been christened the PORT QUEBEC was launched on the 9th August 1937 by Mrs R. H. Senior, wife of the assistant manager in London, who was presented with a silver salver as a memento of the occasion. Her name was shown in full on the ship to avoid confusion with St. John's, Newfoundland.

> "Shipbuilding", said Mr R. Norman Thompson, chairman of Messrs J. L. Thompson & Sons builders of the PORT SAINT JOHN, after the vessel had been launched, "was not easy. There was so much to contend with these days in particularly the great shortage of raw materials that causes delays in deliveries of steel and other finished products. As an example it had been a great disappointment that they have not been able to erect the deckhouses before launching. This was solely due to the fact that they were unable to get delivery of the steel. Steel makers did not seem to realise the progress made in the rate of production of ships".

In the four years 1904-07 the yard at full capacity absorbed 80,000 tons of steel, an average of 20,000 tons per annum. Today with a modern yard and up to date plant and equipment a very much greater quantity can be utilised but the yard cannot even get the 20,000 tons per annum they got 30 years ago. This means that they will launch this year two ships fewer than could been have launched had the steel been available. There is consequentially a loss of employment and disappointment to shipowners.

Every effort has been made to make up for lost time. The first frame on the PORT SAINT JOHN was erected on May 11 so that the launch today is only 11 weeks from that time. This achievement has only been obtained by the wonderful co-operation of our work-people and this effort will, we believe, enable us to deliver the vessel according to contract.

PORT SAINT JOHN sailed from Middlesborough for Louisberg, St. John and Halifax to load a steel cargo for Auckland, Wellington, Dunedin and New Plymouth. She was scheduled to leave Halifax on 25th January 1938 for Australia.

Unfortunately on the 17th January 1938 PORT SAINT JOHN grounded on Petries Ledges at the mouth of Sydney Harbour, Nova Scotia and refloated after eight hours aground. The extensive bottom damage was repaired in drydock at Halifax, Nova Scotia at a cost of £20.000 and resulted in a delay of approximately a month. She left Halifax on 2nd March 1938 and returned the following day owing to a defective thrust block. After relining, trials took place on 10th March 1938. Later in the same voyage on 4th May 1938 she grounded at 9.30 pm on East reef Lady Elliot Island, Queensland, whilst on a voyage from Wellington to Rockhampton in ballast. Two tugs and salvage gear were sent and after an unsuccessful attempt to refloat, a further one was made on the spring tides. She refloated at 8.00pm on the evening of the 13th May and arrived at Sydney on 17th where temporary repairs were carried out to enable her to proceed to England for permanent repair. A court of enquiry blamed Captain Lynd (whose employment was terminated) and 3rd Officer Nickell for the stranding, the latter returned to England on another ship as 4th Officer. In July 1938 the PORT SAINT JOHN obtained a charter from Java to the Mediterranean and returned home. Her troubles were far from over and in April 1939 she was delayed in the Panama Canal with a broken crosshead. During May 1939 it was reported that directors felt that the continuation of trouble with the PORT SAINT JOHN was a distinct reflection on Richardson Westgarth's workmanship and material, and they were thankful that they were not building with them again. In June of the same year cracks appeared in the transverse beams of the main engine and yet again in December she underwent considerable repairs to her bottom plates.

At the Board Meeting in May 1938 the directors heard that both the PORT MONTREAL (1) and the PORT SAINT JOHN had suffered from thrust block trouble, which caused the metal pads in the michel thrust to burn out. This problem was at first thought to be caused by poor quality metal in the pads but it was later thought to be caused by using too light a grade of oil.

9th May 1938 the Directors in answer to a letter from D. H. Bates, Brocklebank.

> "Thank you for your letter of the 6th inst; we all very much appreciate your kind thought in writing to us. Our ships in the M.A.N.Z. Service have been most unfortunate, and we can only hope that their somewhat extended teething troubles will bring immunity in their later years".

During the autumn of 1938, two agreements were entered into in connection with the M.A.N.Z lines by the Port Line Ltd, the New Zealand Shipping Company Ltd, and Ellerman & Bucknall Steamship Company Ltd. The first laid out how the trade should be conducted, stipulating interalia that no shares, or rights or obligations under this agreement should be transferred without being first offered to the remaining original member of the company.

The second instituted a pool of tonnage owned by the three lines engaged in the M.A.N.Z. lines trade. At the same time a two year freight contract to take effect from 1st January 1939 was made between the Australian and New Zealand Lines and newsprint manufacturers of Northern Canada, the rates were 37/6 a ton to Australia and 45/- a ton to New Zealand.

At the same time October 1938 the construction of another new vessel for the M.A.N.Z. Line was approved and in December a tender was accepted from Messrs J. L. Thompson for the construction of a single screw motor vessel at a cost of £205,250.

PORT QUEBEC (World Ship Society Photograph Library)

The new vessel to be called the PORT QUEBEC would be fitted with a 5-cylinder Doxford engine with all electric auxiliaries and electric cargo winches. The proposed engine room personnel of 13 was made up of 6-Engineers, 2-Electricians, 4-Donkeyman Greasers, 1-Storekeeper.

PORT QUEBEC was launched 17th August 1939 by Mrs Warwick Gregory and it was scheduled that she would enter service in early 1940. Unfortunately World War Two disrupted the operations of the M.A.N.Z. Line and it was not until November 1945 that the PORT SAINT JOHN reopened the trade once more.

In 1947 the M.A.N.Z. Line acquired its one and only ship, this was the OTTAWA VALLEY, a standard, war-built "Fort" type steamer of 7,164 tons. The M.A.N.Z. service was maintained by ships from the fleets of the three partners, the Port Line contributing in later years the PORT MONTREAL (2), PORT ALFRED and the PORT ST. LAWRENCE among others.

APPENDIX No. 3 - Port Line Masters in September 1939

PORT LINE LTD

LIST OF MASTERS AS AT 16th SEPTEMBER 1939

BAILEY F W	SS PORT BOWEN
BRADLEY D G H (known as Brad)	MV PORT MONTREAL
BRADLEY J B (known as Bradley)	SS PORT SYDNEY
BROWN A H	MV PORT DUNEDIN
COOPER A A	MV PORT HALIFAX
COTTELL S C	MV PORT TOWNSVILLE
DURHAM R S	MV PORT FREMANTLE
ENRIGHT W J	MV PORT WYNDHAM
GILLING W	MV PORT JACKSON
HALL G S	MV PORT HOBART
HARRIS G T C	SS PORT MELBOURNE
HAZELWOOD G L (known as Hazel)	SS PORT ADELAIDE
HAZLEWOOD H W (known as Wood)	MV PORT SAINT JOHN
HEARN G W	MV PORT HUON
HIGGS W G	MV PORT CHALMERS
HUDSON J J	SS PORT DENISON
JACK J	MV PORT ALMA
JEFFERY H C	SS PORT NICHOLSON
KIPPINS T	MV PORT GISBORNE
LEWIS J G	SS PORT HARDY
RIGDEN T H	MV PORT FAIRY
ROBINSON C A	SS PORT AUCKLAND
STEELE H	SS PORT BRISBANE
SWAN L H	SS PORT DARWIN
SYVRET E J	SS PORT CAROLINE
THOMAS E O	SS PORT WELLINGTON
THROWER C P	SS PORT CAMPBELL
WILLIAMS R	SS PORT HUNTER

Contemplated Changes.

Captain R. P. Fuller to MV PORT HALIFAX (ex Cooper)

Captain A. A. Cooper to MV PORT QUEBEC (Building)

11.1941: Captain Cooper sailed for Canada on board MV NOTTINGHAM to take up new position within M.O.W.T. at Montreal.

7.11.1941 Ship torpedoed by U 74 all lost.

APPENDIX No. 4 - HMS PORT NAPIER

In 1939 it was decided to repeat the 1917 mine barrage between Scotland and Norway. For this task five cargo liners SOUTHERN PRINCE, PORT NAPIER, PORT QUEBEC, AGAMEMNON and the MENESTHEUS were taken up for conversion. Their total capacity was 2,600 mines. It was planned to lay 60,000 mines and a special base was set up in the Kyle of Lochalsh on the west coast of Scotland, which was beyond the range of German aircraft. After Germany invaded Norway in 1940 the plan, by then half complete, was abandoned and instead a barrage was planned beneath the Orkneys and Iceland. Later the area was increased to include the Denmark Strait, (the channel between Iceland and Greenland). The mines had to be laid in often appalling seas, in water as much as 3,000 feet in depth and had to float no more than 10 feet under the surface. Although the cruiser HMS ADVENTURE joined the converted merchantmen and boosted their defences, there were not enough cruisers or destroyers to give the minelayers adequate escort, so the operation was scaled down. In addition HMS PORT NAPIER was lost by fire at her base. The mines were laid in the most likely routes for U-boats. Those laid in the Denmark Strait almost certainly hampered the German battleship BISMARK when she broke out into the Atlantic in 1941. In all, before the barrage was abandoned in 1943 the 1st Minelaying Squadron, excluding the ADVENTURE, laid 110,000 mines of which HMS PORT QUEBEC alone laid 33,000.

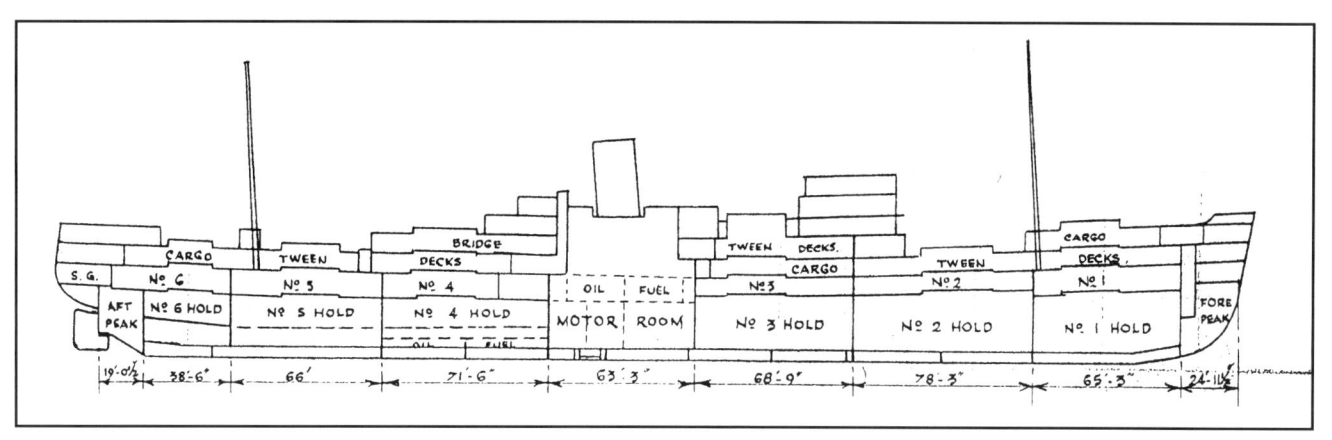

MV PORT NAPIER - original general arrangement.

PORT NAPIER

Letter from J.R.R. dated 29.1.1940

We received on the night of the 27th January 1940 notice AT/RB 2970 that the above vessel has been requisitioned in the Builder's Yard for naval service under T.98 Charter.
We wish to enter a most emphatic protest against the requisitioning of this ship, following so soon after the requisitioning of MV PORT QUEBEC and we should be much obliged if you would arrange for us to have an interview with the appropriate Naval Authorities concerned at the earliest possible moment. We hope that it will be possible for your department and the Ministry of Food to be represented at this meeting.

In the meantime, we desire to make the following points and are sending this letter in duplicate so that you may pass a copy of it to the Admiralty.

1. The PORT NAPIER is a large refrigerated vessel which, in the normal way takes 18 months and probably 2 years to construct and is costing close on half a million pounds.

2. She has been specially designed for the carriage of very large quantities of refrigerated produce from Australia and New Zealand. If her insulated compartments were entirely filled with frozen

sheep she would carry about 200,000 carcasses, or the equivalent in other frozen meat, butter, cheese etc.

3. The vast quantities of timber and cork used for the insulation are already being worked into the ship, and the refrigerating machinery is nearing completion. All this would be rendered useless unless the ship is completed for the purpose for which she was designed.

4. We have every desire to assist the Naval Authorities and indeed, in the case of the PORT QUEBEC we went so far as to suggest they should requisition this vessel in the Builder's Yard as we thought she was more suitable than the PORT SAINT JOHN which they had in mind and which was, at that time, out in Australasia.

5. From the national aspect we cannot believe that the removal of a new refrigerated ship is desirable. There are very few of this type of vessel now under construction and while it is true this Company itself has not lost any ships on the New Zealand coast since the outbreak of war several large refrigerated ships have been lost by enemy action or marine casualty, notably the DORIC STAR, TAIROA, LOCHAVON etc. In addition, several have been severely damaged, such as the MV SUSSEX and put out of commission for some months.

6. From the point of view of the Ministry of Food the loss of the carrying capacity of the PORT NAPIER must be extremely serious. In addition, from the point of view of the Ministry of Supply, the loss of her 200,000 cubic feet of uninsulated space for the carriage of wool etc., is another factor which should be taken into consideration.

7. While we do not wish to press this point unduly, we cannot help commenting on the fact that this Company has, apparently, been singled out to lose its two newest ships which are the first it has built for three years or more. We understand that the alterations contemplated for converting MV PORT NAPIER for naval use are of such a nature as to render her practically useless for our service in the future.

We shall await to hear from you when it is possible for you to arrange the suggested interview with the Naval Authorities.

Chairman of Port Line to The Secretary to the Ministry of Shipping

Confidential Reply from Ministry of Shipping, Berkeley Square House, Berkeley Square, London W1 on 30th January 1940

With reference to the requisitioning of your motor vessel PORT NAPIER for Commissioned Naval Service, I have to inform you that she will be fitted out at the yard of Messrs Swan Hunter and Wigham Richardson at Wallsend-on-Tyne where she is now building.

The vessel has been requisitioned under the terms of the Charter Party T.98. In this connection it will be necessary to agree with the Naval Officer in Charge, Tyne the date on which the vessel was at the complete disposal of the Government.

The Naval Officer in Charge will also arrange with your representatives for a joint On-Survey.

You are requested to supply the vessel with at least 3 months deck and engine room stores. Any equipment not required for the vessel's Naval Service will be stored at Government risk and expense. You may also be required to provide bedding and mess gear for the whole crew (officers and ratings) including the Naval complement; should this be the case the numbers for which bedding and mess gear will be required will be furnished to you later.

It has not yet been decided what the complement of this vessel will be, but the Mercantile Marine Engineers will be asked to volunteer to serve in the ship. A further communication will, however, be made to you in due course as to whether any additional Mercantile Marine complement will be required. It would be convenient if four of the Senior engineers could be retained during the fitting out to care for and maintain the engines. These Engineers should be paid by you until such time as they can sign on Admiralty Agreement T.124, the cost involved being reclaimed from the Government.

In future all mails, including personal correspondence for the crew, should be addressed to the vessel c/o GPO London E.C.1.

From Director of Sea Transport.

Letter received at Port Line London in connection with requisition dated 29th January 1940 and marked Secret

In confirmation of the telegram sent to you on 27th January I am directed by the Minister of Shipping to inform you that the SS PORT NAPIER now building at Wallsend-on-Tyne being required for urgent Government service in the interests of the efficient prosecution of the War is hereby requisitioned.
The following are enclosed for your information and return, where necessary, to the addresses shown thereon.

T.673 Commissioned Mercantile Fleet Auxiliaries memorandum for the guidance of owners
T507 Particulars relating to delivery
T.611 Particulars to enable date of entry into pay to be settled
T.639 Note on claims and accounts
T.401 Claim Form

 payment on account will be made as soon as possible after receipt of a claim.

His Majesty's Government relies on the goodwill of yourselves, your staff and agents in carrying out these instructions and preparing the ship for King's service, especially as regards clearing cargo, fuelling, storing and manning.

PORT NAPIER J 4219 (o/n 7480)

No 1569 Ship Requisitioned by the Admiralty on Jan 27th 1940 and converted into Minelayer. Her original peacetime design was modified fairly extensively to meet the Admiralty's requirements for her use as a minelayer. The area where her holds were was completely decked over, the only exception being a loading hatch near the stern for her deadly cargo of 550 mines. She was fitted out with an array of defensive firepower although, it was hoped that this would not be needed as she was intended to operate under the cover of the main fleets. Two four inch guns were mounted singly side by side on her bow. Four 20 mm anti-aircraft guns were mounted amidships and in addition she was fitted with two single two-pounder anti-aircraft guns and two five inch anti-aircraft guns. Four minelaying doors were cut into her curved stern and narrow-gauge railways were laid in corridors linking these doors with her holds where her cargo of mines would be stored. The heavy mines were set on trolleys which could be moved around the vessel on these rails.
   The PORT NAPIER was launched by Mrs B. Arrowsmith on the 23rd April 1940.
   Launched with Rock Ballast (2001 tons) Steel Drums in Nos. 3,4,5 and 6 Holds (about 300 tons), and practically all side and deck armour on board. Launch weight 9824 tons; Draughts forward 16.0ft, Aft 16.1ft.

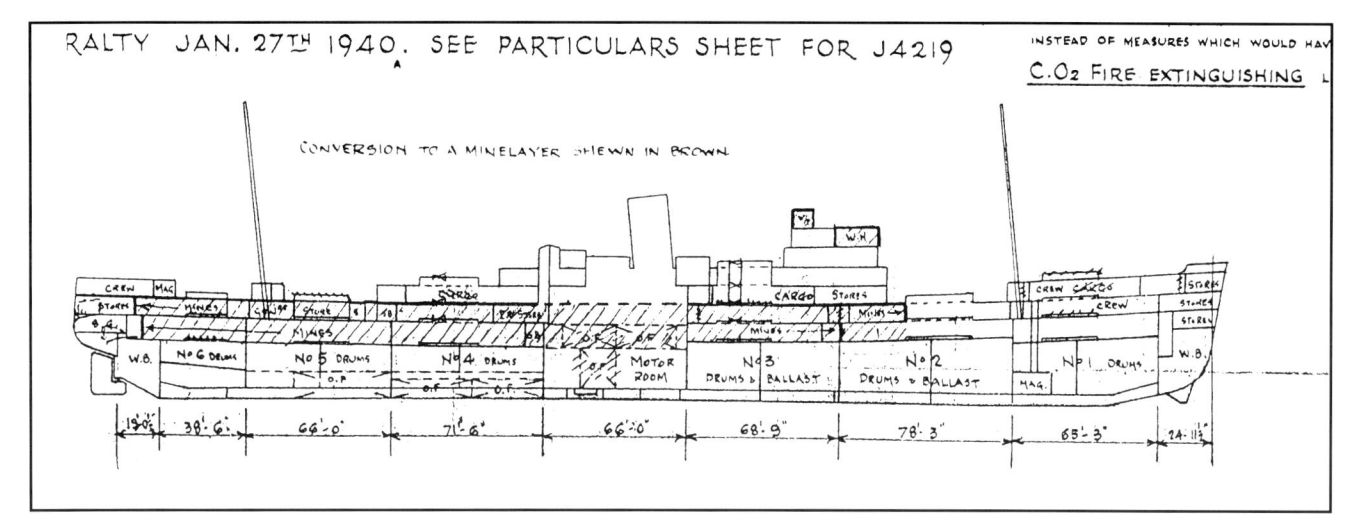

HMS PORT NAPIER - outline conversion arrangement.

SUBDIVISION: Additional Watertight Bulkheads were fitted at middle of holds 1-5 from Tank top to third deck (frames 35,59,108,136 and 163). All hatches on third deck were plated over and the deck made watertight. All holds were fitted with steel drums to give additional reserve buoyancy.

ROCK BALLAST: 2001 tons in Nos. 2 and 3 Holds to give basic light trim and immersion required as minelayer.

PROTECTION: Upper Deck, 2"N.C. Armour was bolted to the steel deck from stern to 132 frame. Nos. 3.4. and 5 Hatchways on the upper deck were removed, beams were fitted and armour laid. Beams were fitted at deck level in No 6 and armour fitted in the hatchway.

SHIP'S SIDE: $1^1/2$"D quality was bolted to shell from upper to 3rd deck level extending from 4 frame above 2nd deck and 6 frame below 2nd deck to 132 frame.

ENGINE CASINGS: 1"D quality was bolted to casings between upper and third decks.

BULKHEADS: $1^1/2$" D quality armour bulkhead fitted at 4 frame in upper tween decks and at 6 frame in lower tween decks. 1" D quality Armour bulkhead fitted at 132 frame in upper tween decks and at 121 frame in lower tween decks. Chart, wheelhouse and transmitting room sides and tops were fitted with 1" D quality, Wood hatch covers were covered with ?" steel plate as protection against incendiary bombs.

UPPER TWEEN DECKS: Two sets of rails each side carrying 78 mines. Rails extending from stern to 132 frame, Cross over rails with turntables fitted just abaft No 132 frame.

LOWER TWEEN DECKS: Two sets of rails converging into one track at the stern. each side, extending to 121 frame. 268 mines carried on 3rd deck. Cross over rails with turntables fitted at frames 55 and 104.

ARMAMENT: Two 4" h.a guns were fitted on the forecastle with a magazine built into after end of No. 1 hold. A $^1/2$" machine gun was fitted on the poop. There was a magazine for the machine gun and small arms on poop. A rangefinder was located on top of the transmitting room at the aft end of flying bridge. There were four paravanes in the forward well. Two 10 inch projectors were situated on flying bridge and a 24" searchlight was fitted on a platform at the base of fore mast. A clump was fitted to the stem for paravane towing. The ship was fitted with degaussing gear.

HMS PORT NAPIER - forward defensive armament (Author's collection)

MINELAYING GEAR: A total of 580 mines was carried.

Holes were cut in shell at stern and sponsons built out to carry tracks clear of ship. Mines dropped from all four tracks on 2nd deck and two tracks on third decks. 2 mining winches fitted aft on each of 2nd and 3rd decks for hauling mines. Mines shipped by ship's derricks and lowered through mine loading hatches cut in decks at 55 and 104 frames. Outer hatches 7'0" x 11'0" feed rails on 2nd deck. Conversion was completed on the 12th June 1940 and trials and delivery to the Admiralty took place on the 16th. She was placed under the control of the Portsmouth Command.

The 1st Minelaying Squadron was formed in June 1940 and HMS PORT NAPIER joined along with HMS ADVENTURE, HMS AGAMEMNON, HMS MENESTHEUS, HMS PORT QUEBEC and HMS SOUTHERN PRINCE (Flotilla Leader).

HMS PORT NAPIER arrived at Port Z.A. (Lochalsh) on 28th June 1940 and from there she carried out six minelaying operational lays in St. Georges Channel, these operations involved a total of 6,331 mines. During September 1940 she went to a shipyard on the Clyde for repairs and alterations. On the morning of Tuesday 26th November 1940 she was to have sailed on Operation SN.11 a minelaying operation in the Denmark Strait, but, during the previous night a gale sprang up and HMS PORT NAPIER dragged her anchor. By the time it was discovered and the engines started, she had drifted close to the collier BALMAHA (1,428g/1924) which she then collided with. Her port propeller became entangled with the collier's mooring cable, and caused her engines to stop. HMS PORT NAPIER was secured without further mishap until daylight and could not accompany the flotilla when it left for sea. Divers spent the rest of the morning freeing the propeller and she was then towed back to her anchorage. On Wednesday, 27th November the tanker RUDDERMAN secured port side to HMS PORT NAPIER to supply her with about 140 tons of diesel oil. Oiling commenced about 12.30 hrs and was completed by about 13. 25hrs. The flexible hoses were disconnected about 13.30 and RUDDERMAN was about to cast off when the Quartermaster of the Watch reported to the Captain, who was in his cabin on the bridge that there was a fire in the engineroom. The pipe " Fire in Engine Room" " Close all Engine Room Ventilation" was sounded. "Action Stations" was also sounded and most of the crew arrived on deck from below to find black smoke pouring from the funnel and ventilators and the order to abandon ship was soon given.

HMS PORT NAPIER - a group of Communications ratings
1-.?., 2 - STAN COLLETT, 3 -PETE RATTUE, 4 - E.D.WALTER.5.- ?.

(E D Walter)

A REPRODUCTION OF A SKETCH OF PORT NAPIER DRAWN BY CAPTAIN TAIT FOR HIS DAUGHTER

The ship was loaded with over 600 mines, so nobody was anxious to stay aboard. Small craft put out from the naval base ashore and secured alongside. Some crew members on the mining deck attempted to push the mines into the sea and several of these were floating around the stern of the ship. One man jumped into the sea and hung onto one of them, and one or two of the others dived in and swam to the nearest shore on the Isle of Skye, although the base was on the mainland at Lochalsh. Ropes and ladders were put down the sides of the ship and most of the crew (around 300) went down these to the boats alongside which ferried them ashore. At first early fears of a massive explosion caused shore units and civilian buildings ashore to be evacuated but, when it was found that undetonated mines burn rather than explode, the fears receded. There were several explosions which seemed to be in the engine room and fuel tanks and gradually the fire engulfed the ship, by which time all the crew had either been taken off, or swum ashore. One or two were injured, but none seriously.

As a result of the growing danger to the town the priority now became to get the burning vessel as far away as possible. HMS PORT NAPIER was cast loose from her moorings and taken in tow away from the town initially, of necessity, in the direction of the small village of Kyleakin of the other side of Lochalsh on Skye. Hurried plans were made for the inhabitants of Portree, Skye's main town 30 miles north to take in the evacuees from Kyleakin, although the evacuation was never put into effect. Whilst under tow the fires continued to intensify and eventually in Loch na Beiste, a small bay about a mile east of Kyleakin and well away from habitation, the burning vessel was let loose and cast adrift.

Shortly afterwards there was a loud explosion which resonated around the nearby hills of Skye and a flash that lit up the night sky momentarily. Part of the central superstructure was blown off the vessel several hundred feet into the air and all the way to the shores of Skye about a quarter of a mile away. The superstructure landed on the beach complete with one gun mounting and a bath. Some of the fragments even ended up halfway up the hill beyond, where they still sit among the trees. The fire could not be extinguished and was now allowed to run its full course. Many of the residents of Kyle noticed the fire and the general commotion down at the pier and congregated at the dock curious to see what was going on. As they pressed forward to watch the fire they had to be held back by police.

None of the mines were detonated although her midships were mangled by the explosion. HMS PORT NAPIER rapidly flooded with water and keeled over to her starboard side in about 20 metres of water with most of her entire cargo of newly loaded mines. Her beam was 68 feet which meant that her port side showed above the water at most states of the tide.

That night because of some German bombing over Ayrshire some 200 miles south a strict security blackout was imposed to keep the loss secret. As a result nothing appeared in any local or national newspapers. As with many other sea losses in both world wars rumours of sabotage were rife. The security blackout probably fuelled these rumours. In the absence of any official explanation people speculated wildly about what had happened and these rumours became more and more exaggerated as they passed around. What probably caused the fire was an alteration in the location of the fuelling pipe. Due to some Admiralty requirement it passed through the engine room in proximity to the oil-fired boiler. The engineer in charge of the oiling apparently failed to shut off when the double bottom tank was 95% full. The pressure caused the pipe to burst and a jet of oil shot across the engine room. A fire quickly followed and in about 20 minutes it was seen that it could not be got under control.

he crew left the base next day on a 24 hour train journey to Plymouth for re-assignment.

Only one officer managed to leave the ship with all his gear, H.B. Walker who transferred a few days before the fire.

It was not until January 1941 that the Port Line learnt officially about the loss of their newest ship in a letter received from The Ministry of Shipping.

> Letter dated 4.1.1941 from (O.J.), Berkeley Square House, Berkeley Square, London, W.1. to Port Line Ltd., Oak Lawn, Leatherhead.
>
> I am directed by the Minister of Shipping to convey to you his regret at the loss of HMS PORT NAPIER. He is however, pleased to state that there were no casualties.
>
> Under the terms of the requisitioning the vessel will be greated (treated) as a total loss and you are requested to make your claim for compensation accordingly to the Accountant General, Ministry of Shipping, Grand Hotel, Blackpool.
>
> The Admiralty are particularly desirous that no account of her loss should be made known and I am directed to ask that this letter be treated confidentially.

Shortly after the sinking two of the stewards called at "Oak Lawn" the wartime headquarters of the Port Line and from them the management learnt some details of the disaster. They also learnt that HMS PORT NAPIER was a very happy and well-run ship. Both stewards who had not received any pay or the return of their discharge books thought that the Chief Engineer had aged a lot since the sinking, but they did not know the cause of the disaster.

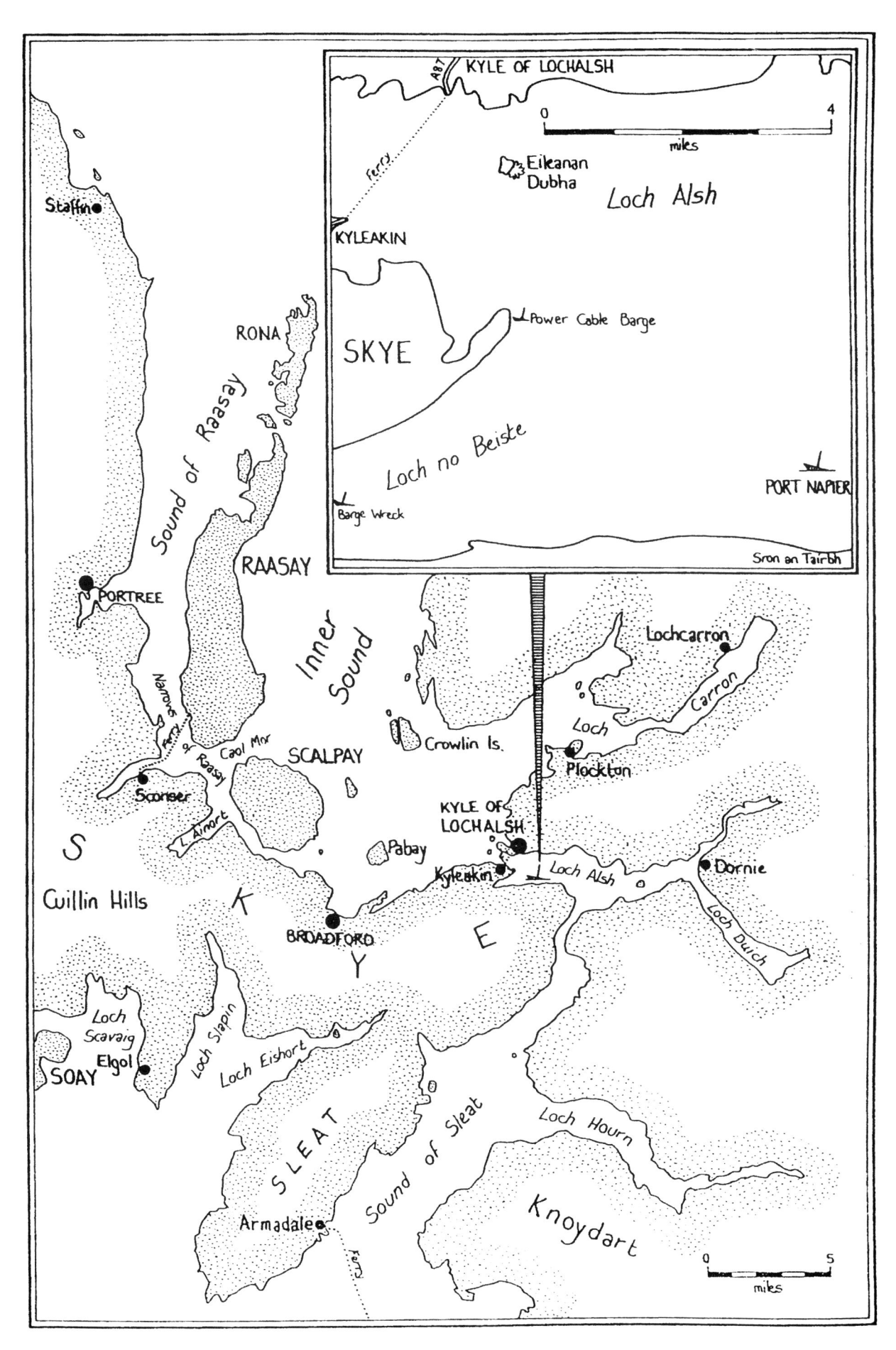

PORT NAPIER - final resting place.

The remains of the ill-fated **HMS PORT NAPIER.** (Author's collection)

HMS PORT NAPIER and her dangerous cargo lay in her watery grave for the remainder of the war. In 1950 the Royal Navy decided to remove the mines to make the wreck safe. After studying the way she was lying they decided on a salvage strategy that would unintentionally elevate her to the status of one of Scotland's greatest wrecks. In 1955/56 a salvage team from the civilian manned HMS BARGLOW under the command of Captain W.R.Fell. C.B.E, D.S.C, R.N. (Retd) removed the entire uppermost port side plating of her hull exposing the inner ribs, bulkheads and double bottoms. By doing this they were able to have Royal Navy clearance divers rig up a lift system and lift the mines vertically up to the surface between each of the decks. 526 mines were removed, 16 were detonated in situ for safety reasons. 4,000 rounds of ammunition were also recovered.

A mine being removed from the wreck, with "Amatol" pouring from the base. (Author's collection)

As the Admiralty were never sure of the exact number of mines originally on her and have never been convinced that they were able to remove all of them they have refused to sell the wreck ever since. The propellers have at some stage been removed by unauthorised salvors and applications have been made to remove prop shafts, wire cable and other deck fittings.

In August 1993 two crates of Whitbread beer were recovered from the wreck of HMS PORT NAPIER by an eight man team from the Hartlepool Diving Club. The beer looked a little cloudy, but it had a good head and a mature flavour. Whitbreads said, "the conditions were dark and cold and the rubber-sealed screw tops prevented any sea water getting inside. If the tops had been cork, contamination would have entered and ruined the beer. Instead it is amazingly drinkable. Beer is not meant to last a long time and normally goes off after about three years. Tests showed the pale ale had an alcohol content of 4.29 per cent, making it stronger than many beers sold today".

Today the wreck of HMS PORT NAPIER lies at latitude 57 15 58.0N and longitude 005 41 11.0W about 350 yards from the shores of Skye. Her uppermost port side shows above the waterline at most states of the tide except high water. She is of great interest to snorklers and divers.

It is still possible to view the remains of HMS PORT NAPIER by taking a trip on the SEAPROBE ATLANTIS, which departs from the pontoons located near the Lochalsh Hotel in Kyle between the months of April and September. This vessel is fitted with glass viewing panels which enable passengers to view both the wreck and the fascinating sea life which resides both in the sunken wreck and its vicinity.

APPENDIX No. 5 - PORT MACQUARIE

When the PORT MACQUARIE was fitted out in 1944, I doubt she commanded the attention normally accorded to a new vessel of the Port Line fleet in peacetime days. The name "Macquarie" is a highly evocative one in Australian lore, but the PORT MACQUARIE was certainly not built in the usual mould of ships bearing well-known colonial governors' names. It is doubtful if she enjoyed even a part of the attention and admiration given to the PORT JACKSON before the war or to the PORT AUCKLAND and PORT BRISBANE built during those euphoric post war years.

She was, in many respects considered as the "ugly duckling" of the fleet except to those who sailed in her and can attest to her merits as a vessel well-suited to her job of carrying cargo. She had few of the fitments that were considered standard in Port Line ships before the war. She was a single-screw motorship of definite utility design, as might be expected of a ship laid down in the bleakest days of WW2. It is likely that the most remembered feature of this ship for people who sailed in her is that she was built with each pair of Samson-posts set at oblique angles in an endeavour to confuse the calculations of U-boat commanders.

The ship sailed on her maiden voyage in February 1944. She left the Tyne where she had been fitting out and sailed in convoy through the Pentlands to Belfast Lough where she joined another convoy to the United States. Her Master on that first voyage was Capt. Hazelwood.

The vessel returned to the UK and afterwards left in convoy to Norfolk, Virginia where she loaded supplies for the American forces in the Pacific. From Norfolk she sailed through the Panama Canal and across the Pacific to the island of Guam that had at the time only just been liberated from the hands of the Japanese. It is thought that she may have been the first merchant ship to visit the island after the liberation - certainly she was a very early visitor. After the discharge of her supplies for the American forces she went to Australia and loaded there for New Guinea where the Australian forces were still involved. At the end of the war she was homeward bound in the Panama Canal.

In the post war period she settled down to the routine of transporting full loads of frozen produce from Australia and New Zealand to ease the stringencies of rationing in the UK and to take full loads of manufactured goods to the Antipodes in return as part of the export drive.

On Monday 26th January 1953, in misty conditions she ran high and dry aground on the shore at Crosby in the River Mersey, very near the present site of the Port Radar Station. In an article in the Liverpool Echo it states that "she ran aground at about 8a.m. on the foreshore at Seaforth near the foot of Cambridge Road with the bow only 20 yards from the edge of the foreshore...."

The entry in the Mersey Docks and Harbour Company Wreck Book relating to the incident states "At

Unexpected visitor- residents of the Cambridge Street area, Liverpool, inspect **PORT MACQUARIE.**
(Company archives)

08:35 hours the MV PORT MACQUARIE outward bound for Glasgow partly loaded with general cargo communicated with the Port Radar Station that she was in difficulty with her compass and requested Port Radar to check her position. At 08:35 hours she was given her position as outside the bouyline between C20 and C22. The vessel then stated she was altering course to port and one minute later stated that she appeared to be aground as she was not answering the helm. Tugs were immediately dispatched but as the time of grounding was at high water they were unable to refloat her. Arrangements were made to discharge her oil bunkers and water ballast and the PORT MACQUARIE was refloated with the assistance of tugs at 8:16 hours on the PM tide, and docked at Sandon Half Tide Dock at 08:45 hours next morning. There was no apparent damage to the vessel.

If an incident was then needed to restore her injured pride then it came just over four years later.

On 11th June 1957 while on a voyage from Panama to Wellington NZ, under the command of Capt. R. H. Webb and with just under 500 miles to go the radio officer received a call for assistance from a passenger ship the CAPTAIN HOBSON owned by the Ministry of Transport and managed by Henderson's of Glasgow. She was on parallel course and had broken down. It was mid-winter in that zone and sea conditions made it impossible for the ship's engineer officers to do any repairs. PORT MACQUARIE turned back 275 miles and went to her aid. The sea had moderated considerably by the time PORT MACQUARIE reached CAPTAIN HOBSON late in the afternoon of 12th June. A rocket line fired from the PORT MACQUARIE by the chief officer, Mr Ballinger straddled the forestay of the CAPTAIN HOBSON at the third attempt and then by a sequence of messenger ropes of gradually increasing size 5^1/$_2$ inch wires were passed from the poop of the PORT MACQUARIE to the forecastle of the CAPTAIN HOBSON. These were made fast to an anchor cable of the CAPTAIN HOBSON and then paid out over the fairlead so that PORT MACQUARIE had about 100 fathoms of 5^1/$_2$ inch wire out and CAPTAIN HOBSON paid out four shackles of cable. There was just enough time to complete the operation before darkness and the tow started at about 18:30 (local time).

On the next day in the early evening the two were joined by the minesweeper HMNZS STAWELL who escorted the two ships to Auckland.

PORT MACQUARIE approaching New Zealand with CAPTAIN HOBSON in tow.   (Company Archives)

For the period of the tow the weather conditions remained fair and the anchorage off Rangitoto Island was reached in five days and one hour. Here CAPTAIN HOBSON was handed over to the tugs and pilot from the Port of Auckland and after a night at anchor to carry out some maintenance PORT MACQUARIE resumed her passage to Wellington.

After this incident life aboard PORT MACQUARIE was the routine of a merchant ship. In 1968 she was sold to shipbreakers in Taiwan and arrived in Kaoshiung for this purpose on 13th September.

APPENDIX No. 6 - M.I.L.A.G.

During World War Two the Germans took surviving crews from Merchant Navy and Royal Navy ships sunk by U-Boat or in action to a prisoner of war camp in Germany, known as Marlag and Milag at Westertimke near Bremen. Nearly 5,000 seamen were interned there.

Unfortunately, many Port Line sea staff, Masters, Officers, Petty Officers and ratings were held in the camp and one, Mr H. Garner then a third officer from the PORT HOBART, played an important part in the organization and welfare work of the prisoners of war. His contribution to the cause of easing boredom and frustration will long be remembered and it was typical of his energy that the thought of holding an Annual Reunion of the ex-prisoners of war from these camps should come from him.

The idea was born one evening in November 1958 on board the PORT SYDNEY where Mr Garner, who was then a member of the Trinity House pilotage service and a "Choice" pilot for the Port Line company, was acting in his new sphere of work. His enthusiasm for a Reunion enlisted the help of his wife as soon as he got ashore and the story is best continued by quoting from a letter received from Captain H Steele retired but himself a prisoner of war in Marlag and Milag, who was present at the first Reunion Dinner held at the Connaught Rooms on 6th July 1959.

"Fifty of the most available P.O.Ws were approached and with their agreement the Connaught Rooms were booked. A thousand pamphlets were printed setting out the proposed procedure. The Marine Superintendents, Superintendent Engineers and Pensions Departments of Port Line rallied with addresses of all 'Port Liners' past, present and retired; also many letters were dispatched to shipping companies asking them to forward pamphlets to any P.O.W. in their employ or on pension. This they willingly did.

It was known that two men had given up the sea and qualified in medicine, and the local librarians assisted in searching the Medical Guide to find their addresses together with the Camp Hospital Staff. Names of others were indelibly printed on our minds but took some running to earth, and it took all the London Directories, followed by those of the Home Counties before some were located.

Fortune aided too - by chance Mr Garner met at Falmouth a P.O.W. (now a local boat owner) which resulted in a letter to the Falmouth Harbour Master who located a P.O.W. and in his turn contacted a large group in the Liverpool area. So well known was the orchestra leader (Neil Block)) that a letter addressed to him care of Postmaster, Minehead, found him.

A letter to the Commissioner of Police Hackney Carriage Department failed to contact a taxi driver but he appeared on the night having learned about the Reunion from another P.O.W., whom he had picked up as a fare. Mr Britten, Secretary, British Ship Adoption Society was of great assistance and it was nice to meet him and his wife at the reception.

Commodore Bailey's camp register in which he kept details of all P.O.Ws. in the camp, became an invaluable guide in classifying some of the replies as some correspondents did not identify themselves by rank, but everyone was listed in the register.

Other valuable contacts were Captain Ashworth, the PLA Health and Sanitary Inspector and an insurance company manager. It was amazing to find so many P.O.Ws, who were now Marine Engineers and Catering Superintendents and they in turn were in a position to pass along the news. The Nautical Magazine was kind enough to include a mention in their 'Gossip Column' and this produced two replies. One from Captain Austin who was an AB in the camp but attended the Camp Navigation School, and was awaiting a new ship in Rotterdam and the other from a carpenter who was now Captain Macfee. Captain Eaddy was located in India, he was then Marine Superintendent for Bank Line and was one of the first acceptors. J. Riddelsdall an apprentice on PORT HOBART was now in Holy Orders and sent his regrets from Kenya where he was a missionary.

Amongst those who served or were still serving Port Line but were prevented attending due to exigencies of the service but sent their regrets were Captains, Fairburn and Hodson, Mr L W Stannard, Mr W Condry in Melbourne, Mr Grover Hooker in Sydney, Mr R Broster in Wellington. Captain George Hall was unfortunately unable to attend.

The Port Line representatives at the Reunion were Mr T. Lockie (Chief Engineer) who came from Greenock, Mr H. (Fritz) Garner, Captain J. Porter, Messrs T. Bowen, J. Gruber, J. Holland, L. Armitage, G. Smith, J. Murray, J. Holman, A. Hendry and Captain H. Steele.

Padre Hall who looked after the religious side of the camp was also there in the same capacity. Those at the reunion were all pleased to see him looking so well.

Those attending numbered 185 P.O.Ws and 100 guests (wives, brothers and sisters of P.O.Ws) and also Mr L. Lockie a passenger in the PORT HOBART when sunk in 1940. Mr F. Vicorani an American who was coming to Europe from New York to join the Ambulance Corps and taken prisoner when the ZAM ZAM was sunk was also present.

The Reception and Dinner was held in the Banqueting Hall, at the Connaught Rooms. We sat at tables with no top table or previously arranged seating and from what was seen everyone thoroughly enjoyed themselves. It did you good to see the look of pleasure as the various guests met, both officers and ratings alike, after a lapse of 14 years. It is hoped that at the next Reunion we shall have the pleasure of seeing some absent ones who were missed this year. Enthusiasm was aroused when a telegram of good wishes was read from Her Majesty the Queen."

Since that time Reunions took place almost annually. The Reunion moved away from London for economic reasons and took place in Plymouth and Bristol. Eventually a more permanent venue at the Crest Hotel at Cardiff was found, with an ex-Port Liner, Jim Waggott, as organiser ably supported by Hubert Hall ex-Blue Star as Treasurer. 1995 saw the celebration of fifty years freedom since the release from Milag and it was decided to call a halt to further reunions in view of the increasing age of those attending. Three years later due to demand another reunion was held which proved to be the last.

Captain H. Steele, who was in command of the PORT BRISBANE at the time of her capture by the German raider PINGUIN in 1940 later becoming Commandant of the Milag P.O.W. camp, died in February 1972. He was the last of the Indra Line officers to serve in Port Line.

APPENDIX No. 7 - Refrigeration

An important trade of Port Line and its predecessors was the carriage of refrigerated cargo. Prior to the introduction of refrigerated machinery to ships, perishable cargoes were either salted or carried packed in natural ice. It was the invention and the subsequent application of practical refrigeration plant that made longer voyages possible for the carriage of easily spoilt goods such as meat, dairy products and fruit. Before the discovery and availability of the Freon refrigeration gases there were three primary refrigeration systems; cold air, ammonia and carbon dioxide. The first successful marine refrigeration plants were cold air machines as fitted to the steamship STRATHLEVEN which loaded its frozen meat cargo at Melbourne in November 1879 and discharged at London in February 1880. This first cargo from Australia had been preceded in 1877 by an experimental cargo of frozen meat from Buenos Aires to Rouen in the SS FRIGORIFIQUE. The ammonia refrigeration machinery had been installed by the Frenchman Charles Tellier, one of refrigeration's early pioneers. About the same time another Frenchman Eugene Nicolle was carrying out pioneering work in Australia and tried to have his equipment installed on the WHAMPOA. Watts, Milburn however, were apprehensive about the use of ammonia and the negotiations were terminated. If this experiment had gone ahead it would have preceded the STRATHLEVEN cargo.

The cold air system had been patented by James Gorrie of Florida in 1850 but it was the collaboration in Glasgow of the Bell Brothers; meat importers and Joseph Coleman that brought about the Bell-Coleman cold air machines suitability for shipboard installation in 1879. The cold air system was successful because of its simplicity; using readily obtainable and safe air. The plant had three stages, starting with the air being compressed in a cylinder to about 45 p.s.i. which caused the pressurised air to rise in temperature. This heat was taken away by cooling with sea water in the next stage and the pressurised air was then expanded in the final stage where there was a dramatic reduction in temperature (as low as minus 80°F). This cold air was delivered via wooden trunking into the cargo space to be cooled and then returned to the machine to be re-cooled, thereby maintaining the cargo at a temperature of about 15°F. The success of the STRATHLEVEN prompted shippers and meat producers in some cases, to supply the refrigeration plant to the ships they chartered. The barque DUNEDIN was chartered in 1882 for the first cargo of frozen meat from Port Chalmers, New Zealand to London. Milburn's FENSTANTON was the first ship of the future "Commonwealth and Dominion" company to be fitted with refrigerated plant and also the first steamer for the New Zealand Shipping Company when she was chartered in 1883 to carry frozen meat from Port Chalmers to London. In 1884 the Derby engineering company of Sir Alfred Haslam bought up the Bell-Coleman patents and produced a number of cold air machinery installations for fitting on board ships. Among the ships fitted were Milburn's "Port" ships and the Federal Steam Navigation Company ships that were ordered in 1896. Corry also favoured this type of refrigeration equipment, but both Royden and Tyser went for the next most popular system that of brine cooled by CO_2.

More efficient refrigeration plant was developed using mediums such as carbon dioxide (CO_2) and ammonia (NH_3). The operation of both carbon dioxide and ammonia refrigeration systems are similar, the main difference being the working pressure; carbon dioxide operates at about 1,000psi and ammonia at about 180psi. These plants consist of a compressor that compresses the gas to the working pressure, the gas then passing into the condenser where it is converted into a liquid. The condenser is circulated with sea-water to liquify the gas by cooling. The liquid is then reduced in pressure via a regulating valve, this reduction causin the liquid to vaporise (change to a gas) and in so doing it extracts the heat required from the brine. The gas then completes its circuit back to the compressor. Ammonia is a very obnoxious substance particularly in confined spaces. The first ammonia plants were installed in well-ventilated compartments on deck near the engine room.

Refrigerated transport by sea proved a success and the cold air machines were slowly replaced by the carbon dioxide and ammonia systems. The cooling medium in this newer system was at first brine (a liquid with a low freezing point) that was circulated through pipes fitted in grid pattern on the sides and overhead in the insulated cargo spaces. The brine transferred the heat from the cargo spaces and was kept cold by the refrigeration machinery. The use of air was not abandoned and some installations combined both air and brine for compartments where different temperatures were required.

The insulating material used in the early days was mainly charcoal but a lot of other materials were tried such as cowhair (felt), sawdust, silicon cotton (slag wool), and even pumice stone was used. These materials were superseded by cork in granulated and slab form. To both protect the cork from damage by normal general cargo and to hold it in position tongue and grooved wood boards were used. Modern developments brought new materials such as fibreglass and plastics in the form of slab and foamed polyurethane, the protection became galvanised steel or alloy aluminium sheeting, but more recent practice was to use plywood panels.

A description of how compartments were prepared for a cargo of frozen meat about the 1890's:- The hold is lined with an ordinary ceiling, this is covered with sheet zinc, then comes six inches of lump charcoal, then solid double battening of two inch thickness and above all inch battens about a foot apart, running transversely to allow an air passage under the cargo. Along the sides close up under the deck in the wings run wooden trunks with here and there holes about six by three inches. Through these the cold air from the refrigerating plant passes into the hold and by, fitting 'twartship battens under the cargo finds its way all over the compartment. These trunks are led into an arrangement known as a snow box, which is entered from the machinery spaces, every four hours during the voyage the engineer in charge checks the trunks making sure that the holes are clear of snow and clearing away as required. Before the meat is received the compartment is thoroughly washed out with soda water.

The success of the FENSTANTON charter prompted Milburns to equip the PORT VICTOR and the PORT PIRIE then building with refrigeration plant. These installations were followed in the early 1890's with the PORT CHALMERS, PORT DOUGLAS and the PORT MELBOURNE. The Australian Chilling and Freezing Company opened a new works at Aberdeen on the Hunter river in 1891, and in February 1892 the PORT DOUGLAS on her maiden voyage took the first shipment of 13,000 carcasses of frozen mutton to London. On her next voyage the PORT DOUGLAS was unfortunately lost off the coast of Africa. However, at this time Milburns also began an important collaboration, with the charter of the PORT PIRIE and the subsequent building of the fully refrigerated ships CORNWALL and her sisters all fitted with cold air machinery for the new Federal Steam Navigation Company. Milburns' opinion of refrigerated cargoes differed from that of their future partners who only built refrigerated cargo ships once they had made the decision, whereas Milburns took an alternative route with their subsequent share in Federal Steam Navigation Company.

In 1887 J. P. Corry made the transition from sail to steam when they took delivery of their first steamship the STAR OF VICTORIA that was also fitted with cold air refrigeration plant. All subsequent steamships built for Corry were refrigerated. Tyser however, entered the refrigerated trade in 1886 by chartering the steamships BALMORAL CASTLE and the ASHLEIGH BROOKE in which they had fitted refrigeration plant. HAWKES BAY, built 1891, was their transition from sail to steam and was fitted with carbon dioxide and brine refrigeration plant. Tyser were particularly associated with the New Zealand trade but were instrumental in combining three of the Commonwealth and Dominion companies before the 1914 amalgamation. Whereas Royden did not build a refrigerated ship until 1896 when they took delivery of the INDRAGHIRI. Although there is no firm evidence the first INDRA may have been fitted with refrigerated equipment when in Royden ownership.

A report in the shipping journal FAIRPLAY of 25th September 1902 attested to the reliability of the refrigeration machinery fitted and also the problems that could occur.

> "As a unique instance of what a good Refrigerating Machine will do, I understand that although one of the meat holds of the S.S. NIWARU on her recent voyage was flooded with sea water, the temperature in the hold was kept down to 19 degrees F. Unfortunately this did not entirely counteract the bad effect of the salt water, which rotted the carcases, and this portion of the cargo was lost. The log shows that same Refrigerating Machine (Hall's Patent CO2 system) maintained the other meat holds of the vessel at temperatures ranging from 5 to 7 degs.F. and as these were not affected by the leakage of salt water into the ship, all this meat was landed in good condition. The Colonial Consignment and Distributing Company, in their September report, referring to this, state that "the upper tiers were so little affected, though permeated with the stench of the carcases below, that North Sea fishing boats were seen to recover much that had been thrown overboard. The damage was entirely confined to one hold; contents of the other holds are being landed in the perfect condition for which this line of steamers is noted, bright and clean and hard as when shipped in New Zealand"'. The maintenance of so low a temperature in a hold under such adverse conditions is believed to be a record.
>
> "The NIWARU is the twelfth ship fitted by J. & E. Hall Ltd, with refrigerating machines for this Company, and another vessel the MARERE is now being fitted."

A record drought in Australia between 1899 - 1905 also interfered with freezing.

By the year 1910, three of the four companies which were soon to form the Commonwealth & Dominion Line were operating 18 vessels in the refrigerated meat trade as follows:

    Indra Line 3 ships   869,000 cu.ft average 289,666 cu.ft
    Star Line   7 ships 1,524,942 cu.ft average 217,848 cu.ft
    Tyser Line 8 ships 1,931,000 cu.ft average 241,375 cu.ft

Chilled beef is superior to frozen and therefore commands a better price at market. Chilled cargoes are carried at a temperature of 28-30°F. When Bell brothers investigated the carriage of meat, mainly from the United States, they were looking to reduce costs. The outcome was the Bell-Coleman cold air system. To demonstrate the practicality of their system they had built in a Glasgow shipyard a typical ships 'tween deck. This was fitted for refrigerated cargo and meat was kept at a chilled temperature of 30°F for ninety days and then sold through the Smithfield market. The Bell-Coleman system was, however, used for frozen cargoes.

The first experiment to bring chilled beef from Australia was carried out in 1894 by the embryo Federal Steam Navigation Company, in the chartered PORT PIRIE. Unfortunately problems arose and the cargo was frozen down during the voyage from Sydney to London.

1911 saw a small-scale experiment with chilled cargo when Tysers MURITAI brought seventy quarters of New Zealand beef to London, but the Nelson-Dicks-Tyser process proved too expensive to repeat. The carriage of chilled beef from the shorter Argentina to London route had commenced in 1901.

It was not until the discovery that a carbon dioxide enriched atmosphere in the cold chambers arrested deterioration of the cargo that the company had success in carrying chilled beef from New Zealand in the PORT FAIRY during 1933. The experimental features were incorporated in the PORT CHALMERS which was delivered in 1933. She was the company's first ship designed to carry chilled beef in gas tight compartments with an enriched carbon dioxide atmosphere.

The apple problems and an increase in fruit cargoes followed by the development of the chilled meat trade highlighted the disadvantages of the brine grid system. After some experiments in the PORT WYNDHAM a decision was made to change over from the brine grid cooling and fit a forced air cooling system. The PORT JACKSON of 1937 was the first ship ever to be completely fitted with this system. It represented the greatest forward step in the carriage of refrigerated cargo since the commencement of the trade. This pioneer development was entirely due to the willingness of the directors to back the enthusiasm of their Superintendent Engineer, Mr H. G. Dearden, working in co-operation with J. D. Farmer of Messrs. J. & E. Hall Ltd., and Dr A. J. M. Smith. (At the time of his death he was Director of the Shipowners Refrigerated Cargo Research Council).

Then came the carriage of cheese at about 45°F. It was kept at this temperature so that immature cheese could be loaded and ripened slowly during the voyage, and this proved quite successful.

Since the 1940's Freon gases have been used in place of the earlier types of refrigerants, and with the introduction of motor ships these machines changed from being steam-driven to electric-driven. Carbon dioxide has in turn given place to a gas known as "Freon". The characteristics of which have so modified the designs of the machinery that it can run automatically. Other developments fitted in PORT NICHOLSON, built in 1962, now permitted the air temperature in the refrigerated cargo spaces to be automatically controlled. The next development was for the temperature in the controlled spaces to be automatically recorded.

APPENDIX No. 8 - PORT VICTOR Correspondence

The following series of letters give an indication of some of the problems encountered in getting a ship to sea in wartime conditions

Letter to the Directors of the Port Line
9th October 1941

1659 - PORT VICTOR

I have been advised by Mr Bocler of Messrs Swan, Hunter & Wigham Richardson that Mr Bryant, Principal Ship Overseer at Wallsend has been given stability particulars of the above vessel in response to a request from Bath.

No hint has been given for the reason for this request. Messrs. Swan, Hunter have promised to advise us immediately if they get a hint of any kind.

B. P. Arrowsmith
Supt Engineer

Letter from Gregson & Company.Ltd.
Shipwrights, Shipjoiners and Insulation Contractors.
Cunard House, Leadenhall Street.London E.C.3
5th August 1942.

1659 - PORT VICTOR

With reference to the question of joiners on the above vessel, we have been through our records and below we give the number of men employed on the various dates : -

June 3rd	-199
July 8th	-274
July 15th	-267
July 22nd	-305
July 29th	-338

Great difficulties are being experienced in obtaining enough labour to complete the job on time.

Letter to the Directors of Port Line.
11th September 1942.
1659 - PORT VICTOR

Present indications are that all work on the vessel will be completed on 9th October.

Cooling down trials will then be held on refrigerated spaces, and if these are satisfactory, vessel will be handed over to the owners on 12th October.

It is suggested that the vessel proceeds from Messrs. Swan, Hunter's to the loading berth and if necessary takes oil bunkers passing down the River Tyne outward bound. (In the case of the "PORT PHILLIP" this vessel proceeded from Messrs. Swan, Hunter's to the oiling berth and was delayed there two to three days owing to high winds).

If the "PORT VICTOR" proceeds to the loading berth from Swan, Hunter's, less risk and less cost will be involved.

B. P. Arrowsmith
Supt Engineer.

Letter to The Management.
Port Line
"Oaklawn"
Leatherhead
Surrey
29th September 1942

m.v. "PORT VICTOR" - Monday, 12th October 1942

Would you kindly give us some guidance with reference to the procedure when the ship is turned over to the Company with regard to the Luncheon to be provided together with refreshments, and if it is to be done by the Builders or the Company. You will doubtless let us know whether it is to be a sit down or a buffet table.

While this vessel is loading at Newcastle I suggest that only Officers, Engineers and Catering Staff are provided with food, and the rest of the ships' personnel commence feeding when the ship signs articles, and until that time they should live ashore, thus taking the same procedure as adopted for the "PORT PHILLIP" as you realise that the ship is starting at zero with no surplus stores and very limited supplies for the voyage out.

If this is agreed upon would you kindly advise the Marine and Engine Room Department in order to avoid any friction.

T. W. Lane

Catering Superintendent

Letter to

Messrs. Shaw, Savill & Albion Company Ltd.,
88, Leadenhall Street,
London, E.C.3

6th October 1942

Dear Sirs,

m.v. PORT VICTOR

We beg to confirm the arrangement made, by which you will load the above vessel from Newcastle on Tyne to New Zealand ports, presumably Auckland, Wellington, Lyttelton and Dunedin, which please confirm.

The following are the arrangements for her loading:-

1. Messrs. Furness, Withy & Company who are your agents at Newcastle on Tyne will attend to all loading arrangements and the outward Customs work of the vessel.

2. Messrs. Wm. Milburn & Company Ltd., our agents at Newcastle on Tyne, will look after all shipowning matters and passengers.

3. The vessel will be consigned to our agents at Curacao, Panama Canal and New Zealand ports.

4. With regard to accountancy, you will render an account to us in London, crediting the freight and debiting all disbursements incurred. Port Line will settle the account with Ministry of Shipping.

5. All cargo documents, mail manifest, etc.will be dispatched by your goodselves or your Agents to our Agents in New Zealand.

6. You will furnish us with the necessary cargo particulars to cable to our Wellington Office.

Will you kindly confirm the above.

Yours faithfully,
PORT LINE LTD

Memo from J. R. R. to Superintendent Engineer and Marine Superintendent. 30.9.1942.

PORT VICTOR
Monday 12th October 1942

Buffet in Smoking Room: Drinks, Hors d'oeuvres, etc. to be ready about 11.45 a.m.

Ordinary lunch to follow in saloon for Mr. Swan, Directors, and maybe one or two naval officers, about 1 p.m.

Only officers, engineers and catering staff to be provided with food until 8 a.m. Monday, 12th October, when all crew are ordered to be on board. Thereafter full meals to be provided, as usual, for full crew.

PORT VICTOR on 6th November 1942 (Ambrose Greenway collection)

APPENDIX No. 9 - Port Line At War

Port Line suffered grievous losses in the Second World War. In 1939 the fleet comprised thirty ships including two nearing completion and of these, twelve or nearly half, were lost through enemy action. Of nine ships managed for the Government, one was lost through explosion.

DATE	SHIP	MASTER	CAUSE
26.09.1940	PORT DENISON	Captain J.B. Bradley	Bombed.
11.10.1940	PORT GISBORNE	Captain T. Kippins	Torpedoed
21.11.1940	PORT BRISBANE	Captain H. Steele	Surface Raider
24.11.1940	PORT HOBART	Captain G.S. Hall	Admiral Scheer
27.11.1940	PORT NAPIER (HMS)	Captain Tait R.N.	Explosion
30.11.1940	PORT WELLINGTON	Captain E. Thomas	Surface Raider
03.03.1941	PORT TOWNSVILLE	Captain T. Kippins	Bombed
28.04.1941	PORT HARDY	Captain J. G. Lewis	Torpedoed
10.06.1942	PORT MONTREAL	Captain J. G. Lewis	Torpedoed
16.06.1942	PORT NICHOLSON	Captain H. C. Jeffery	Torpedoed
11.07.1942	PORT HUNTER	Captain J. B. Bradley	Torpedoed
17.03.1943	PORT AUCKLAND	Captain A.E. Fishwick	Torpedoed
30.04.1943	PORT VICTOR	Captain W. G.Higgs	Torpedoed
14.04.1944	FORT STIKINE	Captain H. J. Naismith	Explosion

MV PORT GISBORNE

The PORT GISBORNE was torpedoed in the Atlantic at 9.15p.m. on the night of 11th October 1940. At the time a strong southerly gale was blowing with high confused seas and poor visibility. The third and missing boat (actually No. 4 of the ship's boats) was on the lee side and did not experience the same difficulty in getting away from the ship as the boats on the weather side. After she had been launched the 2nd and 3rd Officers went into her by going down lifelines. The Captain's reported that No. 4 boat was close to his and flashing signals from time to time. Shortly after, he heard shouting from No. 4 boat and by the aid of a light from a torch he saw two men in the sea. They endeavoured, under very great difficulties to get alongside the men and after a while succeeded. One of them Quartermaster King was pulled on board. The other (the Chief Engineer) could not be rescued. No others unfortunately were seen. There seems little doubt that No. 4 boat was capsized by the tremendous seas and her crew thrown into the water.

The other lifeboat was in charge of S. H. Light, AB who had gone to sea at the age of 13 years and remained at sea until he was 20 years of age. He was at one time an ordinary seaman in the SS PORT HACKING. After leaving the vessel he started coal carting in Great Yarmouth with one cart. This was the basis of his start in life and after a while he had six carts. He then sold this business and started a road transport organization which also did well. AB Light signed on the MV PORT GISBORNE to 'do his bit' during the war. In recognition of his navigating the lifeboat for 11 days, the directors of Port Line presented him with a sextant to replace his which had been lost in the sinking. 11 days after the sinking the survivors were rescued, together with survivors of the Canadian ship ST. MALO by the SALVONIA. Light was a remarkable man, the owner of 25 ton yawl, the licensee of the Southborough Hotel, Kingston By Pass, Surbiton, holder of a pilots license and owner of a couple race horses. Light was awarded both the George Medal and Lloyds War Medal for his War endeavours.

PORT NICHOLSON

PORT NICHOLSON under the command of Captain H. C. Jeffery, left Halifax for New York on 14th June 1942 as part of convoy XB 25. At about 11.18p.m. on 16th June a terrific explosion was felt on starboard side near the engine room. About 20 seconds later another explosion occurred further aft. Captain Jeffery was rendered temporarily unconscious, but arrived on the bridge two minutes later. In the meantime third officer Stansbury fired the two white rockets indicating to the escort that the ship had been torpedoed. Snowflakes were also fired, communications with flooding engine room were broken, the lights failed, and alarm systems were rendered inoperative. The radio-telephone on the bridge was useless and the radio instruments wrecked. "Abandon Ship" was ordered. All hands except 7th engineer McGreavy and Greaser John who were on duty in engine room at the time of the torpedoing arrived at boat stations. No. 3 boat was smashed, but the others were lowered safely and the ship was abandoned for the night. All hands were picked up by the Canadian corvette HMCS NANAIMO (K 101) after about an hour. 4th Engineer Dibley was only stretcher case, but there were several others with minor injuries. (Dibley was trapped in stokehold and badly injured but was rescued by Fireman Blundell at great risk when the ship was obviously sinking). The corvette stood by all night and at about 7.a.m. when Captain Jeffery, Chief Officer Munday and the 1st Lieutenant and five ratings of HMCS NANAIMO, boarded PORT NICHOLSON to investigate, there was little apparent change in the condition of vessel. A wireless message was sent asking for tugs to attempt salvage. About 7.45a.m; the vessel's stern was settling rapidly and the eight men on board were seen to make for and man the cutter which, however, was unable to get clear and was dragged under by the sinking ship. Only 20 to 30 seconds elapsed from the time the stern began settling and the bow, which rose to an almost vertical position, disappeared.

Afterwards 4 men were picked up from the water but as no more survivors were found after a thorough search, the corvette proceeded to Boston. Thus Captain Jeffery and Chief Officer Munday, together with two men from the corvette must have gone down with the vessel, bringing the total of PORT NICHOLSON casualties up to four. Fireman Blundell was awarded the B.E.M and Lloyd's War medal for Bravery at Sea. Captain Jeffery and Chief Officer Munday were both "commended for courage and devotion to duty" (posthumously).

PORT CHALMERS

In London at the end of June 1965 a farewell luncheon was held on board the ship in King George V Dock, at which the principal guests were Admiral Sir Harold Burrough, G.C.B., K.B.E., D.S.O., who was in charge of the close escort for the Malta convoys in 1942, and the High Commissioner for Malta, the Hon. J. F. Axisa, M.B.E.

With Captain W. G. Higgs in command, the PORT CHALMERS was a member of the Malta convoy of July 1941, carrying a full cargo which included 2,000 tons of aviation spirit in four-gallon tins, as well as foodstuffs, ammunition, motor vehicles and aircraft parts. The escort from the United Kingdom to Gibraltar comprised four cruisers, and ten destroyers; from Gibraltar this strengthened as far as The Narrows-the channel between Sicily and the African coast-by a further force which included two capital ships, the aircraft carrier ARK ROYAL, a cruiser and half a dozen destroyers.

The fleet was vigourously attacked by the enemy and one destroyer was hit and completely disabled, eventually having to be sunk by another destroyer. One of the escorting cruisers was also severely damaged and ordered back to Gibraltar; a near miss by a bomb disabled yet another destroyer, which had to be towed for two days, but finally arrived at Malta; and one merchant ship was torpedoed but managed to reach her destination.

Having delivered her cargo at Malta, the PORT CHALMERS left unescorted in September 1941, and despite further attacks by the enemy, arrived back in the United Kingdom undamaged.

By the summer of 1942 however the position of the island fortress of Malta had become desperate, and to bring most urgently needed supplies of fuel and to save the island from starvation and possible surrender, a great convoy, known as 'Operation Pedestal' sailed from Britain.

The Ministry of War Transport gathered together a fleet of 14 of the finest cargo ships afloat, all capable of at least 14 knots. Under the command of Capt. H. G. B. Pinkney, (his first command) he had been chief officer on her previous voyage to Malta, the PORT CHALMERS once again prepared to sail for the 'hot' Mediterranean climes.

Accompanying this convoy was one of the most powerful escorts in naval history, including the battleships HMS NELSON and HMS RODNEY, the aircraft carriers HMS VICTORIOUS, FURIOUS, EAGLE and INDOMITABLE, and a large number of cruisers and destroyers. Leaving the United Kingdom at the end of July, the convoy passed into the Mediterranean in fog on the night of 10th August. The resultant loss of ships was grievous. The aircraft carrier HMS EAGLE was torpedoed and sunk on the afternoon of 11th August, and on the following day the Blue Funnel liner DEUCALION was hit and subsequently sank. During the night of August 12th-13th, when the convoy was off Cape Bon, HMS MANCHESTER was hit and sank later. HMS CAIRO and a destroyer were also torpedoed and had to be sunk later, whilst two merchant ships were destroyed. The BRISBANE STAR, ROCHESTER

CASTLE and the tanker OHIO were all torpedoed but not put out of action.

During fighting in August on 12th and 13th the PORT CHALMERS continued unharmed, fighting back all the time with her own armament. She had, however, one particular moment of breathtaking anxiety. Captain Pinkney, recalled that during the height of the action the starboard paravane of PORT CHALMERS was noticed to be behaving strangely. Paravanes are submerged floats towed from the bows of a ship by wires which stream out at an angle and protect the ship's sides from mines. The ship was slowed down and when the crew had almost wound in the paravane wires they found an unexploded 21-inch torpedo entangled by its propellers. PORT CHALMERS was stopped then she slowly gathered sternway and when the paravane was as far away as the wire would take it, it was cut adrift. Down went paravane and torpedo into the Mediterranean where a great explosion occurred which gave the ship a tremendous shaking but fortunately did no damage.

Enemy attacks resumed again at daybreak on 13th August, when several more ships of the convoy were destroyed. A stick of bombs was dropped on the Shaw, Savill cargo liner WAIMARAMA which blew up and disappeared in a few moments, while the OHIO was torpedoed a second time but struggled on, eventually limping into Grand Harbour, Valetta, supported by HMS PENN and HMS BRAMHAM.

Of the original convoy which left Great Britain, only five merchant ships reached Malta and of these the PORT CHALMERS was the only one to do so without casualties and undamaged.

The bravery of those on board the PORT CHALMERS during the Malta Convoys of 1941 and 1942 resulted in a long list of awards being made, including a D.S.O. for Captain Pinkney (who had already been awarded the M.B.E. while chief officer in the earlier convoy), an O.B.E for Captain Higgs (master on the first convoy), the D.S.C. for chief engineer S. G .L. Bentley and second officer R. Bettess and four Lloyds's Silver Medals for Meritorious Service.

In the course of her career the PORT CHALMERS sailed over 1,800,000 miles, in the course of 66 voyages including her wartime ones.

In the words of the chairman of the Port Line, Mr R. H. Senior, on the occasion of the farewell luncheon on board in London, "she has served us long and well and is a living and lively example of the great shipyard in which she was built, and I am sure you will agree, a credit to her country".

FORT STIKINE

The holocaust of Bombay on the afternoon of the 14th April 1944 was one of immense devastation. Fifteen merchantmen and two warships of the Royal Indian Navy were either sunk or damaged beyond repair. Warehouses over a wide area were burned and shattered. 336 people were killed and over a 1,000 injured. So great was the destruction of foodstuffs in the port area that risk of famine was brought to the region.

The FORT STIKINE blew up in Bombay docks on the afternoon of Friday, 14th April 1944. The explosion devastated a huge area of docks and of the town reducing ships to scrap metal, killing or injuring thousands and rendered countless others homeless and unemployed. The most valuable part of the city was destroyed and life came almost to a standstill.

In wartime many safety factors become overruled, and when this vessel arrived at No. 1 berth Victoria Dock she carried an extremely dangerous and explosive cargo. Nevertheless due to the port arrangements she berthed among many other vessels already lining the quays in this dock and the adjoining Princes Dock.

The FORT STIKINE had sailed from the Mersey on 24th February 1944 her destination "secret" but her cargo clearly marked for Karachi and Bombay. On deck were crated gliders whilst below her Bombay cargo included crated aircraft and shells, torpedoes, mines, rockets, magnesium and bombs totalling 1,400 tons of explosive. Also on board in No. 2 'tween deck were 124 bars of gold worth nearly one million pounds.

North-about around Ireland in convoy, eleven days to Gibraltar and thence unscathed through air attacks in the Mediterranean, she sailed on to Suez, Aden and Karachi. Partial discharge at Karachi was followed by the loading of 9,000 bales of cotton, thousands of drums of lubricating oil (some leaking) timber, scrap iron, sulphur, fish meal, rice and resin. An attempt to load 750 drums of turpentine on top of the coal in the bunkers was firmly resisted.

The FORT STIKINE reached Bombay on 12th April 1944 and despite carrying three categories of explosive and having a priority discharge certificate unloading did not commence until she had been alongside for more than 24 hours.

<u>Disposition of cargo in the holds at the time of her loss.</u>

1. Sulphur, fish manure and detonators.

2. Ammunition on the bottom of the hold, cotton right through to the tween decks. On the wings of the tween decks No. 2 right round ammunition and in the centre tween deck - oil. Some scrap metal. This scrap metal and oil was taken out before the explosion occurred. Also in No. 2 - gold bullion - an Indian found one bar of this gold over $2^1/_2$ miles away from the ship - worth about 90,000 rupees.
3. Main hold right through lubricating oil (petrol). In 'tween decks ammunition on the wings, oil in centre.
4. General cargo in the main hold, also cotton and ammunition again in the 'tween decks.
5. Cotton and timber in main hold, 'tween decks, timber and lubricating oil.

The vessel caught fire in the early stages of discharge. From a sister-ship, FORT CREVIER, berthed 400 yards away, smoke was seen spiralling from the FORT STIKINE's ventilators. Later it was also seen from the steamer IRAN and also by an inspector from the dock police. To no-one did it occur that the ship might be on fire and it was not reported. Some time later the fire was seen by returning stevedores and even then was reported as a routine fire alarm and without any suggestion of undue danger or emergency. This resulted in the despatch of quite inadequate fire-fighting appliances. In the previous five years there had been over sixty fires in ships in Bombay, but only one vessel had been lost although fifteen had carried explosives.

Soon the serious nature of the fire became apparent and every effort was made to contain it. Thirty-two hoses crossed her decks and 1,000 tons of water poured onto the seat of the fire in No. 2 hold. Decks and shell plating grew red-hot.

At 3.45p.m. the explosives caught fire. Five minutes later a great sheet of flame shot up and the ship became a flaming torch. At 4.06 pm the fore part of the ship exploded with a deafening roar. Flaming drums, blazing cotton and white-hot metal cascaded across ships, sheds and the city carving a path of fire, death and destruction.

In the dock a tidal wave lifted the JALAPADMA and dropped her across No. 2 shed. High and dry with her back broken, only her crumpled bows still touched the water. EMPIRE CONFIANCE was towed to safety by a tug, the Norwegian GRACIOSA caught fire, she too exploded and was still burning eight days later. The whole dock area became an inferno.

Under the pall of smoke, eleven vessels were on fire and four sunk. Others were aground, listing and damaged. Dock gates, bridges and berths were destroyed, sheds, warehouses and offices were demolished and the ruins afire. Roads, railways and equipment were a mass of tangled wreckage. No. 1 berth was a devastated crater, very few persons remained alive nearby and smoke and flame enveloped the wreck.

The £1,000,000 worth of gold had disintegrated. In the explosion the fore part of the ship had blown off and sunk. The after part remained afloat and on fire.

Thirty-four minutes later this after part containing 784 tons of explosive also blew up with a blast even more shattering than before. Flying, flaming debris fell again into the dock area and into other parts of the city causing terrible devastation and many more casualties.

Another huge crater was born where the remains of No. 1 berth had previously been. Chaos followed. No organisation was equipped to deal with a disaster of such magnitude and the two docks at the heart of the fire were virtually abandoned. The radius of the fire area was over one mile, hundreds of sheds, the edge of the oil depot and the western part of the city burnt furiously.

In the Alexandra Dock area were three ammunition ships and many sheds filled with explosives. A loaded tanker lay nearby. Fires had to be extinguished and the injured rescued. A central organisation was finally formed and the task of salvage and rescue got under way as confusion turned into efficiency. Subsequently piles of debris were cleared, sunken vessels scrapped or lifted, quay walls, sheds and other buildings repaired or rebuilt. Docks were drained and cleared and other ruins and wreckage swept into the open sea.

Clearance and reconstruction would normally have taken years but wartime requirements called for action on a grand scale and the docks were operating again some six months later.

Allied shipping losses in the Bombay explosion were:
FORT STIKINE, BARODA, TINOMBO, GENERAL VAN DER HEIJDEN, FORT CREVIER, GRACIOSA, ROD EL FARAG, GENERAL VAN SWIETEN, JALAPADMA, KINGYUAN, and the IRAN.

APPENDIX No. 10 - Conversions For War

During the early part of World War Two Port Line placed orders for two twin-screw motor vessels, one from John Brown & Company Ltd, Clydebank, and one from Swan, Hunter & Wigham Richardson Ltd, Wallsend-on-Tyne. While under construction both were taken over by the Admiralty and completed as escort carriers.

HMS VINDEX (Authors collection)

VINDEX - Admiralty Job No 4698

She had been under construction for 3½ months, when requisitioned, therefore some dismantling of the existing structure was needed before the conversion could begin. The original merchant ship structural design was followed except in the region of the upper and second decks where the thickness of the shell was slightly reduced. Internal decks were made watertight and additional transverse bulkheads were built near the bow and stern to improve subdivision. The gallery and flight decks were built above the upper deck with the shell plating carried up to the flight deck. The hangar and flight deck were worked structurally - i.e. no expansion joints were fitted. This new structure was mainly welded.

The hangar extended the full width of the ship and was 231ft x 61 ft x 17ft 6ins. One lift was fitted at the after end of the hangar and this slowed aircraft operation to such an extent that this class never carried more than twenty planes for operational work.

The aviation fuel tanks were surrounded by void spaces, as were the bomb rooms and magazines. One-inch protective plating was fitted over the latter compartments and empty oil drums were used for torpedo protection. No bomb lifts were fitted. Accommodation was all to Royal Navy standards; Hangar etc fitted on deck with flight deck above extending full length of ship and island control station on starboard side. Hold and lower compartments, which where not used for other purposes were filled with buoyancy drums and also 3,000 tons of pig iron ballast was fitted.

A lift manufactured by (Fraser & Chalmers Eng. Works) fitted aft from hangar to flight deck. Eighteen operational aircraft were carried. Arrester gear was fitted on flight deck with operational units below, all supplied by MacTaggart, Scott & Company Ltd. Safety nets were fitted at sides and end of flight deck.

The hull and engine room machinery of the new HMS VINDEX remained as specified by the Port Line. The engine room contained two massive five-cylinder vertically opposed Doxford main propulsion diesel engines capable of 10,700 brake horsepower, three diesel generators, two Cochrane vertical boilers, compressors, evaporators, pumps, heat exchangers and other normal merchant ship installations and fittings. There were also two separate generator rooms, each with an Allen diesel generator and sub station switchboard, and emergency electric motor-driven pumps located outside the engine room. HMS NAIRANA had similar machinery. VINDEX'S Chief Engineer was Commander H. N. Weir, RNR, a Geordie born in Tynemouth of Scottish parents. Both his father and grandfather had served in Port Line. Hector Weir had served his time as an apprentice at the Wallsend Slipway & Engineering Company and at Swan Hunter's. He went to sea and was torpedoed twice during World War One, and after the war he joined the Port Line. Between the wars he became the Port Line's Guarantee Chief sailing with each new ship on her maiden voyage and checking her engine room performance against contract specifications. In 1939 he was standing by the new PORT NAPIER, the name ship of her class which included two Port Line ships also destined to be requisitioned for conversion to escort carriers. After the sinking of HMS PORT NAPIER he joined the armed merchant cruiser ANTENOR, and he was later sent to New York to look after the engines of the first batch of Lease-Lend escort carriers being converted from merchantmen for Britain in American yards. He stood by HMS BITER, and brought HMS DASHER home, but had luckily left the ship to go to HMS VINDEX before HMS DASHER blew up on 27th March 1943, with heavy loss of life. HMS VINDEX was used for both Artic and Atlantic operations and was fitted for both night flying operations and fighter direction. Little was known in 1944 concerning the low temperature brittle fracture characteristics of steel and the riveted hulls of these ships were seen as safer than the all-welded hulls of United States-built ships. While a crack can start in a riveted joint, in a welded ship a crack could travel right round the hull.

The British escort carriers were generally successful as ships but there were a few problems. The increased windage of the hangar structure meant that heavier anchors and cables were needed on conversion. The existing windlasses were retained and these were often overloaded, resulting in frequent breakdowns. The original fit of four arrester wires, one safety wire and a single crash barrier proved inadequate and was increased where possible. Ventilation to living spaces near the hangar had to be improved by fitting forced exhaust.

An enquiry into the loss of the United States-built HMS AVENGER, which blew up when torpedoed, showed that bombs and depth charges were stowed against the ship's side and had been detonated by splinters from the torpedo hit. In all Royal Navy operated ships and some American vessels, longitudinal bulkheads were then built 15 feet in from the side and weapon stowage confined to the spaces between the bulkheads. The cost of conversion of each ship to an aircraft carrier was approximately £1,600,000 per ship. On completion HMS VINDEX was presented with a replica red post office mail box by the foreman carpenter at Swan Hunter. An ensign staff was fitted at the after end of the flight deck to distinguish her from her sister HMS NAIRANA. A large ship's badge inherited from the World War One seaplane carrier HMS VINDEX was also presented to the ship. She operated under T124X articles which meant that Merchant Navy cooks, stewards and engine room ratings were employed. On the 21st November 1943 HMS VINDEX left the Tyne for North Shields and Rosyth to store and ammunition ship. She was under the command of 43 year-old Captain H. H. T. Baylis R.N. previously in command of the escort carrier HMS ARCHER.

On 24th March 1944 HMS VINDEX was damaged when a Swordfish aircraft, carrying two depth charges, crash landed on her when returning from patrol and came to rest about 8ft from the round down of the flight deck. Petrol which leaked from the carburettor was ignited and the aircraft was set on fire. Efforts were made to extinguish the fire but before it could be got under control the two depth charges were burning fiercely and one finally exploded, blowing a hole 8 feet x 4 feet in the flight deck, which temporarily impaired her fighting efficiency but otherwise damage was slight. Temporary repairs to the flight deck were necessary before aircraft could be efficiently operated and she was out of action for three weeks.

In June 1945 Captain Baylis left to take command of HMS VULTURE, the Naval Air Station at St Merryn in Cornwall, and he was succeeded by Commander Williams. With the end of the war in Europe there was nothing for escort carriers to do so HMS VINDEX was sent to join the British Pacific Fleet as a replenishment carrier. She arrived in Sydney on the 13th August 1945, after unloading her consignment of Barracudas at Brisbane, and was once again redundant, although not for long. There was an urgent need for ships to carry people and stores and HMS VINDEX was loaded with food and clothing for Hong Kong. Two voyages were made from Australia to Hong Kong and on the return trips she conveyed a large number of released prisoners of war as well civilian internees who had also been held by the Japanese.

On her return from Australia HMS VINDEX was laid up in reserve in the Firth of Forth for some months and it was while lying there that she was repurchased by the Port Line from the Admiralty and towed to the Tyne to be reconverted into a merchant ship by Swan, Hunter & Wigham Richardson. Arriving on the 4th October 1947, the work took over 18 months to complete.

PORT VINDEX began her first commercial voyage from London to Australia on 22nd June 1949 under the command of Captain H. Hamilton Smith, with Vernon 'Ben' Battle, who had been torpedoed in the Atlantic in the PORT AUCKLAND, as his Chief Officer. After her return from her first peacetime voyage she returned to her builders to have her refrigerating machinery installed, the work taking three months.

Aft on the main deck was the crew's recreation room. This room was in direct contrast to the rest of the ship since it was finished and panelled with material taken from the old PORT MELBOURNE scrapped the previous year. This was purchased by Mr J. R. Rooper one of the directors of Port Line as a memorial to his son who was killed during the war. In 1966 the PORT VINDEX was associated with Glasgow High School for Girls through the British Ship Adoption Society.

"Right a bit" - A rare "pilot's view" of the heaving flight deck of HMS VINDEX (Authors collection)

GENERAL PARTICULARS

13,445 tons (13,660 tonnes) standard: 16,830 tons (17,100 tonnes) deep load. Dimensions: 528.6' x 68.0 x 23.6'. (25.6'deep load) Depth to flight deck 72ft.6ins. Dimensions of flight deck 503.0' x 77.0'. Petrol stowage 52.000 gallons. Fuel 1655 tons. 2.10.1941: Order Placed. 1.7.1942: Keel Laid. 24.10.1942: Conversion to aircraft carrier ordered. 12.12.1942: Allocated the name HMS VINDEX. 4.5.1943: Launched. 15.11.1943: Handed over. 3.12.1943: Commissioned. Complement normal 82 officers and 495 men. Supplementary 96 officers and 612 men. 12.1943: 825 Squadron joins ship. Autumn 1944: 811 Fleet Air Arm Squadron joined the ship at Bangor Bay, Northern Ireland.

During the course of her Naval career, aircraft from VINDEX were involved in the sinking of several German submarines, namely U 344; U 354 and U 394.

HMS NAIRANA (Authors collection)

The John Brown ship, which was to have been called PORT PIRIE, was launched on the 20th May 1943, as HMS NAIRANA. 1.7.1942: Laid down. 20.5.1943: Launched. 12.12.1943: Commissioned.

Her electronic equipment and armament was similar to her sister the HMS VINDEX and was as follows - Electronic equipment: British types 281B, 277 (low-angle search system). 293 radars: YE homing beacon: HF/DF. Guns: two 4in quick-firing MK XV1 high angle guns (twin mounting), sixteen 2pdr pom-poms (four quadruple mountings), sixteen 20mm Oerlikon quick-firing cannon (twin mountings). Aircraft 18. No catapult.

She was slightly larger than her sister and displaced 13,825 tons (14,046 tonnes) standard and 16,830 tons (17,252 tonnes) deep load.

The crest of the ship was an 'Eagle volant affrontee gold field blue', or in plain English a gold eagle with outstretched wings on a blue field.

Her operational duties were similar to that of her sister and as a result of the arduous services which she undertook within seven months HMS NAIRANA was badly in need of refit and her speed was reduced to 15 knots.

HMS NAIRANA SHIPS BELL
(Mrs C. A. Spong)

At the end of hostilities HMS NAIRANA was placed in reserve and on the 20th March 1946 was loaned to the Royal Netherlands Navy. Renamed KAREL DOORMAN and manned by a complement of 558, she was used as a training carrier. Two years later she returned to Devonport and moored alongside HMS VANGUARD while the Dutch transferred their stores to the carrier HMS VENERABLE. On 28th May 1948, the latter was formally handed over by the First Lord of the Admiralty, Viscount Hall, to the Royal Netherlands Chief of Staff, Admiral Jonkheer E. J. Van Holthe. During the ceremony Commander Wood R.N., accepted KAREL DOORMAN from Captain Logger, Royal Netherlands Navy. The lowering of the Netherlands Ensign and the hoisting of the White Ensign on KAREL DOORMAN synchronised with the lowering of the White Ensign and the hoisting of the Netherlands Ensign on HNMS VENERABLE. In doing so KAREL DOORMAN became HMS NAIRANA and HMS VENERABLE the new KAREL DOORMAN. The following day the White Ensign was lowered on HMS NAIRANA and the Red Ensign hoisted on the now M.V NAIRANA.

Port Line representatives had visited her at Devonport on 16th April 1948 and found both her hull and engines in good condition. They decided that it would be better to spend £750,000 on an eight-year-old ship than £1,000,000 on a new single screw smaller ship. Since commissioning she had steamed a total of 110,000 miles of which 30,000 had been whilst under Dutch control.

Shortly afterwards the vessel was taken over by Port Line who had purchased her from the Royal Navy for £50,000. Lifeboats were installed, surveys carried out and the ship, registered and under the command of Captain Bosanquet, left Devonport on 18th June 1948 and arrived at Belfast on 21st June. At the same time the Company applied to the Board of Trade, which, on the 30th June, granted permission to name the ship PORT VICTOR.

As the PORT VICTOR she commemorated the name of the Tyser Line Steamer MURITAI taken over by the Commonwealth and Dominion Line in 1914 and renamed PORT VICTOR, and her successor, a sister ship of the PORT PHILLIP, which was sunk while on her second voyage on 30th April 1943. Messrs Harland & Wolff, Belfast were awarded the contract for converting the vessel. The work of rebuilding then recommenced from plans drawn up for her sister, the PORT VINDEX, similarly undergoing reconstruction in her original builder's yard.

Her reconversion to a cargo liner at Harland & Wolff, Belfast, meant the removal of over 3,000 tons of steel structure forming the flight deck, hangar, bridge-island, internal bulkheads etc. The bridge and flight deck were removed in large sections, some of which weighed 100 tons. About 1,500 tons of new steel was then built into the vessel as new shell and deck plates for poop, bridge and fo'c'sle deck, and for an entirely new pillar and girder system. The main and auxiliary machinery was opened up, overhauled and surveyed. Certain redundant auxiliary machinery was removed, while repositioning of the remaining machinery was carried out. The electrical system was modified and reconstructed. Two 245-kw. generators, originally fitted in compartments forward and aft, were thoroughly overhauled and re-installed at the port side of the main engine room. Two further diesel-driven generators were fitted at the starboard side. A new funnel was erected and alterations made in the pipe systems. The ship was thus entirely reconstructed above the bridge deck, formerly the hangar deck.

When completed, it was possible to trace the PORT VICTOR'S lineage back to the PORT JACKSON completed in 1937, from whose basic design and dimensions eight vessels were built. The midships structure had, on the main deck the accommodation for the crew, with the engineers on the bridge deck, passengers on the boat deck and the Master and mates on the navigating bridge deck. The complement was 78, of which there were 33 in the deck deparment, 28 in the engine room and 17 in the catering departments. Twelve passengers were carried and whenever possible a doctor. There were six holds and the refrigerated capacity was 511,240 cu ft. This in effect meant 4,875 tons of lamb, 8,500 tons of cartoned beef, or 270,000 cases of apples could be carried. The general capacity was 196,750 cu. ft. equivalent to 7,900 bales of wool.

On 6th October 1949 the PORT VICTOR commenced her maiden voyage under the command of Captain E. T. Lawrey, proceeding outwards to discharge at Adelaide, Melbourne, Sydney and Brisbane. On completion she proceeded to New Zealand and loaded at Lyttleton and Port Chalmers for London, where she arrived on 3rd March 1950.

On completion of her fortieth voyage in April 1969, she was chartered by her parent company, Cunard Line, and a voyage of a more interesting nature followed for Cunard-Brocklebank. This was from the Continent and London via Durban to the Seychelles, Red Sea ports, Ceylon and India, from where she returned to the United Kingdom.

In October the vessel was transferred to the Cunard ownership and a Blue Star Port Line charter now followed to Australia, she then crossed to New Zealand to load. On completion of this voyage, PORT VICTOR was redelivered to Cunard and a further voyage was made to the Far East, returning via South Africa, Kingston and Gulf Ports to London where she arrived in December 1970, having during the previous eight months visited no fewer than thirty ports. The vessel now reverted to Port Line, and in charge of Captain D. J. Orr, she sailed outwards to discharge at Apia, Suva, Lautoka, Nelson and New Plymouth, loading at the latter port and Auckland for London, Liverpool and Glasgow. She was sold to Shipbreaking Industries Ltd., Faslane, Scotland on the 22nd July 1971, and ceased to be a unit of the Port Line fleet as from 14.00 hours that day. There were still many years service left in the vessel and her end seemed premature.

A splendid model of HMS VINDEX is on display at the Fleet Air Arm Museum Yeovilton, as are the bells from both HMS VINDEX and HMS NAIRANA.

HMS DEER SOUND entering Malta. (Authors collection)

PORT QUEBEC

Under construction in the Yard of J. L. Thompson & Sons, Sunderland, at the outbreak of the World War Two the PORT QUEBEC was on the point of being delivered when requisitioned by the Admiralty. Taken to the Furness Shipbuilding Company Ltd., Haverton Hill and converted into a minelayer capable of carrying over 600 mines, she joined the minelaying squadron based at Lochalsh which included her larger sister HMS PORT NAPIER. With a naval crew under the command of Captain V. Hammersly-Heenan R.N. but with her own engineers who transferred to the R.N.R. for this service, she continued in this service until October 1943 by which time she had laid 33,494 mines. Sent to John Brown & Company Ltd, Clydebank she was converted into the first aircraft repair ship. Renamed HMS DEER SOUND and under the command of Captain R. H. Johnson, R. N., she sailed for the Far East. She was attached to the Pacific Fleet during the closing months of the war against Japan and, subsequently during the period of gradual occupation of Japanese-held territory. In May 1946 she returned to the United Kingdom and after lying for a considerable time in the Forth, was brought down to the Tyne for de-equipping and re-conversion. Thousands of buoyancy drums were removed from her as well as all the elaborate machinery, lathes, etc which were part of her equipment as a repair ship. She was next moved into Swan, Hunter & Wigham Richardson's drydock where the immense task of removing the armour plate which covered her sides and decks was undertaken. Some 4,000 bolt holes had to be filled in and hatches and hatch-coamings constructed. The entire accommodation was rebuilt to post-war standards, but some connection with her naval career was preserved in the layout of a mess room leading out of a wardroom.

After running trials on the 20th December 1947, the PORT QUEBEC returned to the Tyne to load for Australia. She went to Antwerp and thence to Hamburg and was the first British ship to load in the port for Australia since the war. She completed loading at London, whence she sailed on 21st January 1948 for Adelaide, Melbourne, Sydney and Brisbane.

PORT QUEBEC was under the command of Captain B. P. Fuller, a Canadian, who joined the Port Line service at the time of the formation of the M.A.N.Z Line. The Chief Engineer Officer, Mr G. F. Shields, served in the ship as Lt. Commander (E) when the ship was on minelaying service. PORT QUEBEC remained in service until 1968 and in June of that year left Albany, Western Australia enroute for Taiwan for breaking up.

Authors note: I am indebted to Mr John Fisher who served in the ship from 7th June 1945 to 28th January 1946 as a radar operator and cox'n of the motor boat for the following description of HMS DEER SOUND.

'She carried two LCM (1) under gravity davits forward. I do not recall their numbers, but they were not consecutive, their primary use was to carry aircraft parts to or from HMS PIONEER, to which the HMS DEER SOUND acted as tender. They were also useful for personnel transport as one watch of libertymen could be carried at a time. On the boat deck there was a 32ft motor cutter and a 25ft destroyer type motor boat each side. At the forward end of the after well deck a 27ft whaler was stowed together with a 16ft fast motor boat (skimming dish). I never saw the whaler put in the water, but the skimmer was accidentally sunk in Hong Kong and although divers were sent down it was not found. Visible alterations included a long deckhouse over both No's 1 and 2 holds.

Most of the forward end of this was a recreation space. There was also the canteen, canteen manager's cabin, Master at Arms' office and cabin, and the pay office. The after end consisted of two "arms" just visible in the photo. There was an open upper bridge over the wheelhouse, at the after end of which was the hand-turned type 272 surface radar and its operating cabin. The radar was unpredictable. Once, I picked up a 50ft landing craft at 75,000 yards (37^1/$_2$ sea miles) but another time the set failed to recognise HMS DUKE OF YORK at a tenth of that distance. As it had been broad daylight at the time, no harm was done, but it was highly embarrassing for the operator. The "box" immediately abaft the mast was the W. T. cabin, but didn't look original to me, the large "box" down aft was known as the hangar and it was in here that the aircraft wings, tails and airscrews were repaired. There was usually a strong smell of acetone dope coming from here.

There were two decks in what were No's 1 and 2 holds. The upper contained the Chiefs and Petty Officers' messes and also a properly equipped barber's shop. The seamens' messes were on the lower deck. The Fleet Air Arm ratings messed separately with no direct contact with the seamens' messes. The stokers lived in the poop. There was a laundry inside the old mine chute bulges.

The armament consisted of only thirteen 20mm. Oerlikon guns sited as follows - one each side at the break of the forecastle, one each side on top of a sided extension to the recreation space, one each side abaft the bridge wings, one each side at the after end of the boat deck, four on top of the hangar and one on a raised platform at the stern. The ship sailed to Australia unescorted and the old hands claimed she was the most lightly armed ship to cross the Indian Ocean in wartime. The tall pipe visible abaft the funnel was the auxiliary funnel and was right over on the starboard side. This was always painted aluminium.

During my time on board she was painted in Pacific fleet "camouflage" of a very blue, so-called light and dark grey. Shortly afterwards a new style was ordered. The entire hull, including the forecastle but not the poop, was painted a dark grey, almost the pre-war "battle-ship" with the poop and upperworks a lighter shade.

Even for the lower deck she was a very comfortable ship to serve in. I shall always be thankful for my service in her since she took me to Hong Kong in September 1945 where I found my father and other relatives just out of Japanese P.O.W. camps. I had not seen my father since October 1938, just before my twelfth birthday.

She had a crew of well over 500, the great majority were Fleet Air Arm specialist ratings. The Captain was R. H. Johnson R.N., for many years the captain of the coastal minelayer HMS PLOVER. The National Maritime Museum has a wartime propaganda film of minelaying. Captain Johnson and the PLOVER, both unnamed, feature in it. Captain Johnson joined the Navy as a boy seaman and it was said that he was the first ex-boy to reach four rings having served his time as a warrant officer with acceleration in promotion.

Under the command of Commander Romer R.N she sailed for the Far East and was attached to the Pacific Fleet during the closing months of the war against Japan and, subsequently, during the period of gradual occupation of Japanese held territory. In 1946 she returned to the United Kingdom to "pay-off".

What's In A Name ?

The naming system for the Milburn and Watts vessels evolved as their fleet expanded into two distinct but not exclusive theme's. Some of their ships were given names associated with where the ships traded too, starting with HINDOOSTAN and EASTERN QUEEN and eventually culminated in the well-known PORT prefix. Several vessels were given names of places in China and the Far East, for example CHU KIANG, SINGAPORE and CANTON. The vessels built for the Hamburg-Brazilian operation were suitably named SANTOS, BRAZILIAN and RIO. The second theme was vessels named after English towns and villages, starting with WHALTON and was to include London suburbs beginning with SURBITON a system continued with Watts after 1879. There was also a short-lived group named after places they passed i.e. the prefix CAPE.

Royden utilised INDRA or INVER extensively as a prefix.

Tyser utilised Maori names for their vessels, relevant to the localities to their trading areas in New Zealand, and people therin.

Corry utilised the prefix STAR OF for their vessels followed by a country name.

ACTON	London suburb.
ALABAMA	A state in the south - eastern U.S.A, on the Gulf of Mexico.
ALBERTA	A province in Western Canada.
AMOY	City and port in China (now Xiamen).
ANGERTON	Northumberland village.
ANNE ROYDEN	Named after Thomas Roydens wife.
ARCOT	Madras, India.
ARETHUSA	Nymph in Greek mythology
ASCALON	Ruined city on the coastal plain of Palestine (now Ashqelon).
ASHINGTON	Northumberland colliery village.
BARKHILL	A Mansion situated on Mosely Hill, Liverpool owned by Howell James whose daughter named the Barkhill.
BEATRICE	*nothing located.*
BENWELL TOWER	Bishop of Newcastle's residence (until 1950's).
BERAR	District of the central provinces of India.
BLYTHWOODE	*nothing located.*
BOMBAY	City and port on the west coast of India now called MUMBAI.
BRAZILIAN	Native of Brazil.
BRILLIANT	Intensely vivid.
BUSTON VALE	Low Buston, Northumberland
BUSY BEE	Industrious person.
CACTUS	A plant native to arid regions of the U.S.A.
CANTON	Capital of Kwangtung province (now Guangzhou)
CATHERINE APCAR	Named after the daughter of the original owner.
CAPE CLEAR	South west tip of Ireland (51.26N 9.29W)
CAPE COLONNA	The southern tip of Greece (37.38N 24.01E)
CAPE COMINO	North east coast of Sardinia (40.32N 9.50E)
CAPE COMORIN	The southern tip of the Indian sub continent (8.05N 77.30E)
CAPE CORRIENTES	Western tip of Cuba (21.45N 84.31W)
CARRON	Scottish river/town near Falkirk.
CHARGER	Horse ridden by a knight.
CHARLES TENNANT	A well known Scottish chemical manufacturer (1823-1906)
CHEVIOT	Northumberland mountain
CHIEFTAIN	Leader of people or clan.
CHILENA	Range of mountains in Chile.
CHIPCHASE	Castle in Tyne valley near Chollerford
CHIN KIANG	Port city in China
CHISWICK	London suburb

CHOLLERTON	Northumberland village
CHU KIANG	Port city in China
CLANDON	Clandon Park the Surrey home of the Onslows who held shares in several of the company's ship and the Fourth Earl of Onslow was New Zealand's youngest Governor-General (1888-1892).
CLAREMONT	A mansion situated at Esher, Surrey.
CLIFFORD	Village in Herefordshire.
COLOMBO	Capital of Ceylon
COMPTON	Surrey village
CONISTON	Westmoreland village
CONSETT	County Durham town
COQUET	Northumberland river
CRESCENT	Shape of a waning moon.
CRITERION	Standard by which something maybe judged.
DARLINGTON	County Durham town
DEVONHURST	*nothing located.*
DUNRAVEN	Welsh mining village with a colliery owned by Watts, Milburn
EASTERN QUEEN	*nothing located.*
EMPIRE MOULMEIN	A port in SE Burma.
EQUINOX	Moment or point when the sun crosses the equator
FENHAM	When this ship was built the Milburns moved into a new house in Fenham Terrace, Newcastle.
FENSTANTON	Huntingdonshire village, this ship was launched by Miss Coote whose father was managing director of the Andrew Leslie shipyard at Hebburn and was born in Fenstanton.
FERNWOOD	*nothing located.*
FLODDEN	Northumberland village - site of battle with the Scots 1513
FORT CHAMBLEY	A fort situated on the Richelieu River, Canada.
FORT STIKINE	A fort built in 1834 situated near Wrangell, Alaska.
FOWBERRY TOWER	When built this was the home of Archibald Milburn
FRANKBY	Birthplace of Thomas Royden in 1792.
GILSLAND	Northumberland town
GOSFORTH	Northumberland town north of Newcastle.
GREENOCK	Port on the Firth of Clyde, Scotland.
GUADIANA	Spanish/Portuguese river.
HALICORE	Native of the Indian Seas or Sirenians found in the Red Sea or Indian Ocean.
HANKOW	City in China.
HANNAH PARK	The Wife of the original owner of the vessel.
HARE BELL	A flower, known in Scotland as a bluebell.
HARRY S. EDWARDS	A South Shields shipowner.
HARTLEPOOL	A port on the NE coast of England.
HAVERTON	County Durham village.
HAWKES BAY	North coast, New Zealand.
HERCULES	A Greek or Roman Hero.
HIMALAYA	Snow abode. Mountain range in southern Asia.
HINDOOSTAN	Northern India.
HONG KONG	British crown colony until 1997.
HOWRAH	City in eastern India opposite Calcutta on the Hooghly River.
HUNTINGDON	Huntingdonshire town.
ILDERTON	Northumberland village.
INDRA	Hindu warrior king of the heavens.
INVERCLYDE	River Clyde.
INVERESK	River Esk or an old name for Musselburgh.
ISMYR	*nothing located.*

JAMES CARSON	*nothing located.*
JANE PORTER	Named after the wife of William Corry.
JOHN MIDDLETON	A coal factor.
JOHN STRAKER	*nothing located.*
L'ALLEGRO	Brisk speed.
LA ZINGARA	Region of Argentina.
LARNACA	Port in Cyprus.
LATHOM	Lancashire village.
LEVANT	The eastern Mediterranean.
LIGHTNING	Speed.
LORD COLLINGWOOD	Second in command to Lord Nelson at the battle of Trafalgar, he was also a native of Northumberland.
LOTHIAN	Area of Scotland.
LOWLANDER	An inhabitant of the lowlands e.g. of Scotland.
LUCERNE	Swiss lakeside city.
LUCILLE	*nothing located.*
LUCKNOW	City of northern India.
LURLEI	A rock in the River Rhine near St Goar.
LUTTERWORTH	Leicestershire village.
MAHARAJAH	Hindoo chief.
MAITLAND	A town situated in New South Wales, Australia.
MAKARINI	Maori name.
MANGERTON	Dorset village.
MARCIA	*nothing located.*
MARERE	Maori name.
MARIAN	A devotee of the Virgin Mary.
MIMIRO	Maori name.
MURITAI	Maori name.
NANKIN	City in eastern China on the Yangtze.
NELSON VILLAGE	A village in South Tyneside.
NEREHANA	Maori name.
NINGPO	City and port in China.
NIWARU	Maori name.
NORMANTON	Yorkshire mining town.
NORTH	Lord North, British Statesman.
NORTHUMBERLAND	County in NE England bordering Scotland.
OTTERBURN	Northumberland town.
PEKING	Capital City of China, now Beijing.
PENSACOLA	City and seaport of Florida. U.S.A.
PERSIAN	Native of Persia or nowadays Iran.
PINAR DEL RIO	Town in Cuba.
PLAINMELLER	Colliery village in Tyne Northumberland.
PLASSEY	North west India, scene of a battle in 1757.
POONAH	City in western India. Military and administrative centre when under British rule.
PORT ADELAIDE	South Australia.
PORT ALBANY	A town and port in Western Australia situated on King George Sound. 352 miles S.E. of Perth.
PORT ALFRED	Victoria, Australia.
PORT ALBERT	Victoria, Australia.
PORT ALMA	Queensland, Australia.
PORT AUCKLAND	North Island, New Zealand.
PORT AUGUSTA	Port at the head of Spencer Gulf, South Australia. 259 miles north of Adelaide.
PORT BOWEN	Queensland, Australia, on Port Denison harbour.

PORT BRISBANE	City and seaport of Queensland, Australia.
PORT BURNIE	Tasmania.
PORT CAMPBELL	Victoria, Australia.
PORT CAROLINE	Lacepede bay, South Australia
PORT CHALMERS	Port of South Island, New Zealand. 8 miles north east of Dunedin.
PORT CURTIS	Queensland, Australia
PORT DARWIN	Northern Territory, Australia.
PORT DENISON	Situated on Edgecumbe Bay Central Queensland, Australia a few miles from Bowen.
PORT DOUGLAS	Queensland, Australia.
PORT DUNEDIN	South Island, New Zealand, 8 miles S.W. of Port Chalmers.
PORT ELLIOT	South Australia.
PORT FAIRY	Seaport of Victoria, Australia. 187 miles W.S.W. of Melbourne.
PORT FREMANTLE	Western Australia, 12 miles S.W. of Perth.
PORT GISBORNE	North Island, New Zealand.
PORT HACKING	New South Wales, Australia.
PORT HALIFAX	Capital of Nova Scotia Canada. It is Canada's principal ice free port on the Atlantic coast.
PORT HARDY	New Zealand.
PORT HOBART	Capital and seaport of Tasmania.
PORT HUNTER	Situated on the Hunter River, Newcastle New South Wales, Australia.
PORT HUON	Tasmania.
PORT INVERCARGILL	South Island, New Zealand. 17miles from Bluff Harbour.
PORT JACKSON	Sydney, New South Wales, Australia.
PORT KEMBLA	South Australia.
PORT LAUNCESTON	City of Tasmania, situated on the river Tamar.
PORT LINCOLN	Situated on Eure Peninsula, South Australia.
PORT LYTTELTON	Seaport of South Island, New Zealand.
PORT MACQUARIE	Seaport New South Wales, Australia. Situated at the mouth of the Hastings River on a small bay of the same name.
PORT MELBOURNE	City and port in Victoria, Australia. Situated at the head of Hobson Bay. The north portion of Port Phillip.
PORT MONTREAL	City and seaport of Canada.
PORT NAPIER	North Island, New Zealand. The capital of the Hawke's Bay district.
PORT NELSON	Seaport of South Island, New Zealand.
PORT NEW PLYMOUTH	Town of North Island, New Zealand.
PORT NICHOLSON	New Zealand.
PORT PHILLIP	Harbour of Victoria, Australia. Melbourne stands at the north end of the bay it is the largest indentation on the Victoria coast. It is 30 miles from north to south and 30 miles across at its widest part. Melbourne the capital of the state stands at the north end of the bay.
PORT PIRIE	Seaport on north west shore of Spencer Gulf, South Australia. 40 miles from Port Augusta.
PORT QUEBEC	City and seaport of Canada, on the north bank of the St. Lawrence river.
PORT SAINT JOHN	City and seaport of New Brunswick, Canada.
PORT ST LAWRENCE	Queensland. A general name for ports on the St Lawrence Seaway.
PORT STEPHENS	New South Wales, Australia.
PORT SYDNEY	Capital of New South Wales, Australia.
PORT TOWNSVILLE	Seaport of North Queensland.
PORT VICTOR	South Australia.
PORT VICTORIA	South Australia, but may have been influenced by the Queens diamond jubilee 1897.
PORT VINDEX	A name given in tribute to HMS VINDEX the World War Two aircraft carrier.
PORT WANSTEAD	Port prefix to Watts, Watts chartered ship.
PORT WIMBLEDON	Port prefix to Watts, Watts chartered ship.
PORT WYNDHAM	Western Australia.
PROVIDENCE	State capital of Rhode Island. U.S.A. also to foresee.
RICHMOND	London suburb/North Yorkshire town.

RIO	Rio de Janiero, the principal port of Brazil.
ROSCOMMON	Town and county in Ireland.
ROSEDEN	Northumberland village
ROUEN	Port on the River Seine, France.
ST. BEDE	Northern Saint
ST. CLAIR	River in North America.
ST. OSYTH	Essex village
SABRINA	Latin name for the River Severn.
SAINT GEORGE	Patron saint of England.
SAINT HELENA	Island in the South Atlantic.
SANTA CLARA	Town in Cuba.
SANTA ISABEL	Mexico.
SANTA MARGHERITA	*nothing located.*
SANTA THERESA	Mexico.
SANTOS	Port on the coast of Brazil.
SAVANNAH LA MAR	Town in Jamaica.
SCINDIA	Variant spelling of India.
SHEARWATER	Seabird.
SINGAPORE	City and port in Malaya. Now a country in its own right.
SIR JOHN LAWRENCE	Owner of Ashton Hall, Lancaster, Lancashshire.
SPRINGWOOD	*nothing located.*
STAR OF ALBION	Albion a poetic name for Britain or England.
STAR OF ERIN	Erin a poetic name for Ireland.
SULTAN	Muslim sovereign.
SUMMER HILL	*nothing located.*
SURBITON	London suburb.
TANTALLON	Tantallon Castle, Lothian.
TAUNTON	Somerset town.
TEDDINGTON	London suburb.
TIVERTON	Devonshire town.
TOMOANA	Maori name.
TREVELYAN	Sir George Otto Trevelyan (1838-1928) historian and statesman.
ULRICA	Girls name of Swedish origin.
UNDERWRITER	Person who undertakes liability for a risk.
UNITED KINGDOM	Country of Western Europe comprising England, Wales, Scotland and Northern Ireland.
VALENCIA	Port and region of Spain.
WAR HECUBA	A Trojan woman, the wife of Priam.
WEST STANLEY	County Durham colliery, which on 16th February 1909 was the scene of the worst coal mining disaster in Durham coal mining history. The owner of this colliery was John Henry Burn who was a shareholder in several of the company's ships.
WHAKARUA	Maori name.
WHALTON	Northumberland village.
WHAMPOA	Seaport and city in China.
WILEYSIKE	An area of moor on Northumberland/Cumberland border. Near Gilsland. In Milburns obituary it states 'In his younger days he was considered an excellent shot and he loved nothing so much as a brisk walk with gun and dogs over his moors at Gilsland'.
WOODHORN	Northumberland colliery village.
YANGTSZE	The principal river of China.
ZETUS	The sea Monster which threatened Andromeda also spelt Cetus.

BIBLIOGRAPHY

Appleyard, H. S.,	Bank Line.
Baldwin, C. E.,	The History of the Port of Blyth.
Ballantyne, P. L.,	The Cool Weather Route.
Clarke, J. F.	The Changeover from Wood to Iron Shipbuilding.
Clarke, J. F.,	Building Ships On The North East Coast.
Clarke, J. F.	Power on land & Sea.
Cooper, J., Kludas, A.,& Pein.	Hamburg, South America Line.
Cottrell, P.L.	Shipping, Trade & Commerce
Course, A. G.,	The Deep Sea Tramp.
Craster, H.	History of Northumberland.
Critchell, J. T.	History of the Frozen Meat Trade.
Daunton, M. J.	Coal Metropolis - Cardiff 1870 - 1914
Farnie, D.A.	East And West Of Suez - the Suez Canal and History.
Fell, W. R.	The Sea Surrenders.
Fryer, M.	Newcastle Century
Godfrey, & Lassey	Shipwrecks of the Yorkshire Coast.
Gregory, D.	Australian Steamships - Past and Present
Haig, K. R.	Cable Ships & Submarine Cables.
Hardy, Ivami, E. R.	Casebook on Shipping Law.
Harvey, W. J.,	Head Line (G. Heyn & Sons Ltd)
Hocking,	Dictionary of Disatsters At Sea.
Ingram, & Wheatley	New Zealand Shipwreck 1795 - 1960.
Jones, Geoffrey,	Under Three Flags
Keys, R. E.	The Sailing Ships of Aln & Coquet.
Keys, R. E.	Dictionary of Tyne Sailing Ships.
Laxon, W. A. & Perry, F.	British India Steam Navigation.
Laxon, Farquhar & Kirby	Crossed Flags.
Lewis,	The Rhonda Valleys
Long, A. & R.	A Shipping Venture - Turnbull Scott & Company.
Lubbock, Basil,	The Last of the Windjammers.
Lund & Ludlam,	Night of the U-Boats
Lund	A Glance At The Past.
Maber, John M.,	North Star to Southern Cross
MacDonald, Rod,	Dive Scotlands Greatest Wrecks.
Macrae & Waine	Steam Collier Fleets.
Martin, R.	Historical Notes & Personal Recollections of W. Hartlepool.
McMillen, A. S.,	Port Line Story.
Middlebrook, Martin,	Convoy.
Mitchell & Sawyer,	Empire Ships of World War Two
Mitchell & Sawyer,	The Oceans; The Forts and The Parks.
Poolman, K.,	Escort Carriers of World War Two
Powell, L. H.	The Shipping Federation 1890 - 1950
Rohwer, Jurgen,	The Critical Convoy Battles of March 1943
Roskill, S. W.,	Merchant Fleet in War 1939-1945.
Runciman Sir. W.	Collier Brigs & Their Sailors.
Russell, A. G.,	Port Line.
Smith, P,	Pedestal.
Spalding. Bert,	Shipbuilders of The Hartlepools.
Sullivan, W. R.	Blyth in the 18th Century
Taylor,	Ellermans a Wealth of Shipping
Telford, P. J.,	Donaldson Line
Wallis, J.	The History of Blyth.
Winton, John,	Ultra at Sea.

Other Sources.

British Vessels Lost At Sea (1914 - 1918) & (1939 - 1945), Cassell's World Pictorial Gazetteer, G. W. Z. C.-Port Line Magazine, Liverpool University Archives, Lloyds Collection Guildhall Library, Lloyds Register of Shipping Information Sevices, Lloyds Registers 1825 - 2003, Marine News, Journal of the World Ship Society, Motor Ship, M.I.L.A.G. Association, Mitchell's Maritime Register 1872, National Maritime Museum, Greenwich, New Zealand Marine News, Peabody Museum, Public Records Office, Kew, London - ADM 199/234/444 and BT 107, 108, 109, 110 series, Sea Breezes, Shipbuilding & Shipping Record, Ships Annual 1967, Ships Monthly, The Log - magazine of the Australia and New Zealand W. S. S., The Shipbuilder, Tyne & Wear Museums. Tyneside Industries.

BOLD UPPERCASE names used within the index are those used during involvement by any of the constituent Companies. Lower case are those used previously or subsequently.

INDEX

ACTON. 61	Bougainville 91	**CLIFFORD** 22
Agordat 68	Brasilien. 54	**COLOMBO** 57
Agostino M 91	Bray Head 25	Colonel Vieljeux 200
Akrotiri Express 189	Brazilian. 54	**COMPTON** 62, 63
Alabama. 64	**BRAZILIAN** 54	**CONISTON** 65
ALABAMA 8	**BRILLIANT** 47, 63	**CONSETT**. 58, 63
ALBERTA. 9	Brodfield. 85	**COQUET** 55
Alberto 22	Brodlea. 85	Cornelia Elizabeth 21
Albion Star 196	Brodstone. 25	**CORNWALL** 84
Albionstar. 196	Brodvale. 93	Crescent. 10
Alderminster. 204	**BUSTON VALE** 49	**CRESCENT** 10
Alexandra. 65	**BUSY BEE** 65	**CRITERION** 53
Alfalfa. 26	**CACTUS** 48, 63	Czarita 70
Algeneb 166	**CALLIOPE** 47	Danae. 190
ALN 49	Cambrian Baroness 82	Daphne 189
Amana 194	Cambrian Countess 80	Dargai 77
AMOY. 59, 63	Cambrian Marchioness. . 82	**DARLINGTON** 66
Anar 190	Cambrian Peeress. 29	Darnley 81
Angeliki 193	**CANTON**. 56	**DEER SOUND** 179
ANGERTON 69	**CAPE CLEAR** 73	Delagoa 78
ANNE ROYDEN 21	**CAPE COLONNA** 73	Delmonico 76
ARCHIMEDES 51	**CAPE COMINO**. 74	Demirhan. 200
ARCOT. 92	**CAPE COMORIN** 74	Denton Holme 10
ARETHUSA 47	**CAPE CORRIENTES** . . . 74	**DEVON**. 85
Artemon 194	Capo Nord 94	**DEVONHURST**. 61
ASCALON. 66	Carbella 76	Dona Maria 72
ASHINGTON (1) 66	**CARRON (1)**. 47	Dunnet. 60
ASHINGTON (2) 84	**CARRON (2)**. 49	**DUNRAVEN** 58
Atlantide. 85	**CARRON (3)**. 51	Duns Law. 79
Augusta 86	**CATHERINE APCAR** . . . 57	**DURHAM** 86
Augustus H. Garland . . 199	**CHARGER** 9	**EASTERN QUEEN** 50
Balderton 78	**CHARLES TENNANT** . . . 53	Edith 10
Baltica 190	Chase Side 26	Educator 200
Bankoku Maru 26	Chasehill 92	El Cordobes 26
BARKHILL 21	**CHEVIOT** 55	Elisa. 23
Bassorah 65	**CHIEFTAIN (1)**. 8	Emilia. 52
Beatrice 53	**CHIEFTAIN (2)**. 9	**EMPIRE MOULMEIN** . . 200
BEATRICE 22	**CHILENA** 21	**EMPIRE TREASURE** . . 198
Bedeburn 77	**CHIN KIANG** 58, 63	Empire Wessex 181
Belorussia 78	**CHIPCHASE**. 50	**EQUINOX**. 46, 63
Bendoran 29	Chipchase Castle 84	Euryades 32
Benvannoch 202	Chiswick. 77	Eurybates. 29
BENWELL TOWER. 83	**CHISWICK** 57	Eurydamas. 27
Beppe. 68	Chloe 190	Eurylochus. 31
BERAR. 91	**CHOLLERTON** 67	Eurymachus. 33
Bertha 23	**CHU KIANG** 54	Eurymedon. 28
Betsy Anna. 84	Clan Graham 82	Eurypylus. 32
Bisham Hill 199	Clan Grant 82	Fair Lady 203
Blyth 68	**CLANDON** 62	Falls Of Moness 34
BLYTHWOODE 55	**CLAREMONT** 52	**FENHAM** 53
BOMBAY 91	Clarkspey. 204	**FENSTANTON** 66
Botavon 32	**CLAWDON** 63	**FERNWOOD**. 62, 63

Fidelitas 27	INDRA (2) 26	Kelvinbrae 81
FLODDEN 52	INDRA (3) 32	**KENT** 85
Flora C 204	**INDRABARAH (1)** 29	Kildona 23
FORT CHAMBLY 197	**INDRABARAH (2)** . . 29, 156	Kings Reach 204
FORT STIKINE 197	**INDRADEO (1)** 34	Kirkwall 74
FOWBERRY TOWER . . . 83	**INDRADEO (2)** 29	Kiuho Maru 62
FRANKBY 21	**INDRADEVI (1)** 26	Kongosan Maru 28
Frigida 14	**INDRADEVI (2)** 26	Korio Maru 59
Fukui Maru 25	**INDRAGHIRI (1)** 25	Kostroma 73
Gaeta 83	**INDRAGHIRI (2)** 31	Kronoborg 166
Gamma 52	**INDRAKUALA** 32	Kronshtadt 166
GILSLAND 61, 63	**INDRALEMA (1)** 25	Kronstadt 166
Glacier 76	**INDRALEMA (2)** . . . 27, 156	La Perouse 13
Glorianna 182	**INDRAMAYO (1)** 24	**LA ZINGARA** 21
Golden Dolphin 196	**INDRAMAYO (2)** 28	Laertis 203
Golden Glory 195	**INDRANI (1)** 23	Laleham 81
GOSFORTH 51	**INDRANI (2)** 25	**L'ALLEGRO** 22
Gracia 198	**INDRANI (3)** 31	**LARNACA** 23
GREENOCK 9	**INDRAPURA (1)** 24	**LATHOM (1)** 23
Grid 11	**INDRAPURA (2)** 26	**LATHOM (2)** 23
GUADIANA 48, 63	**INDRAPURA (3)** . . . 30, 156	Legation 176
Guernica 70	**INDRASAMHA** 27	Leif 91
Gustaf 55	**INDRAVELLI** 26	Leme 197
Gustafsberg 55	**INDRAWADI** 28	**LEVANT** 51
HALICORE (1) 46, 63	Indro 26	**LIGHTNING** 92
HALICORE (2) 47, 63	**INVERCLYDE** 33	**LORD COLLINGWOOD** . . 52
HANKOW 59, 63	**INVERESK** 33	Loredano 79
HANNAH PARK 50	**IRTHINGTON** 64	**LOTHIAN** 48
HARE BELL 54	**ISMYR (1)** 21	**LOWLANDER** 196
HARRY S. EDWARDS . . 64	**ISMYR (2)** 22	**LUCERNE** 50
HARTLEPOOL 50	Istambol 65	**LUCILE** 23
Hastier 70	Istanbul 65	**LUCKNOW** 92
HAVERTON 67	Italian 72	**LURLEI** 22
HAWKES BAY (1) 92	J. Jover Serra 73	**LUTTERWORTH** 53
HAWKES BAY (2) . . 97, 161	**JAMES CARSON** 9	Madalena 74
Heimdal 23	James Dixon 51	**MAHARAJAH** 57, 63
HERCULES 8	**JANE PORTER** 10	**MAITLAND** 50
Herefordshire 201	Jeanne Marcelle 68	**MAKARINI** 96, 161
Highland Star 15	Jinbu Maru 25	Maldive Explorer 202
HIMALAYA 91	**JOHN MIDDLETON (1)** . 51	Mana 194
HINDOOSTAN 49	**JOHN MIDDLETON (2)** . 56	**MANAAR** 194
HMS Cyclops 29	**JOHN STRAKER** 64	**MANGERTON** 64
HMS Nairana 186	**JOHN TWIZELL** 46	Manilla 60
HMS Vindex 186	Jolanda 67	Manizadi 200
Hoffnung 31	Joli 204	Mar Bianco 97
HONG KONG (1) 56	Juan 55	**MARCIA** 60, 63
HONG KONG (2) 66	Juan Jose Latorre 52	**MARERE** 94, 159
HOWRAH 91	Jugoslavija 27	Marietta 194
Hughli 196	Julietta 194	Marinula 33
Huntingdon 65	K. Paskhalidis 68	**MARION** 52
HUNTINGDON 65	Kagoshima Maru 74	Maritima 82
ILDERTON 67	Kanaris 200	Marquette 10
Ilena 177	Kaparika 84	Marseilles 14
Inchleana 198	**KARAMEA** 85	Martand 97
Indo Maru 26	Karel Doorman 186	Martano 97
INDRA (1) 23	Kavo Kolones 190	Mashaallah 185

Masir 191	PORT ADELAIDE (4) . . 186	PORT HUNTER (3). 79, 152
Masirah 191	PORT ALBANY (1) . 82, 155	PORT HUNTER (4). . . . 167
Matangi 192	PORT ALBANY (2) 182	PORT HUON (1) 172
MATRA. 195	PORT ALBANY (3) 194	PORT HUON (2) 193
Maud 53	PORT ALBERT (1) 74	PORT INVERCARGILL. 190
McClellan 70	PORT ALBERT (2) 78	PORT JACKSON (1). . . . 68
Merryland. 201	PORT ALFRED. 191	PORT JACKSON (2). . . . 86
Miguel Jover. 72	PORT ALMA (1) 156	PORT JACKSON (3). . . 175
Mill Hill 199	PORT ALMA (2) 173	PORT KEMBLA (1). 81, 154
MIMIRO 94, 159	PORT AUCKLAND (1) . 167	PORT KEMBLA (2). . . . 166
Minasloide 86	PORT AUCKLAND (2) . 185	PORT LAUNCESTON . . 190
Moinho Fluminesse 14	PORT AUGUSTA (1) . . . 70	PORT LINCOLN (1) 81, 154
Mongioia. 85	PORT AUGUSTA (2) 80, 152	PORT LINCOLN (2) . . . 181
Montreal City 35	PORT BOWEN 164	PORT LYTTELTON (1) . 159
MURITAI 96, 160	PORT BRISBANE (1) . . 169	PORT LYTTELTON (2) . 183
Murvet 54	PORT BRISBANE (2) . . 184	PORT MACQUARIE (1) . 82,
Nankai Maru 26	PORT BURNIE 193	 155
NANKIN 58	PORT CAMPBELL (1). . 157	PORT MACQUARIE (2) 180
Nanny 10, 22	PORT CAMPBELL (2). . 167	PORT MELBOURNE (1) . 76
Nausica 199	PORT CAMPBELL (3). . 203	PORT MELBOURNE (2) 158
NELSON VILLAGE 8	PORT CAROLINE (1) . . . 73	PORT MELBOURNE (3) 189
NEREHANA 96, 160	PORT CAROLINE (2) . . . 73	PORT MONTREAL (1) . 176
Nikola Mihanovic 33	PORT CAROLINE (3) . . . 79	PORT MONTREAL (2) . 188
NINGPO 59, 63	PORT CAROLINE (4) . . 164	PORT NAPIER (1) 161
NIWARU 94, 159	PORT CAROLINE (5) . . 195	PORT NAPIER (2) 179
Norbertos 65	PORT CHALMERS (1) . . 75	PORT NAPIER (3) 184
Nordave 192	PORT CHALMERS (2) . . 79	PORT NELSON. 188
Norden 84	PORT CHALMERS (3) . 160	PORT NEW PLYMOUTH 191
Norge 95	PORT CHALMERS (4) . 174	PORT NICHOLSON (1) . 161
NORMANTON. 66	PORT CHALMERS (5) . 194	PORT NICHOLSON (2) . 163
NORTH 92	PORT CURTIS (1) . 81, 153	PORT NICHOLSON (3) . 192
NORTHUMBERLAND . . . 91	PORT CURTIS (2) 165	PORT PHILLIP (1) 68
Ocean Monarch 189	PORT CURTIS (3) 201	PORT PHILLIP (2) 78
Ocean Odyssey. 189	PORT DARWIN (1) 69	PORT PHILLIP (3) 86
Olympia 33	PORT DARWIN (2) . . . 162	PORT PHILLIP (4) . 80, 152
Olympic 11 13	PORT DENISON (1) 72	PORT PHILLIP (5) 179
Oregon Star 198	PORT DENISON (2) 77	PORT PIRIE (1) 70
Oregonstar 82	PORT DENISON (3) . . . 162	PORT PIRIE (2) . . . 81, 153
OTTERBURN 54	PORT DENISON (4) . . . 203	PORT PIRIE (3) 157
P. Claris 72	PORT DOUGLAS 76	PORT PIRIE (4) 186
Parisina 79	PORT DUNEDIN. 170	PORT PIRIE (5) 182
Pei Tai 64	PORT ELLIOT (1). 76	PORT QUEBEC 179
PEKING 66	PORT ELLIOT (2). 156	PORT SAINT JOHN . . . 177
PENSACOLA 59	PORT FAIRY (1). 72	PORT ST LAWRENCE . 192
PERO 46, 63	PORT FAIRY (2). 172	PORT STEPHENS (1). . . 77
PERSIAN 9	PORT FREMANTLE . . . 171	PORT STEPHENS (2). . 157
PINAR DEL RIO (1) 34	PORT GISBORNE. 171	PORT STEPHENS (3). . 202
PINAR DEL RIO (2) 35	PORT HACKING 159	PORT SYDNEY (1) 158
PLAINMELLER. 62, 63	PORT HALIFAX 176	PORT SYDNEY (2) 186
PLASSEY 92	PORT HARDY (1) 160	PORT SYDNEY (3) 189
Plymouth 191	PORT HARDY (2). 168	PORT TOWNSVILLE (1) 175
POONAH 91	PORT HARDY (3). 201	PORT TOWNSVILLE (2) 187
Poredak 78	PORT HOBART (1). . . . 171	PORT VICTOR (1) . 70, 160
PORT ADELAIDE (1) . . . 69	PORT HOBART (2). . . . 181	PORT VICTOR (2) 180
PORT ADELAIDE (2) . . 156	PORT HUNTER (1). 76	PORT VICTOR (3) 185
PORT ADELAIDE (3) . . 164	PORT HUNTER (2). 77	PORT VICTORIA 78

PORT VINDEX 186	**SHEARWATER** 50	**SUSSEX (1)** 85
PORT WANSTEAD 202	Shikishima Maru 61	**SUSSEX (2)** 86
PORT WELLINGTON (1) 169	Shinbu Maru 25	Svea 58
PORT WELLINGTON (2) 182	Sierra Cordova 23	Swat 203
PORT WIMBLEDON . . . 203	Silveroak 202	Switzerland 189
PORT WYNDHAM 175	Singapore 61	Taishikan 173
Praglia 199	**SINGAPORE** 56	Taiyo Maru 59
Pratomagno 26	**SIR JOHN LAWRENCE** . 22	**TANTALLON** 64
Presidente Juarez 76	Skopelo 193	**TAUNTON** 52, 63
Princess Danae 190	Skopelos 193	Teakwood 34
Provencal 64	Sofia Brailli 69	**TEDDINGTON** 65
PROVIDENCE 35	Southern Queen 29	Teni 182
Providentia 35	Spanish Prince 70	Tento 84
Puerto Princesa 188	Splendid Sky 200	Teresia 53
Purificazione 14	**SPRINGWOOD** 21	Tessa 203
QUEEN OF THE WEST . . 9	**ST CLAIR** 63	Tetulia 198
Raeburn 202	**ST OSYTH** 61	**THE DUKE** 21
Ratna Jyoti 201	**ST. BEDE** 51	Therisos Express 190
Ravensworth 79	**ST. CLAIR** 48	Thiresia 53
Raymond 64	St. Pauli 53	Thistledowne 201
Raymondos 64	Stangrant 82	Thorpe Grange 24
Redestos 178	Star Altair 203	Thyra 53
Republica Argentina 77	**STAR OF ALBION** 10	Tinhow 196
Richard Cory 64	**STAR OF AUSTRALIA** . 14,	**TIVERTON** 67
RICHMOND 57	 157	**TOMOANA** 93
RIO 56	**STAR OF AUSTRIA** 13	Tourny 91
Riojun Maru 76	**STAR OF BENGAL** 12	Tower Dale 166
Roger De Lluria 73	**STAR OF CANADA** 16	Trade 32
Romsdal 57	**STAR OF DENMARK** . . . 10	**TREVELYAN** 91
ROSCOMMON 64	**STAR OF ENGLAND (1)** . 14	Trichera 10
ROSEDEN 60	**STAR OF ENGLAND (2)** 17,	Trigonia 33
ROUEN 92	 158	Tudor Star 93
SABA 34	**STAR OF ERIN** 10	Tudorstar 93
SABRINA 22	**STAR OF FRANCE** 13	**ULRICA** 49
Sadokuni Maru 64	**STAR OF GERMANY** . . . 11	**UNDERWRITER** 65
Sagitta 83	**STAR OF GREECE** 11	**UNITED KINGDOM** 8
SAINT GEORGE 83	**STAR OF INDIA** . . . 16, 157	United Vantage 190
SAINT HELENA 8	**STAR OF IRELAND** 15	Unity 58
Sakito Maru 13	**STAR OF ITALY** 13	**VALENCIA** 196
SAMBLADE 199	**STAR OF JAPAN** 15	Vassiliki 199
SAMEDEN 199	**STAR OF NEW ZEALAND** 14	Vianda 27
SAMLEVEN 199	**STAR OF PERSIA** 10	**VIBILIA** 48
SAMPLER 199	Star Of Peru 91	Ville De Diego Suarez . . 200
SANTA CLARA 34	**STAR OF RUSSIA** 12	Vimeira 203
SANTA ISABEL 34	**STAR OF SCOTIA** 10	Vlissingen 92
SANTA MARGHERITA . . 33	**STAR OF SCOTLAND** . . 15,	**VOLANT** 46
Santa Marta 77	 157	Vrontados 74
SANTA THERESA 34	**STAR OF VICTORIA (1)** . 13	Waipara 86
Santi Agostino 52	**STAR OF VICTORIA (2)** 17,	Wanliu 202
SANTOS 53	 158	Wanstead 202
Sardegna 52	Starlight Princess 190	**WAR HECUBA** 196
SAVAN 34	**SULTAN** 48, 63	War Thalia 166
SAVANNAH LA MAR . . . 49	**SUMMER HILL** 9	**WEST STANLEY** 58, 63
Saxon Star 85	**SURBITON (1)** 54	Westminster 24
Saxonstar 85	**SURBITON (2)** 62	**WHAKARUA** 95, 160
SCINDIA 84	**SURREY** 85	**WHALTON** 46, 63

WHAMPOA 60	Wimbledon 203	Yestor 74
Whitgift 26	**WOODHORN** 84	**ZETUS** 48
WILEYSIKE 73	**YANGTSE** 63	Zigurds 77
William C. Lane 182	**YANGTSZE** 57	Zinbu Maru 25

FINISH WITH ENGINES - PORT NAPIER in 1936

PORT CAROLINE the last ship built for Port Line and last to leave the fleet as GOLDEN DOLPHIN (A. Geddes)